FOR REFERENCE

Do Not Take From This Room

LIBRARY LIT. 21–
The Best of 1990

edited by

JANE ANNE HANNIGAN

The Scarecrow Press, Inc.
Metuchen, N.J., & London
1992

ISBN 0-8108-2534-1
Library of Congress Catalog No. 78-154842

TABLE OF CONTENTS

Introduction   vii

Envoi. Bill Katz   xi

Publisher's Note   xv

The Best of Library Literature Jury for 1990   xvii

Notes on Contributors   xix

SECTION ONE: TECHNOLOGY, THE FUTURE, AND LIBRARIES

Magic and Hypersystems: A New Orderliness for Libraries. Harold Billings.   1

Rehumanizing Information: An Alternative Future. John C. Swan.   18

Accuracy of Information Provision: The Need for Client-Centred Service. Paul F. Burton.   30

A New Information Infrastructure. Caroline R. Arms.   49

Decision Factors Favoring the Use of Online Sources for Providing Information. Anne B. Piternick.   68

The Effectiveness of an Online Catalog. Leslie Edmonds, Paula Moore, and Kathleen Mehaffey Balcom.   87

Reclaiming Our Technological Future. Patricia Glass Schuman.   100

SECTION TWO: GOVERNMENT AND LIBRARIES

The National Security Archive: Keeping the
Government Honest. Frankie Pelzman.   117

National Security Restraints of The Federal Government on
Academic Freedom and Scientific Communication in the
United States. Jessica D. Schwab.   127

The "Grey" Ghetto: Key Issues Related to Public Policy
Research Literature. Marc A. Levin.   181

Access to Information for Environmentalists: A Library
Perspective. Susan A. Safyan.   191

Poverty and Development in South Africa and
The Role of Libraries. Mary Nassimbeni.   210

SECTION THREE: SCHOOL MEDIA CENTER CONCERNS

Beyond the Chip: A Model for Fostering Equity.
Delia Neuman.   225

Factors Influencing the Outcome of Library Media Center
Challenges at The Secondary Level. Dianne McAfee
Hopkins.   244

SECTION FOUR: MANAGEMENT APPROACHES

Funding for Public Libraries in the 1990s. Arthur Curley.   279

What Do Our "Senior Citizens" Want From Public Libraries?
Bryce Allen and Margaret Ann Wilkinson.   289

Implications of Tying State Aid to Performance Measures.
Charles Curran and Philip M. Clark.   301

Contents

Ethical Back Talk: Entire Series. Lillian N. Gerhardt.   319

Valuing Corporate Libraries: A Senior Management Survey.
James M. Matazarro and Laurence Prusak.   336

The New Hierarchy: Where's The Boss? Joanne Euster.   351

SECTION FIVE: CHILDREN'S LITERATURE

Killing Books Softly: Reviewers as Censors.   365

Meaning-Making and The Dragons of Pern.
Kay E. Vandergrift.   387

The Purpose of Literature: Who Cares? Natalie Babbitt.   405

A Century of Xenophobia in Fiction Series for Young People.
Paul Deane.   413

SECTION SIX: LIBRARY EDUCATION

Why Library Schools Fail. Marion Paris.   431

"Yes, Virginia, You Can Require an Accredited Master's
Degree for That Job!" Jane Robbins.   442

SECTION SEVEN: HISTORICAL PERSPECTIVES AND COLLECTING

Thomas Jefferson and The Legacy of A National Library.
Douglas Wilson.   457

Collecting Detective Fiction. B.A. Pike.   471

Historical Research in Trade Catalogs. Rhoda S. Ratner.   484

About the Editor   492

INTRODUCTION

The literature of library and information science of 1990 explored a broad range of issues. There is no question that the profession is still concerned with access to information and is more accepting of technology as an ally in that process. At the same time, there is an increase of concern for management approaches to library operations as well as renewed interest in the history and development of collections. Each article included here was reviewed by the jury and discussed at length before being selected for this collection.

Section One, "Technology, the Future, and Libraries," includes seven articles which address issues and concerns in technological applications. Billings compares modern technology to the 16th-century world of knowledge, accepting hypersystems in libraries as a form of memory storage as well as an expansion of it. Swan challenges readers to go beyond our basic craft of making information available to others and "find ways of rehumanizing information, making it again a source of illumination rather than paralysis." Burton suggests that those providing library and information services must improve their accuracy rate and adopt client-centered services in order to operate in a new information marketplace and to meet competition from other sources. Arms provides a sound explanation of BITNET and other networks, such as ARPANET and INTERNET, and their place in research institutions. Piternick lists seven categories such as convenience factors, cost factors, and availability factors that might be used by librarians in determining when to use print or electronic formats in response to client request. Edmonds, Moore, and Mehaffey Balcom report the results of their Baber Research grant that explored the online catalog and its use by children. The importance of the concept of alphabetization is demonstrated and additional issues are raised. Schuman makes a logical and well thought-out case for not being overly impressed by technology. She argues lucidly that we must not be drawn into the technological solutions as a replacement for learning to think. In addition, she throws a gauntlet at libraries and asks us to reconsider our role of service in this important article.

Section Two, "Government and Libraries," includes five diverse articles that address concerns of information access. Pelzman provides a clear exploration of the National Security Archive (NSA) as a staunch information advocate. Schwab addressed two questions: 1.) Will national security actually be endangered by a lack of exchange and communication of scientific ideas? 2.) How extensive is the leakage of national security information in academia? Levin indicates that policy research groups contribute substantially to public problem solving, but their literature presents unique challenges to librarians. Safyan indicates that full access to environmental information is impeded by governments, and by economic inequities and will require familiarity with the crosss-disciplinary and conflicting nature of environmental information. Nassimbeni provides a general overview of the Second Carnegie Report and explores its significance for librarians and, in particular, its impact on library and information services in South Africa.

Section Three, "School Media Center Concerns," includes to research articles of key importance to libraries and schooling. Neuman proposes equity in the access to technology and presents a two-tiered model along with a discussion of obstacles and proposed means of dealing with the situation. Hopkins reports research completed in Wisconsin in 1988 on intellectual freedom and school library media centers.

Section Four, "Management Approaches," includes six different articles addressing a diversity of issues in library administration, including one article devoted to the key concern of ethics. Curley takes a radical posture in opposition to those who believe in performal appraisal and the bottom line, suggesting the alternative path of putting it to the voter—evidence that voters are now supportive of libraries. Allen and Wilkinson analyze data on public library users and indicate a substantial market for public library services to senior citizens. If libraries intend to implement programs and services for senior citizens there appears to be a strong base of public support. Curran and Clark examine the difficult process of deriving any formula for the award of aid and question whether the types of performance measures used by some states have more to do with the educational and economic status of the community than with any characteristics of the library and its services. Gerhardt offers an insightful and practical analysis of the ALA Code of Ethics from the viewpoint of those working with children and youth. Matarazzo and Prusak ask how much value senior executives place on their libraries. Euster describes a knowledge-based library structure and identifies leadership factors of importance.

Section Five, "Children's Literature," includes four articles that address issues of the literature itself, criticism, reader-response criticism and early series books. An editor, practitioner/reviewers, and professional reviewers of books for young people discuss their craft and the effects of reviews on authors, editors, librarians, and ultimately the young audience in "Killing Books Softly." Vandergrift reports on a research project with young people who read McCaffrey's *Dragons of Pern* books. The findings demonstrate that young people do make strong meanings in what they read and that they pay careful attention to details. Babbitt has always responded to those who ask why she doesn't write books about the current social problems of children by declaring, "that is not the purpose of literature." Here she struggles with the question of the purpose of literature and concludes that it is to give pleasure to the reader. Deane maintains the wealth of cultural riches contained in the story of the series books for young people. He uses a number of the best-selling series to investigate and report on "foreigners" in these works, approaching the task more as a social historian than as a literary critic.

Section Six, "Library Education," includes two critical articles in a time of concern for library educatin in this country. Paris writes: "The perception that library schools are out of touch and out of date may be the key to the reality of school closings." She identifies a number of factors that led to schools closings but more importantly characterizes programs that survive and grow. Robbins makes a strong case for educating for a career rather than for the performance of specific tasks. She suggests several actions that could be taken by library educators.

Section Seven, "Historical Perspectives and Collecting," touches upon often neglected areas of collecting as well as placing collecting in perspective in this country. Wilson comments on Jefferson's library which reveals the book collector as well as the informed man. Connections are drawn to the Library of Congress, and it is argued that the Jefferson collection set a tone which Congress has continued. Pile's article on collection of mysteries offers a mapping of the literature. He points out a number of fascinating elements of identification. Ratner makes a powerful argument for collecting trade catalogs as a potential source for cultural and social values.

No book is completed without the support and help of a number of people. I would like to thank the professional community who share their ideas, research, and expertise in our journals and all those who nominate articles for the jury's consideration. The 1990 Jury's diligence in reading the recommended articles and their lively, sometimes arguementative, discussions before closure are greatly appreciated. Finally, I thank all of those contributors who articles were selected for inclusion in this twnety-first volume of *The Best of Library Literature*.

As an editor, it is sad to end a series, but I do so with the confidence that each of the volumes has made a significant contribution to the profession. The juries that selected the articles to be included each year fulfilled a need in capturing a professional moment in time, reflecting both historical context and contemporary issues from a variety of perspectives. Bill Katz, in the farewell which follows, provided not a eulogy on the demise of this series, but an accolade on a past well done.

Jane Anne Hannigan
Editor and Professor Emerita
Columbia University
New York, New York

ENVOI

Bill Katz

LAST WORDS inspired William Saroyan to write: "I was impressed by what people had said at death. I felt absolutely exhilarated by the promise that someday I would die, and say my last words." Well, while not quite prepared personally to sign off in style, a few words about the demise of this series seems appropriate.

The halycon years began in 1970. The idea of celebrating articles of the most original, most dissonant librarians originated with Eric Moon, who had recently moved from the editorship of *Library Journal* to steering Scarecrow Press. Taking a chance on the sales appeal of the aesthetically perfect, Eric and Al Daub launched the anthologies which would embrace us all for 22 years. It is doubtful that the evaluations made a discernible difference to 250 or so million Americans, but it was great fun for the judges, for the readers and, let us hope, for the chosen few. And whatever its strengths and weaknesses, the series did make several valid points:

(1) Comrades and colleagues write with imagination, verve and style. The annual articles are manifest proof that librarians are a beguiling lot with logical, sometimes quarrelsome points to make about the profession. While librarians do not have a cartel on superior thought and expression, they need not apologize to any group for sluggish prose. They match the outlook and posture of any professional, judicious writer. The collection proves it is impertinent and downright wrong headed to take the edge off us all by accusing librarians of repudiation of fine writing.

(2) In its ordered way, the annual collection of some 30 articles incited calm to excited comment. Most readers enjoyed, even celebrated the collection. More combustible critics, particularly those wedded to formula, and desperate for detectable methodology of selection, seemed confused by it all. The notion that three or four people, without benefit of careful research or citation indexes, could

select the "best" of anything, more or less the ruffians of library literature, tended to disturb and upset. Fortunately, the unsociable triflers had no influence on choices. Selection tended to be governed by the judge's staunch allegiance to subjectivity, if not downright treachery. A favored gambit was to vote for the anguished desires of one judge if that judge, in turn, would swing a vote for the ingenious article favored by less than a majority.

The disordered stratagem worked well because the evaluators were all veterans of library warfare, and more important, experts without tinsel. There proved to be a fidelity to quality, to respect for the art of librarianship (or whatever the present neologism), and to librarians rarely found in similar gatherings. Affability and a dash of common-sense helped, too.

(3) From time to time (well, damn near every year) the judges were accused of selection outside of what is indexed as *Library Literature* et company. Determined to define the literature in broader terms than found in the 180 or so periodicals indexed, the only real test was whether or not the article was lively, forceful and illustrative of what nonlibrarians considered the role of the profession. Out of these choices came the obvious conclusion that Americans have a respect for libraries. This measurable well of good will is evident in almost every annual collection.

(4) Those jongleurs of doom who see the end of libraries and librarians might spend a few minutes looking over the past 22 years of *The Best of Library Literature*. The authors represent only a brief, although luxuriant point in an esteemed history which has received and passed over scribes, bards, printers and even "information scientists" to emerge as an energetic and exalted profession. It's a godsend to be a member of such an ancient, such a fortunate group.

Thanks to . . .

Let me thank all of the judges, all of the selected authors, all of the friends who made these great, great years: And with that, a last word from the immortal song, "Shipyard Salley." "Wish us luck, as you wave us goodbye." Eric Moon, William Eshelman and Norman Horrocks who, in that order, represented the publisher in selecting articles. Also, Al Daub of Scarecrow for his support. Particular thanks to the jury members, and especially John Berry, Arthur Curley and Patricia Schuman who gave their time for the last years of the book. Special praise, too, for Jane Anne Hannigan who edited the last numbers.

Then there are all the others, including numerous student assistants who labored at permissions and diplomacy. Here, a word for Robin Kinder, now gainfully employed at Smith, who gave her all and stands as a representative of the best of those student aids.

Of course, the real heroes are the ones who articles were selected each year, who upheld the glories of libraries. Thanks to one and to all. Joe Morehead seems to have been the most sought after author of the lot, appearing in over one-half the annual volumes. I am fortunate to count him as a friend, as I do all of the above.

In this merciful eclipse, "every one is somebody" including you the reader. Hail to you.

PUBLISHER'S NOTE

There is little to add to the Envoi by Bill Katz beyond confirming that this is the last volume to appear in this Series which he and Eric Moon launched in 1971.

A combination of reasons has led to this decision. Obtaining permissions to reprint from publishers has become an increasingly time-consuming chore in many cases. Certain publishers ask for the payment of fees which we consider to be exorbitant. Librarians writing for professional journals might want to question their publishers about the policies for granting reprint permission.

The Jury has continued in its efforts in selecting the best from the year's output, honoring their authors and the editors who published them and giving additional publicity in many cases to journals not so well known as the standard titles. Even so library budgets are declining nationwide and collections of reprinted articles seem to be on the endangered species list for many libraries.

All that is left now is to give the Honor Roll of those who have served on the Jury over the years:

Janet D. Bailey, 1972
John Berry, 1970, 1976, 1982-1990
Deirdre Boyle, 1979-1981
Robert Burgess, Editor 1974
Bertha M. Cheatham, 1982
Mary Kay Chelton, 1981, 1983-1987
Arthur Curley, 1972, 1981-1990
William R. Eshelman, 1970, 1973, 1975, 1979-1985
Barbara Felicetti, 1977
Robert Franklin, 1977
Maurice J. Freedman, 1978
Sherry Gaherty, Editor, 1973
Lillian N. Gerhardt, 1972
Jane Anne Hannigan, Editor 1988-1990
Shirley Havens, 1977
Norman Horrocks, 1974, 1986-1990

Bill Katz, Editor 1970-1987, Juror 1988-1990
Janet Klaessig, Editor 1972, Juror 1976
Cavan McCarthy, 1975
Eric Moon, 1970-1976, 1978
Karl Nyren, 1973
Ann Prentice, 1974
Anne Roberts, 1976
Pat Rom, 1978-1980
Marvin Schilken, 1977
Patricia G. Schuman, 1971, 1976, 1978-1990
Joel J. Schwartz, Editor 1974
Gerald R. Shields, 1974
Jane Stevens, 1971, 1973
Robert Wedgeworth, 1971
Kathy Weibel, Juror 1979-1980, Editor, 1981

Albert W. Daub
President
SCARECROW PRESS, INC.

THE BEST OF LIBRARY LITERATURE JURY
FOR 1990

John Berry, III
Vice President and Editor-in-Chief
Library Journal
New York, New York

Arthur Curley
Director
Boston Public Library
Boston, Massachusetts
Editor of *Collection Building*

Jane Anne Hannigan
Professor Emerita
Columbia University
New York, New York
Chair of 1989 Jury

Norman Horrocks
Vice President, Editorial
Scarecrow Press
Metuchen, New Jersey

Bill Katz
Professor
School of Information Science and Policy
State University of New York, Albany
Albany, New York
Editor of *The Reference Librarian*

Patricia Glass Schuman
President
Neal-Schuman Publishers, Inc.
New York, New York

NOTES ON CONTRIBUTORS

BRYCE ALLEN, Assistant Professor, Graduate School of Library and Information Science, University of Illinois at Urbana-Champaign, Urbana, IL.

CAROLINE R. ARMS, Head, Microcomputer and Media Center, Falk Library of the Health Sciences, University of Pittsburgh, Pittsburgh, PA.

NATALIE BABBITT, Author and illustrator of innumerable children's books including *Tuck Everlasting, The Search for Delicious,* and *Knee-Knock Rise.*

KATHLEEN MEHAFFEY BALCOM, Executive Librarian of the Arlington Heights Memorial Library, Arlington Heights, IL.

HAROLD BILLINGS, Director, University of Texas at Austin Libraries, Austin, TX.

PAUL BURTON, Lecturer at the Department of Information Science at Strathelyde University, Glasgow, Great Britain.

PHILIP M. CLARK, Associate Professor at the Division of Library and Information Science, St. John's University, Queens, NY.

ARTHUR CURLEY, Director of the Boston Public Library, Boston, MA.

CHARLES CURRAN, Associate Professor at the College of Library and Information Science, University of South Carolina.

PAUL DEANE, Professor of English, Bentley College, Waltham, MA.

LESLIE EDMONDS, Coordinator of Youth Services, St. Louis Public Library, St. Louis, MO.

JOANNE R. EUSTER, Vice President for Information Services and University Librarian, Rutgers University, New Brunswick, NJ.

LILLIAN N. GERHARDT, Editor in Chief, *School Library Journal.*

DIANNE McAFEE HOPKINS, Assistant Professor, School of Library and Information Studies at the University of Wisconsin-Madison, WI.

MARC A. LEVIN, Member of the Institute of Governmental Studies, University of California at Berkeley, CA.

JAMES M. MATARAZZO, Professor at the Simmons College Graduate School of Library and Information Science, Boston, MA.

PAULA MOORE, Head of Youth Services, Arlington Heights Memorial Library, Arlington Heights, IL.

MARY NASSIMBENI, Senior Lecturer at the School of Librarianship, University of Cape Town, South Africa.

DELIA NEUMAN, Assistant Professor in the College of Library and Information Services, University of Maryland, College Park, MD.

MARION PARIS, Assistant Professor, School of Library and Information Studies, University of Alabama, Tuscaloosa, AL.

FRANKIE PELZMAN, Free lance writer and regular contributor to *Wilson Library Bulletin.*

B.A. PIKE, Author of *Campion's Career,* and coauthor of *Detective Fiction: The Collector's Guide,* and contributor of reviews and articles.

ANNE B. PITERNICK, Professor, School of Library, Archival and Information Studies at the University of British Columbia, Vancouver, Canada.

LAURENCE PRUSAK, Senior Manager at Ernst & Young's Center for Information Technology & Strategy, Boston, MA.

RHODA S. RATNER, Department Head, History, Technology and Art, Smithsonian Institution Libraries, Washington, DC.

JANE ROBBINS, Professor and Director, School of Library and Information Studies, University of Wisconsin-Madison, Madison, WI.

SUSAN A. SAFYNAN, Graduate of the School of Library, Archival and Information Studies, University of Wisconsin-Madison, Madison, WI.

PATRICIA GLASS SCHUMAN, President of Neal Schuman Publishers, Inc., New York, New York, and President (1991-92) of the American Library Association.

JESSICA D. SCHWAB, Reference Librarian, Wilson, Sonsini, Goodrich & Rosati, Palo Alto, CA.

JOHN C. SWAN, Director of the Library at Bennington College, Bennington, VT.

KAY E. VANDERGRIFT, Associate Professor, School of Communication, Information and Library Studies, Rutgers University, New Brunswick, NJ.

MARGARET ANN WILKINSON, Graduate Student at the School of Library and Information Science, University of Western Ontario, London, Ontario.

DOUGLAS WILSON, Professor of English and Director of the
Seymour Library at Knox College, Galesburg, IL.

SECTION ONE:
THE TECHNOLOGY, THE FUTURE, AND
LIBRARIANS

MAGIC AND HYPERSYSTEMS: A NEW ORDERLINESS FOR LIBRARIES

Harold Billings

The knowledge situation of the late 16th century in Europe was much like the present. That era also was flooded with new information formats, a rapid expansion of knowledge, and efforts to order knowledge through systems that extended the capabilities of the mind. There was a breaching of previously accepted boundaries of place and time, through the introduction of a thought model that accepted and transcended Copernicanism. A comparison of our time with the historical foundations of memory and knowledge systems astir in the 16th century offers insights into the present situation and suggests where our knowledge systems are bound.

The Growth of Knowledge

For all the wider sowing of knowledge the printing press afforded, perhaps its greatest contribution lay in its secularization of knowledge. The place of books in those days was little in the academies and universities, but much within the church. Thought imprisoned by either the Inquisition or the Reformation was dead seed, but printing helped revive it. Dogma was replaced with new intellectual opportunities, and the revolutions in thought that followed should not have

"Magic and Hypersystems: A New Orderliness for Libraries," by Harold Billings in *Library Journal*. Vol. 115, no. 6 (April 1, 1990), pp. 46-52; reprinted with permission from Reed Publishing, USA, copyright © 1990 Reed Publishing, USA.

been surprising. It is certainly not surprising that reactionary agencies of both church and court found an intensely magnified challenge as the printed word and an astonishing new inquisitiveness ran rampant through the intellectual world.

How to organize this flush of books and ideas must have represented a real problem to those institutions and individuals who soon found themselves swamped with printed items. Print had to take its place among the manuscripts of the day, and that added considerably to the space required for storage. The *armarium,* or book chest, was no longer sufficient to hold the library of the time; and an unaided mind or memory was seen as inadequate for all the learning and lore set loose in the world.

Memory Arts in Ordering Knowledge

For centuries, the art of memory had served as a major means for transmitting oral tradition and played a significant part in the art of rhetoric. From the days of the poet Simonides (fifth century B.C.), who, as told by Cicero, introduced the classical art of memory, the memory arts had helped organize knowledge and carry it forward. Memory arts were a major intellectual tool used for 19 light and dark centuries before the Renaissance. It can easily be understood how the memory arts—if generally regarded by the 16th century as a medieval scheme and no longer necessary for carrying the word into the future—nevertheless would early be looked to for help in organizing the storehouses of knowledge that grew so soon from Gutenberg's machine.[1]

The human mind was seen as the device within which the memory arts could organize and relate the knowledge of the times.

Classical mnemonics held as a major principle the role of place and *image* in vitalizing the imagination of the ancient rhetor to recall his text. Simonides was said to have identified for relatives the mangled dead in the ruins of a devastated banquet hall by recollecting where diners had been seated. Thus, in the classical mnemonic, an elaborate building was visually imprinted on the mind, with all its features and furnishings to be recalled turn by turn, so that images in a text could be associated with scenes, and image and embedded text be recollected as each feature of the building was revisited in the memory. A theater or its stage, called to the mind's eye, became common to this classical architectural mnemonic. By the 1530s (when appreciation for the classical arts had come round again) Giulio Camillo of Venice achieved fame for constructing a wooden theater filled with images and boxes, ordered and graded, to function as an elaborate memory system. Several centuries earlier, Ramon Lull laid the foundations for future memory systems by devising an "art" to relate the encyclopedia of knowledge by revolving wheels of divine attributes.

In the late 16th century, Giordano Bruno devised several magic memory systems (conceived on "magical" rather than natural images) that, while based on the ancient precepts of place and image, located astral images on a revolving Lullian wheel. There, virtually "every possible arrangement and combination of objects in the lower world—plants, animals, stones—would be perceived and remembered by their relationship through innumerable metaphysical layers with a mystical, higher unity.

Fifty years later, in the 17th century, Robert Fludd would maintain these common threads by devising a theater memory system that combined a visualization of the stages of "real" public theaters with astrological images.

A wonderful genealogical memory tree could be constructed leading from Simonides through these increasingly magical thinkers of the Renaissance to the eventual spilling out of new "methods" of modern science—still linked to magical memory systems—from the minds of Bacon, Descartes, and Leibniz in the early 17th century.

Under a variety of other codes, concepts of magic seals, astral images, emblems, colors, pictures, mathematical characters, objects, signs, symbols, signals: the visualization of images and places, were incorporated into numerous other efforts at developing memory systems. These attempted to relate and organize the extant universe of knowledge within the human mind: for the retrieval of information, for the discovery of new knowledge, and for bringing the individual closer and more powerfully to the divine.

The late Dame Frances Yates (1899-1981) was a pioneer in the history of the memory arts and did much to relate the topic to the flowering of modern science, though it passed through dark and magical places in doing so. By the 16th century, she writes, "The printed book is destroying age-old memory habits," but adds, "Nevertheless, far from waning, the art of memory had actually entered upon a new and strange lease of life. . . . Through Renaissance Neoplatonism, with its Hermetic core, the art of memory was once more transformed, this time into a Hermetic or occult art. . . . "[2]

Occultism was just as much a part of the learned scene as superstition and magic were part of the warp and woof of all human existence. John Crowley, in an illuminating work on ghosts in Shakespeare, has described a body of common wisdom regarding the supernatural that "extended through all strata of society."[3]

"It should not be forgotten," Crowley says, "that Elizabethan nights were darker than ours, roads longer, Hell nearer. The natural world had not yet divided itself from man's moral apprehension. . . . " Yates characterized the times as a "Renaissance borderland country, half magic, half emerging science. . . . " In the spindrift of ideas thrown off by the Renaissance, real science was never far from pseudoscience, or the two were so commingled that during those times it was difficult to distinguish the two. Astronomy, mathematics, and geometry were not far removed from the alchemical, the astrological, the geomantic, and the hermetic.

Libraries gradually were drawn into this maelstrom of new ideas and a world of knowledge very much at unrest. In the 1550s of the English Reformation, there was a great plunder and dissolution of the cloisters, and the monastery libraries that had guarded what little there was of the written heart of learning for a thousand dark years were almost completely scattered. At particular risk were any works that appeared "popish." Books or manuscripts containing mathematical diagrams were also regarded with peculiar suspicion. It has been estimated that only two percent of the 300,000 volumes in over 800 monastery libraries survived the review of reformers.[4]

Dee and Bruno

Yates not only established the concept of the importance of hermetical influences on the development of modern science, but also named as major catalysts for this movement the two magus philosophers, John Dee (1527-1608) and Giordano Bruno (1548-1600).

Doctor John Dee—astronomer, mathematician, toolmaker, magus, and librarian—suggested to Queen Mary as early as 1556 that the dispersed monastic collections be regathered to form a great National Library, but nothing came of the notion. Dee then began the building of a personal library which by 1583 numbered over 4000 books and manuscripts, perhaps the largest library in England or Europe, and certainly the greatest accumulation of scientific information. By contrast, the library of Sir Thomas Bodley, when he retired in 1587 to "set up his Staffe at the Librarie dore in Oxon," numbered only 2000 volumes.

After generally casual dismissal as a quirky, minor player on the Elizabethan intellectual scene prior to Yates's studies, Dee has been credited in more recent years with being at the very center of an academy of learning in England in the last quarter of the 16th century. Elizabeth, Philip Sidney, and a circle of literary and scientific friends are known to have spent time at Mortlake, Dee's home. But Dee's interest in mathematics, mechanics, and magic was not in the mainstream of the emerging humanist movement, and rather an occult and even dangerous interest to favor in the countryside but not at court.

Still, Dee was an adviser to Elizabethan mariners, worked on scientific instruments, shared his foreign-gained knowledge of geography in advancing navigation, and is credited with spreading a knowledge of Copernican astronomy among English scientists. He composed a preface to the English translation of the works of Euclid which, according to Yates, "As a manifesto for the advancement of science . . . is of greater importance than Francis Bacon's,"[5] while at the same time he composed a description of his attempts to conjure angels through cabalistic numerology. These widely disparate exercises of intellect and ingenuity, while perhaps the most marked signs of a universal Renaissance man, left Dee open to challenge for many years as nothing more than a "conjuror."

At the point of leaving for an extended visit to Europe in 1583 at the invitation of Prince Albert Laski of Poland, Dee produced a catalog of his library. It is one of the first library catalogs known, and one which Yates claims to be an "absolutely basic document for the understanding, not only of Dee himself, but of the courtiers, noblemen, poets, scholars, scientists of the Elizabethan age for whom this was the best library in the country." It also gives us some notion of how the ordering of knowledge and its physical representation was taking form: "partially systematic though the system varies. Some . . . arranged according to size, others according to language . . . subject groupings, Paracelsist books (a large section), Lullist books, historical books, books of travel and discovery. . . . Nevertheless there is nothing haphazard about the catalog; the entries are clearly written and usually include date and place of publication as well as author and title."[6] Among the manuscript books in his library were five on the art of memory, and in his approach to books and knowledge Dee took what could now be perceived as a very modern stance. He was less concerned with how the physical books and manuscripts were arranged than with how their knowledge might be organized and retrieved in his mind. While obviously familiar with the various magical memory methods, Dee was not himself a memory system innovator. However, he helped set in place a role for libraries in preserving learning, enlarged the horizons for Elizabethan exploration by ship and mind, and promoted the new concepts of a Copernican universe—but one whose stars were very much numbered with ghosts and angels as well as the stones of the field.

Meanwhile, to the south in Naples, Giordano Bruno, a young Dominican monk whose influence on European thought would far transcend even that of John Dee's in England, faced with charges of heresy, had broken from his monastic vocation and begun the travels that would carry his versions of Dominican memory systems, and his reframing of Copernican heliocentrism, to Geneva, Paris, London, and Prague.[7]

Copernicus, of course, had argued in his *De revolutionibus Orbium Caelestium* (1543) that the sun lay at the center of our universe, refuting the stubbornly maintained Ptolemaic concept of the Earth as center of all things. But Copernicus believed the stars to be living, bright animals that prowled an outer circular sphere that sealed the universe within. Bruno was greatly affected by Copernicus's ideas, but went beyond them in his interpretations based on the influence of the writings ascribed to Hermes Trismegistus. These suggested the concept of an *infinite* universe to Bruno, an idea that was violently resisted by the Church, but one that would fuel the new mathematics, the philosophies, and the sciences shortly to come.

Bruno's first two works, *De umbris idearum* and *Cantus Circaeus* deal with his theories of magic memory but press far beyond mnemonics into solar magic and talismanic images, by which a thinker might bring those "shadows of ideas" in the archetypal heavens into his own consciousness: "If you embrace in your thought all things at once, times, places, substances, qualities, quantities, you may understand God."

Thus the "ex-friar, infinitely wild, passionate, and unrestrained" (Yates) published his ideas in Paris, solicited the favor of Henri III in the courts of France, then went to London in a rising tumult over his religion to seek the support of Elizabeth and address a challenge to "the most excellent Vice Chancellor of Oxford University and its celebrated doctors and teachers." Bruno argued for an animistic Copernican universe—but an infinite one. For two years he occupied the courtly and supper scenes of London, astounded audiences with memory feats, and published works sharply critical of the Oxford establishment. Those writings were not to lead these unenlightened to a new age of science, but to redirect them to the elder magical religions. Bruno left his influence on the Sidney circles and returned to Paris, Germany, and Prague.

Eventually, Bruno and John Dee would both spend considerable time soliciting the patronage of Rudolf II of Poland, a supporter of studies of the occult. While they apparently never met—for Bruno was in England during two of the six years that Dee was in Europe—they would profoundly enlarge each other's influence, paving the way for a new science to spring from the magics they laid. While each solicited the support of the political rulers of the day, for no philosopher went far without political or theological blessings, each would suffer enormously from the reactions that came with every small intellectual advance.

Dee returned to England in 1589. His champion Philip Sidney was dead in a military foray to the Netherlands. Europe and England were stung by a series of witch hunts, and Elizabeth's coming successor James, the King of Scotland and author of *Daemonologie,* was violently damning anything ascribed to conjuration. Dee found his vast library and collection of scientific equipment vandalized, and lived out his final years in the shadow of disfavor, reputedly selling his books off one by one for his dinners. Bruno foolishly returned to Italy where he was secured by the Inquisition, spent eight years imprisoned under question; and on a cold February day in 1600 he was ridden backwards on a mule, in a white robe, to Rome's Field of Flowers where he was burned at the stake.

A Legacy of Memory Magic

Dee and Bruno each left behind in the works they composed, and in those persons they enchanted new dimensions of thought, a legacy of memory arts-based magic and knowledge systems no longer fettered by a finite, ecclesiastically defined universe. This influence clearly extended into the earliest years of the 17th century advance, as Yates has it, when "the art of memory survives as a factor in the growth of scientific method."[8]

Bacon, Descartes, and Leibniz (who brought us the inductive method, analytical geometry, and a universal calculus) all spent early days awash in the speculations of Dee and Bruno. All three considered the art of memory and how its reformation might influence the new methods from which modern science would so immediately blossom.

Bacon (1561-1626), much in the tradition of the early memory arts, wrote of "prenotions" and "emblems" for place and image as a primitive form of classification in the investigation of natural science.

Descartes (1596-1650) believed that the art of memory could provide "an easy way of making myself master of all I discovered through the imagination . . . through the reduction of things to their causes . . . that out of unconnected images should be composed new images common to them all, or that one image should be made out of which would have reference not only to the one nearest to it but to the all" (*Cogitationes privatae.*)

Leibniz (1646-1716) introduced "characteristica" from memory arts, significant signs or characters, as mathematical symbols; and he called images "notas" which could recall things or words to the calculating mind. The information system Leibniz envisioned was an encyclopedia that would bring together all the arts and sciences known to humankind, with "characters" assigned to all notions, and a universal calculus applied to retrieve this universe of knowledge and solve all problems.[9]

Leibniz even devised a calculating machine, but ultimately had to be satisfied with the library as the means for repositing knowledge. As Daniel Boorstin describes, "Leibniz saw the library as a congregation of all knowledge with the librarian as minister keeping the congregation up-to-date and freely communicating. He pioneered in classification schemes, alphabetical finding aids, and abstracts to help the scholar. The library was his encyclopedia."[10]

So the magics were laid away, or became hidden in the rising arcana of Rosicrucianism. The new sciences and their methods flourished, and memory systems—finding no machine or the human mind capable alone of storing and retrieving knowledge as had been pursued by the magical memory brotherhood— relegated the transmittal of knowledge to the formats and order that libraries grew to provide.

Yates both summarized the influence of the hermetic philosophers on the development of modern science and moved toward prophecy when she observed in 1964, "the Renaissance conception of an animistic universe, operated by magic, prepared the way for a mechanical universe, operated by mathematics. . . . Bruno's assumption that the astral forces which govern the outer world also operate within, and can be reproduced or captured there to operate a magical-mechanical memory, seems to bring one curiously close to the mind machine which is able to do so much of the work of the human brain by mechanical means."[11]

Had Dame Frances been able to follow the development of the "mind machines" she found so curiously close to the memory systems of the Renaissance, and had she done so within the context of the information nova of the late 20th century, she would have found other curious parallels between the knowledge systems and magics of two widely separated centuries.

Modern Magics/Scientific Complexity

As one construes things to be "supernatural" that lie outside the generally accepted definitions of present-day natural science, there is an increasing trend in the late 20th century to achieve some supernatural handhold on current knowledge. One wants to employ fresh language, and images as magical as any of the 16th century, in the attempt to find new order in the structure and complexity of the natural world, to bring new dimensions to the sciences we know.

For example, chaos, an information demon, and new angelic computations are invoked by today's most compelling thinkers in efforts to find meaning in a universe that has become as clouded by doctrinal examination and representation as it was in the days before Renaissance philosophies broke heaven's spherical panes.

One does not ordinarily expect the word "chaos" to define an elegant order, but rather the random, the erratic, and the utter unpredictability of certain natural behaviors. Yet a new science of chaos has offered a fresh approach the past decade, a new way of understanding the growth of complexity in nature. What several scientific disciplines could not descry from their traditional perspectives, new commonalities in the study of chaos are bringing thinkers together (as James Gleick describes) in rapidly "reshapipg the fabric of the scientific society."[12]

Sir James Clark Maxwell, the Scottish physicist who developed the equations governing electric and magnetic fields, posited a thermodynamic paradox in his book *Theory of Heat* (1871). Maxwell suggested a fantastical perpetual-motion device presided over by "a being whose faculties are so sharpened that he can follow every molecule in its course," an imp that was soon dubbed "Maxwell's demon." Maxwell's puzzle of energy creation took over half a century to resolve. Physicists still invoke the demon that early on had raised serious questions regarding the inviolability of the first and second laws of thermodynamics: that energy can neither be created nor destroyed, and that the entropy of any closed system can never decrease.

William Poundstone, in examining the state of information and structure in the universe, turned to a Maxwell's "information demon" and a computer game, "Life," to help validate the overwhelming complexity and richness of a universe that defies any explanation of order within it.[13] Poundstone used the information demon to construct and review an imagined Universal Video Library, defined to hold a copy of *every possible* videotape 100,000 frames long, with each pixel distinguished in all its individuality of color and degree of brightness. While there are no illogics in constructing such a library, the number of videotapes in such a collection can be calculated, and would far exceed the number of atoms in the observable universe, while any effort to locate recognizable objects in the tape library would yield nothing but video snow.

Chance is unable to explain the rich orderliness of the universe, Poundstone contends. He cites the work of the mathematician John Von Neumann on computers and automata that supports the notion that machines can be self-creating and self-improving, that structures can grow richer under physical law.

Similarly, he observes that Claude Shannon, the founder of information theory, working from the similarities between thermodynamics and information proved a growing entropy of information systems—an evolving information complexity derived from a simple, repeating transmittal code. To Poundstone, then, "Complexity is self-generating" and "Creation can be simple." A simple structure and basic physical laws established in a recursive (pattern-repeating) model will generate not only self-reproduction but systems more complex than their parent. An information demon and a computer game say it is so.

The whole field of physics is disquieted because the scientific method is no longer able to keep up with the conjurations of the day; observation can no longer confirm theory. Among some there is concern that the modern body of physics will crumble. Scientists contend in almost theological tones. Recently, in discussing this problem as it relates to "superstring theory" as a theoretical approach to understanding matter, the Nobel laureate Sheldon Glashow observed, " . . . the historical connection between experimental physics and theory has been lost. Until the string people can interpret perceived properties of the real world, they simply are not doing physics. Should they be paid by universities and be permitted to pervert impressionable students? . . . Are string thoughts more appropriate to departments of mathematics or even to schools of divinity than to physics departments? How many angels can dance on the head of a pin? How many dimensions are there in a compactified manifold 30 powers of ten smaller than a pinhead?"[14]

Until risktakers make the effort to break the received tradition, there is never intellectual advance. The deeps of the universe, the boundaries of knowledge, the face of humankind, have always been circumscribed by the conceptual limitations of the human mind. The *thought model* that opened the universe beyond the spheres of Copernicus paved the way for modern science. Dare anyone imagine that the shores on which contemporary science and philosophy have paused are the final beachheads of humanity's knowledge enterprise? Or as Glashow says, "Can anyone really believe that nature's bag of tricks has run out?"

A New Orderliness in Libraries

A thought model that incorporates new electronic information formats, that employs new magics relating image and place to shape the new computations, and that defines a fresh vision of the universe will open a way to the newer sciences undoubtedly to come. Now, as four hundred years ago, the profound influences that are reshaping the contemporary knowledge world have also great potential for affecting the means by which libraries acquire, house, retrieve, relate, and display knowledge and information.

Several library philosophers have begun a rethinking of traditional library programs and procedures given new electronic information formats and the capabilities of the computer to refine the ordering of information knowledge, and the contents of libraries. Libraries may, in fact, be more profoundly affected by new means of "relating" and "displaying" information than by any other changes busy in the new knowledge world.

D. Kaye Gapen, in a talk to the American Library Association annual meeting in New Orleans on July 9, 1988, "Impact of Technologies on Resource-sharing, Linkages, Cooperation," described the changes in libraries, "becoming information systems that address problems, that clarify problems, and that attack problems."[15] Gapen describes three ascending library paradigms in a conceptual model of change: the Library Warehouse Paradigm, an Electronic Information Paradigm, and a third paradigm that will exist, she asserts by 1995, "which will involve the creation of new Knowledge/Thought systems in which the human brain (which has been our primary information processing device) will be complemented by computer software, which will allow not only the rapid storage and transfer of information, but also processing and representation of information in new and different ways."

"Hypertext is the first inkling," she says. "Having gained access to a point in the text you can use hypertext software to jump from point to point to point in the text, or between associated texts, through a web of associations." This will form the basis Gapen asserts, for a synergistic networking of information sources, and a massive transformation of libraries and the information world.

Although the concept of hypermedia—the relating of works and sounds and images—has been with us for 30 years or so, computer software has only recently developed the hypertext capabilities that Gapen describes. The new capabilities are much like those systems the Renaissance memory artists believed would recollect and relate all things, because they will enable the accessing of all related information from any point of entry in a body of information associated by signs and locations. This leads, in turn, to new and striking possibilities.

First, I would suggest that we will move even more rapidly through hypertext concepts toward "hypersystems" in which knowledge and information *systems* themselves, not just information databases, will echo and reinforce one another toward more powerful accomplishments than any one system would allow alone. Traditional information systems—libraries, and their long-established programs and services—will be linked with any number of new "knowledge/

thought" (information and computing) systems through open system interfaces. The result will be an enormous expansion of our capacities for storing, retrieving, representing, and manipulating information, and, therefore, a new order of achievement in the ages-old goal of generating new knowledge.

In the simplest of examples, the present scholarly information systems developing in research libraries represent "hyper" (or extended) relationships between the traditional library model (based on a book and journal collection, card catalogs, reference desk assistance, and interlibrary lending and other standard delivery services) and the heart of a rapidly permuting library system paradigm. Such a paradigm incorporates technologies and philosophies based on electronic information computer assistance networked through campus computation centers and remote databases as well as the local library collection.

John Sculley of Apple Computer has described a future Information Navigator that will allow one to enter an information system at any point and travel throughout it on a hypertext basis, while Steve Jobs's NEXT Computer reflects multitasking and multipath relationships that hint strongly at hypersystem concepts.

Hypersystems will magnify individual system capabilities in ways that will be technically reminiscent of the use of multiple parallel processors in computing, will promote the development of expert systems and artificial intelligence, and will allow for interactivity among knowledge and other systems in ways we cannot yet dream. Interestingly, the binary codes and icon-based commands of modern microcomputers are strikingly similar to the place and image concepts of 16th-century magical memory devices.

Second, and beyond the enormous potential of hypersystems to push us toward a new physics and theology of information, new prospects also appear promising for even the more mundane ordering and reordering of libraries themselves. The latter is suggested in what appears to be a new approach to research librarianship.

The core of this approach lies in how the research library envisions its work, and especially in that respect, how it sees its relationship to research. Francis Miksa, a scholar of classification systems, has examined research patterns within the traditional universe of knowledge orientation of research libraries. He urges the adoption of a revised perspective of the research process that will more adequately provide for its support within the university. Technological innovation is not itself at the heart of the revised perspective, Miksa says, but rather an appreciation of several changes that have taken place in research itself: a shift toward more vigorous and sophisticated research methods, the professionalization of research, and "vastly different and more complex patterns of research information flow."[16]

These factors, and new patterns of research information flow, Miksa says, not only make necessary a striking reordering of research library collection development policies, but even more importantly the establishment of a demand-driven information acquisition and access process. The latter should be focused on "the point of need, rather than on the basis of long-range collecting plans which are themselves based on universe of knowledge parameters."

This rejection of the classic research library worldview of collecting in order simply to represent a mythically stable universe of knowledge will also require the organization of collections on a highly distributed basis, the employment of highly specialized subject experts, themselves broadly distributed at the points where research is being done, and the retrieval of either *sign* or *text* as an option for the scholar.

In other words, the scholar might either review a subject listing (including a bibliographic citation with its attendant descriptive information regarding the text), or would review the text itself in either an abstract or full-text version, before deciding to "acquire" the text through any of several types of delivery systems. Miksa suggests a "find out about" process and a "get" process, "bibliographic control at the source," as a definition for this activity.

In a sense, the scholar makes a conscious choice of what is needed and what is not needed at both extremes of *this search and retrieve* process. Then a hypersystem process, it seems to me, would be applied to this model to help guide and move the user about in the knowledge system and to make selections throughout the information flow.

These points are all brought graphically to focus in a recent news story that describes a new class of microcomputer software that will dramatically extend the usefulness of personal computers, "programs known variously as daemons, sprites, phantoms, dragons or agents. . . . " through which "computer scientists believe that the daemon programs will increasingly evolve into intelligent assistants for computer users." More specifically, with respect to libraries, the article describes a prospective national digital library that would use the concept of daemon programs and a "knowledge daemon" to provide access to a huge array of widely distributed databases, including technical information, card catalogs, and the text of research papers and periodicals, and enable a scholar "to find a document anywhere with a single command to a personal computer."[17] This is clearly the cloak of hypersystems.

All of this calls for a new breed of scholar-librarians who will develop views of their world that are every bit as paradigm-shattering as those promoted by their Renaissance and 17th-century librarian colleagues Dee and Leibniz. This is a new order of memory storage and retrieval systems within a knowledge/thought (hypersystem) paradigm. It represents as significant an opportunity for a new orderliness in libraries as when knowledge was cast out of the monasteries to begin a journey toward different types of storage—toward magic memory retrieval. The result seeded the quickening of new sciences and human advancement.

We have our own Information Demon and memory magics to compare with the pseudosciences and mysteries of Shakespeare's time, in our quest to extend the capacity of the human mind, to relate knowledge, and to bring a new orderliness to libraries. Have we another Renaissance before us? I suspect we do, as new magics charm away traditional acceptations, as the universe rebuilds its recursive richness of human ingenuity, as libraries gather and order human knowledge in new electronic book chests, when the hurly-burly's done.

References

1. Yates, Frances A. *The Art of Memory.* Univ. of Chicago Pr., 1966. Virtually nothing had been done in English on the history of the memory arts and its role in the development of modern thought science until Dame Frances Amelia Yates began serious historical study in the field about

1940. For her extensive body of work on the Renaissance she was made a member of the Order of the British Empire in 1972 and was awarded the Wolfson Prize for historical writing in 1973.

2. *Ibid.,* pp. 127-128.

3. Crowley, John, "Shakespeare's Ghosts." In Sullivan, Jack, ed. *The Penguin Encyclopedia of Horror and the Supernatural.* Viking, 1986, p. 377-379. Crowley, a superb American fabulist, has begun a series of novels based on the mystical lives of Dee and Bruno, the first of which is *Aegypt* (Bantam, 1987).

4. Johnson, Elmer D. *History of Libraries in the Western World.* 2d ed. Scarecrow, 1970.

5. Yates, Frances A. *Theatre of the World.* Univ. of Chicago Pr., 1969, p. 5.

6. Loc. cit., p. 10.

7. Yates, Frances A. *Giordan Bruno and the Hermetic Tradition.* Univ. of Chicago Pr., 1964.

8. Yates, *The Art of Memory,* p. 369.

9. Loc. cit., p. 368-389.

10. Boorstin, Daniel. *The Discoverers.* Random, 1983, p. 535.

11. Yates, *The Art of Memory,* p. 225.

12. Gleick, James. *Chaos, Making a New Science.* Viking, 1987.

13. Poundstone, William. *The Recursive Universe: Cosmic Complexity and the Limits of Scientific Knowledge.* Morrow, 1985, p. 52-77, 90-102.

14. Glashow, Sheldon, "Tangled in Superstring: Some Thoughts on the Predicament Physics Is In," *The Sciences,* May-Jun., 1988, p. 25.

15. Gapen, D. Kaye, "Impact of Technologies on Resource-sharing, Linkages, Cooperation," is an unpublished paper presented at the American Library Association Annual Conference in New Orleans, Louisiana, July 9, 1988.

16. Miksa, Francis. *Research Patterns and Research Libraries.* OCLC, 1987.

17. Markoff, John, "For PC's, a New Class of Software," *New York Times,* Mar. 8, 1989, Section Y, p. 34.

REHUMANIZING INFORMATION: AN ALTERNATIVE FUTURE

John C. Swan

We have a peculiar *relationship* to information—I refer here to human beings in general, not just the subset known as "librarians." Rather, we are unique in that we express our appreciation for the importance of information by converting it into a commodity. In the beginning by means of an oral tradition, and then, when we traded in our memories for the written symbol in order to capture information in material form (the exchange described with such unsettling logic in Plato's *Phaedrus*), we learned how to collect it and parcel it out according to our will.

Collecting information is not, of course, the same as knowing it, but possession confers power. Warehouses of information, however necessary, represent only an early stage of the process of information control. Really efficient subjugation did not begin until we, as good children of the Age of Science, learned that we could master information in much the same manner as other mysteries of nature: by dissection. We discovered we could create multiple forms of access by dividing and conquering, first by arranging the dividends into alphabetical patterns and numerical schedules. Then, after much thought and hard work, we united the fruits of these endeavors with the triumphs of analysis in other areas, chiefly electronics and computa-

"Rehumanizing Information: An Alternative Future," by John C. Swan in *Library Journal*. Vol. 115, no. 14 (September 1, 1990), pp. 178-182; reprinted with permission from Reed Publishing, USA, copyright © 1990 Reed Publishing, USA.

tion. Out of this has grown a combination so potent that its dominance has earned it its own cliché, the Information Age.

Whether or not one accepts the phrase as accurate, there is no denying the power of this fusion of information analysis and the burgeoning capacities of digital storage and retrieval. For all its undeniable instrumentality, it is driven by forces that inevitably favor dissection and displacement over synthesis and stability. The once whole and stable text is now fragmented and dispersed into multiple contexts in the name of increased access, or at least increased impact. Now, the return to wholeness, holistic technologies, and ways of living are all healthy responses to the social fragmentation and alienation observed by even the most Complacent Yuppies among us.

Addicted to Analysis

Every time I open a journal, or find another survey questionnaire in my mail, I am reminded of the fact that this profession is addicted to self-examination, utterly obsessed with the process of seeking itself within itself, and parsing the results into the most elementary constituents. It just may be that a profession that can't find itself in the present will find itself parsed into file clerks, data processors, public relations managers, and baby-sitters by the time we all enter the informational Garden of Eden (or is that the Garden of ALA?).

However, for all the intelligence and progressive insight exhibited in the conferences and literature arising from this self-scrutiny, there are limitations to the process.

A recent survey of academic librarians sought their opinions as to where professional knowledge is best acquired. It began by drawing from a considerable body of library science to provide a distilled list of 56 "knowledge bases" of academic librarianship, that is, "proficiencies, skills, and information possessed by participating librarians." Of the 56, only one refers clearly to knowledge of subject content outside of specifically library-oriented fields; it is called, simply, "Subject field," in the singular. It is hardly startling that the respondents reported that they got most of their knowledge from library school and on-the-job training.[1] This study underscores the fact that

librarians, and not only academic librarians, have an essentially external relationship to knowledge.

Allow me to emphasize this already obvious point by describing
this basic tenet in terms of a few assumptions about the nature of the
librarian's professional responsibility.

- Our role is to provide access to information, not to master that
  information ourselves.

- It follows that we are not expected to have the expertise to
  make direct unmediated judgments about the quality or the
  relevance of the library materials we acquire, organize, and
  otherwise care for. That is, we are generally expected to rely
  on review literature, requests, and other aids, including
  occasionally our personal knowledge if it happens to be
  applicable to a particular subject, but that knowledge is not
  related to our training and roles as librarians.

- We are paid to make information available to others, not to
  interpret that information ourselves.

With suitable hedging and qualifying, these are sound assumptions. One of the ironies of the profession of librarianship is that as it
has become ever more sophisticated in the mastery of the manipulation, storage, and retrieval of data, our professional contact with the
substance itself has necessarily grown less and less intimate. Our
predecessors, from St. Jerome to Justin Winsor, would have found this
exchange of form for content strange indeed.

The problem with it is that in all our concentration upon the
challenge of our craft itself, we are in danger of losing sight of the
dynamic relationship we must maintain between that craft of form
and the actual content.

Out of the Darkness and Into the Data

Before this takes on the appearance of another dire warning of the
evils of technology, let me cite four examples of information problems,
of different types, all of which present certain difficulties to the

librarian who would lead a patron out of the darkness and into data—or beyond.

1. Many of us read Lillian Hellman's moving account of her friendship with the heroic "Julia" in *Pentimento,* that volume of her memoirs that deals with the war years. Many more of us saw the film, with Jane Fonda as the frightened but ultimately brave Hellman carrying out her mission for Julia in Nazi Europe. "What a word is truth," wrote Hellman in the preface to the one-volume version of these best sellers, "Slippery, tricky, unreliable. I tried in these books to tell the truth, I did not fool with the facts."[2] Well, now Hellman has passed on. Her biographer, William Wright, in his *Lillian Hellman: The Image. The Woman* (*LJ,* 11/1/86), demonstrated convincingly that she never undertook the trip to Germany, never went on that desperate search for "Julia's" baby (there never was such a child), and, in fact, never even met the real "Julia." The real "Julia" was Dr. Muriel Gardiner, a genuine heroine who escaped to this country in 1939, eventually to become grist for a personal history that is, it turns out, full of fooling with the facts.[3]

2. Cyril Burt's assertion of the high inheritability of I.Q., based upon his influential studies of separated twins, was taken as all but gospel for many years. Beginning in 1974 and culminating with the devastating critique by Leslie Hearnshaw in 1979, the Burt reputation was effectively and properly dismantled, his studies exposed as fabrications designed to support his own racist preconceptions. Although this was perhaps the biggest scandal in the history of modern psychology, and Burt's name now appears in textbooks principally as an example of scientific fraud, Diane Paul has demonstrated that Burt's data and conclusions are alive and well in current textbooks.[4]

3. In a very controversial and much-quoted paper published by *Nature* (after much delay, and accompanied by criticism and disclaimers), Walter Stewart and Ned Feder examined the trail of error and misrepresentation that extended through over a hundred biomedical research papers, stemming from one man's admitted fraud but in effect including several dozen unwitting coauthors. Given the complexity and specialization of scientific research and its dependence upon mutual trust, as well as the embedded nature of many of the errors, much unease has been generated by the investigators' modestly stated

conclusion: "Certain lapses from generally accepted standards of research may be more frequent than is commonly believed."[5]

4. *American Libraries* reports in its September 1988 issue (p. 640) that the Edmonton Public Library in Alberta, Canada, is now in the midst of controversy because of its policy, begun in 1985, of "balancing" their Holocaust collection with Holocaust-revisionist titles, i.e., those that for the most part deny that it ever took place. Some want these books, such as *The Dissolution of Eastern European Jewry,* removed altogether, but others, such as the Jewish Federation of Edmonton, grant the library the freedom "to buy whatever it likes," but take issue with the manner in which this material is integrated into the collection. For example, the book *Is the Diary of Anne Frank Genuine?* is now cataloged under "Frank, Anne; Jews; Netherlands, Biography." They would rather that it and similar extremist literature be classified in such a way as to reveal it as such, for instance, "Holocaust, Jewish: errors, inventions, etc." and that this material be shelved separately, with labels.

These four instances of the effects of fraud and distortion upon information are not posed here as rare and astonishing. There are more egregious examples occurring daily before our eyes in the area of political information, and, of course, history is full of them—in part, constructed out of them.

A Troublesome Nature

These four accounts were chosen rather as demonstrations of the peculiarly troublesome nature of the information that we librarians are called upon to harness and train. In terms of standard professionalism, and for that matter, common sense, the trouble is manageable, even anticipated. Hellman's book is given its cataloging; Wright's book on Hellman given its places also; and the subject treatment will bring the entries together. The reviews are indexed; the rest is up to the reader, with help, maybe, from the reference librarian, who reads reviews.

Similarly, textbooks with flawed data and conclusions should also be reviewed as such. It is not up to the librarian to know about Cyril

Burt, let alone about corrupt data; people who know how should take the responsibility to write the appropriate reviews, which, again, will be indexed. Though we acknowledge the ambiguities in the notion of a "balanced" collection, we do not, as professionals, interpret it to mean that we are constrained to buy as many lies about the Holocaust as truths. However, given the "slippery, tricky, unreliable" nature of truth, to borrow again from Hellman (an expert), we also avoid categorizing and labeling the materials for our collections according to some standard notion of the facts. We rely on our cataloging and indexing and reference work to aid people in their own struggles to sort them out.

All of these responses to the problem cited are sound, reasonable, and professionally correct; they all recognize and confront on some level the distortions involved, and they maintain the essential externality of the librarian's relationship to the actual substance of the errors and frauds that are the problem. But they are, finally, inadequate, even unrealistic, in the face of the real pressure of the modern information environment and the concomitant demand upon the librarian. The librarian cleaves to the professional goal that distinguishes this profession from all the others in the information game: the commitment to make available the whole fabric of information, rather than bits of data, sound bites, and images torn from it.

The simple fact is that the more a librarian knows about a particular topic, the better access she or he is able to provide to information about it. Knowledge of the real substance of a subject brings with it, one hopes, an awareness of the complexities present. The librarian who actually knows Hellman's books and Wright's biography is less likely to neglect that necessary complexity when the high school student comes to the library. The librarian who understands how bad and fraudulent data cling to life in disguised forms far from its origin is in a better position to use and guide others in the use of reference texts full of authoritative-looking tables and graphs.

Now, it is important to be clear about this: This is not an argument that librarians ought to be taught that which is true and that which is false in order to be able to point their patrons toward the former and away from the latter. I have put a lot of energy into arguing that our deepest professional loyalty must be to access, not to the truth as we or anybody else conceives it.[6] The patron seeking *Is the Diary of Anne Frank Genuine?* has just as much right to it as to the immortal (and true) work itself.

The advantage to knowing the insides as well as the outsides of books is not that the knowledge brings with it the ability to dictate the truth to others. Quite the reverse; the knowledge brings with it a greater appreciation of the nature of the truth.

The common thread of challenge that runs through the four information tales outlined above is that there is a dimension to access that is neglected in our standard conception of professional competence—as we measure it, that is, against those 56 knowledge bases or some other version of the librarians' consensus. In each case the relationship between sources of information, whether relatively simple as in the Hellman case or geometrically complex as in that studied by Stewart and Feder, rapidly becomes the key element in the mapping of a particular stretch of knowledge.

The technology of instant access to purposefully fragmented and disembodied texts and, in another part of our modern electronic forest, the primacy of the similarly disconnected visual images both exaggerate that which has always (since even before Marshall McLuhan) been true about information: changing its context changes its meaning. Destroying or obscuring or rearranging its originating perspectives—all of which we do for the sake of access, subject, and otherwise—can and often does fundamentally alter a package of information. It is not good enough for us to regard that package as a static thing that we can ever more conveniently store and retrieve without regard to its dynamic nature.

Connecting People to Information

We use computers to manipulate information in ways that are based upon our perceived notion of the nature of information. We store vast libraries on small CDs and create and use a growing range of electronic storage media on the basis of the same faith in the simple and discrete nature of the product that facilitated the invention and proliferation of paper indexes. Now, of course, we can do much more with indexes and keywords, but the concepts remain the same.

Establishing access to the world of information by way of subject headings and indexes has, of course, been necessary and wonderful, but as long as we take that accomplishment as the model for the understanding of the real processes of communication and conceptualization, we limit ourselves to static, external relationships with those processes. This grows no less true even as we shorten the time between the creation and the distribution of information, even information delivered in full texts, even information arrayed before the scholar by way of the most user-friendly cross-referencing text retrieval system at the most powerful workstation.

If we are to remain at the nexus of information in all its forms and people in all their forms, it behooves us to look more closely than is our wont at what it really means to connect the former to the latter. It may be, as in the case of the rapidly evolving world of end user searching and the aforementioned workstations, we cannot hope to continue to play such a central role. But I am not ready to concede even that, because the Information Age has given rise to an information need that cannot be addressed, even by the most sophisticated methods of access, as they are now conceived. It is the need to understand information.

The connection between the vastly increased and increasing production of information and the inability to absorb the output was outlined with extraordinary lucidity by Jacques Ellul in 1962. In his classic study of propaganda, Ellul wrote that "Modern man needs a relation to facts, to self-justification to convince himself that by acting in a certain way he is obeying reason and proved experience." He demonstrates that the master propagandists—and surely we recognize that we are surrounded by them—respond to this need with "rational, logical, factual propaganda." In other words, "Propaganda's content increasingly resembles information."

> Except for the specialist, information, even when it is very well presented, gives people only a broad image of the world. . . . A surfeit of data, far from permitting people to make judgments . . . prevents them from doing so. . . . They are caught in a web

of facts. . . . Thus the mechanism of modern information induces
a sort of hypnosis in the individual. . . . The more the techniques
of distributing information develop, the more the individual is
shaped by such information. It is not true that he can choose
freely with regard to what is presented to him as the truth. And
because rational propaganda thus creates an irrational situation,
it remains, above all, propaganda—that is an inner control over
the individual by a social force, which means that it deprives him
of himself.[7]

No one escapes this aspect of the Information Age, not the scholar
and researcher at their workstations, not librarians, not the master
manipulators of the media.

Ellul's point remains, and there is a rather cheerless irony in the
fact that our ever-more-successful "commodification" of information
is resulting in less and less mastery thereof for fewer and fewer people.

What can librarians do about it, we who are as far removed from
said master manipulators or the power structure as the patrons we
serve? We don't generate information; we don't understand it; we just
make it available.

The Teaching Role

Well, it is our problem, however narrowly we tend to define our role,
however external our professional relationship to the commodity in
our charge. Why? Because the real motivation behind all our discoveries and labors to master information, break it down, and create
access to it has been to aid people in the understanding of its content.
Despite our external relationship to our product, we remain the
information professionals with the most serious commitment to the
teaching role in connecting people with what they need to know.

We are not, cannot be content with showing people which keys
to push when. We too are deeply engaged in the computer revolution,
of course, but our perspective is different from that of our information
colleagues whose principal aim is to provide rapid access on the basis
of precisely determined demand. The informational world of the
children's librarian, the reference librarian, the bibliographer, the

cataloger is essentially more broad-gauged than that of the database specialist. The time values are different; the relationship to the patron, or at least the patron's search processes, are more intimate and at the same time less focused and more open to serendipity.

Our real goal must be to trace information to its sources, to illuminate the contexts through which it moves and changes. Further, we must find ways of rehumanizing information, making it again a source of illumination rather than paralysis. No, we cannot master the content itself, but if we cannot convey that content to others in ways that at least allow them better to understand its context, then we are doing no more than our subject access allows us to do now—and machines will do for us soon enough.

The Metaphysical Rant

All of this may be no more than metaphysical rant in the face of pressures that this business of librarianship is powerless to control, except by playing the information game ever faster and more efficiently. But there is a practical side to all of this, if only as an argument for our survival as a species. We can continue to be providers of a unique service, not only by assuring access for those who can't otherwise afford to buy a place in the information revolution, but by offering creative resistance to the fragmentation that that revolution has brought about.

Is this a call to arms against the Information Age and its digitizing powers? Quite otherwise. It is a claim based mostly upon hope that we aren't doing enough with these powers. We manipulate data according to old understandings; they aren't enough, and the more programs we make by bits and bytes, the blinder we are to the picture we create.

One concrete argument that flows from this opposes the two-year master's degree, in favor of advanced work in a subject field: the more actual exposure to real knowledge and its ambiguities a thoughtful person receives, the more that person is likely to appreciate the limitations of the standard tools of access—and therefore be able to use them all the more effectively in communicating that richer context. The machines themselves hold out a good deal of promise: perhaps some future hacker will be inspired to new feats of hypertextualism, multiple forms of access that prompt the user as to the shifting meanings of that which has been called to the screen.

The versions of her life presented by Lillian Hellman and by her biographer and others could be linked in programming that gave the patron the option of comparing them in illuminating ways. The arguments against the existence of the Holocaust promulgated by the fringe could be summoned up, not just as bibliographic records or even texts, but as part of an array of relevant texts and criticisms on the subject. The old problem of labels and their prejudicial effects would disappear in favor of the exact reverse of such censorship: comprehensive and comprehensible access to the full spectrum of ideas and information.

This approach would require a whole new dimension in programming, in addition to the standard levels of processing. It would require a lot of resources, and a lot of motivation, which, given the overwhelming tendency to focus on one small piece of data wanted for one purpose as quickly as possible, is not very likely. But we can hope. There just may be a real librarian among all those keyboard jockeys.

This version of the video display millennium, vague as it is, may never arrive, but that does not let us off the hook. Unless we choose to throw in our lot entirely with the dominant producers and distributors of the commodity—and many of us have and will; the pay is a lot better—we librarians must affirm that our relationship to information is different. To the degree that the Information Age is itself clouding the understanding of its principal commodity, we must offer not only a difference but resistance. Even at the risk of losing our public—and we won't—we must continue to offer the opportunity for discovery, even at the cost of convenience; for depth, even in exchange for simplicity; for richness of perspective, even if it means the loss of precious seconds in our speedy document delivery services. No doubt there are occasions when more information quicker makes a genuinely positive contribution, but I still wonder at the costs, the trade-offs. When someone successfully correlates a rise in computer access to an increase in the collective wisdom, doubters like me will be proven wrong. So far, the signs are not particularly encouraging.

Whatever our ultimate success in bringing the information revolution in line with real human needs, we must not forget that however copious and convenient it is, information without vision is blindness. In a thousand different ways, usually modest and commonsensical, sometimes ingenious, occasionally even wise, we have tried to help them understand what is it they are getting. However external to the act of understanding information we consider ourselves to be professionally, we must insist on a future that preserves that human connection. No one else seems to be up to the task.

References

1. Powell, Ronald R., "Sources of Professional Knowledge for Academic Librarians," *College and Research Libraries,* Jul. 1988, p. 332-340, and its predecessor by Powell and Sheila D. Creth, "Knowledge Bases and Library Education," *CRL,* Jan. 1986, pp. 16-27.
2. Quoted by Geoffrey C. Ward in "Making up the Truth," *American Heritage,* Sept./Oct. 1987, pp. 18-20.
3. *Ibid.*
4. Paul, Diane B., "The Market as Censor," *P.S.: Political Science and Politics,* Winter 1988, pp. 31-35.
5. Stewart, Walter & Ned Feder, "The Integrity of the Scientific Literature," *Nature,* Jan. 15, 1987, p. 207-214.
6. Swan, John C., "Untruth or Consequences," *LJ,* Jul. 1986, pp. 44-52.
7. Ellul, Jacques. *Propaganda.* tr. by Konrad Kellen & Jean Lerner. Knopf, 1986; originally *Propagandes,* 1962, pp. 84-87.

ACCURACY OF INFORMATION PROVISION: THE NEED FOR CLIENT-CENTRED SERVICE

Paul F. Burton

Introduction

The need for objective measurements of the success of library and information services (LIS) has never been greater. With budgets and staffing under pressure, LIS managers must be able to demonstrate effective use of the service in order to prove that it merits continued support. LIS have more than a simple custodial role, and managers must be concerned that resources are being used to the fullest extent possible, consistent with accuracy and the expressed needs of the user.

In the wider context, the potential for competition from other information services available to users can no longer be ignored. The growth of information technology (IT) has meant the development of a new information marketplace: LIS are being forced out of the "self-defined ghetto" (1, p. 204), where they previously enjoyed a quasi-monopoly of information provision, into this marketplace, which resounds to the cries of other information providers making ready use of (and profiting from) electronic sources—a move which also brings a clash of ideologies. Entry barriers to information provision are being lowered and substitute products threaten monopolies, while simultaneously increasing the power of buyers (users) over LIS

(2). LIS must orient themselves towards this marketplace and its requirements: unfortunately, many LIS seem willing to forgo the move (or are reluctant to make it), and there is every possibility that they will be forced into sidestreet operations, to be ignored by the many. The early stages of the process have already been documented:

> Unseen and unheard, the library staff are not automatically seen to be organization's information guardians or advisers: they are the keepers of document collection and are not consulted about information matters outside the library (3, p. 170)

> Libraries are failing to take responsibility for the wider information opportunities (outside the library) that online is clearly opening up for them. (4, p. 149)

With competition growing and continuing pressure on resources, LIS can no longer rely on a monopoly of information provision, but must "deliver the goods" if they are to continue in business. They must move away from function-oriented operations towards more client-centred services, and this is a move which, ironically, can be facilitated by their own growing use of IT (and, let it be said, some innovative and entrepreneurial LIS have made the move). Technical services such as cataloguing and classification become means to the end of client-centred services (which they should have been, but rarely were), which in turn means that public services (the reference desk, etc.) become "front of house" operations which heavily influence the user's attitude to the entire service and require adequate resourcing. Client-centred service implies developing LIS which reflect users' needs for information, not systems which require users to express their needs in terms which the LIS can answer. LIS must concern themselves with both the "longitudinality and laterality" of users, where the former refers to the period of time in which the LIS is interested in its users and the latter to the number of aspect of the user which are of concern. Typically, LIS have high longitudinality but low laterality: "Maximized laterality requires that other behaviour besides that of reading be regarded as organizationally relevant for libraries" (5, p. 182). Information needs arise in a particular environment, not *in vacuuo,* and will be influenced by that environment: a client-centred LIS competing in the marketplace will have to consider the user's environment. Taylor has developed a user-driven model which ensures that the "information use environment" determines the design of LIS and the values which they can add to information:

> The major . . . reason for the existence of an information system is to store and to provide information and knowledge in usable chunks to those who presently or in the future will live and work in certain environments, and who, as a result, have or will have certain problems which information may help in clarifying or even in solving (6, p. 24).

Half-Right Services

Most LIS managers believe that they are running an efficient and effective service, and point to measures of user satisfaction as proof. Unfortunately, most such qualitative and subjective tests are inadequate as measures of the success of LIS, and are frequently at odds with more objective tests which have been applied.

In 1988, there was a brief flurry in the UK professional press over the results of an unobtrusive test of public library reference services. Students from a school of library and information studies asked 12 public libraries of different sizes and in different locations the single question, "What have you got on Robert Maxwell?" Six of the libraries provided "a partial answer," a "success" rate of 50 percent. The publication of the results (7) produced nine letters to the editor expressing reactions ranging from "we must do something" to criticisms of the methodology as superficial and archaic, and one academic library was prompted to carry out an unobtrusive test of its reference service—with essentially similar results (8).

Taken in isolation, that study may not have meant a great deal, but far from being an isolated instance, it forms part of a body of literature which, in general terms, makes exactly the same point—reference services in academic and public libraries provide correct responses to between 50 and 60 percent of the questions put to them by users. So frequently has this result been found that it has been enshrined in the literature as the "55 percent rule" (9, 10). Table 1 summarizes the results of 28 studies of the accuracy of reference services published since 1971: the mean success rate for all studies is 56.7 percent, although if the results for obtrusive testing and those studies which measured *user evaluation* are eliminated, the mean success rate drops to 50.98 per cent: "The evidence is mounting that serious problems exist in the quality of reference desk service in many academic and public libraries . . . " (11, p. 69).

If these results are accurate, then the foundation stone of continued success for LIS—front of house service to users—is demonstrably weak, and we must ask: "Why is the standard of accuracy in reference services so low?" and "What can be done to improve the standard?"

What Is Unobtrusive Testing?

Unobtrusive testing is one of a number of techniques which have been used to test the accuracy of information services. As its name implies, it is based on the principle that LIS staff should not be aware that they are being tested at the moment of dealing with an inquiry (although they may have been informed that testing would take place at some time. Questions are posed, either in person or by telephone, by "proxies," who may play the role of a specific category of user (often a student). The answers to the inquiries have usually been determined by the survey team beforehand, thus providing an objective measure of accuracy, and the team may also ascertain that the necessary reference sources required to answer the question are available. Once the inquiry is completed, the proxy completes a worksheet or questionnaire to provide details of the answer given, and often of other factors such as availability of staff, attitudes to inquirer and inquiry, depth of reference interview, and so on. The studies carried out to date have frequently used inquiries which would elicit short, factual answers, but there is no reason why more detailed and longer questions should not also be evaluated. A recent study of an academic library contained three types of question: questions on library policy, short factual questions, and more lengthy bibliographic questions (8). Unobtrusive testing as a technique in the social sciences is not new: it was first proposed by Webb and others in the mid-1960s (12), and first applied to LIS in doctoral dissertations by Crowley (13) and, later, Childers (14), two studies which were later combined into a single monograph (15). Hernon and McClure have described in detail its application to LIS (16), and it has since been employed in a variety of tests of the accuracy of reference services, with the results shown in Table 1.

There are variations in specific aspects of the tests, such as the number and nature of questions posed, and the criteria on which "success" was judged, which can make direct comparison difficult. In some studies, for example, success was based on the *user's evaluation* as to whether the answer was exactly what was needed, rather than a more objective measure of accuracy (such studies are indicated in Table 1, from which it can be seen that they may result in a higher score). In some instances, a number of questions were asked, while in others only one or two were posed.

Obtrusive testing is a variation in that the LIS staff know that they are being tested. This can be by a third party (a member of the survey team) or by colleagues, and it normally results in a higher level of accuracy (although one such study [17] also found the 55 percent rule to be operative).

Criticisms of Unobtrusive Testing

The results summarized in Table 1 have raised serious questions about the accuracy and effectiveness of reference services. Before going further, however, it is important to be aware of the criticisms which have been levelled at the technique. Some of these criticisms are valid, while some are simply attempts to explain away the results.

Much has been made of the fact that most studies have used short, factual inquiries which, while they are easy to set, control and analyseand therefore facilitate the conduct of the study, are unrepresentative of the true range of questions normally posed to a reference service, since they do not, for example, include the long factual question (a comprehensive bibliography on a subject), the gathering

Table 1: Summary of Results of Unobtrusive Tests of Reference Services

Country	Academic or public library	Reference	Correct answers %
USA	P	Crowley & Childers, 1971 (15)	54.20
USA	P	Crowley & Childers, 1971 (15)	54.75
USA	A	King & Berry, 1973 (32)	60.00
UK	P	House, 1974 (33)	40.00
USA	P	Peat, Marwick, Mitchell, 1975 (34)	40.00
USA	A	Howell, Reeves & Willigen 1976 (35)	84.00a
Aus.	P	Ramsden, 1978 (36)	49.20
USA	P	Childers, 1978 (37)	47.60
Aus.	A	Schmidt, 1980 (38)	13.30
USA	Various	Kantor, 1981 (39)	69.00b
USA	P	Weech & Goldhor, 1982 (40)	70.20
USA	P	Weech & Goldhor, 1982 (40)	85.30c
USA	A	Myers & Jirjees, 1983 (41)	50.40
USA	A	Myers & Jirjees, 1983 (41)	57.10
USA	A	McClure & Hernon, 1983 (42)	37.40
USA	P	University of Illinois, 1983- (43)	80.00d
USA	P	University of Illinois, 1983- (43)	59.00d
USA	P	University of Illinois, 1983- (43)	71.00d
USA	P	Gers & Seward, 1985 (44)	38.20
USA	A	Bunge, 1985 (45)	55.20b
USA	P&A	Hernon & McClure, 1986 (10)	61.80
USA	P&A	Benham & Powell, 1987 (46)	53.00
USA	P	Benham & Powell, 1987 (46)	59.00
USA	A	Murfin & Gugelchuk, 1987 (47)	55.80c
USA	A	Bunge & Murfin, 1987 (17)	55.80c
UK	A (Univ.)	Williams, 1987 (48)	61.10
UK	A Poly.)	Williams, 1987 (48)	64.40
UK	P	Lea & Jackson, 1988 (7)	50.00
UK	A	Bickley et al., in prep. (8)	58.10
		Mean success rate	56.00

Sources: adapted from Crowley, 1985 (28); Douglas, 1988 (29), with additional data from sources listed.

(a) Evaluated by patrons as pinpointing needs very well.
(b) Users completely satisfied or received what was wanted.
(c) Obtrusive testing.
(d) Annual series, questions changed each year.

of views and opinions expressed in the literature of a subject, current awareness and so on. Nor, it is pointed out, do they cover aspects of the reference interview, such as the covert/overt instruction which can take place, and they make no provision or allowance for the service's philosophy on information provision, which might range from the provision of recorded information available within the LIS only to referral to a known expert.

However, short, factual questions are very much part of reference service life, and may constitute a large part, if not the majority, of questions posed by users. Where the criticism is *valid*, however, is in pointing out that results *cannot be generalized to the reference service as a whole*. They should not be allowed, by the process of synecdoche, to represent the entire reference service function (11, p. 73), and until unobtrusive testing examines all the variations in questions, the varieties of reference interview and the service's philosophy of information provision, it is too early to speak of an "unrecognized crisis" (11, p. 69). In the meantime, we must not be sidetracked (panicked) into developing expertise in the short factual question at the expense of the larger problem of diagnosis of information need, and the filtering and synthesizing of information to meet demand.

Daniel has gone further and suggested (11, p. 78) that fact provision should not be seen as a major library service, but as an adjunct to referral and bibliographic provision, because information technology will eventually replace the library in this respect (though this begs the question of the information poor who lack access to the technology). She advocates a limited service for fact provision (say 3 hours per week), but with the important proviso that such service would have a *guaranteed 95 percent accuracy*. The question of guaranteed accuracy is considered below.

Whilst Daniel rightly points out that the "minimal amount of time" spent on the reference interview for factual questions (a criticism made by some studies) is due to the nature of the questions and not to some limiting factor (an internal clock) imposed by the library staff, her further comment, that "perhaps the questions were not intrinsically interesting enough to challenge the mettle or engage the interest of the librarian," is itself open to criticism. Whilst acknowledging that an interesting question may spur staff to additional effort, intrinsic merit or interest of questions have no influence whatsoever on the effort put into answering inquiries—or do they?

A further factor is the need to distinguish between the *absolute* and *relative* accuracy of answers. LIS staff, the argument runs, may have an ideal of absolute accuracy (which unobtrusive testing seeks to establish) and which they use to evaluate results, but users are willing to accept less accurate responses, which staff would judge as failures of the service. This is not borne out by studies of reference service provision which have found a close match between the evaluation of an answer by staff and by user, but it suggests that the task is, in fact, to upgrade user expectations (11, p. 79).

There is a low expectation of service sector provision (which includes LIS), a factor often used in arguments in favour of charging—nobody rates a free service very highly. Charging, however, is a side issue here. If expectations of quality of service are raised, then what level of accuracy would be acceptable, and what are the associated resource implications? What, for example, if LIS were to guarantee 80, 90 or even 100 percent accuracy in its answers (11, p. 77)? Why, indeed, do LIS not already give such guarantees, staffed as they are by highly qualified individuals, with a string of post-nominal letters? Why is the level of service not comparable to those services provided in the commercial sector, which, for a price, guarantee 100 per cent success (18)—the important point being that many customers are willing to pay the price?

Attempts to *justify* the 55 percent success rate (rather than to question the results) centre on the nature of the task. The sheer range of questions with which a reference service can be faced in the course of a typical day is said to be a root problem: "Reference librarians . . . cannot transmute themselves into instant experts on every subject, *mutatis mutandis,* 20 or 50 times an hour" (11, p. 71). It seems a fair point, but is it? Do we not, as information professionals, follow Dr. Johnson and claim that, although we do not know an answer ourselves, we know where to find it?

For others, the problem lies in the conflicting priorities of library service and the belief that staff have assigned the wrong priority to reference work. Reference work is "stigmatized" and those who are required to spend lengthy periods "at the reference desk" come to consider themselves as martyrs or scapegoats for others who are thus freed to attend faculty seminars, committees and "one-on-one database search appointments" (11, p. 72). If there is any element of truth in this (and an intuitive reaction says there is), we should ask whether we are putting the right people into this upfront operation so important to the service and its image, for if we are not, what does this do for users' expectations of the quality of service?

Numerous reports have indicated that a significant impact of automation. in LIS is on technical services such as cataloguing and classification procedures. The use of bibliographic utilities for cataloguing has eliminated the need for many professionals in technical services (19; 20; 21; 22) and paraprofessionals are capable of doing much of what remains: at Penn State University Library clerical staff carry out copy cataloguing with OCLC and LC MARC, while paraprofessionals deal with incomplete records and supervise the clerical staff. Professionals supervise the paraprofessionals, assign subject headings and *work in public service areas in a liaison role.* The result: 5000 more titles per year processed by 25 percent fewer staff: 91 percent of users prefer the online catalogue, despite (staff) concerns over less than perfect records. "Thus, there is some preliminary evidence that the existence of some inconsistencies in the online catalogue is offset by the efficiency and convenience of online access to all library holdings" (19, p. 148).

When a Danish university library went for quick and dirty cataloguing in a bid to reduce a backlog caused by too high a standard of cataloguing, users did not even notice the difference in the level of cataloguing (23). Users, it seems, prefer quality of service over arcane systems used to maintain the mystique of cataloguing (24). Indeed, on reflection, it seems ludicrous that users are kept waiting (sometimes for months) for new monographs simply because it takes so long to catalogue them.

Automated LIS have fewer "work activities" and need 24 percent fewer staff, but the use of IT can lead to more activities (all those tasks that no one had time to do because of the basic routine), so technical services professionals can be moved into public services (25). By reducing the resources required for technical services, there can be a redistribution in favour of public services, and an opportunity to develop client-centred, rather than function-centred, services, providing visible and effective access to information and improving the LIS's awareness of users' needs. Unfortunately LIS have failed to develop a long-term strategy for IT. To date, its introduction has been simply to reduce routine or to speed up certain processes. Only recently has the notion of using IT for advantage in the information marketplace been suggested. Properly applied, a long-term strategy ensures that the redistribution of resources is directed towards the active development of client-centred services.

When LIS had a virtual monopoly in information provision, there was no pressure to abandon the minutiae of cataloguing and classification, and the objectives of technical services displaced public service objectives—but those days are drawing to a close, even though cataloguing staff may display a tendency gradually to increase the level of cataloguing (23).

But is it sufficient (even with the laudable aim of avoiding redundancies) simply to transfer technical service staff to front of house operations where they will sit uncomfortably on public view? How "good with the public" is someone trained in the details of AACR2 and DC20? Can they be retrained? Is the stigma of the reference desk due to an earlier emphasis during the education of LIS staff on the "professionalism" of cataloguing and classification *vis-à-vis* other work, or is it also due to differing personality characteristics? The abilities and characteristics needed of those working in reference services are very different from those required in technical services such as cataloguing and classification. Introverted bibliophiles make poor communicators and lack the interpersonal and communication skills required at the reference desk, yet communication skills were rated highest of seven qualities sought by both personnel managers and heads of information services when recruiting information workers (26, pp. 35-6). Similar results were obtained by Moore: "About half [of the employers] thought that skills in organizing and retrieving information and interpersonal communication skills were *essential* for the jobs. Overall, more than 80 per cent thought that such skills were desirable" (27, p. 37, original emphasis).

If the emphasis of the future is to be on communicators with interpersonal skills *and* a knowledge of reference work, the schools of library and information studies must grasp the nettle and ensure that their graduates and diplomates have those skills enhanced by their education and training, and that, in turn, has implications for the type of applicant which the schools should be accepting into their courses.

The problem is exacerbated, suggested Shapiro (11, p. 75) by the problem of burnout and the higher turnover of reference staff caused by the "continuous barrage of questions," and this may be related to the concept of unsuitability for reference work. She feels that throwing (in-house) training programmes at the problem is not enough and that we must identify the root causes of the problem and consider questions such as: why is there a lack of familiarity with basic reference publications, why is minimal time spent on the reference interview (would staff prefer not to work with the public, or are there queues building up?), why do staff appear not to know (ineptitude, inadequate training, pressed for time?), why are some staff "abrasive" with the public (personality flaws or burnout?). Some of these questions are obviously related to points made earlier.

A major criticism of unobtrusive testing (though not, it should be noted, of the results) concerns its ethnics: comments are similar to those which have been raised over any form of covert observation. Crowley suggests that there is risk of psychological damage to self-esteem when library staff learn that they have given inaccurate information (28, p. 64). Is it ethical to observe staff at work without their knowing about it? Should staff know that they are being monitored, even though it has been shown that, when staff are aware of testing being carried out, they perform noticeably better, the implication being that they increase their efforts for the duration of the study and then lapse back to conform with the 55 percent rule?

Whilst there may well be some psychological damage to staff (nobody likes to be told they are wrong 45 percent of the time), what of the damage to the users? The problem is that we may rarely know the consequence of the information we provide: that should not make us complacent, and with the growth of competition the consequences will soon be obvious—users will vote with their feet and go to the competition.

Finally, the studies have been criticized for not indicating what remedial action should be taken, and for not providing guidance on the causes of failure: are resources inadequate or policies on information provision inappropriate (29)? This criticism is largely justified, though others have taken up the challenge.

Douglas himself has extracted a number of themes relating to reference service failure and suggested appropriate remedial action, mainly in the form of monitoring and evaluation and the development of suitable in-house policies which would result in greater improvements than episodic testing alone. He categorizes failures under six headings, ranging from "wrong information" to "query not accepted (because the client is not a member)," and suggests that we can develop policies for improvement.

Others have suggested that the answer lies in improved education and training, both by the schools of library and information studies and the LIS themselves (workshops, seminars, etc.) (10), or in the provision of a three-tier reference service, in which an information desk handles only directional and routine inquiries (with guaranteed accuracy?), while more complicated questions are passed to the other tiers to be dealt with by subject experts (11, p. 76). This would go some way to alleviating the problem of the "instant expert," though it presupposes the presence of subject specialists at all times.

In more general terms, the answer is to identify the qualities associated with a good reference service and then to develop a set of indicators for those standards which could be used in evaluating the work of reference staff and enabling them to develop and improve. Schwartz and Eakin outline three broad characteristics (behaviourial, knowledge, and reference skills) with a total of 31 specific characteristics, and then develop a set of standards or service objectives from those characteristics (30). The method has been used in the reference service of the University of Michigan's Medical Library (where a three-tier reference service was established), and the experience has been judged to be a positive one.

No single approach is sufficient, however. LIS have a portfolio of assets such a stock, property, professional skills, goodwill, IT base and heritage items, and the task is to maximize those assets (18), to ensure maximum exploitation of stock and the skills of staff. Standards of service are undoubtedly required—how else to evaluate provision of information? In-house monitoring will indicate areas where those

standards are not being met, and policies will indicate the necessary
remedial action, which may include in-house training programmes.
A major step towards improving the accuracy rate must come from
the schools of library and information studies, who must recognize
the new market in which LIS operate and must select and educate
students accordingly, not only in the use of information sources but
also in communication skills, in the role of information in the user's
world, and in the techniques of asset maximization.

Conclusion

In general, few of the criticisms which have been levelled at unobtrusive testing affect the results which have been reported, and we must
continue to be concerned by those results.

We claim to be a profession, and use that claim to justify our status
and our salaries (and implicitly or explicitly the value of our services).
Can we hold on to that claim when we are found to be operating below
the high levels which most people assume of "the professions"? If the
doctor, surgeon or lawyer were to work at the level of accuracy
suggested, there would be an outcry, as 45 percent of their clients were
wrongly diagnosed, died on the operating table or were unjustly
incarcerated—indeed, look at the outcry which develops when these
professions do get it wrong! At least one commentator has suggested
that, on the basis of the results of the Lea and Jackson study, there is
no case for librarians being better paid (31). Surely we do not subscribe
to the belief that, because an inaccurate answer is not life-threatening,
we do not need to maintain higher standards? How do we know the
consequences of our mistakes? We need more research into the
contribution of information to work which users do and the environment in which their information needs arise. It is not difficult to
hypothesize about some of the consequences of inaccurate information: presumably half of Lea and Jackson's students would have failed
that part of their course which was based on an essay on Robert
Maxwell!

A number of crucial questions must be answered in order to improve reference services (11, p. 70). In summary form, these questions (with some suggested answers) are:

1. Should the profession be satisfied with 55 percent accuracy? (In general terms, this is unacceptable: in a competitive market it is suicidal).
2. To what extent is accuracy a high priority, in the light of other job responsibilities? This suggests the wrong priorities: accurate information provision must have the highest priority).
3. What degree of accuracy can we expect for in-depth questions or questions requiring the use of non-paper formats? (There seems to be no prima-facie evidence for suggesting that in-depth questions, etc., should not be answered with the same high level of accuracy as the short factual question, and if the LIS utilizes IT for factual questions, then it can concentrate its resources on the in-depth problems.)
4. (a) What are the role and responsibility of staff and professional organizations for training and improving the accuracy rate?
   (b) What long-term programmes of education and training are appropriate?
   (c) Is there now a need for a national programme of continuing education? (All three are relevant to the problem. The initial education and training provided by the schools must be complemented by focused in-house training and opportunities for continuing and mid-career education of LIS staff.)
5. Has there been an inappropriate allocation of resources, e.g. to collection building, bibliographic control and networking, rather than to strengthening the provision of accurate information? (In general, and with the benefit of hindsight—yes, as a result of the pressures of the times in which these decisions were made. The times now demand a new allocation of resources more fitted for the new marketplace.)
6. To what extent is a "half right" service attributable to staff competency, administrative policy or education? (All three have played a part: earlier answers are relevant.)

Now that LIS recognizes the futility of holding comprehensive stocks and the importance of cooperation, and with the opportunity to reallocate resources from back of house operations, the time has come to concentrate efforts and reallocate priorities on the maximum effective and accurate exploitation of information resources, regardless of where they are held:

> managers can determine how well their reference staff perform existing services and meet formal objectives. They can reexamine library reference service and, where necessary, develop specific strategies to better meet the present and future information needs of library clientele. Such service, in the information age, must provide accurate bibliographic and physical access, and offer referral to a more diverse range of information resources and formats—housed internally and externally. (11, p. 71)

To date, we have been rearranging the deckchairs on the *Titanic*: it is time to set a new course which will take the LIS around the icebergs—and into new waters.

References

1. Seeger, T. Changes in the occupation and profession of information work: the impact of the new communication technologies. *Social Science Information Studies*, 1983, 199-208.
2. Porter, M.E. *Competitive advantage: creating and sustaining superior performance*. Collier Macmillan, 1985.
3. Nicholas, D., Erbach, G., Pang, Y. W., and Paalman, K. *End-users of online information systems: an analysis*. Mansell, 1988.
4. Nicholas, D., Harris, K., and Erbach, G. *Online searching: its impact on information users*. Mansell, 1987.
5. Hanks, G., and Schmidt, C. J. An alternative model of a profession for librarians. *College and Research Libraries*, 1975, 36 (3), 175-87.
6. Taylor, R. S. *Value-added processes in information systems*. Ablex, 1986.
7. Lea, P., and Jackson, L. The exception or the rule? The quality of reference service in public libraries. *Library Association Record*, 1988, 90 (10), 582-5.

8. Bickley, J., Craig, S., Kennedy, A., and Burton, P. F. Unobtrusive testing of enquiry services. In preparation.

9. Durrance, J. C. Reference success: does the 55% rule tell the whole story? *Library Journal,* 1989, 114 (7), 31-6.

10. Hernon, P., and McClure, C. Unobtrusive reference testing: the 55% rule. *Library Journal,* 1986, 111 (7), 37-41.

11. Hernon, P. Library reference service: an unrecognized crisis. A symposium. *Journal of Academic Librarianship,* 1987, (2), 69-80.

12. Webb, E. J. *Unobtrusive measures: nonreactive search in the social sciences.* Rand McNally, 1986.

13. Crowley, T. The effectiveness of information service in medium size public libraries. Ph.D. dissertation, Rutgers University, 1968.

14. Childers, T. Telephone information service in public libraries: a comparison of performance and descriptive statistics collected by the State of New Jersey. Ph.D. dissertation, Rutgers University, 1970.

15. Crowley, T., and Childers, T. *Information service in public libraries: two studies.* Metuchen, 1971.

16. Hernon, P., and McClure, C. *Unobtrusive testing and library reference services.* Ablex, 1987.

17. Bunge, C. A., and Murfin, M. E. Reference questions: data from the field. *RQ,* 1987, 27 (1), 15-18.

18. Cronin, B. *Libraries 2000 AD: the skills requirement.* Keynote address to Colleges of Further and Higher Education Annual Study Conference on Personal Management Skills, Glasgow, April 1990 (in press).

19. Bednar, M. Automation of cataloging: effects on use of staff, efficiency and service to patrons. *Journal of Academic Librarianship,* 1988, 14 (3), 145-9.

20. Dakshinamurti, G. Automation's effect on library personnel. *Canadian Library Journal,* 1985, 42 (6), 343-51.

21. Waters, D. Assessing the impacts of new technology on library employees. *LASIE,* 1986, 17 (1), 20-7.

22. Waters, D. New technology and job satisfaction in university libraries. *LASIE,* 1988, 18 (3), 103-8.

23. Cotta-Schonberg, M. von. Automation and academic library structure. *Libri,* 1988, 39 (1), 47-63.

24. Sanders, G. Tasks, technicians and tenosynovitis: the impact of technology on job design in libraries. *Australasian College Libraries,* 1985, 3 (3), 107-14.

25. Dehennin, W. Aspects of organization in a computerised library. *Liber Bulletin,* 1988, (31), 117-30.

26. Angell, C. *Information, new technology and manpower* (Library and Information Research Report 52). British Library, 1987.

27. Moore, N. The emerging employment market for librarians and information workers in the UK. *Journal of Librarianship,* 19 (1), 31-40.

28. Crowley, T. Half-right reference: is it true? *RQ,* 1985, 25 (1), 59-68.

29. Douglas, I. Reducing failures in the reference service. *RQ,* 1988, 28 (1), 94-101.

30. Schwartz, D. G., and Eakin, D. Reference service standards, performance criteria and evaluation. *Journal of Academic Librarianship,* 1986, 12 (1), 4-8.

31. Harvey, T. N. Letter to the editor, *Library Association Record,* 1988, 90 (12), 705.

32. King, G., and Berry, R. *Evaluation of University of Minnesota Libraries Reference Department telephone information study: pilot study.* University of Minnesota Library School, 1973.

33. House, D. Reference efficiency or reference deficiency. *Library Association Record,* 1974, 76 (11), 222-3.

34. Peat, Marwick, Mitchell & Co. *California Public Library Systems: a comprehensive review with guidelines for the next decade.* Peat, Marwick, Mitchell & Co., 1975.

35. Howell, B. L., Reeves, E. B., and Willigen, J. van. Fleeting encounters: a role analysis of reference librarian-patron interaction. *RQ,* 1976, 16 (1), 124-9.

36. Ramsden, M. *Performance measurement of some Melbourne public libraries: a report of the Library Council of Victoria.* Library Council of Victoria, 1978, 51-79.

37. Childers, T. *The effectiveness of information in service in public libraries: Suffolk Co. Final Report.* Drexel University School of Library and Information Science, 1978.

38. Schmidt, J. Reference performance in college libraries. *Australian Academic and Research Libraries,* June 1980, 87.

39. Kantor, P. B. Quantitative evaluation of the reference process. *RQ,* 1981, 21 (1), 43-52.

40. Weech, T. L., and Goldhor, H. Obtrusive versus unobtrusive evaluation of reference service in five Illinois public libraries: a pilot study. *Library Quarterly,* 1982, 52, 305-24.

41. Myers, M. J., and Jirjees, J. M. *The accuracy of telephone reference/information services in academic libraries: two studies.* Scarecrow Press, 1983.

42. McClure, C. R., and Hernon, P. *Improving the quality of reference service for government publications.* American Library Association, 1983.

43. University of Illinois, Library Research Centre. *Illinois Library statistical report.* Illinois State Library, 1983-.
44. Gers, R., and Seward, L. J. Improving reference service: results of a statewide study. *Library Journal,* 1985, 110, 32-5.
45. Bunge, C. A. Factors related to reference question answering success: the development of a data-gathering form. *RQ,* 1985, 24 (4), 482-6.
46. Benham, F., and Powell, R. R. *Success in answering reference questions: two studies.* Scarecrow Press, 1987.
47. Murfin, M. E., and Gugelchuk, G. M. Development and testing of a reference transaction. *College and Research Libraries,* 1987, 48 (4), 314-38.
48. Williams, R. An unobtrusive test of academic library reference services. *Library and Information Research News,* 1987, 10 (37/8), 12-40.

Bibliography

Bath, F. Uneven reference service: approaches for decreasing the source of conflict at the reference desk. *Reference Librarian,* 1985 (12), 49-63.

Birbeck, W. P., and Whittaker, K. A. Room for improvement: an unobtrusive testing of British public library reference service. *Public Library Journal,* 1987 2 (4), 55-60.

Bunge, C. A. Measurement and evaluation of reference and adult services. *RQ,* 1983, 22 (3), 251-4.

Craghill, D., Neale, C., and Wilson, T. D. *The impact of IT on staff deployment in UK public libraries* (British LIbrary Research Paper 69). British Library, 1989.

Gapen, D. K. Transition and change: technical services at the center. *Library Resources and Technology,* 1989, 33 (3), 284-96.

Goldhor, H. An analysis of available data on the number of public library reference questions. *RQ,* 1987, 27 (2), 195-201.

Hansel, P. J. Unobtrusive evaluation: an administrative learning experience. *Reference Librarian,* 1987, (19), 315-25.

Hernon, P. Utility measures, not performance measures, for library reference services. *RQ,* 1987, 26 (4), 449-59.

Jones, D. E. Library support staff and technology: perceptions and opinions. *Library Trends,* 1989, 37 (4), 432-56.

Kemp, J., and Dillon, D. Collaboration and the accuracy imperative: improving reference service now. *RQ,* 1989, 29 (1), 62-70.

Kesselman, M., and Watstein, S. B. The measurement of reference and information services. *Journal of Academic Librarianship,* 1987, 13 (1), 24-30.

Kiesler, S., Obrosky, S., and Pratto, F. Automating a university library: some effects on work and workers. In Kiesler, S., and Sproull, S. (eds.). *Computing and change on campus.* Cambridge University Press, 1987, 131-49.

Klerk, A. de, and Euster, J. Technology and organizational metamorphoses. *Library Trends,* 1989, 37 (4), 457-68.

McClure, C. R., and Nernon, P. Unobtrusive testing and the role of library management. *Reference Librarian,* 1987, (18), 71-85.

Marchant, M. P., and England, M. J. Changing management techniques as libraries automate. *Library Trends,* 1989, 37 (2), 469-83.

Martin, S. K. Library management and emerging technology: the immovable force and the irresistible object. *Library Trends,* 1989, 37 (3), 374-82.

Miller, W., and Gratch, B. Making connections: computerized reference services and people. *Library Trends,* 1989, 37 (4), 387-401.

Murfin, M. E., and Bunge, C. A. Paraprofessionals at the reference desk. *Journal of Academic Librarianship,* 1988, 14 (1), 10-14.

Olsgaard, J. N. The physiological and managerial impact of automation on libraries. *Library Trends,* 1989, 37 (4), 484-94.

Olson, L. M. Reference service evaluation in medium-sized academic libraries: a model. *Journal of Academic Librarianship,* 1984, 9 (6), 322-9.

Peake, D. The impact of information technology on librarians and society, *LASIE,* 1988, 19 (1), 10-16.

Powell, R. R. An investigation of the relationships between quantifiable reference service variables and reference performance in public libraries. *Library Quarterly,* 1978, 48 (1), 1-19.

Prince, B., and Burton, P. F. Changing dimensions in academic library structures: the impact of information technology. *British Journal of Academic Librarianship,* 1988, 3 (2), 67-81.

Rodger, E. J., and Goodwin, J. To see ourselves as others see us. *Reference Librarian,* 1987, (18), 135-47.

Seggern, M. von. Assessment of reference services. *RQ,* 1987, 26 (4), 487-96.

Strong, G. E. Evaluating the reference product. *RQ,* 1980, 19 (4), 367-72.

Thompson, J. Unobtrusive reference service testing at Auckland Public Library. *New Zealand Libraries,* 1987, 45 (6), 117-19.

Whitlach, J. B. Unobtrusive studies and the quality of academic library reference services. *College and Research Libraries,* 1989, 50 (2), 181-94.

A NEW INFORMATION INFRASTRUCTURE

Caroline R. Arms

The decade of the eighties transformed the world of the librarian. When the decade began, integrated library systems and online catalogs were in their infancy, and CD-ROM was still in the back rooms of the Sony Corporation and Philips N.V. When it came to an end, many smaller libraries had discarded their card catalogs, and almost every library was promoting end-user searching of bibliographic databases, whether by supporting user-friendly interfaces to remote online services, mounting databases locally on minicomputers or mainframes, or installing CD-ROM systems. The decade to come may see an even more fundamental transformation.

While the librarian's environment was changing, the environment of the researcher in many disciplines was changing even more dramatically, due to the emergence of personal computers and networks that link scholars across campus, across the country, and across the world. An engineer or scientist now needs a computer and links to national networks to keep abreast of developments in his or her field. In several disciplines, working papers mounted for access over the national networks and informal discussions by electronic mail with peers around the world are more important for current awareness than reading the published journals. By the time an article appears in print, the research is old news. Meanwhile, scholars in less technical disciplines are realizing that the personal computers they use for writing also can be a gateway to information, providing access to resources of all kinds without leaving the office, without a trip to the library.

Librarians must respond to this challenge by adapting their services and applying their expertise in this new environment. In *Campus Strategies for Libraries and Electronic Information* ten academic libraries discuss the challenge, the opportunities it affords for better service, and specific steps they have taken [1]. A first step is the provision of access to online catalogs over campus networks. For many institutions, the next is to add other bibliographic and reference databases to their local online service or to support access to commercial services through local facilities. Now that scholars can locate materials in the collection from their desktop, some libraries accept loan requests by electronic mail, and deliver materials by campus mail or fax.

A more subtle (and probably more important) step is one that librarians can take as individuals: to familiarize themselves with the new "wired" environment. Scholars in many fields use the national networks routinely, to communicate with fellow researchers and for access to special resources. The resources may be general-purpose, but scarce, like supercomputers that support computer-intensive simulations of molecular structures or meteorological models; or very specific, such as SCIPIO, a database of catalogs from art sales from the sixteenth century to the present, which is accessible through the Research Libraries Group (RLG/RLIN).

The networks of primary interest to the academic and research community are BITNET and the Internet. Each of these networks reaches several hundred universities and research institutions nationwide, and has links to other networks around the world. Non-academic organizations can also apply for network connections if they are involved in or support research. Obvious examples are corporate research laboratories, equipment suppliers, and government funding agencies, but the range and the number of non-academic affiliates are both growing rapidly.

What is a Network Anyway?

To avoid confusion, a little clarification of terminology is in order. For most librarians, the word "network," even when applied to networks of computers, has had a meaning subtly different from that used in the computing world. Librarians are familiar with the network established by OCLC, and similar networks established by RLG and other library consortia to provide access to a shared resource. Each of these networks had a single purpose: to link terminals to a host computer that provided a particular service (or set of services provided by a single organization). To the librarian, the service and the network were almost indistinguishable.

In the computing world, a network is like a highway system, a general-purpose system for carrying traffic, independent of the services that can be offered by third parties because it is there. A highway system supports a variety of services, such as buses, taxis, and long-haul trucking, as well as private vehicle traffic. Similarly, a computer network can support different types of service, offered by anyone with access to the network who chooses to provide them. On the academic networks, there are guidelines that restrict the offering of services unrelated to research or education, but the restrictions are administrative not technical.

In that they support services offered by independent providers, the Internet and BITNET are more like Telenet and TYMNET than like the OCLC network. In another respect, they are very different. For most users, Telenet and TYMNET provide a single type of service: linking terminals to host computers. Both BITNET and the Internet are computer-to-computer networks; users at terminals (or personal computers acting as terminals) are not directly connected, but can gain access by logging on to one computer on the network, from which they can reach others. Both networks support a variety of services, including (but certainly not limited to) electronic mail, the transfer of files between computers, and access to stored databases.

A computer network consists of computers linked together, usually by cables of copper or optical fiber. However, attaching a cable between two computers does not create a network, because it does not guarantee useful communication. There needs to be an agreed coding scheme for signals transmitted on the cable, and a recognized procedure for taking turns to transmit. The rules that govern computer communications are known as communication "protocols." For a non-technical introduction to networking protocols, see the chapter on "Protocols and Standards" in *Campus Networking Strategies*[2].

Each network, whether it is a local area network serving a department, a campuswide network, or a long-distance network, is characterized by the set of protocols on which its services are based. Networks that use the same protocols are straightforward to link together, but links between networks using different protocols are usually limited in functionality. BITNET and the Internet are based on different underlying protocols. Electronic mail can be sent between them, but other functions, such as file transfer, operate only within each network.

Newcomers to the networks are often surprised bv their decentralized nature and perplexed by differences between BITNET and the Internet. A brief history will provide an explanation. For a fuller version, see my chapter, "National Networks," in *Campus Networking Strategies*, from which the two following sections are an updated summary [2].

The Internet—A Network of Networks

The Internet is a group of interconnected national, regional, and campus networks that use the same communications protocols. With support from the National Science Foundation (NSF) and the Department of Defense (DoD), and technical development projects at many research universities, the Internet is becoming the dominant network.

The history of the Internet begins with a 1969 project funded by the Defense Advanced Projects Research Agency (DARPA) to explore the feasibility of a long-distance packet-switching network. On packet-switching networks, messages are sent as individually addressed packets; long messages are broken into short segments and sent as sequences of separate packets. Packets from different communication sessions can be interspersed on the same line, and if equipment fails, packets can be rerouted individually without affecting the sessions.

The prototype packet-switching network was successful. Known as the ARPANET, it has served as the basis for continuing networking research and development sponsored by the DoD. One important development, around 1980, was the design and testing of "internet" protocols for linking independent networks. These protocols, Transmission Control Protocol (TCP) and Internet Protocol (IP), were adopted by the DoD in 1982 as parts of its networking standard. The protocols are usually referred to jointly as TCP/IP. Associated with TCP/IP are protocols that support electronic mail (SMTP), file transfer (FTP), and terminal sessions to remote computers (Telnet— not to be confused with Telenet, the commercial network). A TCP/IP network can support many other functions, but they may not be implemented on all computers on the network. It is usually assumed that any computer on a TCP/IP network will let a user send mail, transfer files, and access remote computers interactively.

The ARPANET itself (or the Defense Data Network, of which it is now part) is not open to all academic institutions. It is a network that connects organizations involved in government-sponsored research in networking and computer science. The importance of the ARPANET to the academic world in general is as the source of the TCP/IP protocols, which have been widely adopted by other networks. Other early funding for networks linking universities was also focused on computer science research groups. In 1981, the NSF funded the establishment of CSNET, a network to allow collaboration among engineers and computer scientists at all institutions (not just those with DARPA research projects). Much of CSNET uses the TCP/IP protocols, and agreements between NSF and DARPA ensured the accessibility of relevant resources on the ARPANET to CSNET users. In 1985, CSNET became self-supporting, with member organizations paying annual dues, and in 1989, CSNET merged organizationally with BITNET.

In 1984, the NSF began a more ambitious project, establishing a number of supercomputer centers and designing a network to provide access for any NSF grant recipient to any of the centers and to support communication between members of the scientific community.

TCP/IP was chosen as the underlying protocol, and the network design explicitly incorporated a linked hierarchy of networks at the national, regional, and campus level, all based on the same protocol. The NSFNET itself is a very high speed backbone (currently 1.5 megabits/second, but soon to be raised to 45 megabits/second) that links the supercomputer centers and a number of mid-level networks. Mid-level networks are independently funded and operated (although several had some initial support from the NSF) and most are state or regional networks. Attached to the mid-level networks are campus networks; universities are responsible for providing access to the network facilities for their communities.

Each mid-level network has its own policies and charges for connections. The NSF is currently offering grants toward the cost of equipment and line charges for an academic institution to connect to a mid-level network. Many mid-level networks encourage industrial participation for corporations whose scientists and engineers collaborate with academic researchers. For example, a number of computer manufacturers are members of CSNET, Kodak is a member of NYSERNet, and Alcoa of PSCnet. Mid-level networks vary in organizational structure, services, and level of central support. NYSERNet, one of the pioneers, may be a model for future developments. NYSERNet, Inc. is a non-profit corporation in New York State that supports research, development, and education. The group that formerly provided technical network operation within NYSERNet has recently become a commercial organization, Performance Systems International (PSI). PSI provides networking services to NYSERNet and to other clients. One interesting service offered by PSI in certain cities is dial up access to the Internet for individuals and for organizations that cannot yet justify the cost of a dedicated line.

NSFNET, its associated mid-level and campus networks, and the Defense Data Network are all part of the Internet. Agreements between NSF and DARPA allow traffic between their networks, and a user with a personal workstation connected to a campus TCP/IP network can reach resources anywhere else on the Internet, which also incorporates TCP/IP networks in other parts of the world, such as NORDUnet in Scandinavia, JUNET in Japan, and ACSnet in Australia.

Bintet—a Cooperative

The first network "for the rest of us" (rather than computer scientists) was born in 1981, when the first link of BITNET was installed between IBM mainframes in computer centers at Yale and City University of New York (CUNY). Ira Fuchs, then Vice Chancellor of University Systems at CUNY had seen an informal electronic mail network spread within the IBM corporation using standard IBM software and leased telephone lines. He envisaged a similar cooperative network between universities, with each site responsible for its connection to a site on the existing network, and agreeing to allow at least one new member to link through its facilities.

BITNET was to be accessible and affordable to all universities. Network speed should support electronic mail, but not necessarily the instantaneous response needed for interactive sessions. After eighteen months, BITNET reached twenty universities, including a link from New York to California. During the next few years the number of BITNET sites doubled each year. BITNET now has over 500 member sites in the United States, and is linked to networks using the same protocol in Canada (NetNorth, with 110 sites), Europe (EARN, with 650 sites), Asia (65 sites), and South America (20 sites).

Starting in 1987, BITNET, like CSNET, has levied annual membership fees (from $750 to $8,000, depending on an institution's annual budget) to support the growing administrative and technical burden of support. But the central staff is small; BITNET still relies heavily on the voluntary efforts of its member institutions for improved software and new developments.

In 1989, BITNET, Inc. became the Corporation for Research and Educational Networking (CREN) and the new organization also took over responsibility for CSNET. Day-to-day operations and information centers for the two networks are still separate, but policies and strategy will be coordinated. The commitment to a national network that supports inexpensive access for the whole higher education community remains.

The Convergence of Bitnet and The Internet

As networking has become more widespread and a factor in all aspects of academic life, demand has grown for links between the national networks. Since the underlying protocols are very different, a simple merger is not technically feasible. For some years, mail "gateways" have allowed users on BITNET to exchange mail messages with Internet users. To simplify the process, BITNET is ercouraging the adoption of the same addresses and addressing scheme that is in use on the Internet. For mail, at least within the United States, the two networks will soon appear as one. However, direct file transfer between the networks is not possible, and the BITNET protocols will never support interactive access to remote computer systems. Some BITNET members are now operatmg new protocols that allow traditional BITNET procedures to be handled over Internet TCP/IP links. This eliminates the cost of separate sets of connections, but the two networks still appear independent to the user.

Another example of the growing convergence between the national networks is the administrative merger of BITNET with CSNET (part of which is a mid-level component of the Internet). However, there is a fundamental distinction in mission between BITNET and the NSFNET. NSF is the National *Science* Foundation, charged with supporting scientists and maintaining the nation's leadership role in science and engineering. CREN's aim is for networks to reach the widest community possible, supporting university faculty, staff, and students in all disciplines and all aspects of research and education. Unless or until the federal government funds a comprehensive network whose charter is to serve both communities (and perhaps more—what about public libraries and secondary schools?), a need for at least two networking organizations will remain, even if they share technology and operate over the same hardware infrastructure.

Decentralization—Pros and Cons

Decentralization, and the entrepreneurship it has encouraged, has been essential to the vigor of both BITNET and the Internet. Member institutions were able to take the initiative to develop improved software and new services, using their own resources for facilities that would be of particular benefit on their own campus. Once developed, the software was usually made available to other institutions free of charge or for nominal cost. Formal support for such software was not necessarily provided, but expertise was shared informally, usually over the networks themselves. This spirit of cooperation permeates all aspects of network use. Individuals and institutions contribute time and energy to developing network services and giving assistance, knowing that they will be rewarded by appreciation, by professional recognition, and through services and assistance offered by others.

However, decentralization has disadvantages too. Librarians might assume that the resources on the networks are all described and cataloged in some central location. But they would be wrong. Since there is no centralized control or registration process for services- (even the registration of network addresses for individual computers is decentralized to campuses), identifying valuable resources can take detective work or access to an appropriate grapevine. When the networks were small, and the available services few, the grapevine was reasonably effective; but success and growth generate new challenges.

Recently, several attempts have been made by various groups and individuals to collect information on resources—a big improvement over the situation a year or two ago. Some of these are listed in the Appendix: "What's Out There." One reason for librarians to get involved with national networks is to bring their expertise to bear on the problem of providing the equivalent of bibliographic access to the growing body of bulletin boards, databases, specialized computing resources, and other services that the networks can bring to the scholar's desktop. Another is to draw on their experience of patrons' information needs to suggest and develop new resources.

A National Research and Education Network

What will the future hold? Academic and research networks are here to stay. Exposed to the excitement and the benefits to scholarship that they offer, researchers in many fields now find them essential tools. However, the current organizational structure of the Internet emphasizes research, with more general support for education being only a byproduct. Libraries must join other organizations that represent the educational community as a whole to be sure that "the rest of us" are not overlooked in the push for ever more powerful networks for the scientists and engineers.

The Department of Defense and the NSF fund manage key portions of the current Internet as part of their specific missions. The Department of Energy, the National Aeronautics and Space Administration, and the Department of Health and Human Services also run networks with overlap in mission and in clientele. In December 1987, these five agencies established the Federal Research Internet Coordinating Committee to formalize the informal cooperation that had existed for several years. Important motives were the pressure to cut costs, and the need for a single body to participate in international networking arrangements.

A report on high-performance computing issued a month earlier by the Federal Coordinating Council for Science, Engineering, and Technology (FCCSET, which operates out of the Executive Office of the President of the United States) urged the establishment of a general national research network [3]. The report stressed that "the United States faces serious challenges in networking technology that could become a barrier to the advance and use of computing technology in science and engineering."

Gore's Proposal: An Online Highway System

For the first time, a comprehensive national computer network was being discussed seriously in government circles. In 1989, Senator Albert Gore introduced a bill (S.1067) known as the "National High-Performance Computer Technology Act of 1989." In his introductory statement, he urged the need for the government to act as a catalyst by developing an information infrastructure to "get companies interested in those information networks and show them that there is a market out there." He drew an analogy with the Interstate Highway System, introduced thirty years ago, which boosted productivity of private industry through improved transportation.

Gore also pointed out that the network he proposed would cost less than one Stealth bomber. His bill would charge the NSF with establishing a three-gigabit/second National Research and Education Network (NREN) by 1996. The very high speed (2,000 times the speed of the current NSFNET backbone) is important to researchers in fields like astronomy, meteorology, and high energy physics, who can always take advantage of more computing power and higher data transfer rates to develop more detailed models.

For the average academic and for librarians, the important aspect is that the bill specifies that the network should link "government, industry, and the *higher education community*," not only the scientific and engineering research community [italics mine]. A proposed advisory committee would include "university and college educators" and "librarians involved in electronic data storage and retrieval." The act does not include specific recommendations about the offering of commercial information services over the NREN, but does specify that it should support accounting mechanisms, and that it should "be phased out when commercial networks can meet the networking needs of American researchers."

The NREN is only a proposal, but the Internet, on which it would be based, is a reality. It is clearly crucial for librarians to participate actively in planning for future network developments.

Libraries and the NREN

Library organization are laying the groundwork for participation. In March 1990, the Coalition for Networked Information was founded by the two major associations concerned with the management of information technology in higher education (EDUCOM and CAUSE) and the Association of Research Libraries. Institutions that belong to any one of the founding organizations can join the coalition, which will operate through a task force. Two individuals from each institution can be appointed to the task force, one representing libraries, and the other representing information technologies. Sixty universities had committed to joining the coalition before its official formation.

Primary concerns will be increased availability of information resources, improved and wider access to those resources, and the integration on campuses of library and computing resources. The coalition will be loosely patterned after EDUCOM's Networking and Telecommunications Task Force (NTTF), founded in 1985 to address common interests in the evolution of computer networks at campus and national levels.

In August 1989, the National Library of Medicine published a long range plan, which included a proposal that it should participate in planning for the future national network "so as to ensure fulfillment of the biomedical community's need for access to these advanced communications networks and to reflect biomedical priorities as the design options are taken" [4].

An article by Steve Cisler in the Spring 1990 newsletter of the Library and Information Technology Association (LITA) stresses the importance for libraries of their representation in the development of the NREN [5]. Participation in higher level planning and design will be more effective if it is based on experience of what is already possible. By exploring today's national networks, librarians can help shape the library of the future.

The Library of the Future

One design for a library of the future has been proposed by the Corporation for National Research Initiatives [6]. Robert E. Kahn and Vinton G. Cerf are taking a long-term view, looking ahead to what might be possible in fifteen or twenty years. They are not new to ambitious, long-term projects, having helped to establish the ARPANET and to develop the TCP/IP networking protocols that are the basis for the current Internet. The Digital Library System, as they call it, will be a collection of cooperating computers on a high-speed network.

The user will have a workstation attached to the network; this workstation will hold a personal library system that integrates today's tools for creating, storing, and retrieving information, such as word processor, spreadsheet, graphics software, and bibliographic file manager. The personal library system can communicate with servers on the network to retrieve additional information. Standard communication procedures will be the glue that binds the digital library together, but the personal system can be customized to the interests and whims of its owner.

Imagine:

Twenty years from now, John Smith is writing an article about the history of world networks. He discovers an article from a 1990 issue of *ONLINE,* and while reading it (on his computer, since screens of photographic quality make online browsing a pleasure), he says, "Find any other articles or books about networks by Caroline Arms, that I don't already have a copy of. Retrieve copies of the articles and tell me the easiest way of accessing the books." (Voice input is standard.) His personal library system gets to work. John reads on, undisturbed by the hidden activity.

First, the system sends a message to the "index, catalog, and reference server" to request citations and locations for any articles that I have written on networks. Going through the retrieved citations, the personal library system discards those for documents that it already holds, and those for which a bibliographic record shows that John has a paper copy. Then it sends out requests to the relevant database servers for the remaining articles, and, knowing that John often still prefers to read longer works in print form, checks the catalogs of the campus library and other libraries that can deliver books quickly.

After a while, the library system signals, by an unobtrusive sound or a visual signal on the screen, that progress has been made. John asks for details. He is informed that the articles are in his in-tray, and that although it will take four or five days to get a

print copy of *Campus Networking Strategies,* it is online on the
Digital Press server. Since John is cost-conscious, he has instructed the system always to consult the "accounting server" for
costs of online access and to compare them with charges for
interlibrary loan. (His campus library has recently raised the
charge for interlibrary loan for books that are available online.)
In this case, the royalty costs for online browsing are two cents
a page, and interlibrary loan costs $10. Since he would like to
take the book to his cabin in the woods next week, John asks for
the interlibrary loan anyway, and turns back to the article on his
screen.

On today's Internet and BITNET, early prototypes of components of this design can be seen. Database servers accept and respond
to information requests by electronic mail. New distributed applications give users who run special software on their workstations flexible
tools for retrieving and manipulating information from remote
sources and integrating it with their personal work. Operating systems
exist for personal computers that support several tasks simultaneously
and allow information to be transferred easily between the application
those tasks.

Kahn and Cerf are not merely visionaries; they are working at
finding partners and funding for projects that will build experimental
versions of systems that support more powerful access to a wider range
of information. A key part of their design is an open architecture that
encourages independent, but compatible, developments through ad-
herence to a set of conventions and standards. Their system also would
allow interaction with other autonomous library systems that do not
adhere to those particular standards. The time is ripe for experiments
in a variety of libraries, to explore key factors for addressing the needs
of different clienteles.

Initial developments probably will concentrate on the user's access
to information already stored, but several servers will relate primarily
to the initial processing of an item to be stored in the library. A
document would be sent initially to an "import/export" server, which
would enlist the assistance of a "representation transformation server"
if the document was not in a standard format ready for storage. The
document would then be submitted to a "registration server" that

would record the acquisition, pass it to the "index, catalog, and reference server" for classification and cataloging, and sent details of any royalty arrangement to the "accounting server." Once cataloged, the document would be stored in the appropriate database server. There is no reason for all servers to be totally automated, although automation of routine processing tasks should be feasible. To deal with exceptions, some servers will pass requests to human specialists: for instance, to supplement automatic indexing or reference systems, or to check the legality of an unusual royalty arrangement.

From Dreams to Reality

With the development of national and campus networks over the last decade, the vision of the scholar with instant access from his desktop to a wide array of relevant resources regardless of their physical location is becoming a reality. On some campuses, the network reaches every office and every dormitory room. At Dartmouth College, the slogan is "a port for every pillow." Some universities are working with telephone operating companies to evaluate services (such as ISDN, Integrated Services Digital Network) that use existing telephone lines for simultaneous voice and data communications. With this type of service, faculty can bring the campus network into their homes at speeds greater than provided by conventional modems.

In this "wired" environment, the scholar in search of information beyond the books at hand turns first to the computer: to send an electronic note, post a query on a bulletin board, or search a catalog or database. The proposed National Research and Education Network is intended to serve the general national interest and bring the same environment to a wider community than today's academic networks. Librarians without access to today's national networks can work through professional organizations to press for extensions to support education in the very widest sense. Librarians who have access today can explore the new environment and contribute to it, involving themselves directly in shaping the information infrastructure of tomorrow.

REFERENCES

[1] Arms, Caroline R., ed. *Campus Strategies for Libraries and Electronic Information,* EDUCOM Strategies Series on Information Technology. Bedford, MA: Digital Press, 1990.
[2] Arms, Caroline R., ed. *Campus Networking Strategies,* EDUCOM Strategies Series on Information Technology. Bedford, MA: Digital Press, 1988.
[3] Executive Office of the President, Office of Science and Technology Policy. "A Research and Development Strategy for High Performance Computing." November 1987.
[4] National Library of Medicine (U.S.), Board of Regents. "National Library of Medicine Long Range Plan: Improving Health Professionals' Access to Information." Bethesda, MD.: U.S. Dept. of Health and Human Services, National Institutes of Health, August 1989.
[5] Cisler, Steve. "NREN: The National Research and Education Network." *LITA Newsletter.* Issue 40, Vol. 11, No. 2 (Spring 1990): pp. 1-2.
[6] Kahn, Robert E., and Vinton, G. Cerf. "The Digital Library Project, Volume 1: The World of Knowbots." Corporation for Research Initiatives. March 1988. Draft report.

Appendix: What's Out There? A Network Resource Guide

Joining Instructions

* For procedures for joining the Internet and for names and administrative contacts for mid-level networks contact Merit/NSFNET Information Services at 800-66-MERIT.

* For information about NSF sponsorship for joining the Internet and about grants for links from universities to mid-level metworks, contact Brenda Peterson or Douglas Gale at the NSF at 202-357-9717.

* For information about joining BITNET, call the CREN Information Center at EDUCOM at 202-872-4200.

Information About NSFNET

There are two primary sources of information about the NSFNET:

* The NSF Network Service Center at BBN Systems and Technologies Corporation through "infoserver@nnsc.nsf.net" with the lines: REQUEST: nsfnet TOPIC: nsfnet-help

* Merit/NSFNET Information Services. For instructions, send mail to "nis-info@nis.nsf.met" (Internet) or "nis-info@MERIT" (BITNET) with the message HELP; or use anonymous FTP with the password "guest" to "nis.nsf.net" (35.1.148), and the message: GET READ.ME (use upper case).

Merit/NSFNET publishes a newsletter about NSFNET developments called *The Link Letter*. Back issues can be obtained by anonymous FTP from "nis.nsf.net." Subscription requests should be sent to "nsfnet-linkletter-request@merit.edu."

List of Lists

The master list of bulletin boards on the Internet is maintained at the Defense Data Network Information Center. Because of the size of the file, it is divided into sections for more convenient downloading. The files are in the "netinfo:" directory as "interest-groups-m.txt," where m runs from 1 to 10 (or more, since the file is continually growing).

To get the introductory section, use anonymous FTP to "nic.ddn.mil" (192.67.67.20), and give the commands:

CD netinfo: (Remember the colon.)
GET interest-groups-1.txt

or send mail to "service@nic.ddn.mil" with the message **netinfo interest-groups-1.txt** in the *subject* field.

The INTERNET Resources Guide

This guide is a catalog with entries in a standard format. Entries are based on contributions from representatives of organizations that maintain resources accessibly over the Internet, such as databanks, supercomputers, and online library catalogs. Designed to be kept in a loose-leaf notebook, the guide can be downloaded by entry, since each entry is in its own numbered section. Each section is available as plain text or in PostScript format. The table of contents and other front matter are in the resoucr-guide directory. Entries are stored in a subdirectory by chapter, with each chapter including resources of a certain category. For example, the chapter.2 directory has entries for online library catalogs.

The guide can be downloaded using anonymous FTP from "nnsc.nsf.net."

Subscriptions of two types are also available: the first will send you a copy of each new or updated section automatically; the second will notify you when a revised chapter is available for downloading. If you wish to be added to the mailing list for either of these subscription services, send a message to "resource-guide-request@nnsc.nsf.net."

Library Catalogs Accessible Over the INTERNET

A listing, with detailed instructions, is maintained by Art St. George at the University of New Mexico. The list can be retrieved by sending the message get internet library to LISTSERV@UNMVM (on BITNET).

Files Accessible on the INTERNET

For a list of sites with files for public access that accept anonymous FTP, send mail to BITFTP@PUCC (on BITNET) with the word FTPLIST.

Resources on BITNET

Check with your local computing organization before downloading these documents. They may have been downloaded and mounted locally, or equivalents tailored to your campus or organization may have been prepared. Useful sources of information about BITNET are at the BITNET Network Information Center at EDUCOM, and Yale University. The following files can be retrieved by sending a one-line message to LISTSERV@BITNIC or LISTSERV@MARIST (at Yale) with the word GET followed by the two-part filename (with a space between the parts):

BITNET USERHELP
    (A document for new BITNET users)
BITNET SERVERS
    (A list of servers on BITNET)

The file MAIL MANNERS contains some useful guidelines for using electronic mail. To retrieve it, send the message GET MAIL MANNERS to LISTSERV@BITNIC.

Christopher Condon at Yale publishes a monthy newsletter about BITNET. NETMONTH has information about new bulletin boards or servers. To subscribe, send mail to LISTSERV@MARIST with the words

SUBSCRIBE NETMONTH Your full name
    (Use your own name)

For a complete list of BITNET bulletin boards, send mail to LISTSERV@BITNIC or any other LISTSERV with the words: LIST GLOBAL.

DECISION FACTORS FAVORING THE USE OF ONLINE SOURCES FOR PROVIDING INFORMATION

Anne B. Piternick

There are an increasing number of reference sources available online, either as remote or on-site databases or as CD-ROM, as well as in print. In some cases, a source is available in more than one format. In other cases, reference sources are available online that are unlike the printed sources traditionally available.

Experienced reference librarians are becoming comfortable with the new sources, and are regularly making decisions about which source is appropriate to answer a particular reference question or request for information. These decisions may be based on quite a complex series of factors although the consideration of such factors may be made almost instinctively or unconsciously by the librarian. To the novice, however, the choice may seem baffling, especially since opting for online may involve a charge—either to the library or to the patron. If a source is locally available on CD-ROM, or mounted on site, a charge will likely not apply, but the librarian will still be faced with choosing the best alternative. The problem may be compounded when dealing with students or other library users. It has been recognized that library users who search on CD-ROM or other online systems may not always be getting the best results; in some cases they would be better off using a printed source.[1] The question of which type of source to use is something that cannot be avoided in planning bibliographic instruction, at least for instruction which goes beyond sessions on how to use the OPAC, how to use MEDLINE on CD-ROM, or how to use other sources in machine-readable format, and asks the question "Why?"

The author has had to face this problem with classes of library school students. Although in our program students are well versed in the technologies available for library and information services, and the use of the computer is integrated into all courses dealing with library functions and services, nevertheless we teach separate courses in reference sources and in online searching, both at the introductory and advanced levels. Bridging the gap between such courses, and helping the student feel comfortable in making choices between printed and online sources is not a simple task.

Finally, experience in handling a mix of online and printed sources should definitely be helpful in making decisions on purchase, lease, or payment for the use of reference sources. Comparative evaluation of the different formats in the context of reference services has been discussed by Large.[2] He makes the point that opting for online access to a source rather than purchase of a printed, or even a CD-ROM version, may mean committing an unknown amount of money to be spent on searching rather than spending a known amount on outright purchase. CD-ROM products cost more than their printed counterparts, but offer searching capabilities similar or identical to those provided by remote online systems. Selecting the option that will yield the best value for money is not easy. Tenopir offers useful advice in choosing among alternatives.[3]

Online Use for "Ready Reference"

During the early 1980s a number of reports were published on the use of online searching for "ready reference " or "quick reference" questions.[4] All of them provided some indication of the type of question that could be best handled online, and some also specified general conditions appropriate to online searching. The most comprehensive set of "Guidelines for Questions to Be Answered Online" was compiled by Sieburth, as part of her recommendations for ready-reference searching.[5] These are as follows:

1. The information cannot be found in a printed source.
2. Very specific information is needed such as dates, events, or data.
3. A database will provide a quick answer to a question that would take a long time to research in a printed source.
4. The most recent information is requested or a span of years must be searched.
5. The printed index does not yield satisfactory subject access.
6. The patron's information is incomplete and a search will quickly provide an answer.
7. Printed sources are unavailable—in use, at the bindery, or not owned by the library.
8. A more comprehensive source of addresses, telephone numbers of companies, associations, or individuals is needed.
9. A citation must be verified or completed.
10. New, colloquial, very specific terms, or acronyms cannot be found under standard indexing.
11. A database represents a source for which there is not print version available.
12. Students need help finding relevant citations.
13. Concepts must be combined that are treated separately in indexes.
14. Subjects are interdisciplinary and it is difficult to find good coverage in standard indexes.[6]

In a further chapter entitled "Online at the Reference Desk," Sieburth also gives examples of "specific instances when searching an online database can be an efficient method of answering a question."[7] The aim of the present paper is to develop a systematic, comprehensive range of factors that might affect the choice of online over printed sources for answering requests for information of all kinds: it is not limited to the context of ready reference. Focus is not on the type of question to be answered, or purpose of the search (although that may be readily deduced in some cases), but primarily on the characteristics and capabilities of online sources that make them different from printed sources. It is hoped that this approach will also assist novice searchers and reference librarians in formulating a systematic framework for the pre-search interview.

Differences in Approach in Using Printed and Online Sources

This is not the place for an exhaustive comparison of all the differences between print and online sources, including comparative costs, equipment, telecommunications, and so on. However, it seems appropriate to discuss two differences in approach to using print and online sources. The first concerns the structure of the sources themselves; the second concerns the process of searching.

Marcia Bates has proposed a definition of a reference source that is based on its organizational structure. In her terms, reference books are "books that contain a substantial percentage of their length . . . in files and/or lists."[8] This is best illustrated by a concordance: by changing the organizational structure of the text on which it is based (the Bible, Shakespeare's plays, etc.) a reference source has been created. In a similar way, the computer can now take a text in machine-readable form and make a reference source of it by transforming it into a machine-readable file. Full-text files of newspapers have thus become reference sources, presenting alternatives to newspaper indexes, and alternatives that are much more up-to-date, as well as different in character. Law reports and statutes, medical textbooks and similar manuals have likewise become reference sources. A completely new range of sources to use in reference work is now available.

The computer has also created more powerful versions of reference sources that have been used for years. A typical example is a bibliographic database, equivalent to an abstracting service. *Resources in Education,* in its printed version, boasts several indexes in each issue: subject, author, institution, publication type, and a cross-reference index from Clearinghouse number to ERIC Document (ED) number—the number used to file the set of ERIC documents on microfiche. In the machine-readable version on Dialog (available on disc as well as online) the following additional indexes are searchable: Clearinghouse code (that can be used as a subject or "quality" indicator), words in title, words in abstract, publication year, sponsoring agency, grant/contract number (that could be used to find all reports on a particular funded project), availability (that could restrict a search to documents in the ERIC microfiche set), language, country/state of publication, and level of government involved. The number of descriptors is also significantly increased over the ones used as subject headings in the printed version and a distinction is made between "major" and "minor" descriptors. This kind of extra search capability for online bibliographic databases is something to which reference librarians have become accustomed.

A much more extreme example of the power of online searching is the online version of the *American Library Dictionary* as it is mounted on Dialog. Access to the information in the printed version is virtually limited to geographic location—the system used to arrange the entries—or to the name of the institution, which can be located in an alphabetical index. The Dialog database, however, boasts 36 searchable indexes to "general information," plus a further 32 indexes to information on holdings, collection, and services, and 19 more to information about budget and expenses. Most of the indexes for the last two categories provide access to numeric data making it possible to search the directory for libraries that have collections, or budgets, or periodical subscriptions, or numbers of branches, within a certain range, of which spend a certain amount of money on professional staff, AV equipment, or manuscripts, and so on. With tools like this available, it becomes imperative for reference librarians and researchers to recognize cases where online searching means that quite different kinds of searches are possible, not simply that we now have a easier or more effective way of searching a file.

Finally, it must be noted that there is access to a wide range of databases, especially in the area of business and finance which have no printed equivalents, and which can only exist because of the power of the computer for storage, searching, and updating of files. At the same time regular use is made of a vast number of sources that are only available in print and may never be converted to machine-readable form. It is important that neither category be rendered "invisible" to the librarian, student, or researcher because of the medium in which it exists.

A second difference relating to approach concerns the way in which a search is conducted manually and online. In a manual source the search is hierarchical: first, a single access point is selected that locates a number of entries, then a term or equivalent that will make it possible to refine the search to a smaller number of entries, and so on until the final entry(ies), or the abandonment of the search. Thus the search proceeds by selecting a subject heading, moving to a subheading, and then scanning the entries under that subheading for relevant words in the titles. Or we select an author's name for our access point, and scan the titles by that author until location of the document wanted. If the hierarchy does not arrange the search categories in the way required, the search becomes difficult. Thus it is difficult to search on printed *Resources in Education* for documents on a particular topic that relate to, or were produced in, Canada, because the indexing does not allow for subheadings, and the entries under subject are title entries, so a scan for publication information is not possible. The hierarchical nature of searching in printed sources thus limits their usefulness to searches where there is not a requirement to combine a number of concepts and/or qualifiers.

In an online search the process is based on the intersection of sets using Boolean operators. Provided that the appropriate searchable fields are available, sets can be created based on subject, country of publication, language, and so on; combining the sets creates a final set of records that correspond to all the search parameters, making it possible to conduct a search for "Canadian" documents in the *Resources in Education* subfile of the ERIC database. Technically speaking, the number of concepts and qualifiers that can be combined in an online search is very large—thus the use of online searching for complex topics.

It has been noted in numerous publications that manual and online searches by subject will produce different results, since there are differences between hierarchical searches based on controlled vocabularies of various kinds, and Boolean searches, which may combine controlled descriptors. In some cases the controlled terms do not appear in the printed sources as title words or words in abstracts, or even perhaps codes or other subject designators. Carol Tenopir indicated that the capability of searching the full text of the *Harvard*

Business Review online made it possible to retrieve more relevant documents than resulted from searching controlled vocabulary terms or abstract words.[9] Nevertheless, she notes that: "Total reliance on one search method in HBRO precludes a comprehensive search in many cases."

Online searching greatly simplifies citation searches, and recent experiments have compared this method of searching with Boolean searching on subject terms. Again, the results have shown that different groups of documents are retrieved.[10] It should be clear from all this that, where a comprehensive search for all documents on a particular topic is concerned, no one method can be relied on, and both printed and online versions of a reference source may have to be searched.

Decision Factors

Bearing all this in mind, an attempt has been made to identify a number of factors that affect the decision regarding whether to use an online source in responding to a request for information. The factors that are identified fall into seven groups: availability factors, cost factors, convenience factors, bibliographic factors, subject specification factors, factors relating to information not indexed in printed sources, and special qualifying factors.

Availability Factors

Use online source if:

1. No printed equivalent to the database exists.
2. Printed source is not held by library or is temporarily unavailable.
3. Printed source is not as up-to-date as online and current information is required.
4. Material is included in database that is not in the printed equivalent.
5. Database includes searchable text of documents.

These factors have counterparts that favor the use of printed sources. Print is favored if no adequate database exists for the topic; if the backfile on the online database does not go back far enough; and if material included in the printed source is not available online. Any factor or its counterpart can help to determine quickly whether print or online is appropriate for a particular search, or whether it may be necessary to use both. It is important to keep informed of what sources are available, of the length of the backfile on a database—especially on CD-ROM—or of what is included in a particular source. Even when the print and online sources each have a common parent and bear the same title, it is important to check for content. The PsycINFO database includes book reviews, which are not included in *Psychological Abstracts*.. Pagell has noted that some full-text databases are more full than others.[11] To date, without special imaging software it is usually not possible to display illustrations online, although online searching may be used to locate works that contain illustrations.

Cost Factors

Use online source if:

1. Database is available in library on CD-ROM.
2. Unlimited database use is allowed because of contract with vendor.
3. Library mounts database on in-house system.
4. Database is available through low-cost version of vendor system.
5. Estimated cost of search will be below threshold for free searches.
6. Patron is willing to bear cost of search.

Certain conditions mean that cost need not be a negative factor in deciding whether or not to go online. In some cases, the library pays "up front" for the costs of searching in order to obtain unlimited use. These cases are presented as factors 1-3 above. (Note that a contract for unlimited database use could still involve royalty charges for records printed out.) Libraries have also made use of low-cost vendor systems such as BRS/After Dark or Dialog's Knowledge Index as a means of providing ready-reference service online without charge, or of making free or cheap searching available for end-users. Front-ends or gateways such as EasyNet may also help to reduce the cost of searching vendor systems.

In all these cases there may be limits on the number and kinds of databases that can be searched, and/or the capabilities of the searching system. The search software available for some CD-ROMs and for After Dark and Knowledge Index is not as powerful as that on the standard vendor systems, and an in-house system may be even more restrictive. The time spans covered by databases on these systems are also likely to be limited.

Convenience Factors

Use online source if:

1. Fast processing of search is desirable.
2. Search of printed source would involve handling many physical volumes.
3. No one source adequately covers the subject.
4. Search involves broad range of years.
5. Search will result in a large amount of information, or large number of citations to be copied.
6. Results must be sorted or tabulated in a particular way.
7. Article required is not in library but is in a full-text database.
8. Item searched may be ordered from a document supply source accessible online.
9. Results require editing, annotating, etc., using a microcomputer.
10. Search results can be downloaded to the patron's file/transmitted by email.

The factors identified as "convenience" factors are helpful in determining whether or not an online search is going to save the time and effort of the reference librarian or the requestor. In either case, it may be worth the money to conduct an online search because of the speed and ease with which a large file may be consulted, and/or the results may be sorted, printed, edited, transmitted, or ordered. Multidisciplinary searches are simplified because search strategies can be saved and run against two or more databases. Some vendors (e.g. Dialog, MEDLARS, WILSONLINE) now permit simultaneous searches on multiple files. BRS will merge outputs from different databases. Sorting capabilities allow printouts to be ordered to suit the needs of the patron: arranging citations by journal title, for example, saves time in consulting the volumes in the library. Report formats make it unnecessary to manipulate and tabulate data from a large number of records. Mailing labels may be ordered off-line for addresses extracted from directory databases.

For interlibrary loan purposes, online searching saves time and effort by making it possible to verify and order a copy, or locate a holding library and request a copy or loan, during the same terminal session. If the need for a document is very urgent, a full-text database may provide an instant copy.

On the other hand, in many cases, it is going to take longer and be less convenient to sit at a terminal or a CD-ROM workstation, log on, and conduct a search, than to pick a volume off the shelf and make a quick check for information.

Bibliographic Factors

Use online source if:

1. Search involves a nondistinctive personal name.
2. Search is for specific item where approximate title but not author is known.
3. Search is to verify garbled or incomplete citation.
4. Date of item sought is uncertain.
5. Search is for item appearing in specific journal or conference proceedings.
6. Search involves corporate name.

Many abstracting and indexing services have no authority control for names; in some cases, names are "standardized" by being reduced to initials. To search a non-distinctive name in a printed source is a disheartening experience, but an online search can combine a name with some other access point such as title word or affiliation. Word indexing of titles makes it easy to retrieve a citation using significant words or phrases from the title. Because an online system can search a wide span of years in one pass, it is ideal for searches where the date of an item is uncertain; alternatively, publication date can be used as an additional term to identify a publication. Many bibliographic databases include source—journal title, CODEN or ISSN—or conference as a searchable field, although there is a marked lack of standardization among the different databases.[12] When combined with author or title data, these fields make it possible to identify an item that appeared in a particular serial or proceedings volume. All of these reasons make online the choice for verifying incorrect and incomplete citations.

Similar problems may exist for locating names in directories: where they can be combined with fields such as city, profession, field of research, etc., a search for the right person is simplified. Searches for corporate names may also be simplified if the field is word-indexed in an online system; this makes it possible to search fragments of names. In full-text databases, parts of names or "popular" company names can be combined with other terms. The *PTS Corporate Thesaurus* available on several databases not only serves as an authority for corporate names, but also indicates relationships between companies. Thus the unknown or approximate name of a subsidiary of/parent of Company A can be rapidly identified. Online searching may also permit the use of stock exchange ticker symbols, DUNS numbers, etc., as substitutes for corporate names.

Subject Specification Factors

Use online source if:

1. Printed source is poorly indexed.
2. Vocabulary in printed source is not sufficiently up-to-date to reflect new terminology .

3. Controlled vocabulary term does not reflect earlier terminology required for retrospective search.
4. Controlled vocabulary term is not specific/broad enough for topic.
5. Jargon terminology is used.
6. Search is for definition of new word or phrase not found in dictionary or thesaurus.
7. Patron can identify a known item that can be displayed online to check for search terms.
8. Search is complex, involving combination of multiple concepts.
9. Search involves both class and all members of class.
10. Search is for compound/product/industry that may be identified by a code or standard number.
11. Citation search is required, involving two or more authors.

The ability to search the text of titles, abstracts, or complete articles makes it possible to identify terms that are not represented in the controlled vocabulary used for subject indexing, or when the vocabulary used or indexing of the source is substandard. Truncation helps to compensate for lack of standardization of spelling or of word form in such searches, and proximity operators help in searching phrases. Knapp has identified cases in which searching of text words is appropriate.[13] Text words may be particularly important in searching a topic that is not yet so widely recognized as to be represented by an index term. Early articles on President Reagan's "Star Wars" initiative were not initially indexed using this term.[14] At the same time, where terminology has changed, text-word searching may be used to retrieve early articles that were indexed under out-of-date terminology. Sometimes older records are re-indexed in the online database; changing the indexing is not possible in a printed source, although thesauri may indicate terms that have been replaced.

If a full-text database is searched, the earliest record in the set may provide a definition of a new term. This is particularly easy to do if the searching system highlights terms used in searching, and will display paragraphs where the search terms occur. As an example of such a search, a definition of "posslq" (an acronym standing for "persons of opposite sex sharing living quarters") was quickly found in the "Magazine Index" database on Dialog.[15]

Sometimes a topic may be clarified because the patron can identify an item on the subject that has already been published. Such an item can be simply and rapidly called up online to check what terms have been used to index it, these terms may then be used as the basis of an online or manual search.

Where a topic is complex and can only be adequately defined by a combination of concepts, an online search is indicated. Precision of results may also be enhanced by combining a set with a broad concept term that will provide "context" for the search: a Cardalert code on COMPENDEX, for example, or a Clearinghouse Code on ERIC.

Online searching makes it particularly easy to search simultaneously for a class plus all the members of the class, usually by means of codes or class numbers (although this may be transparent to the searcher). Thus a search may be conducted for documents on injuries to the brain that will automatically include documents on injuries to any part of the brain, or for documents indexed by a general concept such as "milk products" as well as those relating to specific milk products such as yoghurt, whipping cream, ice milk, etc. This can make an enormous difference to the speed and efficiency with which a comprehensive search of this kind can be carried out. In some cases the database producers offer ready-made strategies or "hedges" that include all specific terms representing a broad concept. These "hedges" can be called up and automatically searched online. For example, PsycINFO provides one that covers all terms relating to substance abuse (23 terms) and another covering all journals published by the American Psychological Association (15 titles); COMPENDEX provides one that covers every possible term (86 in all) for any kind of building or structure.

In chemical databases, names of compounds may be searchable by word fragment. This makes it possible to retrieve records relating to compounds belonging to a chemical "family" by searching word roots.

Online databases often contain approaches to subject information that is coded. The PTS family of business databases use Standard Industrial Classification codes for industries and products, as well as codes for geographic areas and "events," such as strikes, mergers, etc. Such codes offer an alternative kind of controlled vocabulary for a search, and are particularly useful if they are standardized across several databases—as, for example, the Chemical Registry Number, which is used as a standard number to represent chemical compounds that may appear under different chemical names. Where the codes are hierarchically structured, they can be used for the class/members of class type of search described above.

Finally, cocitation searching is virtually impossible to carry out manually. It is a means of subject searching where two or more cited authors or cited references are used in combination as search terms to bypass problems with vocabulary. Procedures for cocitation searches, as well as for searches in which cited references are combined with other access points, are discussed by Bawden.[16]

Factors Relating to Information Not Indexed in Printed Sources

Use online source if:

1. Search involves articles by person who may appear as joint author in multi-authored publications.
2. Search involves papers published by different authors affiliated with the same institution.
3. Search involves name of person, place, or thing that may be mentioned in the text of a newspaper or article but not indexed.
4. Required information may appear in abstract without being indexed.
5. Topic is unlikely to have been the main thrust of articles published to date.
6. Patron requires an article that includes special features, such as illustrations.
7. Search involves quantifiable data: number, size, rank, etc.

Special conditions exist where information may be somewhere included in a printed source but is not accessible because it is not indexed. There is often a limit on the number of author names that will be indexed for multi-authored papers. Both source and cited articles in the printed Citation Indexes can only be searched under first author, and up to 1977 Index Medicus had a limit of three authors, whereas all were indexed in the MEDLINE database. (There is now a limit of 10 in both.) Some printed sources will index by affiliation—for example, the "Organization" index in the Citation Indexes—but others include corporate names only if no personal author name appears on a title page. A search for work done at X University or by the research division of the Y Company cannot therefore be carried out in most printed bibliographic sources.

Because of the cost of printing, paper, binding, and mailing, printed sources also limit subject indexing. Online sources may include index terms that do not appear in the printed equivalents, and these terms may index "secondary" information that does not constitute the main thrust of an article. The "minor descriptors" in the ERIC and MEDLINE databases are examples of such indexing. Also, a search of the text of articles or abstracts using uncontrolled terms may reveal information that has not been assigned any index terms. Belanger and Emmick cite an example of a name that could not be found in the Wall Street Journal Index because the indexing was not specific enough; an online, search readily provided the answer.[17]

Features such as illustrations are searchable in some online databases, but may only be identified by scanning entries in a printed source. And, as noted above with reference to the American Library Directory, some quantifiable data that is not indexed in a printed source may be searched online. The INSPEC online database, for example, includes numerical indexing that makes it possible to search for physical properties such as frequency, wavelength or temperature, greater or less than a specified amount or falling within a specified range.

Special Qualifying Factors

Use online source if:

1. Search must include/exclude certain categories of documents: in/not in English; dealing with animals/humans, specific age groups, etc.

2. Search is for particular type of document: review (of books, movies, restaurants, etc.), bibliography, theoretical or experimental study, etc.
3. Search is for items published in a specific year, within a range of years, or for the most recent publications.
4. Search involves factors relating to quality, or intended audience.
5. Patron wants articles that are in journals held by the library, in core journals in the field, etc.
6. Bibliometric data is required.

These factors make it possible to save a great deal of time and effort by weeding out items that have undesirable characteristics or conversely by restricting a search to items that possess desirable characteristics. In many online databases, for example, it is possible to limit a search to documents that are in English, or that are not in a particular language. In databases that deal with experimentation on human or animal subjects (PsycINFO, MEDLINE), it is possible to limit results to one category or the other. It is also possible on databases such as MEDLINE to limit a search to cases involving subjects in specific age groups.

The ability to restrict a search to items published at a particular time is important. Manual searching can be inconvenient if there are delays in indexing or cataloguing items; this results in a lack of correspondence between the publication date of the item and the issue date of the index or catalog. Searching the "update" portion of the database is the basis of SDI services, and this or some other date restriction may also be useful for running updates to searches carried out sometime previously.

As noted above, the printed version of *Resources in Education* has an index by document type, yet this is most unusual for a printed source. Although special indexes exist in some fields for reviews, in most cases it is not possible to restrict a manual search to other types of document, or to documents that take a particular approach—historical, theoretical, experimental, etc. A similar difficulty exists for documents intended for a particular audience (professional, lay, student) or that include ratings (movies or restaurants rated as "Grade A"). This kind of qualification is possible in a number of databases.

Although it costs time and money to create, a search strategy can be formulated that represents the journal titles held by a branch or small library, or ones that are considered the core journals in a field. Such a strategy can be formulated as a search "hedge" and stored online, to be applied automatically as a qualifying factor to a search if appropriate. (The journal subject categories used by the Citation Indexes are coded by BRS and Dialog and may thus be used as ready-made core journal lists.)

Finally, because vendor systems normally provide occurrence counts, online searching may be used to provide bibliometric data. The extent to which this is possible will depend on whether or not the sample to be studied is adequately covered in online databases. But where statistical data on publication is required, online should always be explored. It has, of course, been used extensively for citation analysis, but other types of studies have been suggested, such as collection management, trend analysis, questions involving institutional or corporate research productivity, and issues management.

Conclusion

Although any one of the factors identified here may be conclusive in a decision on whether or not to use online sources (especially factors on availability and cost), in many cases more than one factor will apply. As an illustration of this, the matrix indicates factors which could or would apply in several different kinds of requests for information (figure 1).

Cost has been omitted here, since it can be assumed to apply, as a positive or negative factor, in every case. Availability factors are included only where they are obviously involved in a particular type of search.

How might the system of decision factors presented here best be applied in the field? It may be useful in the following situations:

- reference and/or online courses in library school
- in-house training of novice reference staff

- staff orientation when online services are being introduced or expanded
- bibliographic instruction programs including discussion of online sources, either remote, on-site, or CD-ROM
- promoting online services to potential users
- preparation of a case for access to, or purchase of, online sources.

It is also hoped that it may serve as a "refresher" for librarians who are not involved in online searching on a regular basis.

References

1. Carol Reese, "Manual Indexes Versus Computer-Aided Indexes: Comparing the *Readers' Guide to Periodical Literature to Info Trac II*," *RQ* 27:384-89 (Spring 1988).
2. J. A. Large, "Evaluating Online and CD-ROM Reference Sources," *Journal of Librarianship* 21:87-108 (Apr. 1989).
3. Carol Tenopir, "Decision Making by Reference Librarians," *Library Journal* 113:66-67 (Oct. 1, 1988).
4. Judith B. Broessler and Julia M. Rholes, "Online Services at the Reference Desk: DIALOG, RLIN and OCLC," *Online* 7:79-86 (Nov. 1983); Eileen Hitchingham, Elizabeth Titus, and Richard Pettengill, "A Survey of Database Use at the Reference Desk," *Online* 8:44-50 (March 1984); Sara Brownmiller, A. Craig Hawbaker, Douglas E. Jones, and Robert Mitchell, "Online-Ready-Reference Searching in an Academic Library," *RQ* 24: 320-26 (Spring 1986); James Markewicz and Linda Guyotte Stewart, "Quicksearch: Computer Searching for Undergraduates at Cornell University," *Journal of Academic Librarianship* 10:134-36 (July 1984); Sandra E. Belanger and Nancy J. Emmick, "Use of Ready Reference Searching in Business Reference," *Journal of Academic Librarianship* 12: 298-303 (1986).
5. Janice F. Sieburth, *Online Search Services in the Academic Library: Planning, Management, and Operation* (Chicago and London: American Library Assn., 1988).
6. Ibid., p. 159-60.
7. Ibid., p. 227-29.

8. Marcia J. Bates, "What Is a Reference Book? A Theoretical and Empirical Analysis," *RQ* 26:37-57 (Fall 1986).

9. Carol Tenopir, "Full Text Database Retrieval Performance," *Online Review* 9: 149-64 (Apr. 1985).

10. Katherine W. McCain, "Descriptor and Citation Retrieval in the Medical Behavioral Sciences Literature: Retrieval Overlaps and Novelty Distribution," *Journal of the American Society for Information Science* 40: 110-14 (1989); Miranda Lee Pao and Dennis B. Worthen, "Retrieval Effectiveness by Semantic and Citation Searching," *Journal of the American Society for Information Science* 40: 226-35 (1989).

11. Ruth Pagell, "Searching Full Text Periodicals: How Full is Full?" *Database* 10:33-36 (Oct. 1987).

12. Martha W. Williams and L. Lannom, "Lack of Standardization of the Journal Title Data Element in Databases," *Journal of the American Society for Information Science* 32:229-33 (1981).

13. Sara D. Knapp, "Free-Text Searching on Online Databases," *The Reference Librarian* 5/6: 143-53 (Fall/Winter 1982).

14. Anne B. Piternick, "What's in a Name? Use of Names and Titles in Subject Searching," *Database* 8: 22-28 (Dec. 1985).

15. In this connection, see also Hikomaro Sano, "Online Databases as Sources of Linguistic Information," *Online Review* 12: 15-23 (1988).

16. David Bawden, "Citation Indexing," in C. J. Armstrong and A. J. Large, eds., *Manual of Online Search Strategies* (Boston: Hall, 1987), p. 44-83.

17. Belanger and Emmick, "Use of Ready Reference Searching."

18. For example: Loene Trubkin, "Building a Core Collection of Business and Management Periodicals: How Databases Can Help," *Online* 6:43-49 (July 1982); Katherine E. Clark and William R. Kinyon, "The Interdisciplinary Use of Physics Journals," *College & Research Libraries News* 50: 145-50 (Feb. 1989); Donald T. Hawkins, "Unconventional Uses of On-line Information Retrieval Systems: On-line Bibliometric Studies," *Journal of the American Society for Information Science* 28: 13-18 (Jan. 1977); Jack E. Hibbs, Ronald R. Bobner, Isadore Newman, Charles M. Dye, and Carolyn R. Benz, "How to Use Online Databases to Perform Trend Analysis in Research," *Online* 8: 59-64 (March 1984); F. W. Lancaster and Ja-Lih Lee, "Bibliometric Techniques Applied to Issues Management: A Case Study," *Journal of the American Society for Information Science* 36: 389-97 (1985).

THE EFFECTIVENESS OF AN ONLINE CATALOG

Leslie Edmonds, Paula Moore, and Kathleen Mehaffey Balcom

A 1982 nationwide survey of library users commissioned by the Council on Library Resources[1] concluded that there is widespread public acceptance of the online catalog. The research also conjectured that the key issue for librarians is not whether to adopt an online catalog, but how to proceed. The survey included public library users, but reached only a small number of users under the age of fourteen. A literature search indicates that no systematic study of online catalog use by children has ever been reported. To date, automation research has made only brief reference to this user group and then the focus has been primarily on acceptance of technology, not the effectiveness of it. Librarians must evaluate the skill levels required by software design to be assured that children's access to materials is not hindered by the introduction of an online catalog.

If public libraries are going to convert to the use of online catalogs for public access, it is important to look carefully at the use of such Catalogs by children. The need for evaluation of online catalogs goes beyond acceptance or comfort in the use of the computer. It may be assumed that younger library patrons are more accepting of computer technology because they learn to use computers in school. The more important question is whether children can use existing online programs to find needed materials. Of particular concern are developmental skills required by the interactive software. Can children understand information presented on the screens with a program now available? Are they generally capable of understanding search methods used in a program? Does the online catalog offer any advantages or disadvantages as compared to the traditional card catalog? Answers to these questions will help program designers and librarians define the parameters of effective use of online catalogs by children and plan modifications in the online catalog, in bibliographic instruction, and reference/reader's advisory services.

This study evaluates children's use of an online catalog to gain bibliographic access to materials at the Downers Grove Public Library (DGPL). To provide a basis of comparison, the study also evaluates children's ability to use the DGPL card catalog. Although most libraries close their card catalogs when introducing an online catalog, the DGPL chose to maintain its card catalogs pending resolution of some specific problems connected with the online database. DGPL touch screen terminals were used to access CLSI's Online Public Access Catalog (OPAC terminal). A specific set of tests was developed to determine if children have the necessary developmental skills to effectively locate and interpret bibliographic information as presented by both forms of the catalog.

Overview

With the cooperation of Downers Grove Elementary School District #58, a sample of children in the fourth grade (9- to 10-year-olds), sixth grade (11- to 12-year-olds), and eighth grade (13- to 14-year-olds) was tested to see if their skill development would allow them to follow the online catalog protocols and interpret information presented on the screens in order to identify materials in the library's collection. In addition to observing student use of the library's online and card catalog, general skill levels were measured by a written test. Texts pertaining to the design of instructional programs to teach media skills suggest that 4th-8th graders should have mastered alphabetizing skills as well as basic use of the card catalog. Therefore, it is reasonable to focus on basic alphabetizing skills and knowledge of simple filing rules as prerequisites to effective catalog use and as developmentally appropriate for the children in this study. Three tests were developed to measure the children's skills and their understanding of and preferences in the use of the card catalog versus the touch screen online catalog. During a visit to the DGPL, children took part in the following activities:

1. *Skills Test/Skills* included:

   a) The alphabetizing of individual words, names and phrases.
   b) The application of simple filing rules to locate titles, authors, and subjects; for example, knowing when to ignore articles and how to interpret spaces and punctuation.

2. *Preference Survey.* A survey was taken of the children's preferences between the card catalog and the online catalog.

3. *Observation/Interview.* Students, selected at random, demonstrated actual skills in manipulating the card or online catalog. The research observers noted:

   a) Ability to find call numbers for items owned by the DGPL.
   b) Efficiency in finding bibliographic information in a known item search.

The research focused on collecting data to answer the following questions:

1. Do older elementary school children use a touch screen online catalog as effectively as a card catalog?
2. What are the impediments to effective catalog (online and card) use by children?
3. Which kind of catalog do children prefer to use? What aspects of the catalog (both online and card) do children identify as helpful or easy to use? What aspects of the catalog (online and card) do children identify as difficult to use or understand?

4. Are there changes in software design, bibliographic instruction or other public library practices that would make the online catalog easier for children to use?
5. Is independent (unassisted) bibliographic access improved or diminished for students if the library converts from the card catalog to the online catalog?

Children were considered effective or successful in using the catalog if 80% or more of the searches resulted in the identification of the call number. They were considered moderately successful if between 60% and 79% of the searches resulted in identification of the correct call number; they were considered unsuccessful with a rate below 60%. Data were also collected to describe the techniques children employ when using a library catalog. The data on the techniques were used to get a sense of the efficiency of the children's searches. When they search a catalog in normal, non-experimental settings, their searches may be ultimately successful even if errors or mis-starts are made. However, their frustration or difficulty with searching may cause them to give up the search and choose other ways of accessing materials at the library.

Methodology

In testing, a great deal of care was taken in selecting the items students would search for during the study observations. A pool of fifteen search items was compiled consisting of five authors, five titles, and five subject headings. Items were chosen that would be understandable to the students and that represented "clean" searches in both the card catalog and the OPAC. Titles of children's books were selected that contained easily understood words. The authors' names were distinct yet uncomplicated, i.e. neither "Smith" nor "Mikolaycak" was considered. The subject headings used were all either two or three word phrases that appeared a relatively few number of times in either catalog. Each chosen item was judged to be straightforward and to require only basic knowledge of filing rules to locate. Because the DGPL is part of a cluster of libraries using the same OPAC data base, each item was checked to ensure that the OPAC screens shown during the search contained no typographical errors. Five OPAC searches required a minimum of eight touches of the terminal screen for successful completion. Another five required nine touches, and the last five required at least ten or eleven. The fifteen search items were also checked against the card catalog to ensure that there were no irregularities or errors in filing or in the card format.

The DGPL's children's services coordinator set up a schedule for the class visits during October and November of 1986. Classes of fourth, sixth, and eighth grade students were invited to the public library to participate in the research project. While the nature of the research activities was explained to the teachers of the participating students, the teachers did not direct their students to prepare for their library visit. A signed parent consent form was obtained for each student prior to the library visit.

Staff from the DGPL and students from the University of Illinois Graduate School of Library and Information Science were trained to administer the skills test and to record observational data consistently. Both the administration of the skills test and the observations were conducted with a high degree of consistency and without difficulty.

Classes visited the library one at a time. Upon arrival, students received a brief explanation of the activities planned for their visit. The class was randomly divided into two groups. The first group was given the preference survey and the paper-and-pencil skills test. While a half hour was allotted for completion of the skills test and survey, students were neither timed nor rushed. Students were able to finish this written work in the time provided.

The second group was segregated in a room adjacent to the children's services area. Students in this group were randomly selected to conduct searches at either the card catalog or the online catalog. Before beginning a search, students who were chosen to do an OPAC search were shown a sample entry in the online catalog format. The students who were to be observed at the card catalog were shown a sample card entry for the identical title. The observers asked students to identify the author, title, and call number for the sample entry.

Next, students were given a card with a title, author, or subject heading printed on it and were instructed to find either the specific title, any book by the listed author, or any book on the specific subject. Each student selected for observation was given the opportunity to do a title, author and a subject search, but all three searches had to be conducted with the same catalog. The order of the search cards alternated between author, title and subject searches. Students could decline to do more than one search. In the case of the online searches, the observer excused students after the first or second search if they were unable to experiment with the OPAC, or when the number of touches to the OPAC screen indicated that improvement or success was not likely. For searches on either catalog, students were asked to find the call number when search item was located. If the student said the call number aloud or pointed to it, the search was considered a success.

Halfway through the class visit, the activities of the two groups were switched. In this way, all students visiting the library completed the skills test and survey, while the majority of students were observed using either the card catalog or the online catalog.

Analysis of Results

Data collected for this study was designed to answer five research questions. Results were also analyzed for performance variations between grades as well as between males and females. Findings related to each question will be discussed in this section.

Research Questions

1. *Do older elementary school children use a touch screen online catalog as effectively as a card catalog?*

Based on the data collected, children do not use the online catalog as effectively as a card catalog. About 65% were successful in the card catalog searches, whereas about 10% were successful in the online searches. While children made errors in each step of both types of searches, those using the card catalog made fewer errors than those using the online catalog.

2. *What are the impediments to effective catalog (online and card) use by children?*

There seem to be several impediments to use of library catalogs by children. First, some of the students studied lacked many of the basic skills necessary to use catalogs of either type easily. These students were generally unsuccessful at alphabetizing full words and were similarly unable to demonstrate mastery of common filing conventions. They also exhibited some problems in correctly identifying titles, authors, and call numbers.

A second impediment involved the use of both the card catalog and the online catalog. Because there is a series of steps involved in using either catalog, children were presented with a sequence of problems to solve. The sequential nature of successful searching appeared to be difficult for younger children (ages 8-12) to master due to their age and, thus, stage of development. Sequential searching was also problematic for older students. There were simply too many opportunities for error in the process of using a catalog, between file selection, choosing the correct catalog drawer, or in narrowing down the online alphabetical lists and then locating the search item.

A third hindrance to effective catalog use was the students' inability to conceptualize what letters or words fall *between* entries. This was demonstrated in the scores on Question 7 of the skills test which replicated card catalog drawers: *"Pretend these are labels on the card catalog. Write down the drawer number where you would look for each author or title."* In trying to identify the correct drawer in which various authors and titles were filed, less than half the students scored within the skilled range and fully one-quarter proved unskilled. Their difficulty in visualizing made the task of searching for entries online particularly hard, since searching depended so heavily on the concept of selecting the item that came directly before the search item in each of the OPAC alphabetical lists.

A fourth difficulty was that students could not follow the online protocols to conclude their searches and identify the DGPL call numbers. Of the 35.09% who reached the general entry for their search item online, only 10.3% were actually able to name the call number.

3. *Which kind of catalog do children prefer to use? What aspects of the catalog (both online and card) do children identify as helpful or easy to use? What aspects of the catalog (online and card) do children identify as difficult to use or understand?*

The students preferred to use the card catalog (68%) over the online catalog (16%). (See Table 1.) Another 16% had no preference. Familiarity seemed to be the only common reason that children gave for their preference. The students were not very articulate in explaining their choices ("It's easy." or, "Because I like it."). It is likely that children preferred the card catalog because they had used one in their school library. The online catalog may not have been preferred simply because students were unfamiliar with it. If students had had equal experience with both catalogs, the preferences might have been more balanced.

Table 1: PREFERENCE BY TYPE OF CATALOG BY GRADE

Catalog Format	Grade			Total
	Fourth	Sixth	Eighth	(N=207)
OPAC	9	17	7	33
Terminal	11.11%	26.56%	11.29%	15.94%
Card Catalog	60	38	421	40
	74.07%	59.38%	67.74%	67.63%
No Preference	12	9	13	34
	14.81%1	4.06%	20.97%	16.43%
Total	81	64	62	207

4. *Are there changes in software design, bibliographic instruction, or other public library practices that would make the online catalog easier for children to use?*

Several things could be done to improve children's use of both types of catalogs. First, no matter which catalog is to be used, children should have more effective and directed instruction. The public library will need to cooperate with the schools to devise ways to reinforce instruction for children in basic alphabetizing skills and filing rules. Particularly if the card catalog is to be used, this instruction would seem to be the best way to improve student performance, since changes in the design of the card catalog are impractical. The public library staff needs to make a commitment to tutor students in the use of the catalog as part of their reference or readers' advisory service. The library might choose to provide a written instruction sheet for students to help them use the catalog. Such instructions could break down the series of problem-solving steps to ensure success at each level.

For use of the online catalog, instruction is also necessary, but schools may have trouble implementing bibliographic instruction if they don't use the same online system. A public library might assist in preparing an instructional unit on the online system for use in the schools. The benefit of class visits must be examined carefully because of the expense and lower likelihood of success. Individual instruction to young patrons and simple, written instructions for the use of the online catalog could also be undertaken by the public library.

While changing the design of the online catalog can be difficult, it is both technically possible and feasible. Online catalogs are an emerging technology and as such, the design of the software will continue to evolve. For children, a better design could eliminate some of the problem-solving steps. There needs, for example, to be fewer screens per search and fewer items on each screen (a smaller percentage of the screen used). The bibliographic entry should be shortened and made easier to read. The DGPL online screens were too cryptic for students to interpret, even when the entry elements were clearly identified. Children would be aided by the use of natural, concise language and clearly written messages. User errors should be tagged so that children know when an error has been made, and so that the mistakes can be easily corrected without returning to the first screen. The great promise of the online catalog is that it can be redesigned, whereas the card catalog cannot.

5. *Is independent (unassisted) bibliographic access improved or diminished for students if the library moves from the card catalog to the online catalog?*

If the library does not provide personal assistance to students using the online catalog, bibliographic access by students is greatly reduced by the introduction of an online catalog. However, it must be stressed that fourth grade students did not appear to have mastery of the card catalog either. For younger students, the choice of catalog would not really affect their access, since they require assistance in using either catalog.

Conclusions

The results of this research study raise several important issues which need to be explored, both as explanation of the data and as a basis for decision-making in the public library setting.

The pattern of performance on both the skills test and in the observation of subjects followed the anticipated developmental model. That is, the younger children did less well on almost every measure. Overall, the fourth graders differed dramatically in their performance, while the sixth and eighth graders were more similar. This would also be expected since the fourth graders would be conforming to Piaget's concrete operations stage and the sixth and eighth graders would be moving into the formal operations stage of development.

One would expect that students at the concrete stage of reasoning would rely on trial-and-error problem solving, e.g., using such techniques as card-by-card comparisons or looking inside each drawer to see what part of the alphabet is inside. Fourth graders used these techniques to a greater extent. At the concrete operations stage, children need to depend on manipulation of physical items. While they can understand comparisons between items and changes in items (conservation and reversibility), it is difficult for the child at the concrete stage to use rules, to generalize, or to apply logic to problem solving. It is surprising, therefore, that the fourth graders need to actually look at each card or check individual drawers as a way of using the card catalog. Nor is it unexpected that the OPAC is almost unintelligible to the fourth graders since it is doubtful that the younger children have any way of understanding the size of the database. The format of the screens does not help children "see" what decisions need to be made. Although the OPAC allows patrons to page item-by-item, it is difficult to tell how many items fall between the item presented and the item desired. Since the patron can see how many drawers the card catalog has and how many inches of cards are in each drawer, the card catalog provides this information at a glance. Thus, the patrons can adapt their searches with this information.

The fourth graders' mastery of either library catalog could be improved with instruction and practice and they will naturally need to use a less-efficient approach which allows them to manipulate cards or helps them to see online entries as separate physical items.

The transition to formalized thinking begins at age eleven or twelve—the final developmental stage that continues through adulthood. Formal thinking is characterized by the ability to use logic, apply rules and to use conditional (if/then) thinking. These skills are needed for catalog use. Students no longer are dependent on what they see or sense for what they know. The formal operations thinker can "visualize" the alphabet and select where to start looking for an entry without having to see physical cards or compare actual entries. The sixth and eighth graders would both be at the beginning of the formal stage and thus have some mastery of how to apply rules and use conditional logic. It would be expected that the older students would be capable of "figuring out" how to use the catalog given the rules for catalog use. Since older students only had knowledge of the rudimentary rules of catalog use, they may not have had enough knowledge to be successful. Also, students at the beginning of this stage are still learning applications for logic, so they are not always able to apply the correct rules or interpret rules correctly.

Another level of concern is the experience, training and sophistication of the users of library catalogs. Patrons must be able to remember and apply the correct rule or rules, perform several steps (by applying several rules) in sequence and utilize rules accurately and precisely. A basic concept or rule that needs to be mastered is that of order. Essentially, the catalog users have to understand the concept of alphabetization and be able to locate words and phrases that fall between two points in an alphabetic sequence. To do this, users have to be able to identify what items come before or after a fixed point in the alphabet. The catalog in either format presents an extraordinarily complex set of rules of order to master. While we might think of the task as "knowing the alphabet," it is apparent that the task is closer to acquiring a working knowledge of AACR2.

Catalog users, thus, have two challenges. They must know the rules and also understand the logic or the organizational structure on which the rules are based. If users understand the structure but don't know the rules, they may be able to figure out how to do a search but it would not be particularly efficient. If the users know the rules (or many of the rules) but not the structure, any exceptions to known rules will present insoluble problems and it will be difficult to keep all the rules straight.

The children in this study did not have knowledge of many rules, nor did they seem to be able to easily understand the concepts. Naive users of any age will need to increase knowledge, practice sequencing, and concentrate on accurate task performance. The students did not demonstrate understanding of the concepts involved in alphabetizing. Moreover, they did not know many rules and were unable to accurately perform the several steps included in catalog use without making errors. The older students were better able to correct errors and were more knowledgeable than the younger students, though few students really demonstrated sophistication in using the catalog.

Use of the catalog is dependent on developmental level, experience and training. Because catalog use can be complex, it is important to recognize that children who are not yet developmentally capable of mastering the necessary logic for the catalog may require simpler library catalogs. Another alternative may be providing children with assistance in the use of the existing "adult" catalog. Thus, our findings suggest that in order to improve children's use of library catalogs, the catalog needs to be simplified (the total number of rules reduced). In addition, better training and guidance must be furnished to these young library patrons.

A Follow-up

Although CLSI is no longer marketing the particular software package used at Downers Grove, the research presented in this study can be replicated with public access online catalogs currently in use. Librarians who are not yet using an online catalog will find it of value. Also, since research determining student success in using card catalogs is sparse, the methodology used in the Baber research will offer librarians an opportunity to assess student effectiveness in traditional card catalog as well.

As a result of the Babar research project, a balance was struck in the library's children's service department in providing staff assistance at both catalogs. When working with students in grades six through eight, the staff introduces them to the OPAC rather than the card catalog for author and title searches. The inherent problems within the library's database would render subject searches incomplete and inefficient, however by utilizing the OPAC and describing the search strategy in an informal, narrative style, students can receive the training and practice necessary for successful OPAC searches. A model for an effective OPAC demonstration still needs to be developed, tested, revised and implemented.

Instruction presents a unique set of difficulties in the broader perspective of the school's catalog and a public library's online catalog. It is unlikely that the school library will have an online system that is compatible with a public library's catalog system. Moreover, the school media program of bibliographic instruction does not easily lead to effective use of the public library's catalog; teaching a separate set of skills, either through class visits or through limited opportunities for student practice may prove ineffective. In addition, the expense of supplying online terminals to local schools is prohibitive (this may be the case in other school districts). Therefore, it is essential that school and public librarians work together to bridge the gap in technologies and existing instructional programs so that children can become effective catalog users.

References

1. Joseph Matthews, Gary Lawrence, Douglas Ferguson, eds. *Using Online Catalogs: A Nationwide Survey.* Neal Schuman Publishers, 1983.

RECLAIMING OUR TECHNOLOGICAL FUTURE

Patricia Glass Schuman

It is easy to get the impression that the future of libraries and librarians depends on new technology. We read the predictions in the literature. We hear them at conferences. We budget more and more money. We plan our services based on them.

Predicting the future is tempting. The future is, after all, where we are all going to live—soon. Predictions seem to abound at the end of every decade as we look ahead to the next. Why? As Ambrose Bierce once said: "The future is that period of time in which our affairs prosper, our friends are true, and happiness is assured."

Predictions, particularly predictions about electronic technology, too often cause us to assume that the future will just happen, not that we can play a key role in inventing it. These predictions, combined with very real social and technological trends, can both comfort and frighten. We often cope with trends and the predictions based on them by envisioning a future that connects events and developments that might otherwise seem random.

"Reclaiming Our Technological Future," by Particial Glass Schuman in *Library Journal*. Vol. 115, no. 4 (March 1, 1990), pp. 34-38; reprinted with permission from Reed Publishing, USA, copyright © 1990 Reed Publishing, USA.

Prediction and Fantasy

This vision comprises a series of collective—almost unconscious fantasies. These fantasies influence our interpretation of reality. The power of fantasy lies both in its simplicity and its broad scope. Fantasy evokes both fear and hope. It shapes our collective judgment, and it often drives our philosophy.

Our collective fantasies go something like this:

- We are in the midst of an information explosion. Our only hope for controlling this explosion is through the use of technology.

- New technology will provide users with greater access than ever before. Individuals will easily and directly access information to fill their needs from their homes and offices.

- Librarians could be key players in the information marketplace—or they could become obsolete. Our challenge is to figure out what business libraries are in: the book business or the information business?

Two major assumptions are at work here. The first is that we are moving toward a paperless society. Books will soon be historic artifacts, and full-text electronic publishing will hold sway. The second assumption is that hardware and software will be readily available, usable, affordable, desirable, and satisfying to everyone.

Our fantasies envision a world of accessible electronic information and an ever-increasing number of workstations, complete with artificial intelligence systems. Well-trained end users with well-defined information needs will access the world's information store with little more than a keystroke.

Our fantasies are as seductive as a love affair. There is the hope of enchantment, the possibility of dependence, and the fear of betrayal. Fantasies often contain truths; they strike some note of recognition. But they are oversimplifications of reality. Nevertheless, fantasies often influence both our public philosophy and our decisions about programs and services.

Access to Excess

Take the information explosion fantasy. The statistics are dramatic.

- Americans bought 13.2 million tons of newspapers in 1988.
- Over one million books are published annually; over 1000 per day worldwide.
- A weekly edition of the *New York Times* contains more information than the average person was likely to come across in a lifetime in 17th-century England.
- The English language now contains 500,000 words, five times more than in Shakespeare's time.
- The collections of large research libraries have doubled in the past 14 years.

We may readily throw out with our nightly garbage more print than past generations dreamed it was possible to own. But what are these statistics really dramatizing? They tell us that there is more data than ever before; not that there is better data, more relevant information, or even a more knowledgeable society.

More than 60 percent of the content of a typical newspaper is advertising. A typical American reads three books a year. What we are actually experiencing is not an information explosion. It is an explosion of data. Some scientists now claim that it takes less time to do an experiment than to do the research to find out whether or not it has been done before.

Richard Saul Wurman, author of *Information Anxiety,* calls what is happening the "non-information explosion." Data provide neither enlightenment nor knowledge. Words like "mis-information," "dis-information," "meaning-glut," and "info-lag" are entering our vocabulary. What we are really experiencing may be access to excess. The mere fact that there is more data available does not mean that people either want it or can use it meaningfully.

An individual must be literate in order to negotiate our complex social, political, economic, and work environment. But print illiteracy is almost a national disease. Twenty-three million Americans cannot read above a fifth grade level; 20 percent of all Americans are unable to write a check that a bank can process. An individual must not only be print literate. He or she must be culturally literate, visually literate, and computer literate. With all these skills, the individual might then have a chance at being "information literate."

An educated user also needs an awareness of the value of information and the financial wherewithal to use it. What does our fantasy about direct home delivery of information services really mean in a society where 25 percent of households below the poverty line have no telephone? Only 13 percent of U.S. households own a personal computer. Only ten percent of these have modems. Seventeen percent of all white children use a computer at home, while only six percent of black and Hispanic children do.

Rather than universal delivery, there is a very real possibility that technology could widen the gap between the information rich and the information poor. We may fantasize about universal access, but the threat of narrow control in an information society is all too real.

The Information Oligopoly

While the computer can conceivably sort through and select information in a matter of minutes, some human being somewhere has to feed the databank. The question is not just access. What will we have access to? Do we know who is feeding the data banks that have multiplied like rabbits in the last decade? Not exactly. What we do know is that the number of companies that control information is shrinking.

Eighty-five percent of existing databases are in the Northern hemisphere; 70 percent are in the United States. One company, IBM, is responsible for manufacturing two-thirds of the world's computers. Eighty percent of the market for workstations is controlled by four companies: Sun Microsystems, Apollo Computer, Hewlett-Packard, and Digital. In April 1989, Hewlett-Packard announced plans to buy Apollo.

Five commercial database vendors account for over 90 percent of the sales and uses of database services: Mead Data Services, Maxwell Communications, Knight-Ridder, West Publishing Company, and STN.

Once an industry made up of independent, family-run companies, trade-book publishing is now dominated by a handful of corporations: Advance Publications, Hearst, MCA, The Pearson Group, Time-Warner, Bertlesmann, and Paramount Communications.

Hachette, Inc., a French company, is the world's largest producer of magazines and reference books. Rupert Murdoch is the largest newspaper publisher in the world. He also has extensive holdings in Fox Broadcasting and 20th Century Fox—not to mention Harper &

Row, *TV Guide,* and other magazines. Murdoch is the largest publisher of evangelical Christian books in the United States.

The current serials crisis libraries are facing is largely caused by a few multinational publishers. Robert Maxwell is one. His many holdings include Pergamon, ORBIT, BRS, and numerous scientific journals. Maxwell recently laid out his approach to publishing in an interview in his own new journal, *Global Business:* "I set up a perpetual financing machine through advance subscriptions—as well as the profits on the sales themselves. It is a cash generator twice over. It's no use trying to compete with me."

Maxwell plans a chilling future for us. He says, "I am determined that Maxwell Communication Corporation will be one of what I expect will be only ten surviving global publishing companies."

Journalist Ben Bagdikian's June 12, 1989 *Nation* article, "The Lords of the Global Village," documents a global media oligopoly that is largely invisible to the consumer. It controls newspaper, magazine, and book publishing, as well as broadcast stations, film studios, and software and hardware companies.

> Bookstores and libraries still offer miles of shelves stocked with individual volumes . . . but if this bright kaleidoscope suddenly disappeared and was replaced by the corporate colophon of the few who own this output, the collage would go gray with the few media multinationals that now command the field.

Bagdikian warns,

> Neither Caesar, nor Hitler, Franklin Roosevelt, nor any Pope, has commanded as much power to shape the information on which so many people depend to make decisions about everything from whom to vote for to what to eat.

Ian Reinecke, author of *Electronic Illusions* and an admitted "technoskeptic," concurs:

> The evidence is that the unholy alliance of the technocrat and the accountant that rules over major publishing groups will not be the best guardians of editorial quality. . . . Although computer

data banks may amass information at an astonishing rate, and
the information industries may churn out vastly greater quantities of it, ordinary citizens may grasp little of it. . . . There is no
evidence that the growing conglomeratization and privatization
of information will be either efficient or equitable.

Our fantasy tells us that new electronic technologies will help to
widen access. In reality the potential control of information access is
in the hands of media conglomerates and technology producers.

The Full-Text Fallacy

What about the paperless society fantasy F. W. Lancaster and others
propound? This fantasy is based on the notion that books will become
obsolete. Full-text electronic materials will easily be accessible via
workstations, and no one will really need to visit a library at all.

I disagree. To paraphrase Mark Twain: Rumors of our death are
greatly exaggerated. If you think we are on the fast track moving
toward a paperless society, just take a look at your desk. Several fallacies
underlie the fantasy of the quick demise of books and libraries. This
fantasy is dependent on the notion that all information will be
produced, stored, organized, and manipulated electronically. The
reality is that the quantity of printed information is doubling every
five years. While most publishers now use electronic means to typeset
books, journals, and newspapers, very few of these will ever be offered
for electronic distribution.

Print publishers are using technology because it's cheaper. For
many, it's cheaper only because they can use computer disks that
authors supply to them. Any publisher will tell you that while technological costs are dropping, the costs of intellectual labor are rising.

Electronic publication requires a different intellectual design than
a book. Books and journals are specific intellectual containers. Like
databases, they too have access points: tables of contents, chapter
headings. running heads, indexes, etc. Each of these is a conceptual
package that is not necessarily enhanced by—or transferable to—elec-

tronic media. Do we really need to read *Real Men Don't Eat Quiche* at a workstation?

For most publishers, electronic publishing is conceptually uncertain at best and economically risky at worst. Newspapers and many magazines depend on advertising for a substantial portion of their revenues. The price of a page of advertising is usually based on the number of people who buy or subscribe. Full-text technologies, like CD-ROM, do not yet include graphics. Even if they did, how could electronic publishing—which is geared for individual, on-demand use—guarantee circulation numbers for advertisers?

Book and journal publishers receive payment up front upon purchase by the consumer. With technological dissemination, the publisher is paid only upon use. How can a publisher predict the demand for a specific article or chapter? There is also a morass of other complications like the question of copyright, ownership, and textual integrity.

Full-text availability online as a replacement for paper may be somewhere off in the distant future. But although all Neal-Schuman books and journals are now typeset electronically, as a publisher and librarian I have little faith in an electronic distribution system that pays a royalty per use for a publication. That is not to say we might not publish software—or a large database—along with our books and journals. But I have no idea how a user might access a single part of a 300-page book—or how often. I have no idea how to find out. And I am not alone.

As a publisher I attempt to publish not just data, but information and knowledge within a conceptual framework: a book or journal. The organization, design, and content are of a piece that I, for one, do not wish to see either fragmented or condemned to total oblivion. Our books and journals are designed not just for data retrieval, but for browsing, thinking, reading, and connections between people and ideas.

Remember the prediction that film would replace books? That television would replace radio and film? Instead, what generally has happened during each new stage of communications technology is that the possibilities have expanded, not contracted.

Part of the fantasy is that technology is always successful and generally accepted. That's just not true. Remember the Betamax video format? Or videodisc?

Remember automats—those self-service restaurants that were considered great examples of labor-saving technology in their time? You looked through small windows; behind each was a dish of food. You made your choice and put your coins in a slot, the window opened, and out came your selection.

Restaurateurs who thought they were in the food delivery business fantasized that these self-service restaurants would eliminate a whole class of workers: waiters and waitresses. They could cut down their personnel costs and deliver more food to more people more quickly and cheaply.

How many automats are around today? The proponents of automats forgot one thing—the importance of human contact. Diners want to be able to ask someone: "How's the fish?" "What's the special today?" "What wine do you recommend?"

There will no doubt be new information products produced that you and I have never even imagined. But that is not a corollary to the fantasy that print will die.

Without the reality of the paperless society, there is little chance that libraries will shed what some call their "edifice complex" very soon. We know that the rate of obsolescence of equipment and software is about three to five years. And we think we have a problem with brittle books?

Even if the amount of electronic information expands dramatically and becomes crucial to the average individual, many people will choose to access databases from the library. They will choose to use libraries because they do not own a computer or because they want librarians, who are expert at searching, to act as intermediaries between them and the electronically packaged data.

The Business Fantasy

Which brings us to the next, and perhaps the most dangerous, of our fantasies. This is the fantasy that says: libraries must decide whether they are in the book delivery business or the information delivery business.

The business proposition is often urged upon librarians. The most frequent metaphor used to illustrate the argument is that of the railroad companies that failed to realize that their business was not trains but transportation.

The metaphor is a glib one. But libraries are not in either the book or the information business. Nor should they be *in* business. They cannot hope to compete with the Maxwells and the Murdochs, nor with AT&T nor IBM, all of whom claim that they are in the information business.

Adopting the vocabulary and methodology of business can be a dangerous game for the library profession. This fantasy can lead us to follow the agenda of the marketplace rather than to forge our own. The production, management, and sale of information is something quite different from the provision of access. It implies efficiency, not equity. Just look at what the concept of managing information has done to public access to government information: cutbacks, privatization, increased user fees, and, generally, less access to less information.

Conversely, private sector, profit-oriented companies that are in the so-called information business do not—and cannot—compete with libraries: not with library services, not with library programs, not with library collections, not with the expertise of librarians.

Their computers can certainly collect data. They can store it. They can manipulate, organize, and transmit it. But knowledge is a human achievement. It is not always immediately profitable in the marketplace.

Workstations—or any technology, for that matter—are a means for extending the capacity of the human brain. They do not replace it. "User-friendly" is not synonymous with responsiveness. Those ubiquitous bank teller machines, for example, provide simple, preprogrammed answers to a limited number of questions. Most individual information problems are not so well defined either by subject or scope. The user often does not articulate a specific need that can be filled by a single source. Solving simple problems is not adequate reference services. Personal communications with computers is not individual conversation. It is, in fact, programmed response.

What about the promise of expert systems and artificial intelligence? Thomas Anantharaman, co-inventor of Deep Thought, a computer that can play chess at about the level of a Grand Master, is quoted in a recent issue of *Discover*. He says:

> Few problems are as well-defined as they are in chess. Computer chess will give you an idea of how to approach a problem . . . but it won't solve the problem completely. I can't think of a single real-world problem that has been solved by artificial intelligence.

So much for the artificial intelligence fantasy. Systems are programmed. They can't take initiative. Libraries can. And they must.

We know libraries are not self-sufficient or self-sustaining. How can we expect a user with a workstation to be? We have never even been terribly successful teaching people to use reference books. Our most successful technique is the in-depth reference interview.

People only use technology on a regular basis if it is simple, unobtrusive, and satisfying. I haven't got a clue about how my television works. I merely pick up a receiver to dial my telephone. I put a videotape into my VCR and push "play." Computers are not yet that simple. The promise is that they may be. In the meantime, there are bugs in my software. My manual is unintelligible. I don't understand the DOS commands.

Some members of the profession may fantasize that technological devices and business methods will change the image of libraries and improve our status as librarians; that the management and merchandising of information should be our new role. Some also fantasize that charging fees will increase the user's recognition of the value of library services. The underlying logic is faulty. I know the value of a Mercedes Benz. So what? I can't afford one. This is like saying that if we charge people for borrowing books, more people will read.

We in the library profession will make a grave mistake if we persist in the marketplace fantasy. Certainly, we must understand that libraries are a market—a large consumer of information services and products. But libraries have no business *in* business.

Understanding Through Knowledge

Libraries are service organizations. Librarians are service-oriented professionals. Our business is not information. Our mission is to facilitate understanding through knowledge.

A telephone operator fills an information need; and telephone operators are gradually being replaced by computers. Postal workers deliver documents; computers and FAX machines often do so more efficiently. Both provide information delivery—even access of a sort—to very limited kinds of data and documents. The mission of librarians is not just to simply fill specific information needs. Our mission is to solve information problems.

The business fantasy suggests that instead we must transfer the cost—and possibly even the necessity for information skills—back to the user. A dentist does not expect a client to fill his or her own teeth; the medical profession does not advocate self-diagnosis and treatment.

Rather than attempting to be entrepreneurs who believe, as the former head of the British Lending Library Maurice Line does, that "We can have our cake—and eat it, too—if we sell it," librarians should stop trying to compete in what we fantasize as the great information technorace. Instead, we must move beyond fantasy and deal with reality.

The reality is that there is a discrepancy between what is technically feasible, what is practical, and what is actually happening. Computers don't think. Neither does a library. Creation of services is a human function. The future direction of library services is largely up to librarians. No technology can beat the highly developed skill of a librarian who can analyze an information problem, figure out the real underlying questions, and match those questions with answers.

No machine can compete with a creative, knowledgeable, flexible professional librarian, one who provides interpersonal interaction, information evaluation, communication, synthesis, and judgment. No software is better than a librarian who demands a say in future technological developments that affect library services, and who is not a passive recipient of vendor-driven technology and services. What actually happens will depend not just on technological innovations, but on our human creativity and ingenuity. "Libraries provide not only—but also," says Lester Asheim.

> Society, certainly a democratic one, needs some communication agency which judges the importance of an idea on the basis of the individual who might be touched by it and not by the particular mechanism on which it happens to be carried, or by the size of the audience that is willing (or able) to pay for it.

Far from wiping out the need for librarians, technological tools can be a means that help us to develop whole new levels of service. Business equates information with profit. Librarians must equate information with understanding.

The role of the librarian is to distinguish between data and information, between facts and knowledge. Librarians must be concerned not only with the what and the how but with the why. Access means more than mere physical location. It means the connection of ideas to people.

Our challenge is not just to provide more information, or even just the right answers. Our challenge is to help people formulate the right questions. When Albert Einstein was asked what single event was most helpful in developing the theory of relativity, he is said to have answered, "Figuring out how to think about the problem."

Helping others to do the same is the challenge before us if we truly have a commitment to excellence.

Bibliography

Asheim, Lester, "Means and Ends in Librarianship," in Edelman, Henk. *Libraries and Information Science in the Electronic Age.* ISI Pr., 1986, p. 100-165.

Bagdikian, Ben, "The Lords of the Global Village," *The Nation,* Jun. 12, 1989, p. 805-820.

Interview with Robert Maxwell, *Global Business,* Spring 1988, p. 41-44.

Lancaster, F. W. *Libraries and Librarians in an Age of Electronics.* Information Resources Pr., 1982.

Line, Morris B. *The Research Library in the Enterprise Society.* Univ. of London Library Resources Coordinating Committee Occasional Publication 8, 1988.

Reinecke, Ian. *Electronic Illusions: A Skeptic's View of Our High-Tech Future.* Penguin, 1982.

Waters, Tom. "Computer Watch," *Discover,* May 1989, p. 26-30.

Wurman, Richard Sau. *Information Anxiety.* Doubleday, 1989.

SECTION TWO:
GOVERNMENT AND LIBRARIES

THE NATIONAL SECURITY ARCHIVE: KEEPING THE GOVERNMENT HONEST

Frankie Pelzman

If the National Security Archive were a quasi-independent federal agency, the descriptor would be "lean and clean." If it were a library, the category would be "research/depository." If it were a policy institute, the heading might be "information/advocacy/current." NSA, of course, is all three. It has developed a complex, multifaceted character in a few short years.

In 1985 two Washington reporters, Scott Armstrong and Ray Bonner, working independently on foreign policy books, realized they both had amassed boxes of good stuff—archival material of potential value to other chroniclers of contemporary history.

"We should agree on a place to put it all when we're done" was a natural thought. If an old-fashioned attic had been available, there might be no NSA. Instead, that casual conclusion eventually became a small institution with an imposing mandate, respected and established, one of the swarm of gadflies that are movers and shakers of the Washington establishment. Less well known than any part of the Nader conglomerate, nonetheless in some Washington circles—and among some librarians, NSA is synonymous with information.

"The National Security Archive: Keeping the Government Honest," by Frankie Pelzman in *Wilson Library Bulletin.* Vol. 64, no. 9 (May 1990), pp. 31-36+; reprinted with permission from *Wilson Library Bulletin,* copyright © 1990 by *Wilson Library Bulletin.*

Not Just an Archive

NSA has initiated or participated in important litigation related to access to information, to the definition of public information, and to the broadest reading of the Freedom of Information Act. At the same time, it has created a central repository of contemporary history for scholars and journalists, set up an independent publishing operation, and, most recently, signed a contract with publisher Chadwyck-Healey of Alexandria, Virginia, that is making NSA's rich resources available on microfiche with printed, two-volume indexes.

Under the series title The Making of U.S. Policy, previously classified documentation from federal and private sources is now available to libraries everywhere, to scholars and researchers, and to any student for whom the actual script of history is critical. Available now are *The Cuban Missile Crisis, 1962, El Salvador, 1977-1984,* and *The Iran-Contra Affair, 1983-1988.* Titles yet to come include *The Berlin Crisis, 1958-1962; Nuclear Nonproliferation, 1955-1988; Iran: The Making of U.S. Policy,* and *Afghanistan: The Making of U.S. Policy.*

On the handsome flyers promoting the series, there is the following description of NSA: "The records in the Archive's collection are obtained through Freedom of Information Act declassification requests and legal suits, as well as through many other channels: government reports released without classification, donated record holdings and oral histories, Congressional reports and testimony, official court records, and Presidential Libraries." It almost makes it sound easy.

Scott Armstrong is sitting on a bench on the campus at American University. It is a spring day that January has dealt unexpectedly, and there are coats discarded under the trees and arcs of Frisbees crisscrossing the open yard. Armstrong looks like a middle-aged preppie, slightly round in outline, or a popular teacher at a small New England school. He looks tired, and exhilarated. He recently has left NSA as director, although he remains as an adviser, and he is stirring the soup for a new venture at AU, a Center for International Journalism. He hopes to get back to the book that he was writing in 1985 and he is excited at the prospect of a new venture. He feels pain at exiting the institution he founded, uncertain not as to its future but, perhaps, as to whether the original passion can be maintained with change and success. There is no doubt that Scott Armstrong is passionate about information.

Clearly NSA is at a pivotal moment In its institutional life. Its board is conducting a search for an executive director at a time when some members are leaving, tired of stress and pressure, and when NSA faces important decisions about funding and future policies. Success, as well as failure, is an institutional problem and the next months will be important for the Archive.

If NSA had been content to fill only its information role—receiving, evaluating, and computerizing information documents given to it by others or collected through its own painstaking research procedures, publishing careful chronologies of the history revealed by those documents, evaluating what needs to be saved and made accessible to future generations—it could have become a quiet haven for scholars that might eventually have found a formal home in some academic library or archival office.

It developed, however, that FOIA and NSA were made for each other, and that has made all the difference.

Using FOIA

There are three principal statutes related to the dissemination of information and privacy issues; the most familiar is the Freedom of Information Act. It, in theory, is the most often used and the simplest to exercise. The rules for implementing the act, related to a federal agency's response time and to what the requester must pay for, are set out in the *Code of Federal Regulations*. If you want some information about the deliberations carried out at the Federal Aviation Administration related to guidelines in rulemaking for the use of infant seats, for instance, you could write a letter to the agency and request information under FOIA. In theory, again, the agency must respond within ten days—although that deadline is often the first thing to get lost in the government quadrille.

The costs of FOIA requests are of considerable concern to NSA, which is aggressive in its voluminous requests for information. In

1986 FOIA amendments added to a narrowly germane bill by Senator Orrin Hatch (R-Utah) made it difficult for NSA to qualify for preferred, i.e., reduced, rates for FOIA requests. The Hatch modifications were intended to restrict reduced rates to only two categories of requesters, and neither of those was "any non-profit group that intends to make information available." The omission of that category would have meant hundreds of thousands of dollars in additional costs for NSA, which has a staff of around thirty and an annual budget of $1.5 million. Ultimately, in July 1989, in the lawsuit *Armstrong v. Bush et al.,* Judge Douglas Ginsburg of the U.S. Circuit Court of Appeals for the D.C. Circuit, writing for a three-judge panel, while denying NSA status as an educational institution, accepted the group as a representative of the news media because of its publications. The decision, of course, represented an important victory not only for the Archive but for free-lance journalists and writers, who often have been denied FOIA fee reductions, particularly at the State Department.

Every federal agency has a FOIA office; many do a terrific job. According to Scott Armstrong, both the departments of Defense and of Health and Human Services, with huge burdens—HHS answered 125,759 FOIA requests in 1989—manage to respond within the time frame. "Then there's an agency like State," Armstrong commented. "In one year, as I remember it, the State Department never answered one FOIA request on time." There are simple tricks of the trade e.g., an agency may answer a respondent on day ten with a letter stating it will be unable to provide the answer on time. Many agencies, including the FBI, are "starved for resources," according to Representative Don Edwards's (D-Calif.) statement at a recent House oversight hearing. The FBI has lost forty-three staff positions, while the number of annual requests has grown from 12,000 to over 16,000. Yet it is hard to feel that the FBI meets the intent of FOIA when its own data show that the Bureau's average response time last year for requests requiring more than inserting a piece of paper in an envelope was 326 days, more than double the response time in 1983.

The rules, of course, permit an agency to deny or answer a request in part or full, giving the reasons for its decision. The reason often turns out to be "CLASSIFIED"; in certain more tense situations the response can have ominous explanations, such as "National Security" or elegant ones like "Executive Privilege." NSA learned, not surprisingly, that, particularly at Defense, the "Classified" stamp was used like an involuntary muscle: a request more often than not was followed by a twitch that said, "No." Large groups of employees at Defense are engaged in reviewing and evaluating material; it may seem just as simple to stamp the cover "Classified" and call it a day. It is possible to request the group's supervisor to review the decision, but often in those instances it seems easier, or more politic, for the supervisor to support a staff call.

Once NSA began to compile chronologies related to Iran-Contra, or El Salvador, the Archive early on took the position that much of what was classified was light years from "top secret"; most would be open at the National Archives twenty years later. "We just decided to push the deadlines a little," Armstrong says.

Information Advocates

In that process, NSA became the plaintiff in a series of cases, a chain of information that continues today and almost certainly changes the character of how NSA will be thought of in the future. The image of a rocking chair repository has been overshadowed by the aggressive image of an information advocate. The issues are meaty enough to have attracted some of the city's top legal talent pro bono, and Armstrong credits Ralph Nader's Public Citizen Litigation Group, Hogan & Hartson, Wilmer Cutler & Pickering, and others for much of NSA's success in court.

Librarians and the American Library Association, of course, are most familiar with the NSA in regard to the FBI's Library Awareness Program. Following the hearings held by Representative Don Edwards and the subsequent program guidelines that the agency and the congressional oversight committee seemed to agree upon, there was a period of quiet that suggested the FBI had turned in its library card. Last December, documents obtained by the Archive in a FOIA lawsuit revealed the subsequent background searches conducted by the agency on 266 people connected to the Library Awareness Program. NSA's analysis of the stack of documents handed over by the FBI determined that approximately 100 of those investigated were librarians. (NSA and some of its staff are ALA members.)

The documents also make it clear that although the FBI had told ALA that the visits had stopped after December 1987, they had, in fact, continued through 1988 and 1989. The ALA/NSA litigation continues in an effort to retrieve information that was excised or deleted from the documents released by the FBI. Originally ALA and the Archive filed FOIA requests with the FBI in July and September 1987; they filed suit in 1988 after the FBI failed to respond.

Despite the 1,200 pages of documents released by the FBI in December 1989, NSA believes what was withheld is likely to be equally revealing. Assisting NSA Counsel Sheryl Walter in future phases of the litigation is pro bono counsel Martin Wald, of Covington & Burling, Washington, with financial help from People for the American Way.

This network of legal and funding assistance is basic to NSA's operations. From its earliest days it has gotten more bang from the buck through outside legal assistance and generous support of its goals from a number of major foundations and sponsors. Support for The Making of U.S. Policy/Chadwyck-Healey Inc. document sets alone comes from over twenty-five foundations ranging from Ford and MacArthur, to the Rockefeller Family Fund, to the Philip M Stern Family Fund, to the Ottinger Foundation and from "dozens of individuals and law firms who have donated money, pro bono services and in-kind equipment to make the Archive possible." A line of credit from the Ford Foundation is a financial lifeline for the Archive. Armstrong, NSA Deputy Director Tom Blanton, and the organization's distinguished twenty-two-person board (chaired by John Shattuck, vice-president for government, community and public affairs, Harvard University) have been extremely skilled at what any organization most needs from is board: the ability to tap those organizations committed to similar goals.

Tom Blanton took some time to discuss the process that takes place at NSA, the levels of information that accrue around the particular matters that the Archive decides to focus on at a given time. According to Blanton, in any one year NSA has about sixteen ongoing projects, "with perhaps seven going through at full speed," and publications produced for about five of these. Outside sources may donate documents. NSA may bring in an expert to advise on what kind of FOIA request to file, what documents it should be asking for to fill in the gaps in the documents that are publicly available. At the same time, the Archive may be involved in twelve to fifteen lawsuits, usually with other groups.

As information develops, it is computerized and cataloged with indexing by names and dates to produce a primary glossary, organizational glossaries, and indexes. Researchers who go fishing can come up with person, place, time, documents, and more—whatever the bait.

Before the agreement with Chadwyck-Healey, NSA already had done considerable publishing independently. Most familiar, perhaps, are the NSA Chronologies. These fat paperbacks exemplify Tom Blanton's remark that "our research is devoted not to coming to conclusions about the event, but to pointing to the government document(s) about the event, and bringing that out to the public."

In 1987 Warner Books published *The Chronology: The Documented Day-by-Day Account of the Secret Military Assistance to Iran and the Contras.* Its 657 pages take the reader from January 1980 to April 8, 1987. Its 12-page cast of characters runs from "Abrams, Elliott (Assistant Secretary of State for Inter-American Affairs. Previously served as Assistant Secretary of State for Human Rights and Humanitarian Affairs. Coordinated inter-agency support for the Contras. Worked closely with Lt. Col. Oliver North on the contra aid program, helping to solicit funds from third countries, including Brunei)" to "Weir, Benjamin (Kidnapped May 8, 1984, in Beirut. Released on September 15, 1985, after Israel shipped 508 TOW missiles to Iran. President Reagan is not sure whether he approved this shipment)."

In his introduction to *The Chronology,* Washington journalist Seymour Hersh wrote, "*The Chronology* tells us what happened, but not why. Its dry recital of events poses some questions that must be answered by the official investigators. . . . Why was [Congress] so slow to learn and act? How valuable are the intelligence oversight committees whose function seems to be little more than to help the [Reagan] Administration provide a smokescreen for its real policies? Similarly, why didn't the press do more to penetrate government secrecy?" No one can say NSA tries to duck the important questions.

The Oversight Function

In conversation, both Blanton and Armstrong come back again to the question of congressional oversight, not in a single policy matter but from an overall historical perspective. Both refer to a quotation (Woodrow Wilson, *Constitutional Government,* 1885) that they have obviously used before:

> The informing function of Congress should be preferred to its legislative function. The argument is not only that a discussed and interrogated administration is the only sure and efficient administration, but more than that, that the only really self-governing people is that people which discusses and interrogates its administration.

When you listen to Armstrong or Blanton, you hear a deeply felt concern not only that Congress ignores and thereby dilutes its oversight function, but that we as a society are less and less concerned with the discussion and interrogation of our administration. As Frances FitzGerald wrote in her *New Yorker* piece "Iran-Contra" (October 16 1989), "It has been three years since the first news of the Iran-Contra affair broke, and still the story is incomplete. New documents and new details continue to make their way into the public domain, now in scraps, now in volumes. The trial of Oliver North filled in several pieces of the vast puzzle. Yet by this time the public has grown weary; the audience drifts away."

NSA, on the other hand, hangs in there. On January 18, 1989, two days before he was to leave office, President Reagan instructed White House staff to erase their computer message system. This electronic message system, called PROFS (Professional Office System), has replaced memo pads in sophisticated institutions; although Colonel North had instructed that his PROFS messages be destroyed, he was unaware that they were magnetically stored. Much of the Iran-Contra puzzle was able to be put together only because of the existence of these centrally stored tapes. NSA requested, and got, a temporary restraining order blocking the White House erasures. Administration counsel argued that the two million pages worth of notes from the administration s last month were no more than jottings of the "Let's change lunch to Tuesday" ilk. NSA's counsel, Katherine Meyer of the Public Citizen Litigation Group, argued that these messages were part of presidential history and as such should be archived and ultimately made accessible. Many of the messages, she continued, are presidential records under the Presidential Records Act and, by destroying them in the past, the White House routinely broke the law. The suit, *Armstrong v. Bush*, also named as a defendant Don Wilson, the U.S. Archivist, for failing in his duties by allowing such records to be erased. NSA was joined in this suit by the American Historical Association, ALA, the Center for National Security Studies, and Gaylord Nelsol, the former Democratic senator from Wisconsin who cosponsored the Presidential Records Act in 1978.

Librarians need to be cognizant of the language of that act, which defines "presidential records" as "documentary materials . . . including electronic materials . . . created or received by the president, his immediate staff, or a unit or individual of the Executive Office of the President . . . which relate to or have an effect upon the carrying out of the constitutional, statutory or other official or ceremonial duties of the president." (The act excludes agency records, which are subject to FOIA.) The wording suggests a signpost for the era we are just entering, when we are likely to see the definition of information broadened even beyond our twentieth-century imaginations.

Blanton noted that NSA is uncertain whether the case will be heard in the Court of Appeals. What is more important, he said, is our lack, under the law, of any guidelines for preserving this type of material. His hope is that the lawsuit may help to jump start the process. If it wins the case, NSA may not get to see the electronic records for twelve years. but they will still exist. And we would have established precise federal regulations that would apply to archival materials whatever their format.

Keeping the Pressure On

At the same time that access to information at the highest level is frontpage news, NSA also has taken on a lot of FOIA requests for people whose original requests go back eight or ten years and have never been satisfied. The decision in these instances turns on requests that still are open and relate to subjects in which NSA has a particular interest. Why not let tired old FOIA requests fade away? Read Taylor Branch's comments in his preface to *Parting the Waters: America in the King Years, 1954-63.*

> I regret having to leave the record on Stanley Levison slightly ajar. Since 1984, I have sought the original FBI documents pertaining to the Bureau's steadfast contention that King's closest white friend was a top-level Communist agent. On this charge rested the FBI's King wiretaps and many collateral harassments against the civil rights movement. In opposing my request, the U.S. Department of Justice has argued in federal court that the release of thirty- to thirty-five-year-old informant reports on Levison would damage the national security even now. Almost certainly there is bureaucratic defensiveness at work here—and also, I suspect, some petty spy rivalry with the CIA—but so far the logic of secrecy has been allowed to reach levels of royalist absurdity. . . . [T]he material being withheld denies the American public a common ground for historical discussion.

Changes may be ahead for NSA. With a "second generation" of leadership, there may be a greater emphasis on management efficiency and less on passion—not necessarily a negative, but change nonetheless. Yet NSA's agenda is unlikely to shift dramatically.

Devoted to research, collection, and indexing and its role as library, litigant, adversary, and advocate, NSA is shaping a distinguished place for itself in enlarging that "common ground" where information flows freely to those who need it professionally, and to those who need it in order to participate fully in an informed democratic society.

NATIONAL SECURITY RESTRAINTS OF THE FEDERAL GOVERNMENT ON ACADEMIC FREEDOM AND SCIENTIFIC COMMUNICATION IN THE UNITED STATES

Jessica D. Schwab

Introduction

Academic freedom and national security are two principles that historically and presently are in a continual state of conflict. The attempt to balance these issues in society, with their opposing goals and philosophies, produced an inevitable struggle. It is difficult for experts in national policy to make decisions on academic freedom, and it is likewise difficult for leading scientists to decide what constitutes a threat to national security.

Academic Freedom/Scientific Communication

Arthur O. Lovejoy provided a timeless definition of academic freedom:

National Security Restraints of the Federal Government on Academic Freedom and Scientific Communication in the United States," by Jessica D. Schwab in *Government Publications Review.* Vol. 17 (1990), pp. 17-48; reprinted with permission from Pergamon Press, Inc., copyright © 1990 by Pergamon Press.

> . . . freedom of the teacher or research worker in higher institu-
> tions of learning to investigate and discuss the problems of his
> science and to express his conclusions, whether through publi-
> cation or in the instructions of students, without interference
> from political or ecclesiastical authorities, or from the adminis-
> trative officials of the institution in which he is employed, unless
> his methods are found by qualified bodies of his profession to
> be clearly incompetent or contrary to professional ethics [1].

An alternative way of defining academic freedom is to divide the idea into three separate concepts:

1. The specific work of the professor: The freedom to teach, do research, and publish without interference.
2. Protection of individual professors and allowing them to exercise the same civil and political rights as other citizens without endangering their academic status.
3. A set of practices guaranteeing the autonomy of the academic profession as a whole [2].

For the purposes of this discussion the main focus will be on the first concept: the professor's right to pursue research and publish without interference.

The principle of academic freedom originated in the United States as an official doctrine of the American Association of University Professors (AAUP). In the AAUP's founding document, the 1915 Report of Committee A on Academic Freedom and Tenure, a code was established concerning scholarly behavior and developing the procedures for ensuring that the enforcement of the code would be in scholarly hands [3]. In other words, before the outside world could exert political pressures, the university would police its own. This often has meant the sacrifice of an individual for the good of the academic institution.

Indeed, academic freedom is still evolving and must maintain a delicate balance among the individual, university, and government [4]. An important consideration is the reluctance of the courts to interfere with institutional autonomy even to protect individual rights. This posture of the courts is known as academic abstention or the doctrine of judicial noninterference [5]. Scientific communication has been an important aspect of the recent controversy between national security and academic freedom. Obviously this is the academic area where national security concerns would be concentrated because of the potential revelation of information, including critical technologies and leading-edge innovations that constitute a potential threat to national security.

Scientific research by its very nature is dispersed, interdependent, and a cumulative enterprise [6]. It is of prime importance that there be open channels for both formal communication (conferences, symposia, etc.) as well as informal communication (personal communications, working papers, preprints, etc.). Such exchange of scientific information occurs mainly in the academic setting. It is difficult to impose restraints when there is a tradition of openness and freedom of the exchange of information.

First Amendment Issues

The judicial issue that has become important is whether there should be First Amendment protections for scientific inquiry and/or communication. The argument is that scientific expression is protected by the free speech clause of the First Amendment. The Supreme Court has on several occasions *implied* that scientific speech is a protected form of expression [7]. However, it seems that the Supreme Court is developing a hierarchical view of the First Amendment and assigning different levels of constitutional protection to different levels of expression [8]. For scientific expression this involves a three-pronged test that will determine value, hence the constitutional status, of a given form of expression [9]. The three tests are: an individual interest in self-expression; a general social interest in the free flow of information; and a more specific social interest in enlightened public decision making [10].

When applying these tests to scientific expression it quickly becomes evident that scientists have strong individual interests in the free exchange of scientific data and ideas; that the general public also has a vested interest in the free flow of scientific information because discoveries of science will advance society as a whole; and that the use of scientific information for deciding specific questions of national security, the environment, energy, health care, education, and agriculture will aid an informed public in participating in the decision making process.

Scientific inquiry does not have the same first amendment protections as scientific speech because it is seen to be *noncommunicative conduct*. There is support for the idea that if "scientists are precluded from pursuing lines of investigation, they are restrained in their ability to engage in free expression" [11]. With this in mind it is necessary to determine just how much protection is merited under the free speech clause of the U.S. Constitution. Under what circumstances may the government permissibly constrain the research activities of scientists?

The problem is rooted in the fact that "the Supreme Court has never developed a comprehensive set of tests to determine the validity of a governmental action which abridges speech" [12]. In the area of national security, the Supreme Court has held that the mere assertion of some general danger to national security is not sufficient to justify a prior restraint of speech [13]. The two criteria that must apply to justify a prior restraint are that the injury must be certain to occur and that the harm must be irreparable [141].

The government may decide to assert that if information generated by scientific inquiry is obtained by a hostile foreign power, it is possible that the information would upset the international balance of power, or that the scientific information could be utilized to develop technologies militarily advantageous to enemies of the United States [15]. In either case, the government is required to assume the burden of establishing that such injury is certain to occur; it is mandatory that proof be provided that prior restraint is necessary.

National Security

American national security policy has developed and evolved as a result of international political and military developments, domestic politics, and technological advancements [16]. The interplay between the first and third categories is important to this discussion. This interdependence has evolved into the idea that American national security since World War II has depended largely on technological superiority [17] .

During World War II universities became engaged in activities that were basically narrow in scope and applications oriented in support of the war effort. By necessity, these activities were classified and secret. Immediately following the war, the federal government and the academic community agreed to continue the federal support of basic research in university settings [18] and to remove most classified projects to off-campus sites. As a result of this partnership there has been an implicit understanding that the government would not interfere in basic research that was not directly related to national security.

With the postwar onset of the cold war there was a growing concern to protect scientific information. "From 1949 to 1969 the basic legislative framework for export controls related to the protection of national security" [19]. With this a precedent was set for the use of export controls to control technological information and, ultimately, scientific communication. More recently, there has been concern that the Soviets are taking advantage of the openness of U.S. society in general and of freedom in the university settings in particular, to acquire technological information. According to a 1982 report to the U.S. Senate Committee on Governmental Affairs [20], among the basic techniques that the Soviets allegedly use to obtain U.S. technology were: bribery, blackmail, and extortion; obtaining information from government publications available through U.S. agencies or technical journals; the promotion of student exchanges (there are restrictions on Soviet participation in these exchanges because restraints are not stringent regarding Soviet bloc students); scientific exchanges possible through bilateral agreements with the Soviet Union on scientific and technical subjects; and the covert purchase of American high technology. More recently, in 1988, the Federal Bureau of Investigation waged a "Library Awareness Program." This program involved enlisting librarians to observe and inform FBI officials regarding any suspicious behavior of Soviet nationals. The librarians were supposed to be on the lookout for Soviet nationals who might be recruiting other library patrons to become spies or checking out and using highly technical *sensitive* materials. Thomas E. DuHadway, deputy assistant director of the FBI's intelligence division, said that the FBI has contacted approximately 25 libraries in this campaign [21].

Four types of scientific or technological information may be of use to foreign governments—

- scientific theory;
- knowledge of activities and progress in specific scientific fields;
- information that is embodied in scientific and technical equipment; and
- experimentation and procedural know-how—detailed knowledge, much of it gained through direct observation and experience with scientific and technical techniques [22]—is transferred in a different manner.

The first two types are usually transmitted in written or oral formats that are exchanged freely among researchers. The third type of information usually involves the physical transportation of equipment. The fourth type of information, involving know-how, is usually transferred by way of an "apprenticing" experience, which frequently involves long-term scientific exchanges involving actual participation in ongoing research [23].

Officials in U.S. intelligence agencies have maintained that only a small fraction of the overall Soviet bloc intelligence collection effort is directed at U.S. universities [24]. The specific incidents involving collection of militarily relevant information in a research setting have usually involved episodes in which visitor status was abused by Eastern bloc scientists. These incidents have included a visitor's technical activities and studies going beyond the agreed field of study; a visitor's time being poorly accounted for, including reports of excessive time spent collecting information not related to his or her field of study; visitors, either successfully or unsuccessfully, attempting to evade visa or exchange agreement restrictions imposed on his or her itinerary;

and, in one or two incidents, visitors participating in clearly illegal activities of an intelligence nature [25].

U.S. International Scientific Standing

Another important consideration is that if the U.S. restricts scientific exchange, inquiry, and communication, will it be isolated to the point of hurting national security by impairing scientific achievement? In other words, "if 'national security' is understood in military, economic, cultural, and psychological terms, then it may be argued, as many scientists do, that security results from achievement and not from concealment" [26]. The United States does not hold a monopoly on scientific information. In fact, only about 37 percent of the articles in scientific journals are authored solely by U.S. scientists [27], while 47 percent of the scientific journal literature are authored solely by scientists from countries other than the U.S., and the remaining 16 percent are coauthored jointly by scientists from both the U.S. and other countries [28]. It is important to realize that there is a true international community of scientists. National security in the United States is bolstered by and supported by the international forum of scientific exchange.

Conflict

National security concerns and scientific communication often overlap and conflict. This is particularly true when the federal government, through the Department of Defense, sponsors research and development on university campuses. For the fiscal year 1986, the Department of Defense dispensed prime contract awards totaling 2.712 million dollars for research, development, testing, and evaluation to educational and nonprofit institutions. Two hundred and eight educational institutions received 52.2 percent of the 2.712 million dollars in funding [29]. Three areas of concern for the Department of Defense regarding university research are:

- The degree to which government review of proposed publications will be required in projects of the kind undertaken by university investigators.

- The degree to which participation of foreign nationals in research will be restricted.

- The definitions and government guidance for determining what technological areas and what state of application and development will require extraordinary controls [30].

It is apparent that there is room for genuine conflict when contrasting the Department of Defense's areas of priority and the earlier cited AAUP guidelines [p. 2. footnote 2].

The McCarthy era was a time that such conflict actually existed; it provided a true test for the principles of academic freedom. There was considerable pressure exerted from outside the university setting, and often dissenters suffered dismissal from their academic positions. Disciplinary action came from the coerced academic establishment as a result of outside political influence. The interference of outsiders with the autonomy of the academic profession because of the actions of an individual, was not something that academia could tolerate. Responding to these outside pressures, academic institutions required the signing of loyalty oaths and assembled internal investigating committees.

Academic freedom deteriorated to the point that professors were dismissed for simply taking the Fifth Amendment when questioned about their membership in the Communist Party by the House Un-American Activities Committee (HUAC). There was also an academic blacklist in operation. If a professor lost his position as a result of a congressional investigation, he would have a difficult time finding a new one [31]. This blacklist was operative for years; for some people it began in the late 1940s, and for others it continued throughout the fifties and often into the sixties [32]. The AAUP "refused to modify its opposition to the firing of Communist teachers, and it took equally strong stands on loyalty oaths, censorship, and the Fifth Amendment. But it did not censure any school which violated those principles" [33].

Academic freedom was not defended by the very association that should have been its strongest proponent. This past tragedy may well serve as a lesson to the academic community that if its members are to enjoy principles of academic freedom, it may be necessary for them to defend and support these principles by protecting the individual rights of their community.

Another vulnerable area for conflict between academic freedom and national security is the differing political atmosphere between wartime and peacetime. In times of national crises such as wars, there is a tendency to redraw the boundaries of acceptable professional behavior so as to come to terms with the prevailing political consensus [34]. During World Wars I and II, professors were disciplined by their academic administrations for their politically unpopular opinions [35].

Recent Trends Affecting the Conflict

The three major operative issues precipitating government concern about the outflow of academically generated information are:

- The Changing Nature of Military Technology—Military power is now highly dependent on advanced commercial technology. To further complicate matters, much of the technology that is now useful from a military point of view is also useful in the commercial sector. Before, research on military-specific technology was somewhat contained in government and industry laboratories and on a selected number of university campuses. With few exceptions, the development of high technology, whatever the source, has military impact.

- Changing Interest of University Researchers—Universities have entered a new era in which applied research in certain fields is receiving pronounced attention.

- Emerging Concept of Militarily Critical Technology—The DOD has spent a great deal of time and effort defining what technologies are important militarily, and what transfer of

information or know-how would substantially benefit
potential adversaries [36]. (See Appendix)

Vehicles for Restraint on Academic Freedom/Scientific Communication

History of Controls

Export control policy emerged in the United States after World War
II. This control policy was in response to the strategic threat of the
Soviet Union and other new communist states. In 1949, the U.S.
Congress passed the Export Control Act of 1949 (50 *U.S.C.* Sections
2021-2032; P.L. 81-11; Ch. 11, 63), Stat. 7) to insure that nothing
of military or strategic significance was exported to communist states.
This act was to be the central export control policy for the next two
decades. The Department of Commerce issued export licenses that
could fall into the category of either *general* or *validated.* General
licenses required no formal application procedures and were usually
reserved for exporting goods to allies. Validated licenses were usually
required when exports were sent to the Soviet Union or other communist countries. When a validated license was required, the exporter
formally applied for the license, which then underwent a governmental review for approval or rejection.

The United States also organized the multilateral Coordinating
Committee (COCOM) of the NATO states (excluding Iceland, but
including Japan) in an international attempt to regulate strategic
exports to the Soviet bloc. COCOM constructed a commodity control list and an exemption review process designed to enlist the
voluntary participation of the member states. This organization is still
in existence, but the members are not bound by treaty or executive
agreement; they consider themselves to be brought together by mutual
security interests in the face of a mutually perceived communist threat
[37].

The Mutual Defense Assistance Control Act of 1951 (the Battle
Act), (22 *U.S.C.A).* App. 1611-1613d; P.L. 82-213; Ch. 575, 65 Stat.
644), required an embargo on the shipment of arms, ammunition,

and other strategic products and materials to any nation or nations, including the Soviet Union and countries under its domination, that threatened the security of the United States. This legislation was instituted by the Congress in order to provide a vehicle for supporting the control policies of COCOM. The Battle Act was also used as a coercive tool to influence other governments to adopt the U.S.-sponsored control proposals.

The Export Control Act and the Battle Act together constituted the main force of the United States export control policy until 1969 [38]. There were, however, several other laws that also had influence on government control of information. The Atomic Energy Act of 1946 (P.L. 79-585; Ch. 724, 60 Stat. 755, 766-68 (1946)), reflected a legislative assumption that all significant atomic energy information is produced and owned by the federal government. The Invention Secrecy Act of 1951 (35 *U.S.C.*, Sections 181-188 (1976); P.L. 82-593; Ch. 950, 66 Stat. 805 (1952)), with its permanent emergency measures rooted in World Wars I and II, authorized the Commissioner of Patents and Trademarks to keep secret any private patent application that, if disclosed, would be "detrimental to the national security" [39].

In the 1950s and 1960s there was considerable pressure to loosen the restrictions of the export control policy in the United States as a result of the resurgence of the European and Japanese economies, increased communist interest in trade with the market economies, and the early stages of detente between the U.S. and the USSR [40].

Export Regulations

The Export Administration Act of 1979 (EAA) (50 *U.S.C.* App. Section 2401 et. se8.; P.L. 96-72; 93 Stat. 503 [1979]) governs the export of articles or information with both military and civilian applications. There are three principal reasons for the imposition of the export controls: to further national security, to foster foreign policy, and to protect the domestic economy from the drain of scarce materials. The Department of Commerce is responsible for enforcing the EAA through a comprehensive set of regulations, the Export

Administration Regulations (EAR) (15 *C.F.R.* Sections 368.1-399.2 [1982]). The EAR set guidelines for an elaborate system of licenses to control exports or re-exports of tangible items to third countries. These guidelines include a Commodity Control List (15 *C.F.R.* Section 399.1 (1982)) that identifies the specific items that are to be controlled. The extent of control over the item depends on the nature of the article, the country of destination, and the end use of the goods. In addition to controlling tangible items, the EAR also exerts control over *technical data*. The definition of what constitutes an export of technical data includes situations in which there is an actual transmission of data out of the United States, a release in the United States with the knowledge that the data will be shipped out of the country, or a release abroad [41]. The regulations also define what is meant by release of technical data:

- Visual inspection by foreign nationals of U.S. equipment and facilities;

- Oral exchanges of information in the U.S. or abroad; and

- The application to situations abroad of personal knowledge or technical experience acquired in the U.S. [42]

There is evidence of a shifting interest that involves emphasis on controlling the design and manufacturing know-how of technology rather than the physical product. In 1979, Congress directed the Secretary of Defense to develop a Militarily Critical Technologies List (MCTL) (Initial MCTL: 45 *Fed. Reg.* 65,014-65,019 (1980)) and, after review with the Department of Commerce, to incorporate this list into the control system. The MCTL is not publicly available; parts of it are classified because it is considered possible that adversaries might consider it a shopping list of technologies. It covers over 700 technologies, many of which are thought to have substantial or primarily nonmilitary applications.

The second influential export control is the Arms Export Control Act (22 *U.S.C.* Sections 2751-2794) and its concomitant regulations, International Traffic in Arms Regulations (ITAR) (22 *C.F.R.* Sections 121.01-130.33 (1978)). The Department of State administers the

ITAR and issues licenses. The DOD is usually consulted when licensing decisions are made. The controlled list of arms, ammunition, and implements of war are designated on the United States Munitions List (22 *U.S.C.* Section 2778). As in the EAR, the Arms Export Control Act is meant to control the release of *technical data.* The State Department regulations define controlled *technical data* as including not only information that can be used or adapted for use in the design or production of arms, ammunition, or implements of war, but also information that may be used or adapted for use in the overhaul, operation, or maintenance of such items [43]. There is also a wide interpretation of the term *export* to include disclosure of information during visits abroad by American citizens or disclosure to foreign nationals in the United States [44].

When comparing the two sets of laws and regulations, it becomes clear that although the scope of information subject to ITAR is narrower than that covered by EAR, the controls are more far-reaching [45].

The Atomic Energy Act of 1954 (42 *U.S.C.* Sections: 2011-2296 (1976) and Supplement IV (1980)), restricts a narrow range of national security information relating to nuclear energy. Under the act almost all information relating to nuclear weapons and nuclear energy is designated *restricted data* [46]; such information is born classified. The chief problem with this type of restriction is that it is applied to nuclear information with no consideration of where the information originated. In other words, it does not matter if the information is in the public domain; if it has not been declassified by the government, it is *restricted data.* To follow the letter of the law adversely affects scientific communication because scientists are deterred from dealing with atomic energy information.

In the past decade, as the United States has refined and developed its export policy, there has been pressure from the U.S. for COCOM (discussed earlier) to consider proposing an international version of the militarily critical technologies list. Controversy over this proposal has surfaced for several reasons: the MCTL has not replaced the Commodity Control List or the COCOM list of actual physical commodities; there is considerable debate as to what should be included on the control lists; and it has not made the job of controlling technology transfer any less difficult [47].

Other problems have arisen over the fact that U.S. exporters feel that the controls are unilateral and that there are unfair opportunities for competitors at the cost of U.S. exports and jobs. It is also argued that the actual administrative procedures governing the implementation of the lists should also be more similar [48].

Classification Controls

The most recent and wide-ranging classification control is Executive Order 12356 (3 *C.F.R.* 166 (1983)), which was signed by President Ronald Reagan in April 1982. The order appears to have reversed a trend of the last 30 years toward narrowing the basis for assigning official secrecy to government records [49]. The general policy statement in E.O. 12356 states, "when there is reasonable doubt about the need to classify information, it shall be safeguarded as if it were classified" [50]. There is also less stringent restraint on classifying documents—there need only be evidence that its disclosure "(could) reasonably . . . be expected to cause damage to national security" [51]. E.O. 12356 designates three new categories of information to be considered for classification, and in the declassification procedures there has been an elimination of the mandatory review of a document's classification after 20 years. The balancing test of former President Carter's version of classification control E.O. 12065 (3 *C.F.R.* 190 (1978)), which permitted the classifier to consider the public's interest in disclosure, has been revoked. These additional restraints have particular implications for government restriction of scientific and technological information. The Order, "may prompt frequent widespread application of official secrecy to scientific research produced by and for the government" [52].

In E.O. 12356, for the first time, there is a warning to contractors, licensees, and grantees that they shall be subject to appropriate sanctions for improperly handling classified information [53]. Scientists may face classification of their government-funded studies and they may be restrained in discussion of their findings with anyone except those who have been properly approved to receive such information.

Controls on Foreign Visitors

Controlling visits of foreign scholars and scientists, either through the issuance of visas or the implementation of particular exchange agreements, is another vehicle for restraint on scientific communication. Visa controls originate from the Immigration and Nationality Act (8 *U.S.C.* Section 1101 et. seq.). Those who have grounds for admission that are important for scientific communication are bonafide students pursuing a full course of study at an established institution of learning and the temporary visitor "who is a bonafide student, scholar, trainee, teacher, professor, research assistant, specialist, or leader in a field of specialized knowledge or skill, or other person of similar skill" and who is a participant in certain exchange programs designated by the Secretary of State [54].

The visa system has been seldom used to inhibit technical communications because of workload considerations and a lack of information about visa applicants and unresolved questions of policy as to whether visas can be denied for reasons of technology transfer [55]. This policy appears to be changing (See Appendix I where six incidents of the use of denial of visas or restriction on foreign scientists participating in scientific exchanges are noted). In fact, in May 1983, William Schneider, Jr., Under Secretary of State for Security Assistance, Science and Technology, released a statement indicating that "the State and Justice Departments have been directed to apply the appropriate provisions of the Immigration and Nationality Act to deny or restrict visas when there is reason to believe that an alien is seeking to come to the United States to acquire controlled strategic technology illegally" [56]. Such restrictions are problematical when the universities are expected to control and monitor the actions of visiting scholars who are on restricted visas. The campus is usually decentralized and is neither structured nor staffed to police the flow of visitors [57].

Another problem with these possible restrictions concerns the high percentage of foreign nationals who are studying science and technology on United States campuses. Nearly half of the recipients of doctorates in engineering are foreign nationals [58], as are 70 percent of the postdoctoral scholars [59]. In the period from 1976 to 1979, the number of U.S. full-time graduate students in science and engineering declined slightly while the number of foreign nationals increased by 29 percent [60]. Such large percentages indicate that if foreign students were seriously restricted on U.S. campuses, the result would be a major setback for scientific and technical research in the United States. It would be extremely difficult to monitor the informal scientific interaction that normally goes on among university research groups where there is constant intellectual exchange and wide discussion of research results among its students and faculty [61]. Therefore, it is not likely that it would be possible to pursue a research project subject to controls on the transfer of information to foreign nationals in a department having foreign students [62].

Since 1972 there have been bilateral U.S.-USSR intergovernmental agreements in the areas of science and technology. These programs were reduced as a result of the Soviet invasion of Afghanistan, and by 1980 the number of visits that took place under these exchanges had dropped by 75 percent. The Department of State, acting with advice from the interagency Committee on Exchanges (COMEX), evaluates the scientists from communist countries who are involved in exchange programs. COMEX includes the Departments of Justice and Defense as well as the Director of Central Intelligence. Recently, COMEX has established an advisory committee of academic scientists.

Contact Controls

The federal government is a major source of funds for university research, and, for the most part, the university research considered militarily critical is funded by the DOD. If the research is being funded by the DOD it is reasonable to assume that the information will be monitored for national security infractions. In fact, there could be controls established in the original contract and this would offer the university the option of voluntarily withdrawing from the agreement if it was felt that the contract was overly restrictive in regards to academic freedom.

The federal government funds approximately one-half of the total research and development expenditures in the United States [63]. Approximately $3 billion is expended on academic research in the fields of natural sciences and engineering [64], the larger part of which is used for basic, rather than applied research [65]. It is obvious in examining these statistics that the potential threat of withdrawal of such substantial federal funding would probably compel universities to comply with federal restrictions and controls.

The Department of Defense in the *Report of the Defense Science Board Task Force on University Responsiveness to National Security Requirements* [66] has established suggested guidelines for the release of information in DOD-university contracts. To assure the university community that a broad restriction on the flow of scientific information is not being sought, the DOD offers the following clarification:

- DOD-funded research constitutes only a part of the overall university research budget.

- Within DOD-funded unclassified research, only manufacturing and process-oriented research (as opposed to basic research) are of concern.

- Even with process-oriented research certain information could be released generally to the scientific community after thorough review.

- Even information that could not be released publicly could be circulated within a selected subgroup of the scientific community [167]

There was also a list of considerations that would simplify the relationship between the DOD contract monitor and the university contractor:

- The university and the individual scientist would know in advance what was expected in terms of information release.

- The export control/release of sensitive information guidelines would simply be an add-on to the existing contract procedures.

- The State and Commerce Departments would not be flooded with unnecessary license requests from the university sector.

- Those license applications received from the university sector would be more focused and therefore more substantive since they would have already passed through a process of review of the military significance of the data release.

- Judgment as to what is militarily critical would remain with DOD.

- The system could operate with personnel and structures already in place at DOD, State, and Commerce. [68]

Voluntary Prepublication Review

Contract controls are a form of voluntary prepublication review because the university is requested to voluntarily submit to possible future restrictions on the contracted research. There is also the possibility that the government might request prepublication review for reasons of national security without funding the project (for example, cryptography).

The National Security Agency's (NSA) responsibilities include safeguarding the secret communications of the United States. Therefore, the agency is concerned with the study and discoveries in the field of cryptography because advances might imperil national security. Several incidents occurred in the late 1970s where NSA attempted to suppress presentations of cryptography papers at scholarly symposia. There was concern on the part of NSA and the scientific community over this issue, and as a result there was a formation in 1980 of the Public Cryptography Study Group (PCSG). This nine member group consists of mathematicians and computer scientists nominated by various professional societies, university administrators, and the general counsel of NSA. The group's goal is to find a way to satisfy NSA's concerns about the publication of cryptographic research papers without unduly hampering such research or impairing First Amendment rights [69].

The PCSG recommended that on a trial basis there be a system that would involve authors submitting their cryptography manuscripts for prior review to NSA at the same time that the manuscripts are submitted to journals. NSA would determine the research areas to be covered by the system after consultation with the appropriate technical societies. This proposal was accepted by all members of the PCSG except one. As of May 4, 1984, out of 200 papers reviewed, nine have been challenged, six modified and three have been withdrawn [70]. Whether this proposal would be applicable to other fields is open to debate. The field of cryptography is unique for several reasons, and this would have to be considered when applying the model to other fields. First of all, cryptography involves only a few dozen researchers and the publication rate is less than 100 papers a year. Secondly, the agency with the principal interest in cryptography, the NSA, is both technically competent and mission-oriented. Lastly, the frequency of problem papers—that is, papers that would interfere with NSA's mission—is small. These characteristics do not prevail in other areas of science and technology [71]. It is likely that this system of voluntary prepublication review would not succeed in other areas of science and technology.

Implementation of Gray Area Criteria

The *Corson Report (Scientific Communication and National Security: A Report)*, prepared by the Panel on Scientific Communication and National Security, Committee on Science, Engineering, and Public Policy, National Academy of Sciences, National Academy of Engineering, Institute of Medicine. (Washington D.C.: National Academy Press, 1982) was produced by a group of concerned scientists who set guidelines and recommendations for the federal government and the scientific community enabling both groups to protect scientific communication without endangering national security. An important theme of the *Corson Report* reveals the need to build tall fences around narrowly circumscribed technologies that could be identified as meeting four gray-area criteria:

- The technology is developing rapidly, and the time lag from basic science to application is short;

- The technology has identifiable, direct military applications or it is dual-use and involves process- or production-related techniques;

- Transfer of the technology would give the USSR a significant near-term military benefit; and

- The U.S. is the only source of information about the technology, or other friendly nations that could also be the source have control systems as secure as those in the U.S. [72].

The government is not following these criteria and is generally moving toward a broader approach regarding restraints of critical technologies. There has been little progress in streamlining the MCTL. In fact, a new, unclassified Militarily Significant Emerging Technologies Awareness List (METAL) [73] is being created for monitoring purposes that will identify certain technologies just appearing on the horizon but not yet embodied. Continuing efforts are also under way within the Coordinating Committee for Multinational Export Controls (COMEX) to identify additional technologies that are to be proscribed or restricted for export to Warsaw Pact countries [74]. Furthermore, the definition of *threat assessment factors* proposed to the DOD Steering Committee on National Security and Technology Transfer for identifying militarily significant emerging technologies is substantially more comprehensive than the Corson Panel criteria.

Has the Government Followed the Guidelines of the Corson Report?

The recommended preferable form of control that the *Corson Report* proposed was through research-funded contractual restrictions. However, the government has implemented such contractual controls more stringently and in a manner more far-reaching than was originally recommended. If the new technical data regulations are implemented into EAR, then export controls would eventually replace DOD-imposed contractual controls, which would be contrary to the initial recommendations of the Corson Panel [75].

There is also continuing confusion and lack of coordination between various executive agencies and their respective policies regarding technology transfer. Lack of government-wide coordination concerning technology transfer will eventually result in the government's losing credibility with the research community.

Leakage of technological information and the positive or negative effects of control measures are also little understood. Are government imposed controls actually preventing the transfer of valuable national security related knowledge? It is difficult to determine if the previously leaked information has actually contributed to Soviet military superiority.

If the controls are too strict then there will be a lack of publication, and this will result in a general decline of scientific innovation. There may be an exodus of the superior scholars from the fields that are the most strictly controlled. Another consideration is that the scientific fields that are controlled are also the most instrumental in sustaining U.S. technological lead time over the Soviet Union.

Problem with the Controls on the Export of Technical Data

The major problem with the technical export system is that it is complex and confusing. It is difficult to understand what the various regulations intend to accomplish, and it is also difficult to determine which agency has jurisdiction over each incident of technology transfer. The agencies that deal with the export controls are understaffed, which leads to delays that penalize legitimate trade.

Regulations on export do not solve the problems of theft and other covert intelligence activities. In fact. there is a possibility that the export regulations may very well influence the Soviets to resort to covert operations. Ironically, the United States provides high technology in a pure military form to other countries throughout the world and many of these countries do not protect these technologies from export to the Soviet Union as strictly as does the U.S.

Conclusion

The current controls on technology are attempts to compensate for past laxity instead of dealing with the problem in its present context. One of the current problems involves the technology leaks that result because there are graduate students who travel back and forth between the United States and Warsaw Pact countries. There are strict controls over student exchanges from the Soviet Union and from China, but the Warsaw Pact countries do not come under the same scrutiny.

The MCTL list (700 technologies) is too long, and the categories too broad. Present policy risks inhibiting the flow of technology for the day-to-day operations of U.S. companies with multinational branches.

The U.S. industrial and university communities and the federal government should work together to more carefully define critical technologies and the methods of protection that should be used. There should be an effort to improve industrial security and counterintelligence efforts so that the theft of technology does not render the controls on sales meaningless.

A number of organizations are attempting to resolve these issues of national security and the free flow of scientific communication. They are:

1. the National Academy of Science's Committee on Scientific Communication and National Security (*Corson Report*);
2. the DOD University Forum;
3. Multi Association Policy Advisory Group (a group which solicits reviews of MCTL from industry);
4. COCOM;
5. the Defense Department-Industry Group; and
6. COMEX.

There are possible solutions to the complicated problems involving export controls. The regulations should be revised so that they are less confusing and more easily understood. Adoption of a true list of militarily critical technologies that can be used as a basis for future export controls is necessary. Within this revised list there should be a prioritizing of the controls.

Academic freedom is essentially the freedom for scholars to pursue their research and teaching without outside interference. This paper has dealt mainly with one aspect of academic freedom, the freedom of scientific communication and exchange. This freedom is threatened by the use of national security restraints.

Scientific freedom and national security are two ideals that inevitably clash. In recent years, there has been ample evidence (see Appendix), that national security concerns were of primary interest to the Reagan administration. The emphasis in policy has been such as to risk the disruption of scientific communication. This turn of events will ultimately result in a loss of national security for the United States, because the United States will lose its critical technological lead over the Soviet Union. The United States has achieved its edge in technology because of the openness and exchange of information between its scientists and the international scientific community. It is critical that the current administration assess and balance the legitimate concerns of national security with the equally imperative concern of scientific communication and exchange.

Notes

1. Arthur O. Lovejoy, "Academic Freedom," in the *Encyclopedia of Social Sciences* (New York: Macmillan, 1930), vol. 1, 384.
2. Craig Kaplan and Ellen Schrecker, eds., *Regulating the Intellectuals* (New York: Praeger, 1983), 26.
3. See generally, Committee on Academic Freedom and Academic Tenure, "Report," AAUP Bulletin 1 (December 1915).
4. Virginia Davis Nordin, "Autonomy, Academic Freedom, and Accountability: The University, the Individual, and the State," in *Whistle Blowing in Biomedical Research,* ed. Judith P. Swazey and Stephen R. Scher (Washington, DC: Government Printing Office, 1981), 32.
5. Nordin, 32.
6. Paul E. Gray, "Technology Transfer at Issue: The Academic Viewpoint." *IEEE Spectrum* 19 (May 1982): 65.

7. See, for example, *FCC v. Pacifica Foundation,* 438 U.S. 726, 746 (1978); *Miller v. California* 413 U.S. 15, 34 (1973); *Roth v. United States* 354 U.S. 476, 484 (1957).

8. James R. Ferguson, "Scientific Inquiry and the First Amendment," *Cornell Law Review* 64 (April 1979): 645.

9. Ferguson, 748.

10. 425 U.S. at 761-65.

11. Ferguson, "Scientific Inquiry," 651.

12. Norm Dorsen, Paul Bender, and Burt Neuborne, eds., *Political and Civil Rights in the United States* (Boston: Little, Brown, 1976), 51-59.

13. David Faure and Matthew McKinnon, "The New Prometheus: Will Scientific Inquiry be Bound by the Chains of Government Regulation," *Duquesne Law Review* 19 (1981): 688.

14. *Near v. Minnesota,* 283 U.S. at 716.

15. Faure and McKinnon, 689.

16. Amos A. Jordan and William J. Taylor Jr., *American National Security* (Baltimore: John Hopkins University Press, 1984), 58.

17. Panel on Scientific Communication and National Security, Committee on Science, Engineering, and Public Policy, National Academy of Sciences, National Academy of Engineering, Institute of Medicine, *Science and National Security: A Report* (Washington DC: National Academy Press, 1982), 10. (Hereafter referred to as: *Corson Report.*

18. Gray, "Technology Transfer," 64,

19. John F. Murphy and Arthur T. Downey, "National Security, Foreign Policy and Individual Rights: The Quandary of U.S. Export Controls," International and Comparative Law Quarterly 30 (1981): 729.

20. U.S. Congress, Senate, Committee on Governmental Affairs, *Transfer of United States High Technology to the Soviet Union and Soviet Bloc Nations,* 97th Cong., 2d sess., 1982 (S. Rept. 97-664), 9-12.

21. Gordon Flagg, "Transcript of Closed NCLIS Meeting Details FBI's 'Library Awareness Program,'" *American Libraries* 19 (April 1988): 244.

22. *Corson Report,* 15.

23. *Corson Report,* 15.

24. *Corson Report,* 17.

25. *Corson Report,* 17-18.

26. Harold Relyea, "Controls and Scientific Communication," in U.S. Congress, Joint Economic Committee, *East-West Technology Transfer: A Congressional Dialog with the Reagan Administration* (*S Prt* 98-277), Washington, D.C.: Government Printing Office, 1984), 111.

27. *Corson Report,* 24.

28. W. D. Cooke, T. Eisner, T. Everhart, F. Long, D. Nelkin, B. Nidom, and E. Wolf, "Restrictions on Academic Research and the National Interest," in U.S. Congress, House, *1984: Civil Liberties and the National Security State, Hearings Before a Subcommittee on Court Civil Liberties and the Administration of Justice,* 92d Cong, 1st and 2nd sess., 1985, 762.

29. U.S. Department of Defense, *Educational and Nonprofit Institutions Receiving Prime Contract Awards for Research, Development, Test, and Evaluation: Fiscal Year 1986,* (Washington, DC: Government Printing Office, 1986), 2-12

30. David A. Wilson, "National Security Control of Technological Information," *Jurimetrics Journal* 26 (Winter 1985): 111.

31. Ellen W. Schrecker, *No Ivory Tower: McCarthyism and the Universities (New York: Oxford University Press, 1986),* 265.

32. Schrecker, 265.

33. Schrecker, 314.

34. Kaplan and Schrecker, *Regulating the Intellectuals,* 30.

35. In World War I, the first such crisis occurred. Political opinion was divided about the war, and, as a result, there was considerable suppression of dissenting viewpoints. The university setting was no exception. Professors were dismissed for voicing their positions. For example, at Columbia University James McKeen Cattell was dismissed because he petitioned Congress for the passage of a law exempting unwilling draftees from having to fight in Europe. (Kaplan and Schrecker, *Regulating the Intellectuals,* 30). In the aftermath of the 1940 Nazi-Soviet pact, there was a fervor against the Communist Party. There were universities which caved into the pressure and dismissed professors who were members of the Communist Party. One of the most extensive examples of this occurred in New York City College where the Rapp-Coudert Committee questioned dozens of professors and forced the city to dismiss more than 40 of them. (Kaplan and Schrecker, *Regulating the Intellectuals,* 31). These actions were to set the stage for academic policy for the next 15 years.

36. "Export Control and the Universities," Jurimetrics Journal 23 (Fall 1982): 41.

37. Gary K. Bertsch, "U.S. Export Controls: The 1970's and Beyond," *Journal of World Trade Law* 15 (Jan/Feb 1981): 68.

38. Bertsch, 69.

39. 35 *U.S.C.* Section 181 (1976).

40. Bertsch, "U.S. Export Controls," 69.

41. 15 *C.F.R.* 379.1, (b) (1).

42. 15 *C.F.R.* 379.1, (2).

43. 22 *C.F.R.* Sections: 125.01, 125.02.

44. 22 *C.F.R.* Section 125.03.

45. *Corson Report,* 33.

46. Mary M. Cheh. "Government Control of Private Ideas— Striking a Balance Between Scientific Freedom and National Security," *Jurimetrics Journal* 23 (Fall 1992), 4.

47. Gary K. Bertsch, *East-West Strategic Trade, COCOM and the Atlantic Alliance* (Paris: The Atlantic Institute for International Affairs, 1983). 48.

48. Bertsch, 49.

49. Relyea, "Controls and Scientific Communication," 112.

50. E.O. No. 12356 Section 1.1 (c) 3 *C.F.R.* 166, 137 (1983).

51. E.O. No. 12356 Section 1.3 (b).

52. Relyea, "Controls and Scientific Communication," 112.

53. Relyea.

54. 8 *U.S.C.* Section 1101 (15) (F),

55. *Corson Report,* 37.

56. William Schneider, Jr., U.S. Department of State, Press Statement, Washington D.C., May 5, 1983, 3.

57. "Export Control and the Universities," 45.

58. Peter D. Syverson, "Statistical Profile of Doctorate Recipients by Racial or Ethnic Group and U.S. Citizenship Status, 1981," in *Summary Report 1981: Doctorate Recipients from United States Universities,* [Office of Scientific Personnel, National Research Council] (Washington, DC: National Academy Press, 1981), 40.

59. National Research Council, Committee on a Study of Postdoctorals in Science and Engineering in the United States, *Postdoctoral Appointments and Disappointments: Report of the Committee on the Study of Postdoctorals in Science and Engineering in the United States* (Washington, DC: National Academy Press, 1981), 201.

60. "Full-time Graduate Science/Engineering Enrollment in Doctorate-Granting Institutions by Citizenship," in *Foreign Participation in U.S. Science and Engineering Higher Education and Labor Markets* (Washington, DC: National Science Foundation, 1981), 5.

61. W. D. Cooke *et al.,* 5.

62. Cooke *et al.,* 15.

63. Gary C. Hufbauer and George N. Carlson, "United States Policy Toward the Transfer of Proprietary Technology: Licenses, Taxing and Finance," *Vanderbilt Journal of Transnational Law* 14 (1981): 338.

64. *Sloan Commission on Government and Higher Education: A Program for Renewed Partnership,* (Cambridge, MA: Sloan Commission on Government and Higher Education, 1980), 164.

65. *Sloan Commission on Government,* 165.

66. U.S. Department of Defense, "Report of the Defense Science Board Task Force on University Responsiveness to National Security Requirements," In U.S. Congress, House, *Hearings on Military Posture and H.R. 5968 (H.R. 6030), Department of Defense Authorization for Appropriations for FY 83, Part 5: Research and Development, Title II,* 97th Cong., 2d sess., 1982, 163-354.

67. "Export Control and the Universities," 45.

68. "Export Control and the Universities," 45.

69. Mitchel B. Wallerstein, "Voluntary Restraints on Research with National Security Implications: the Case of Cryptography, 1975-1982," *Corson Report,* Appendix E, 123.

70. Wallerstein, 125.

71. Mitchel B. Wallerstein, "Scientific Communication and National Security in 1984," *Science* 224 (May 4, 1984): 464.

72. *Corson Report,* 125.

73. METAL is an unclassified watchlist to which a technology might be assigned during the period that it was still in the stage of basic research. (Subcommittee on Monitoring of Emerging Technologies, "Report to the DOD steering committee on national security and technology transfer," Department of Defense, Washington D.C., 29 December 1983).

74. Wallerstein, "Scientific Communication," 465.

75. Wallerstein, 465.

Appendix*

The following is a partial list of events covering the years from 1980 to early 1988. These events include prepublication review, the removal and suppression of papers from conferences and symposia. denial of visas to visiting scholars, and restriction of foreign students in certain laboratory situations on campus.

February 1980   The American Vacuum Society (AVS), organizer of a conference on magnetic bubble memories, was pressured into disinviting Soviet bloc nationals and requiring registrants from over a dozen foreign countries to sign a letter of assurance [Nicholas Wade, "Science Meetings Catch the U.S. Soviet Chill," *Science* 207 (March 7, 1980) : 1056].

February 1980   Soviet scientists were denied visas to attend a conference on laser fusion under the auspices of the Institute of Electrical and Electronics Engineers (IEEE) and the American Vacuum Society [Nicholas Wade, "Science Meetings Catch the U.S. Soviet Chill," *Science* 207 (March 7, 1980): 1058].

December 1980   The National Science Foundation included in a grant award letter a "reporting" clause requiring the grantee (in an area of cryptographic research) to delay the publication of research results which might require classification until they are cleared by the National Security Agency [Mitchel B. Wallerstein, "Voluntary Restraints on Research with National Security Implications: The Case of Cryptography, 1975-1982," in *Corson Report,* Appendix E, 120-125].

Early 1981   A Hungarian scientist was scheduled to visit Cornell to study electronic circuitry. He decided to cancel his trip because of restrictions imposed by the State Department. He could receive information only in classroom settings,

---

* This appendix was also published in a similar form by the American Libraries Association in "Less Access to Less Information By and About the U.S. Government." The author has included information from that publication but has also reexamined the original sources and supplemented the outline with further research.

	he would not be permitted to attend private seminars, and he could not receive prepublication copies of research papers [Gina Kolata, "Attempts to Safeguard Technology Draw Fire," *Science* 212 (May 1, 1981): 523-524].
February 1981	The Public Cryptography Study Group, whose nine members come primarily from the academic community, voted to recommend a purely voluntary system of prior restraint on the publication of research in cryptography. Although it considered a statutory system of prior restraints, possibly to go into effect if a voluntary system failed, the group rejected this approach. The National Security Agency (NSA) will be the monitoring agency [Gina Kolata, "Prior Restraints Recommended," *Science* 211 (February 20 1981): 797].
July 1981	At the Ottawa Economic Summit, President Reagan asked for greater cooperation among the International Coordinating Committee for Multinational Export Controls (COCOM) allies in restricting technological flows to the Eastern bloc. This resulted in the first high-level meeting of COCOM in over 20 years [*Corson Report,* 106].
December 1981	During 1981, numerous universities received letters from the Departments of State, Commerce, and Defense noting the existence of the export control laws and asking for information about the activities of Chinese scholars [Kim McDonald, "Universities Charge U.S. Presses Them to Restrict Activities of Foreign Scholars," *The Chronicle of Higher Education,* 9 December 1981, 1].
Early 1982	Stanford University reacted strongly to restrictions the State Department requested regarding the visit of Soviet scientist, Nicholay V. Umnov. Umnov is an expert in robotics and as part of the National Academy of Science's exchange program, he requested visits to several universities. The State Department felt that he would learn about important computer technology. Stanford also questioned the role of the NAS in transmitting the State Department's restrictions [Gina Kolata, "Stanford Protests Restriction," *Science* 215 (February 5, 1982): 638].
February 1982	The number of Soviet and American scientists involved

in official exchanges dropped from 104 in 1977 to 30 in 1981. Government screening of applicants is apparently higher, with outright rejections having increased from 0 in 1978 to 14 in 1981 [John Walsh, "New Pressures on Scientific Exchanges," *Science* 215 (February 5, 1982): 637].

February 1982   The State Department denied a Soviet arms-control expert permission to participate in a panel at Stanford ["State Department Rule Forces Stanford to Cancel Panel," *Washington Post,* 3 February 1982, sec. A, 18].

April 1982   The President signed Executive Order 12356. This order substantially increases the amount of information that can be classified. (April 6, *Federal Register,* 14873-14884). Critics see the executive order as a reversal of a 30-year government policy of automatic declassification of government documents. Although the National Archives still has the authority to review classified documents, budget cuts are likely to limit the ability of National Archives to carry out this function effectively [Kim McDonald, "New Secrecy Order Will Limit Access to Papers, Historians Say," *The Chronicle of Higher Education,* 14 April 1982, 1, 14].

April 1982   The Institute for Scientific Information (ISI), was informed by the U.S. Customs Service that one of the weekly tapes of the *Science Citation Index* that the Institute had been sending to the Library of the Hungarian Academy of Sciences had been confiscated because ISI had no export license for Hungary. The tapes had been shipped for many years to Hungary and Eastern bloc countries. ISI was informed that it would be able to obtain a license for Hungary but not for Poland or the Soviet Union. The reason given for the distinction pertained to the technology of the computer tape itself rather than the information contained on it [*Corson Report,* 106].

May 1982   Surprise inspections of cargo bound for Eastern Europe and the Soviet Union and special searches of the personal effects of foreign nationals as they leave the U.S. were part of a new effort by the U.S. Customs Service under the code name "Operation Exodus." An example of this

	involved some Chinese graduate students waiting to board a flight in New York who were detained and searched. Nothing of a sensitive nature was found [*Corson Report*, 106].
August 1982	The Society of Photo-Optical Instrumentation Engineers (SPOIE) at an international technical symposium was ordered to withdraw more than 100 papers which had been cleared for presentation. These orders came from the Pentagon [Joel Greenberg, "Remote Censoring: DOD Blocks Symposium Papers," *Science News* 122 (September 4, 1982): 148].
October 1982	The Optical Society of America was ordered by the Pentagon to disallow six papers on laser communications because of the national security problems these papers would present [Kim McDonald, "Pentagon Blocked 6 Scientists, Optics Researchers Charge," *The Chronicle of Higher Education*, 3 November 1982, 1].
November 1982	IEEE, in an international conference, was requested by the Air Force to withdraw three previously approved papers from the program. This request was later rescinded after adverse publicity [*The Institute* 7 (January 1983):1].
March 1983	Immigration and Naturalization Service (INS) published a final rule in the *Federal Register* on March 11, 1983 that requires the INS to terminate "the nonimmigration status of any Libyan national, or of any other foreign national acting on the behalf of a Libyan entity, who is engaged in aviation maintenance, flight operations or nuclear-related studies or training" (8 *CFR* 214, *Federal Register* (March 11, 1983), 10296-297.) This regulation marked the first time that U.S. universities have been required to discriminate based on nationality among foreign students who have legally entered this country. The government has used the rule mainly to deny visas to Libyans who have not previously studied in the U.S. [Melvyn B. Nathanson, "Academic Freedom Versus Nonproliferation: The Libyan Case," *Bulletin of the Atomic Scientists* 41 (March 1985): 29].

July 1983   IEEE, in a joint meeting with the Polar Research Board
                   and the National Academy of Sciences—National
                   Research Council was requested to withdraw six Depart-
                   ment of Defense sponsored papers because of possible
                   national security implications [Ross Gelbspan, "One
                   Case of Papers Being Withdrawn," *Boston Globe,* 22 Jan-
                   uary 1984, 7].

September 1983   Prior to a conference on aerospace systems, the chairman
                   of the Institute of Electrical and Electronic Engineers
                   was requested by the Air Force to destroy all records and
                   to cancel all presentations of certain papers that were
                   considered to be compromising national security. The
                   chairman responded by saying he would do so if the Air
                   Force would bear the burden of the estimated $25,000
                   to $50,000 that this tardy request would cost. A day
                   later the request was withdrawn [American Association
                   for the Advancement of Science, Committee on
                   Scientific Freedom and Responsibility, *National Security
                   and Scientific Communication Professional Society Chronol-
                   ogy,* April 1984, A-4].

November 1983   At the annual meeting of the American Vacuum Society,
                   Alfred Zehe, an East German physicist and an exchange
                   scholar at the University of Puebla in Mexico, was arrest-
                   ed by the FBI and charged with espionage. A week
                   before the conference the FBI had asked for six FBI
                   agents to be given credentials to attend the conference
                   under false names. After Zehe was arrested the FBI
                   requested a list of the 2,600 individuals who attended
                   the meeting, threatening to subpoena the list if it was
                   not supplied [Colin Norman, "To Catch a Spy," *Science*
                   222 (November 25, 1983): 904].

November 1983   IEEE at a national telesystems conference, was informed
                   by the Air Force that William Hurd of the Jet Propulsion
                   Laboratory would be required to delete a three-word
                   phrase from his paper on digital systems. This was
                   requested even though Mr. Hurd had never signed a
                   contract with the Air Force *The Institute* 8 (March
                   1984): 1].

January 1984	At a UCLA sponsored conference on Arms Control, the Air Force attempted to prevent a political scientist from presenting a paper on satellite systems. This did not succeed because the author of the paper contended that he had received all his information from publicly available sources [Lee Dembart, "Air Force Fails in Effort to Muzzle Speaker at UCLA," *Los Angeles Times*, 27 Jan. 1984, sec. 2, p. 1].
March 1984	There was concern in Britain that because of national security restrictions in the area of materials science, British researchers were not gaining access to the latest U.S. research results. There was also concern about restricting any scientist who was not an American citizen from attending academic activities. An example of this took place at UCLA where a short course on matrix metal composites was restricted to U.S. citizens [Jon Turney, "How American Security Hits British Research," *Times Higher Education Supplement*, 9 March 1984, 1].
April 1984	The Administration considered implementing a directive that would require university scientists working on Pentagon-sponsored projects to submit papers to the Department before they were to be presented for publication in learned journals. Work regarded as sensitive would be blocked. There was vocal criticism from three of the nation's leading universities: MIT, California Institute of Technology, and Stanford. The presidents from these three universities warned President Reagan's science advisor that they would stop doing sensitive research for the Defense Department if their freedom was curtailed. This had already occurred at Cornell where administrators turned down a $450,000 Air Force contract for research in electronics because the Defense Department had demanded an unrealistic degree of secrecy [Peter David, "Reagan Proposes to Censor Defense Study, *Times Educational Supplement*, 13 April 1984, 17].
April 1984	Vice Admiral R. A. Miller, Vice Chief of Naval Material, issued a memo prohibiting Navy civilian employees from actively participating in non-DOD-sponsored symposia, conferences or similar forums on weapons

and technology-related subjects [Eliot Marshal. "Do Seminars Leak Navy Secrets?" *Science* 224 (June 29, 1984): 1409].

May 1984   Europeans were concerned that U.S. restrictions on access of foreign scientists to strategic areas of American research will endanger efforts to increase international collaboration in scientific activities. A British computer company, International Computers Limited (I.C.I.), complained that the company has been required to apply for export licenses on knowledge contained in the heads of American research workers who have been recruited to work in Britain. There is concern that if the U.S. continues to disallow European research workers access to the most up-to-date American information in technical fields such as large scale integrated circuits or computer-aided design, Europe will develop their own systems which may be incompatible with U.S. computer technology [David Dickson, "Europeans Protest U.S. Export Controls," *Science* 224 (May 11, 1984): 579]

May 1984   U.S. Congress conferees agreed while rewriting the Export Administration Act to codify the Department of Defense's recent shift of internal authority over export controls from the research and engineering to the policy office. (Department of Defense Directive 2040.2, signed by Secretary of Defense, Caspar W. Weinberger, 1983). The research and engineering office was seen industry-wide as technically better qualified to evaluate security risks of sensitive technology. The codification eliminated the possibility of a future administration shifting the authority of export controls back to the research and engineering office ["Conferees Codify Defense Export Controls Directive," *Aviation Week & Space Technology* 120 (May 28, 1984); 27].

June 1984   National Academy of Sciences postponed its visit to the Soviet Union. The purpose of the visit was the exploration of possibilities of expanding scientific links with the Soviet Academy of Sciences. Academy President Frank Press said that discussions would be impossible "given the deep concern the members of the U.S. National Academy of Sciences have about the circum-

	stances of Foreign Associate Andrei Sakharov" [Colin Norman, "Academy Cancels Visit to Soviet Union," *Science* 224 (June 22, 1984): 1324].
July 1984	Defense Department announced that it will rescind its long-standing proposal to require 60-day submission of sensitive but unclassified research manuscripts written by university researchers under contract to DOD. There was no agreement between defense and university officials on a proposal to require 90-day prior submission of sensitive but unclassified development work manuscripts, with defense officials retaining the right either to impose prepublication changes or to block them outright [Paul Mann, "Pentagon drops Report Screening Plan," *Aviation Week & Space Technology* 121 (July 23, 1984): 119].
September 1984	President Reagan announced on August 3, 1984 that the U.S. was willing to resume intergovernmental scientific exchanges with Poland that had been suspended in 1981 as result of the Polish government's declaration of martial law. Two million dollars was held in reserve for this purpose, but Congress voted to use those funds to pay U.S. costs of scientific exchanges under a bilateral agreement with Yugoslavia [John Walsh, "Details Delay Resumption of Polish-U.S. Exchanges," *Science* 225 (September 7, 1984): 1004].
November 1984	DOD issued one directive and prepared to issue a second that would restrict the release of unclassified and previously available information about weapons and other military systems. The new rules applied to technical information generated by DOD, military contractors, research organizations, universities and anyone under contract to the Pentagon. Critics said that the directives were worded so broadly that they could also be used to restrict the flow of embarrassing information about weapons performance. DOD officials sought to assuage fears that the new directive would be used to cut off technical information to Congress or to hide mistakes by pointing to specific provisions forbidding such actions [Fred Hiatt, "Pentagon Seeks to Curb Release of Information," *Washington Post,* 8 November 1984, A4].

November 1984   Defense Department expanded labeling system it uses to distribute technical documents produced by and for department research programs. The scientific community was concerned that labeling may keep researchers from sharing unclassified findings with professional societies and associates. The new labels can be attached to unclassified technical documents, informal working papers, memoranda, or preliminary reports, either in-house or contractor-produced, if they are not already in the public domain [Paul Mann, "Strictures on Non-Secret Data Concern Scientific Community," *Aviation Week & Space Technology* 121 (November 19, 1984): 24].

January 1985   A 32-page report prepared by John Shattuck, Harvard's Vice President for Government, Communication, and Public Affairs, asserted that the controls on academic research, "threaten to erode the American tradition of academic freedom." The document was prepared at the request of Derek C. Bok, Harvard's president. The material for the report came from Harvard's own files and from previous studies of academic censorship by the government, in particular from two reports on scientific communication and national security issued by the National Academy of Sciences. The report discussed several incidents that were widely published regarding DOD suppression of technical papers at scientific meetings. Other incidents that were not widely publicized include denial of visas by the State Department to foreign scholars. The most surprising assertion of the report was that the requirements of prepublication eview reach several federal departments and agencies which have no relationship to national security matters [Kim McDonald, "Government Efforts to Muzzle Researchers Are Growing, Harvard Report Charges, *The Chronicle of Higher Education*, 9 January 1985, 1, 13].

February 1985   Representative Jack Brooks (D., Texas), reintroduced legislation that would prohibit the executive directive signed by President Reagan in 1983, requiring a lifetime of commitment by more than 100,000 federal employees to submit their writings to the government for review before publication. The directive expanded the CIA's prepublication agreement to an estimated 156,000 federal employees who held "sensitive compartmented information" clearances. Reagan rescinded the directive, but several government agencies have gone forward with its recommendations [Howard Fields, "Bill to Kill Prepublication Review Introduced," *Publishers Weekly* 227 (February 8, 1985): 29].

February 1985   There may soon be an effort to limit access to the Commerce Department's National Technical Information Service (NTIS). A February memorandum by Commerce Secretary Malcom Baldridge suggested that "new legislation, new Executive Orders, and coordinated government-wide regulations" might be required to stem what he called the "hemorrhage" of information through NTIS. Baldridge wanted authority to screen documents containing potentially sensitive information whether they were classified or not [Colin Norman, "Commerce Secretary Wants Technical Data Restricted," *Science* 227 (March 8, 1985): 1182].

March 1985   Increasingly, scientific and engineering societies have limited attendance at their conferences to U.S. citizens. The societies were practicing self-censorship because of past restraints by the government. These societies included: the Society of Manufacturing Engineers, the Society for the Advancement of Material and Process Engineering, the American Institute of Aeronautics and Astronautics, and the American Ceramics Society [Kim McDonald, "Scientific Organizations Move to Limit Conference Attendance to U.S. Citizens," *The Chronicle of Higher Education,* 6 March 1985, 5, 7].

April 1985   The DOD told the Society of Photo-Optical Instrumentation Engineers, sponsors of an April technical symposium in Washington, that it must cancel the presentation of approximately a dozen unclassified research papers because the information might help the enemies of the U.S. In addition, DOD ordered the Society to restrict the audience that attended the presentation of two dozen other technical papers that also were unclassified. The authority cited was the Export Control Act, which bars export of sensitive technology without a license. DOD maintained that if foreign scientists were present, the result might be an unauthorized export of information [David Burnham, "Pentagon acts to Curb Science Parley Papers," *New York Times,* 8 April 1985, A15].

April 1985　The Reagan administration was drafting guidelines to classify all national security-related information throughout the federal government, including civilian agencies, as part of an effort to increase computer and telecommunications security. Much of this information in government computers is unprotected and widely available. One result of this measure is that sensitive information stored in civilian agency computers would fall under a new national security classification [Michael Schrage, "Government is Drafting Electronic Security Rules," *Washington Post,* 18 April 1985, A11].

April 1985　The Department of Energy issued final regulations in the April 22 *Federal Register,* 15818-29, to prohibit the unauthorized dissemination of certain Information identified as Unclassified Controlled Nuclear Information (UCNI). The regulations set guidelines for determining what should be UCNI, established minimum protection standards, specified who might have access to UCNI, and specified penalties [*Federal Register,* 15818-29, April 22, 1985].

May 1985　According to the annual report of the Information Security Oversight Office, the total number of "classification decisions" in fiscal year 1984 was 19,607,736, an increase of nine percent over the year before. The systematic declassification of old records decreased under the Reagan E. O. 12356, but proceeded faster in 1984 than in 1983 [George Lardner Jr., "Administration Keeping More Facts Secret," *Washington Post,* 8 May 1985, A21].

July 1985　On July 8 the American Institute of Physics issued a statement that said it would not hold restricted sessions at any of its meetings in order to permit the presentation of unclassified papers that the DOD deems militarily sensitive. The institute's executive director, H. William Koch, said that the statement was issued in part to encourage the organization's nonmember societies to

adopt similar policies of their own [Colin Norman.
"Physics Institute Will Not Restrict Meetings," *Science*
229 (July 19, 1985): 253]

September 1985   Some university scientists questioned whether the results
of basic research done for the Star Wars program could
actually remain free from interference by the Pentagon,
especially if the results could be directly applied to
development of the proposed missile-defense system.
James A. Ionson, who directed the Innovative Science
and Technology Office of the Strategic Defense
Initiative Organization, assured the scientists that he had
no intentions of imposing any restrictions on fundamental research supported by his office [Kim McDonald,
"Pentagon Vows Not to Restrict 'Star Wars' Work,"
The Chronicle of Higher Education, 25 September 1985,
1, 2].

September 1985   In a September 17 letter to Defense Secretary Caspar W.
Weinberger, the presidents of 17 American scientific and
engineering societies accused the DOD of creating a
new system of classification of research and declared that
their organizations would no longer sponsor restricted
sessions at their meetings. The effect of this group action
would be to shut out from their meetings the papers of
any defense-funded scientists working in sensitive but
unclassified areas [Michael Schrage, "Scientists Defy
Pentagon on Research Restrictions," *Washington Post*, 21
September 1985, A11]

September 1985   Agreement was close between the federal government
and four university centers on how much access foreign
nationals should have to supercomputers. The proposal
to control access to the supercomputers was originally
made by DOD officials [Judith Axler Turner, "Settle-
ment Seen Near in Controversy Over Use of Supercomputers," *The Chronicle of Higher Education*, 18
September 1985, 34].

October 1985   In a 34-page report, *Soviet Acquisition of Militarily
Significant Western Technology: An Update*, the Pentagon noted that in the late 1970s and early 1980s the
Soviet Union had drawn up a list of all the universities
that had information it needed. The response from the

academic community was varied, but generally it was thought that the report was issued in order to create confusion and fear that would in turn lead to improvident restrictions on the exchange of scientific and technical data [Stacy E. Palmer, "Campuses Fear Pentagon Move on Exchanges," *The Chronicle of Higher Education* 2 October 1985, 1, 8].

December 1985 A group of 15 independent documentary film makers and production companies filed suit on December 5 in the Los Angeles Federal District Court charging that the federal government had severely limited the distribution of their films abroad because of differences in political ideology. The United States Information Agency (USIA) was hindering the distribution of the films by not issuing a certificate stating that a film was educational, scientific, or cultural in nature. The problem arose because if no such certificate was issued by USIA, the films were subject to high import taxes from the foreign countries and voluminous paper work that makes distribution to schools and libraries virtually impossible [Marcia Chambers, "Suit Says U.S. Curbed Films Over Ideology," *New York Times,* 6 December 1985, C16].

December 1985 After it was revealed in the news media on December 11, the White House announced that President Reagan signed a secret directive requiring thousands of Administration officials and perhaps some cabinet members to submit to polygraph tests as part of a counterespionage crackdown throughout the government. The President signed National Security Departmental Directive 196 on November 1. It applied to officials with access to sensitive compartmental information (SCI); more than 182,000 federal employees and contractor personnel would be subject to the tests. [Patrick E. Tyler, "Wider Polygraph Testing Approved by the President," *Washington Post,* 12 December 1985, A4]. [Don Oberdorfer, "Schultz Says He Would Quit if Required to Take the Lie Test," *Washington Post,* 20 December 1985, A1, A50]. Don Oberdorfer, "President Sharply Restricts Polygraph Tests for Officials," *Washington Post,* 21 December 1985, A1, A8]. ["Reagan Called Aware of Scope of Directive,"

Washington Post, 25 December 1985, A16]. National Security Departmental Directive 196 is classified; thus it is not known whether it contains a prepublication review system for speeches and writings of current and former government employees. However, such a system is already in effect. According to a June 1984 General Accounting Office report, every employee with access to SCI is required to sign a lifelong prepublication censorship agreement, Form 4193 [U.S. Congress, House, News Release, in general, "GAO Update on Administration Lie Detector/Censorship Status Reveals Reagan Promise of Suspension Has Little Effect; Brooks Calls for End to Programs, Prohibition by Law," released June 13, 1984].

February 1986   Department of Defense proposed new rules for clearing research papers for presentation at scientific meetings. These rules applied to papers originating from research performed in DOD labs or under contract to the department. Scientific organizations generally agreed that these rules would prevent papers from being withdrawn at the last minute from scientific conferences but there was concern that the rules would lead to further attempts to require that some unclassified papers be presented only in special export-controlled sessions. The main thrust of the rules is that the DOD will be required to meet tight deadlines when reviewing papers. Abstracts must be reviewed within 10 working days, papers scheduled for open sessions must be reviewed within 20 working days and all other papers must be cleared in 30 working days [Colin Norman, "DOD Proposes Rules for Reviewing Scientific Papers," *Science* 231 (February 28, 1986): 915].

March 1986   After many months, U.S. federal government did not come up with a final policy regarding access of Soviet bloc scientists and exchange students to university supercomputers. Universities and the National Science Foundation have reluctantly accepted visa controls keeping Soviet bloc researchers away from federally funded facilities leaving to the government the responsibility for enforcing the visa controls. There was still contention over restricting registration of foreign students in courses that utilize the supercomputers ["Tighter Controls on Supercomputers," *Science News* 129 (March 22, 1986): 185].

March 1986   DOD and the Central Intelligence Agency initiated a disinformation program covering 15-20 programs, six or seven of which are DOD projects. Deliberately false, incomplete, and misleading information, including altered technical information, would be released in order to impede the transfer of accurate technological inform- ation to the Soviet Union. A DOD official said, "If some of the results of the disinformation activity on a partic- ular program get passed on to Congress through hear- ings or other means, there are channels on the Hill that can be used to get the correct information to the people who need to know" [David M. North, "U.S. Using Disinformation Policy to Impede Technical Data Flow," *Aviation Week and Space Technology* 124 (March 17, 1986): 16].

May 1986   Donald A. Hicks, Under Secretary of Defense for Re- search and Engineering was the first Pentagon official to suggest in public that his department offer proof of its concern regarding limiting access to U.S. super- computers by Soviet Bloc scientists. There were current negotiations between the Defense Department and five university-based supercomputer centers which were sponsored by the National Science Foundation. The Foundation was seeking an exception for course-related work and certain scientists on a case-by-case basis [Judith Axler Turner, "Aide Urges Pentagon to Explain Why it Should Bar Soviets from Computers," *The Chronicle of Higher Education*, 14 May 1986, 1, 34].

May 1986   "The Pentagon, concerned with the flow of high tech- nology to the Soviet bloc, is trying to limit foreign access to government and commercial computer data bases that contain sensitive technical information. A range of legal and technological options are now under exploration, from licensing access to high tech data bases to planting special computer programs within the data bases to monitor who is seeking what information. Government officials concede, however, that they face formidable obstacles in devising a workable system, including such questions as whether data bases enjoy the same constitutional protections as other media and how to implement restrictions in ways that won't deny data-base benefits to American users" [Michael Schrage, " U.S. Seeking to Limit Access of Soviets to Computer Data," *Washington Post,* 27 May 1986, Al, A18].

May 1986   There was concern in Britain about restrictions the U.S. was imposing on supercomputers delivered to Britain. Richard Field, director of the computer center at the University of London, stated that there was a list of conditions from the U.S. upon delivery of the Cray I supercomputer. Mr. Field said British universities could not be bound by American restrictions. He also stated that his center had monitored closely the supercomputer it already had, a Cray l-F, checking for any signs of non-academic use [David Walker, "Britons Upset by U.S. Attempts to Restrict Use of Imported Supercomputers," *The Chronicle of Higher Education,* 28 May 1986, 29-31].

June 1986   The National Academy of Sciences signed a new two-year agreement on scientific cooperation with the Soviet Union on April 1, 1986. The agreement calls for regular meetings of officers of the two academies, exchanges of academy members, workshops, cooperative research in areas to be specified and exchanges of individual scientists. NAS President Frank Press said the agreement was concluded without specific approval from the Reagan administration but the State Department was informed. The new agreement differs from earlier agreements because it places more emphasis on regular meetings of academy officers and lays out specific agendas for the meetings [William Sweet, "US and Soviet Academies Sign Agreement," *Physics Today* 39 (June 1986): 67].

July 1986   The Massachusetts Institute of Technology, a university that spent $38 million in 1985 on defense-related research, considered withdrawing its ties with the Pentagon. MIT faculty put together a special inquiry called the "Ad Hoc Committee on the Military Presence at MIT," chaired by economist Carl Kaysen. The report found widespread uneasiness among faculty over the government's push for a narrow, more applied focus in military research. The study devoted special attention to attitudes regarding Strategic Defense Initiative because there was fear that the DOD will ask for specialized weapons research. MIT's increased reliance on funds from DOD and SDI is the fastest growing segment of DOD research. The study made no suggestions for solutions to the problem, but it was passed to MIT President Paul Gray who will create another committee to decide what the university should do [Eliot Marshall, "MIT's Faustian Bargain: Signs of Malaise," *Science* 233 (July 25, 1986): 416].

August 1986   Following the announcement that the U.S. and Soviet Union have agreed on 13 new exchanges covering a range of cultural, educational, and scientific contacts, there was concern that the Soviet Union will initiate a return to pre-1979 levels of cooperation. U.S. critics of exchanges said that in the 1970s the Soviets largely set the agenda. The interagency Federal Coordinating Council for Science, Engineering, and Technology will be given the task of developing government-wide policy to guide agency activities in the science exchanges. The two criteria that will be implemented are that the U.S. will want to be certain that the exchange projects have scientific value for this country and that strategically ensitive technology will not be lost to the Soviets [John Walsh, "U.S.-Soviet Exchanges—Redefining Coexistence," *Science* 233 (Aug. 22, 1986): 833].

September 1986   The administration announced that it suspended NSDD 196. This was a reaction to widespread criticism. According to a September 1986 General Accounting Office *report, Information and Personnel Security: Data on Employees Affected by Federal Security Programs* (GAO/NSIAD-86-189FS), there were still more than 290,000 present and former federal employees who were affected by the previously mentioned Form 4193, which meant submitting to prepublication review. Not included in the figures were the CIA and National Security Agency, which set similar requirements for their employees. The number of books, articles or speeches submitted for review was rising: 12,934 in 1984 and 14,144 in 1985. According to GAO, in 1985 the number of known unauthorized disclosures of classified information made through published writings or speeches by then current employees was five and by former employees was two.

September 1986   Twenty national organizations banded together to fight Reagan administration restrictions on access to federal data by forming the Coalition on Government Information. The participants, such as the American Civil Liberties Union, the American Association for the Advancement of Science, the American Library Association and People for the American Way, identified areas of immediate concern: the proposed privatization of the National Technical Information Service, the draft amendments to the Freedom of Information Act, and the inaccessibility of local housing statistics collected by the federal government ["20 National Groups to Fight Curbs on Federal Information," *American Libraries* 17 (September 1986): 576].

November 1986   The Reagan administration proposed that American scientists undertake a design study with the Soviet Union, Japan, and the European Economic Community to test the possibility of constructing an Energy Test Reactor. Originally, there was hope that the U.S. and the Soviet Union would work together closely to develop the reactor but the DOD opposed any international collaboration with the Soviet Union that entails actual construction and engineering [Mark Crawford, "Researchers' Dreams Turn to Paper in U.S.-U.S.S.R. Fusion Plan," *Science* 234 (November 7, 1986): 666].

December 1986   The House Committee on Government Operations report indicated that three days after being informed of new regulations permitting the release of former President Nixon's papers, the White House took action that led to the Justice Department's issuing a memorandum that would permit Nixon or any incumbent president to block their release. The committee report said that the courts have already held that the archivist has the right to make decisions on the release of presidential papers [Dale Nelson, "The Nixon Papers

Shuffle," *Wilson Library Bulletin* 61 (December 1986): 30].

December 1986   "In 1980, the Office of Management and Budget under the Paperwork Reduction Act, got the authority to review all data collection efforts of executive branch agencies. A pattern of obstructionism, barring certain types of data collection, has been charged by many agencies, and now the House Committee on Science and Technology has asked the General Accounting Office to investigate. Allegations of improper use of its powers include OMB's hostility to any data collection dealing with minorities and discrimination, questions concerning the environment and public health, and social science research generally. In matters calling for medical or other special scientific expertise, unqualified OMB officers are charged with overruling qualified agency scientists. The specific agency accused is OMB's Office of Information and Regulatory Affairs (OIRA)" [*Library Hotline,* Dec. 15, 1986].

December 1986   The Defense Department created a National Telecommunications and Information Systems/Security Policy (NTISSP), which will restrict access to national security information. A memorandum signed by the President's former National Security Advisor Vice Admiral John Poindexter was about "a national policy on the protection of sensitive but unclassified information in the federal government telecommunications and automated information systems." There was concern among the private sector that utilize government databases that there will be sanctions if NTISSP is not followed. Jack Simpson, president of Mead Data Central, said that "DOD's theory is that if information in print form is unclassified, it becomes classified as soon as it's gathered in pieces and put in a computer" [Willie Schatz, "The Chilling Effect," *Datamation* (December 15, 1986), 28].

Winter 1987   Some examples of alteration of government information as a result of budgetary restrictions on federal agency publication programs follow: *The Handbook of Labor Statistics* did not appear in 1986 and its future publication is unsure; *International Economic Indicators* was discontinued in 1986 because of inadequate funding; after being discontinued in 1979, the *Federal Statistical Directory* is now published by the private sector at three times the government price; there has been a reduction in the detailed data collection for *Vital Statistics of the United States*; the periodical *American Education* was discontinued in 1985. Much of this information, which is no longer available in the printed format, appears in electronic databases which restricts access to this important information to people who have the expertise and the money to search these expensive databases [Arnold Lewis and Margaret S. Powell, "The Silent Threat: How Federal Policy Stifles Scholarship," *Educational Record* 68 (Winter 1987):18].

January 1987   National Academy of Sciences released a report (*Balancing the National Interest: U.S. National Security Export Controls and Global Economic Competition*) criticizing recent federal government efforts to restrict foreign and domestic exchange of unclassified information. The report's main recommendations included: export controls governing communication among scientists in countries allied with the United States should be kept to a minimum; the Department of Defense should utilize its power sparingly, to restrict the spread of data from studies it has paid for, unless the data would fall under normal guidelines for security classification or export control; and controls on the international exchange of data for commercial or research purposes should not be expanded [David L. Wheeler, "Science Academy Criticizes Federal Efforts to Curb," *Chronicle of Higher Education* 21 January 1987, 4].

February 1987   Jack Simpson, president of Mead Data Central, was visited by agents of the Air Force, the CIA, the National Security Agency and the FBI. All of these agents requested the identities of the company's 320,000 subscribers. They were interested in possibly blocking certain subscribers from using the databases, or they wanted Mead to tell the government which information those subscribers requested. This action was not an isolated one. The administration was interested in

limiting the U.S. scientific information available in
commercial and government databases in order to keep
the information out of the hands of foreign competitors
and adversaries. There was general concern in the
academic community that if the information was
restricted on databases there would be no opportunity
to search for possible duplication of research. Mead
decided to police itself by dropping Energy Department
reports and other research by NTIS [Bob Davis, "Federal
Agencies Press Data-Base Firms to Curb Access to
'Sensitive Information'," *Wall Street Journal,* 5 February
1987, 25].

April 1987   In a speech on the floor of the House of Representatives,
Rep. George Brown (D., Calif.) called for an end to the
tight security surrounding U.S. photoreconnaissance
satellites. He suggested the following three changes:
relax the existing limit of 10-meter resolution on civilian
remote sensing satellites, initiate discussions within the
U.S. and with other nations on an international arms
control treaty verification organization, and remove the
"veil of secrecy that has been draped for far too long
over the National Reconnaissance Office and its
operations" ["Congressman Urges Public Disclosure of
Spy Satellite Data," *Aviation Week and Space Technology*
126 (April 6, 1987): 30].

May 1987   Howard Baker, Jr., the new presidential chief of staff,
revoked the memorandum issued by Vice Admiral John
M. Poindexter, "National Policy on Protection of
Sensitive but Unclassified Information in Federal
Government Telecommunications and Automated
Information Systems." The policy would have allowed
the National Security Agency and the Defense Department to review what goes into the electronic databases
and also to have access to records of who would be
using government sponsored operations such as the
National Technical Information Service, the National
Science Foundation's supercomputer centers and the
National Library of Medicine's Medline [Irwin Goodwin, "In Rough Waters, White House Cancels Controls
on Databases," *Physics Today* 40 (May 1987): 66].

May 1987   The Department of Energy instituted a program known as SAFE (Security Awareness for Employees). SAFE was initiated at the Lawrence Livermore National Laboratory in Livermore, California in 1986 and is expected to be implemented throughout the rest of DOE's laboratories and contractors. SAFE's ultimate goal is to inform scientists that though they may be working on unclassified projects it is possible that the work is subject to export controls and the information should not be revealed to foreign colleagues in casual conversation. The DOE would like to inform the scientists that ignorance of possible export controls will not protect them against felony prosecution if they are caught. Robert I. Park, executive director of the American Physical Society's public affairs office, is a leading critic of government controls on nonclassified data. Park charges that if the SAFE program includes lab personnel whose work is not subject to censoring controls then it risks "imposing on them a chilling effect" with regard to the normal free flow of scientific information. Another government restraint on information occurred late in 1986 when Michael Radnor, director of Northwestern University's Center for the Interdisciplinary Study of Science and Technology (CISST), learned that NASA had included him on its little-known "No-No List," which includes individuals and companies that would not be allowed to subscribe to *NASA Tech Briefs*. This journal offers nonclassified descriptions of new technologies resulting from NASA research. The reason for cancellation of Radnor's subscription is that CISST ran a technology-transfer program with Japan [Janet Raloff, "Coming The Big Chill?" *Science News* 131 May 16, 1987): 314].

May 1987   The Justice Department filed papers in a lawsuit seeking to overturn a 1986 federal court ruling that narrowed Richard Nixon's right to keep secret 44 million pages of documents and more than 4,000 hours of tape recordings of conversations that had taken place during his administration. Thirteen years later virtually all the tapes and more than 95 percent of the documents are inaccessible. In a Justice Department memorandum dated February 16, 1986, Charles Cooper, Assistant Attorney General for the Office of Legal Counsel, argued that the National Archives should not have a final say on the issuance of presidential papers. "[An] incumbent President should respect a former President's claim of executive privilege." The probable result of this memorandum is that Nixon does not have to fight against the disclosure of his papers, but any interested scholar, journalist or other interested party must file suit in order to view any of Nixon's presidential documents ["History Deleted," *Nation* 244 (May 23, 1987): 669].

June 1987
The National Security Council, under pressure from the Department of Defense, moved to block U.S. support of multilateral environmental research programs that include scientists from the Soviet Union and other socialist countries. One of these research programs is the Ocean Drilling Program (ODP), which is a basic research effort that has uncovered valuable information involving the long-term history of global environmental change. Another environmental research program under scrutiny is the International Institute for Applied Systems Analysis (IIASA), which is a think tank that conducts policy-oriented research on problems of the environment, population, and technological change. There have been reviews by the Department of State, other federal agencies, and the scientific community as to whether there are any security risks involved in these two environmental projects and despite the collective failure of these agencies to find any security risks, the NSC has persisted in refusing to allow the research [William C. Clark, "National Security and the Environment," *Environment* 29 (June 1987): 1].

June 1987
The University of California at Berkeley announced in January 1987 that it would close a 1-MW research reactor. In December 1986, Berkeley physicist Charles L. Schwartz charged that the reactor had been used for military research by private contractors Lockheed and Aerospace in violation of a university rule that no classified research be done on campus. University

officials said that the main reason for shutting down
the reactor was the low usage of the reactor for research
and the university's need to house the computer science
unit of its electrical engineering department in a new
building over the reactor [William Sweet, "Research
Reactor Closed at Berkeley for Mixed Reasons," *Physics
Today* 40 (June 1987): 56].

July 1987   Frank Press, president of the National Academy of
Sciences, and other leaders in the American scientific
community contend that the Japanese have not been
open about technological research done in their laboratories. Very few American scientists have been able to
conduct research in Japan, in contrast to the hundreds
of Japanese who have studied at the best American
laboratories. White House science advisor, William
Graham, proposed strong measures directed at the
Japanese government. These included a demand that the
Japanese government commit itself to enlarging its
support of basic research, which U.S. researchers might
then tap; a demand that Japan pay for U.S. scientists to
learn the Japanese language so they can keep abreast of
cutting-edge research in Japanese laboratories; and a
demand that research positions in those labs for U.S.
scientists also be subsidized by the Japanese. The White
House Economic Policy Council decided not to adopt
these measures because it was believed that the measures
would have damaged current joint scientific endeavors
with Japan [Marjorie Sun, "Strains in U.S.-Japan
Exchanges," *Science* 237 (July 31,1987): 476].

July 1987   William Graham, the President's science adviser, decided
to exclude noncitizens from a mass meeting on superconductivity on July 28, 1987. The program was
sponsored by the White House Office of Science and
Technology Policy, four federal agencies, the National
Academy of Sciences, and the National Academy of
Engineering. The apparent reason for excluding foreign
scientists was to deny information to America's
competitors in trade [Eliot Marshall and Marjorie Sun,
"Stumbling on Superconductors," *Science* 237 (July 31,
1987): 4771].

August 1987   David A. Wilson directed the Export Controls Information Project for the Department of Defense-University Forum. The project has produced a set of publications explaining government policy on national security and export controls as it affects university research. During the last year the issues have become less confused, but several of the export-control issues have not yet been resolved. The government task force responsible for deciding how to handle foreign access to supercomputers cannot reach an agreement on the issue; the Export Administration Regulations, after two years, are still in draft form; government officials may seek further revisions in the International Traffic in Arms Regulations; and the debate over setting security standards for unclassified but "sensitive" data in computer databases is not resolved ["Export Controls and Research Results," *Science News* 132 (August 1, 1987: 73].

September 1987   The North Atlantic Treaty Organization (NATO), directly finances more scientific exchanges than any other organization. More than 250,000 scientists have participated in its programs over the past 30 years. The NATO Science Committee, unlike the other NATO programs, consists of scientists appointed from each member country rather than government officials. NATO contributes a major share of support for international scientific meetings. sponsoring some 60 to 70 Advanced Study Institutes for postdoctoral students and 20 to 30 workshops each year [Colin Norman, "Unsung Force in Science Exchanges," *Science* 237 (September 4, 1987): 1113].

October 1987   FBI agents have visited approximately 20 libraries, mostly academic, asking librarians to cooperate with agents in a "Library Awareness Program" which is part of a national counterintelligence effort. The FBI claimed that the program was aimed mostly at diplomats. When questioned about the need to recruit librarians to watch for suspicious characters, James Fox, director of the New York FBI office, said that most libraries have computer links to "sophisticated research and information banks" that could provide "sensitive information, even if it is not classified." He also said that libraries are excellent sources for names of technical experts to recruit as agents [Graceanne A. DeCandido, "FBI Agents Ask N.Y. Librarians to Spywatch," *Library Journal* 112 (October 15, 1987): 12].

October 1987 The American Library Association has accused the FBI of attempting to infringe First Amendment privacy rights of library patrons because of recent attempts by FBI agents to convince librarians to watch out for spies attempting to gain access to information that could be potentially harmful to U.S. national security. The ALA protested the FBI approaches and has asked Congress for an investigation of the matter [Howard Fields, "ALA Protests FBI's Attempted Surveillance of Library Patrons," *Publishers Weekly* 232 (October 30, 1987): 12].

January 1988 As the FBI continued its "library awareness program," an incident occurred at the Brooklyn (N.Y.) Public Library where a library staff member was approached by an FBI agent who asked the librarian to report any suspicious behavior of patrons gathering information that might be detrimental to national security. Larry Brandewein, Brooklyn Public Library Director, responded to the FBI inquiries by saying "We have refused to cooperate with such inquiries, which we regard as illegal and improper" ["FBI Persists in 'Awareness Campaign,'" *American Libraries* 19 (January 1988): 8].

April 1988 After initial incidents of FBI agents approaching librarians at fewer than 20 New York City libraries to aid the agency by watching out for suspicious characters researching subjects crucial to national security there was a follow-up interview with FBI Director, William Steele Sessions. During the interview Sessions said that for the past 10 years the FBI has sought assistance of special librarians in technical libraries asking the librarians to watch out for foreign, hostile intelligence persons seeking both information and to recruit people who will be agents for their country. The justification for this ongoing program was, "The potential hostile presence in this country includes 20,000 students from

Communist countries, 9,000 visitors from Communist countries and over 4,000 Communist diplomats and commercial representatives based in the U.S. One-third of these diplomats and commercial representatives are believed to be involved in intelligence gathering efforts. We do not have enough personnel to keep track of everyone who comes into the country with an intelligence gathering mission, and therefore public awareness is important to our efforts" [Natalie Robins, "The F.B.I.'s Invasion of Libraries," *The Nation* 246 (April 9, 1988): 481].

April 1988   In a closed meeting between FBI agents and the National Commission on Libraries and Information Science there was discussion on the "library awareness program." Thomas E. DuHadway, deputy assistant director of the FBI's intelligence division, claimed that there have been incidents of foreign agents recruiting librarians. He went on to say, "We've had Soviets tell us that they think it's better to recruit two librarians in a science and techno-logical library than it would be to recruit three engineers who could put together a system, because those librarians have access to people, places and things that can front for the Soviets that the engineer can't." NCLIS Chair Jerald C. Newman supported the Bureau's actions saying, "We have the responsibility . . . of being sure there's freedom of access of information, but I think we have another responsibility in upholding the Constitution of the United States." Several brief passages in the transcript of the meeting were blanked out by the FBI as sensitive or classified [Gordon Flagg, "Transcript of Closed NCLIS Meeting Details FBI's 'Library Awareness Program'," *American Libraries* 19 (April 1988): 244].

THE "GREY" GHETTO: KEY ISSUES RELATED TO PUBLIC POLICY RESEARCH LITERATURE

Marc A. Levin

"Grey," "ephemeral," "fugitive," and "non-trade" are terms used to describe the unique publications issued by American private public policy research organizations. These research organizations often publish the best and brightest analytical thinking about public problem-solving and wield considerable influence in the process of national policy-making. Information professionals, responsible for social science collections, have for decades agonized over issues related to acquiring, cataloging, and organizing this unorthodox literature. Librarians have traditionally viewed this body of literature as too difficult and laborious to locate and inferior by library standards to sit on open shelves among the general collection.

To illustrate the complexity, consider the array of issuing agencies: think tanks, government consulting firms, pressure groups, professional and trade associations, university and private research institutions, watchdog and public interest groups, citizen research committees, blue-ribbon study commissions, and specialized research and development laboratories. These policy research groups contribute substantially to public problem-solving through the dissemination of vital information in the form of specific data, new evidence,

"The 'Grey' Ghetto: Key Issues Related to Public Policy Research Literature," by Marc A. Levin in *Collection Building*. Vol. 10, no. 1-2 (1989), pp. 29-33; reprinted with permission from Neal-Schuman, Publishers, Inc., copyright © 1990 by Neal-Schuman Publishers, Inc.

alternative hypotheses, or policy evaluation studies. The literature issued by such organizations strives to link research with theory as applied to public problems or focuses new attention on the causal explanation of social phenomena.

On the eve of the November 1986 general election, a significant national public opinion poll was released that reported where Americans get their political information. It revealed that libraries were rated as the least common place to locate such information.[1] These findings raise serious questions about our ability to provide the public with the necessary information for effective citizen participation in the political process. As information providers we cannot overlook this situation. Instead, we must correct it by improving and expanding library services that promote access to information by citizens who want to increase their understanding of public issues. The importance of public policy research literature to professional social inquiry, scholarly communication, student research, citizen awareness, and the policy development process is notable, yet, this body of literature is often neglected, even shunned by librarians.

To rectify our history of neglect, we must understand the key issues associated with the literature disseminated by policy research organizations. Clarifying the issues will permit us to elevate our critical consciousness and lead to the development of a model of library services for fugitive materials.

The Role of Policy Research Organizations

No discussion of grey literature would be complete without first examining how information disseminated by public policy research organizations affects the policy-making process. A policy research organization can be broadly construed to mean an organization that does research bearing on governmental policies and programs in the public interest. Such organizations form what some observers have called a "shadow government"; yet their exact role in the political process is not altogether clear. In fact, the estimates of such research organizations varies. Using the broadest definition, there are approximately 10,000 private organizations with some potential for public policy research or policy advocacy. Ideally, such research organizations are nonpartisan, independent entities, operating free from government supervision and public scrutiny, yet influential to the policy process. Their main purpose is to stand above specific economic, political, or class interests and to speak for the general welfare of society. These organizations do not decide policy as that remains the task of our elected officials. Instead, they formulate, recommend, and evaluate policy initiatives, serving in an agenda-setting and advisory role.

The original concept of a nonpartisan public policy research organization, operating free from government supervision and domination by special interests, is uniquely American. The historical development of these organizations was based on the belief in nonpartisan expertise, and faith that public policy could be depoliticized. Charles B. Saunders, in his history of the Brookings Institution, described this reform movement for rational public problem-solving as based on two essentials:

1. through the application of scientific inquiry to achieve knowledge of the best methods for maximum effectiveness and minimum waste in the conduct of governmental affairs; and
2. the development of active public interest in administrative efficiency.[2]

Out of this spirit of reform during the late nineteenth and early twentieth centuries arose hundreds of organizations dedicated to the fundamental commitment to make social science research useful to leaders throughout society. During its first 50 years, according to Saunders, the Brookings Institution was responsible for establishing a modern federal budget system, for drafting major sections of the New Deal legislation, and the founding of the United Nations[3] These accomplishments testify to the enduring influence such institutes have had upon national policy-making.

Since the mid-1960s there has been a proliferation of policy research organizations, due mainly to massive federal spending aimed at solving societal problems. In more recent years, numerous policy research organizations that are more openly partisan have risen to new prominence casting aside the cloak of political neutrality. The spectrum includes groups such as the American Enterprise Institute for Public Policy Research and the Heritage Foundation as conservative in policy outlook; the Cato Institute as libertarian; and the Institute for Policy Studies and the Center for National Policy as liberal in policy direction. As if in a "war of ideas," these organizations strongly advocate their own points of view as the appropriate version of the public's interest.

Regardless of partisanship, these organizations serve to bring together the leadership of foundations, mass media, prominent intellectuals, influential public officials, and corporate and financial institutions in an effort to research policy issues and develop policy consensus.[4]

Characteristics of the Literature

The ultimate goal of policy research groups is the diffusion of new knowledge. To accomplish this, their publications are actively promoted to key policy-makers. Policy analyses and recommendations, backed up by empirical evidence, are designed to advance a certain policy choice. In commenting on the value this literature offers policy-makers, Alice M. Rivlin, the former director of the U.S. Congressional Budget Office, stated:

> We now know as never before just who the poor are, where they are, and what it is they lack. More than ever before, we know which parts of the nation are growing and which are not; which parts of our cities are less or more troubled by street crime or urban decay; who among the nation's children are, or are not learning to read.[5]

While some of the literature pushes for specific practical solutions to well-defined problems, a common goal of these publications is to illuminate alternatives and/or to reconceptualize old problems.

In general, policy research organizations tend to publish both monographs and periodicals. Monograph subjects are diverse, ranging from rent control to birth control to arms control. The periodical literature is likewise varied, ranging from academic journals, such as the *Cato Journal* and *Urban Land,* to less substantial newsletters and bulletins, such as the *Conservation Foundation Letter* and the Tax Foundation's *Tax Features.* Many organizations publish series of working papers or discussion papers that reflect new and dynamic thinking on the most immediate and pressing issues confronting policy-makers. Typically, this literature is printed on poor quality paper with soft covers, often mimeographed or photocopied—all for the sake of rapid dissemination.

How These Publications Influence Policy

To form a better understanding of the influence this body of literature seeks to exercise, one must understand the policy-making process.[6] There are three recognized political concepts that attempt to explain how policy is determined in our system of government:

- the pluralist democracy model
- the administrative efficiency model
- the elitist model.

A fourth model, referred to as the participative model, is still struggling to emerge and gain popular acceptance.

Briefly, the theory of pluralist democracy envisions a political model in which multiple centers of power, such as politicians and special interest groups, bargain and compromise to produce decisions that are acceptable to many competing interests. The administrative efficiency model can be characterized as policy dominance by experts and professionals, such as bureaucrats and policy analysts, who rely on rational, objective decision making. The elitist model contends that issues and elections may come and go, but a stable group of individuals, often referred to as the governing elite, continues to exercise a disproportionate influence over public policy. In all of these models, policy questions are decided by political surrogates, not by popular influence.

This leads us to the fourth concept which attempts to reestablish popular control of a system in which policy-making is dominated by special interests, experts, and elites. The participative model, promoted by Professor Douglas Yates of Yale University, advocates greater citizen involvement in the policy debate through greater dialogue between citizen and government.[7] This model emphasizes interactive problem-solving that values expertise for discovering policy options, but not at the expense of the public will. I believe this model offers the best potential for reducing public alienation from government, as expressed by record low voter turnouts, and it acknowledges that social problems can most effectively be solved through human interaction and dialogue among a knowledgeable citizenry.

Implications for Information Professionals

Which one of these models thrives depends on the ease of access to vital policy information. This is where the information professional can make a difference. One of the best sources of high quality, specialized policy-related information is the literature issued by policy research organizations. We can assist directly with the development of a participative model by making available the information necessary for citizen involvement. In 1980, the U.S. Advisory Commission on Intergovernmental Relations (ACIR) extensively studied the role of citizen participation in the governmental process. A significant finding of the ACIR study was that citizens often do not have information necessary for meaningful participation.[8] As information professionals we can help remedy this situation by building library collections rich with the specialized knowledge so critical for the public's emerging role in the interactive problem-solving process.

Two related trends add additional impetus to this mandate. First, there is an escalation in the privatization of government research activities. More and more surveys, statistical compilations, consumer studies, program evaluations, and data collection activities are being conducted under government contract by the private sector. Often, the literature issued by these organizations is the only source of this vital information. In the past, we could rely on the government to distribute information through the depository library system. In recent years the program has been curtailed. If we fail to actively collect information as it is produced, it is unlikely to reach the mainstream of public knowledge. Second, there is increasing use of the initiative and referendum process in which citizens are asked to decide complex and crucial public matters. For example, during the November 1986 general election, Californians were asked to decide on such complex public issues as the quarantine of AIDS-virus carriers, groundwater protection from toxic wastes, and English as the official state language. Often literature issued by policy research organizations is the only source of independent information that objectively evaluates important policy questions before the electorate.

An Agenda for Professional Action

In light of these assumptions and trends, our task is to develop an agenda that elevates policy research literature into greater prominence in our collections. Whether our users are actual policy-makers, scholars, researchers, students, or ordinary citizens, we must recognize the value this literature offers society. It contributes to an informed and enlightened public, which is the foundation of democracy. The modern information professional is fast assuming the role of ombudsman between the information seeker and the available resources. Thus, access to information is now the key issue before us.

There are three areas of professional activity that I suggest can be undertaken in our institutions to improve access to this body of literature:

- collection development
- bibliographic control
- research

For starters, a major problem is locating grey literature, as it is not actively marketed to libraries. Nor are there any commercially produced finding aids that include this literature. Yet, specialized research collections have for decades successfully captured these fleeting publications. Unlike other library-related problems, failure to collect this literature is not due to financial limitations. Since the main objective of policy research organizations is to disseminate information to influence the policy process or develop critical thinking on a policy problem, publications are marginally priced or free. However, titles go quickly out-of-print due to limited press runs, so swift ordering is essential. To accomplish this, acquisition systems must be streamlined, efficient, and flexible. Complex acquisition systems that require detailed bibliographic information are too slow. In most cases, these publications can be ordered by sending a simple request letter providing enough identifying information to describe the desired item. Incomplete author, title, imprint, or other bibliographic information is quite acceptable, as long as it is intelligible. Standing orders are also sometimes available.

Discovering the existence of this literature will require a dedicated effort by the information professional to scan the policy-focused information environment. This involves reading the same literature geared for policy-makers and scanning several influential newspapers on a regular basis. Both types of sources are excellent for discovering new and emerging policy studies. Several of the larger policy research organizations, such as AEI, Brookings, Rand Corp., and SRI, have publication catalogs available for the asking. Numerous research collections around the nation have for decades distributed regular library accessions lists of newly acquired items along with pertinent ordering information. Exchange agreements are also possible provided your institution publishes significant items that may be of interest to a policy research organization. Under these agreements, institutions send each other their new publications free of charge, serving a depository function as well. Lastly, outreach programs to local policy-makers or influential faculty members can be developed by agreeing to have the library accept the policy research literature they receive, often unsolicited, in the mail.

Another problem we have to overcome involves the bibliographic control of grey literature. At present, there is no national bibliography of past or current titles issued by policy research organizations. Indexing and abstracting services have largely ignored this literature, with the possible exception of the *Government Reports & Announcements Index* and the *Public Affairs Information Service.* Shared cataloging systems, such as OCLC and RLIN, contain only limited holdings for many of these publications. Undoubtedly, there is room for vast improvement and innovative solutions. Because this literature is difficult to catalog, libraries have ranked it very low in cataloging priority, often relegating it to pamphlet files or the abyss of Government Documents collections, with few or no bibliographic records. We must collectively agree to process these materials through shared cataloging systems meeting full bibliographic input standards. Once this literature is identified through automated cataloging systems, it can be accessed by users. The subject searching capabilities now available through many of these national online databases, such as OCLC's Gateway System loaded on BRS, will permit offsite access to these holdings via inter-library loan transactions.

Finally, collecting and cataloging this special literature is not the end of the problem. Research projects should be initiated to better identify what we already have in our collections, how to preserve the existing historical literature for future generations, and how users go about seeking this information. I believe this literature warrants long-term retention as it serves a valuable research function—documenting the historical policy development and policy intent process. Citation studies, survey research, compilation of bibliographies, and catalog use studies would increase our ability to cope with the myriad of problems generated by the literature. With answers to these perplexing questions, we could proceed to develop cooperative agreements among interested institutions for specific collection development and shared cataloging responsibilities.

Conclusion

Information disseminated by public policy research organizations is concerned with building on fundamental knowledge and educating the public to enable them to participate in policy problem-solving. We have a special obligation to place this information in the public domain where people grappling with these issues can access it and use it for social betterment. This is not an easy task. It will take research, ingenuity, and commitment. If we begin now to take up the challenge of actively cataloging and collecting, within the next ten to twenty years this body of literature may no longer be considered "fugitive."

References

1. Lawrence Kilman, "Where Public Gets News of Candidates," *San Francisco Examiner* (3 November 1986): A-9.
2. Charles B. Saunders, Jr., *The Brookings Institution: A Fifty-Year History* (Washington, D.C.: Brookings Institution, 1966): 12.
3. *Ibid.*, 3.
4. Donald T. Critchlow, *The Brookings Institution, 1916-1952: Expertise and the Public Interest in a Democratic Society* (DeKalb, Ill.: Northern Illinois University Press, 1985): 9.
5. Alice M. Rivlin, *Systematic Thinking for Social Action Research* (Washington, D.C.: Brookings Institution, 1971): 5
6. Thomas R. Dye, "Oligarchic Tendencies in National Policy-Making: the Role of the Private Policy Planning Organization," *Journal of Politics* 40 (May 1978): 310.
7. Douglas Yatff, *Bureaucratic Democracy: The Search for Democracy and Efficiency in American Government* (Cambridge, Mass.: Harvard University Press, 1982): 6.
8. U.S. Advisory Commission on Intergovernmental Relations, *Citizen Participation in the American Federal System,* A-73 (Washington, D.C., U.S.G.P.O., 1980): 12.

ACCESS TO INFORMATION FOR ENVIRONMENTALISTS: A LIBRARY PERSPECTIVE

Susan A. Safyan

Many Canadians feel that no issue today is more important than the environment (Ludlow 1989). Membership in environmental groups grows as more citizens become actively involved in cleaning up the refuse of industrialized society, and in slowing the destruction of the planet's forests, oceans and ozone layer.

Librarians and environmentalists share a fundamental commitment to the principle of access to information. At present, however, full access to information is impeded by a number of factors, some intrinsic to the complexities of the literature itself, others imposed by governments, or the result of economic inequities. But if information is a prerequisite for any type of effective change, librarians need to renew their commitment to the principle of access by becoming familiar with the major sources of environmental information.

"Access to Information for Environmentalists: A Library Perspective," by Susan A. Safyan in *Canadian Library Journal.* Vol. 47, no. 5 (October 1990), pp. 337-343; reprinted with permission from the Canadian Library Association and *Canadian Library Journal,* copyright © 1990 *Canadian Library Journal.*

The Principle of Access

Both American and Canadian Library Associations have articulated their positions on access. CLA has stated that "it is the responsibility of libraries to guarantee and facilitate access to all expressions of knowledge and intellectual activity" (CLA 1985). The ALA has made access to information its "highest priority' (Durrance 1984) and has explicitly linked access to information with the principles of an informed democracy (ALA Commission on Freedom and Equality of Access to Information 1986).

Libraries can be seen, from this perspective, as guardians and advocates of the public's right to know, particularly in such matters of public policy as protection of the environment. R. G. Macfarlane has argued that "librarians should work with social change agents (such as environmentalists) in their lobbying for freedom of access to information, realizing that they are the major beneficiary of this effort" (Macfarlane 1986). Macfarlane further recommends that librarians "make every effort to determine the information needs of social change groups in their neighborhood and assist in filling them" (Macfarlane 1986).

For librarians, commitment to access to information should implicitly involve understanding the specific information needs of special interest groups. In the case of environmental information, this means becoming familiar with a literature that has been characterized as prolific and rapidly expanding; almost without standards; vulnerable to ideological manipulation; and difficult both to obtain and use.

Information for Environmentalists

The complex information needs of environmentalists are determined by the structure of a field of study whose focus is often simultaneously global and local, technological and aesthetic, political and transnational, legal, scientific, economic, and usually controversial. Information scientists have concluded that "the concept of environmentalism, as it is widely held today, is a fusion of scientific and social thought, with roots ranging from religious and philosophical values to politics and economics on to the biological and physical sciences and engineering" (Freeman and Smith 1986). Thus, a study of the environment is, in library terms, a tour through the Dewey Decimal classification system.

This diffusion of information within the library itself might be seen as an impediment to accessing information, particularly in areas that are fundamentally cross-disciplinary, such as the environment. In fact, a study of citizen groups' information needs revealed that "scattering of information" (Durrance 1984) was the most commonly reported obstacle to obtaining data.

The problem may be especially acute for environmentalists whose sources include various levels of government; industry- and environmentally-aligned scientists; public policy experts; and the myriad environmental groups themselves. Some of these sources issue regular publications such as periodicals or annual reports; others publish studies irregularly or disseminate unpublished, written information. Both electronic and informal information dissemination are also common.

The very high volume of environmental information produced is daunting; for example, an online search of selected Canadian databases, limited to the subject of acid rain, yielded over 900 documents totalling nearly 100,000 pages of material, yet there are hundreds of databases covering both

specialized and general environmental and related topics (Joy, Eaton and Goins 1989). Robert L. Smith has commented on "the exponential growth in ecological research" and has noted that "it is nearly impossible ... for a library to own even a fraction" of what has been published (Smith 1986).

Sources of Environmental Information

Some of the information types and sources available to environmentalists within a library context include information originating from environmental groups, from the Canadian government, and from the scientific establishment. Information from these often-conflicting sources must be accessible at least through (if not in) the library (i.e., through online databases or inter-library loan) if the library is to serve environmentalists adequately.

Moreover, it is necessary when speaking of environmentalists to distinguish between two levels: 1) subject specialists employed by large organizations such as Greenpeace, or by government agencies such as Environment Canada, and 2) community-based, nonprofessional citizen activists. From the perspective of most public libraries, the former function more often as a potential information source, while the latter constitute a definable group of information seekers

Two professional environmentalists, interviewed by the author for this article, state that the information available in public libraries is generally neither current enough nor of adequate depth (Bechler, Lyons 1989), and two others admitted that most of the information needs of their organization were not met by either public or academic libraries (Carr, Yeats 1989). These same four specialists agreed that a major source of information for environmentalists is the network of environmental groups themselves. First-hand observation and infor-mal information gathering were cited as important environmental sources.

This perception is supported by the research of Anna de Soledade Vieira who studied environmental information in the Third World. She concluded that "informal channels of communication have major importance in the field, but librarians are still not prepared to use them to their advantage" (Vieira 1985). Greenpeace researcher Bob Lyons observed in an interview that since both libraries and environmental groups are "publicly funded" (albeit the former through taxes and the latter through voluntary donations), one role of the public library could be to "help build databridges between environmental groups" (Lyons 1989).

One way in which libraries might facilitate access to the informa-tion found through the environmental network is by setting up an information and referral (I & R) service. This would mean developing and providing access to organized files of contact information for environmental groups, many of which have special libraries. Possible starting places for such information include the *Directory of Canadian Environment Experts,* which lists over a thousand individuals and organizations, or the *Canadian Conservation Directory,* which includes contact information for international organizations as well.[1] Public librarians might also liaise between the public and those special libraries which provide only limited, on-site access to the information they house.[2]

Grey Literature

Information produced by environmental groups often appears in the "grey literature" and cannot be "readily retrieved through conventional bibliographic or acquisition procedures" (Lovenburg and Stoss 1988). Although environmental "grey literature" may require a special effort to obtain, it offers the researcher current, specific information which is usually written for the nonspecialist. It can also "provide a range of subjective viewpoints, perceptions and options on environmental issues" (Lovenburg and Stoss 1988). Lovenburg and Stoss advocate the use of a vertical file for acid rain grey literature and propose the use of the classification scheme developed by ARICA, the Acid Rain Information Clearinghouse, shown in Table 1. Such classification schemes exist for other areas of environmental research (i.e., the *Environmental Microthesaurus: A Hierarchial List of Indexing Terms Used by NTIS*). Applying them to the organization of environmental vertical files would greatly enhance the bibliographic accessibility of the information both produced and used by environmental groups.

Table 1: ACID RAIN CLASSIFICATION SCHEME

General Works (reviews and overviews)
Nontechnical reviews
Professional / technical reviews of a general nature
Nonprint materials
Information sources
Education resources

Environmental Effects
Aquatic ecosystems
Terrestrial ecosystems

Health effects
Effects on materials

Air and Atmospheric Processes
Emissions
Meteorological considerations (weather, scavenging)
Transportation (long-range transport) deposition; atmospheric
    modeling
Monitoring programs

Socio-Economic Aspects; Political Aspects
Laws; regulation
Government policy
International relations
Economic aspects
Public participation
Industry perspective

Mitigation and Control Technologies
Emission reduction
Liming
Biological control

Source: Lovenburg, Susan L., and Frederick W. Stoss. "The Fugitive Literature of Acid Rain: Making Use of Nonconventional Information Sources in a Vertical File." *RSR* 16 (1-2): 103.

Government Literature

Much of the information required by environmentalists is generated at some level of government. The federal government of Canada has acknowledged that it is "perhaps the most important single institutional repository of information about our society and its political, social, economic and environmental problems" (Roberts 1977). But despite its primary role as a repository of environmental information, access to that information is often seriously impeded by the government itself.

Scattering of information is one obstacle to access. Environmentally significant information originates, at the federal level, not only from Environment Canada, but also from Forestry Canada, Indian and Northern Affairs Canada, and from the Departments of Fisheries and Oceans, and Energy, Mines and Resources. The *Microlog* index to government publications concludes succinctly that "jurisdiction over environmental matters . . . does not fall exclusively under any of the powers assigned to either the federal or provincial governments under the Canadian constitution" (*Microlog* 1989).

Joan Durrance's citizen group study found that "groups concerned with environmental problems . . . were . . . likely to experience the problem of not knowing if information was available . . . This is due, at least in part, to the multiple governmental agencies with which citizens must interact in seeking this type of information" (Durrance 1984). Libraries might facilitate access to government information by mediating between environmentalists and information specialists in those government agencies where members of the public have restricted access.

Large public and academic libraries often function as depositories for government publications, both federal and provincial, which can be accessed through such indexes as *Microlog* or *Government of Canada Publications*. But these documents and even the indexes themselves may not be available outside large libraries in metropolitan areas; and because not all government reports are published, the problem of uncertainty as to the existence of information is further exacerbated.

However, unpublished documents containing information significant to the environmental movement may be available through the Access to Information Act. For example, Greenpeace was able to obtain government studies which revealed the presence of dioxins in shellfish in B.C.; and West Coast Environmental Law Association obtained access to information, not available through the provincial government, on pulp mill pollution in B.C. (Lyons, *Dire Straits* 1989). On a practical level, most librarians do not actively advocate the use of the Access Register. But as equitable access to information is fundamental to librarianship, the limits of the Act should be understood by librarians.

The Access to Information Act

The Act has been criticized (by proponents of access to information, and by environmentalists among others) for a number of weaknesses, including poor indexing, time delays in release of information, inconsistencies between federal departments on release of records, and the quality or usefulness of records released (Rubin 1984). Much information is kept secret under the numerous exemptions to the Act.

In the environmental field, the public's right to know is often in conflict with the government's structure of secrecy. A librarian committed to facilitating access to information for environmentalists may, therefore, encounter political or ideological barriers to that information.

In the U.S., for example, a Greenpeace report revealed that the Environmental Protection Agency (EPA), in collaboration with the American Paper Industry, attempted to violate freedom of information laws in order to suppress a study on dioxins (von Stackelberg 1989). The Sinclair Report (*Controlling Pollution from Canadian Pulp and Paper Manufacturers,* which contains "massive documentation of constant violations [of pollution laws]" by the pulp and paper industry, was kept a secret from the public by Environment Canada (under still undetermined exemptions) until leaked to Greenpeace (Lyons *Dire Straits* 1989). Environmentalists from that organization concluded that "scientific overviews and information embarrassing to either the government or industry are unlikely to surface until there is a major change of attitude on the part of governments. This will only come about with persistent public pressure" (Lyons, *Dire Straits* 1989)—precisely the kind of pressure an organization of information specialists such as librarians could articulately exert.

Provincial Excess

At the provincial level there may be no access legislation, further restricting access to information. In B.C., the Ministry of the Environment conducts studies funded with "public money, ostensibly to protect the public," but often keeps the results "the private property of industry and government departments" (Lyons, *Dire Straits* 1989).

In contrast, the Manitoba government has created a "public registry network . . . under the new Manitoba Environment Act" (Robson, 1988). Selected information on development projects, such as environmental impact assessments, have been located in a government registry and in eight public libraries in the province. The provincial Environment Department reasoned that locating this information in public libraries would improve its accessibility. Similar liaisons between the Ministries of Environment and libraries in other provinces could be established, perhaps through the provincial Library Services Branch, were both agencies willing to improve access to environmental information.

Scientific Sources

Environmentalists, particularly the specialists, also use the publications the scientific establishment as sources. Libraries can provide access to this information in several formats, including print reference monographs and journal articles, accessed through abstracting and indexing tools. The latter are often additionally or, occasionally, exclusively available in electronic format.

The scientific literature on the environment is problematic, however, and librarians providing access to this literature need to be aware of inherent complications and impediments which cannot always be adequately compensated for solely within the library context. Henry T. Blanke has observed: "In a society increasingly reliant on science and technology, matters involving political values are redefined as problems to be addressed by technical expertise. The crucial question in such a situation becomes 'Who owns the experts?; " (Blanke 1989).

Blanke's question is particularly relevant in the area of environmental information generated by scientific experts.

The question of the reliability of scientific data is closely connected with the conflicts that arise over the methods of presenting and interpreting that data. Environmental groups have attempted to "develop meaningful standards for environmental information representation and exchange" (Freeman and Smith 1986) but a comparative examination of recent news coverage on environmental matters , reveals the highly contentious nature of environmental research.

Industry and government studies tend to minimize the significance of results emphasized by environmentalists, or to omit contextual information considered crucial by them. Environmentalists charge that reports from industry and government "routinely describe" pollutants in terms of "micrograms per litre" but do not report that "the factory in question is spewing out many millions of litres [of these toxic substances] per day" (Lyons, *Dire Straits* 1989). A report produced by the Woodfibre pulp mill, for example, a dramatically reduced level of dioxins in effluents, yet, as one environmentalist pointed out, failed to mention that "there are probably a thousand toxic compounds being dumped by pulp mills, and dioxins are just part of the problem" (Bohn September, 1989).

The interpretation of scientific data is also contentious. An Environment Canada report on marine pollution used many of the "same scientific reports as a study prepared by Greenpeace, but because the findings were interpreted differently, the two studies came to opposite conclusions on the environmental health of the marine environment (Bohn November, 1989).

While the public confers the highest credibility on the opinions of the scientific establishment, scientists have been criticized, on the one side, for "publish[ing] papers about isolated aspects of pollution only, without drawing clear conclusions about the human and environmental consequences," (Lyons, *Dire Straits* 1989) and, conversely, for subjecting pure data to "interpretation and value judgments when it becomes involved with social issues" (Freeman and Smith 1986).

Corporate Sources

Environmental groups are often skeptical of the information produced by the corporate sector on the environment. MacMillan
Bloedel and the B.C. Council of Forest Industries are currently
spending a combined total of $4.5 million to convince the public to
support their current logging practices. An environmental journal
reports:

> The overall industry strategy for winning the hearts and minds
> of British Columbians includes educational displays at shopping
> malls, life-size posters at bus stops, ads inside the buses and a
> "Forests Forever" supplement to most households in the prov-
> ince. There is even a $3,000 prize for high-school students with
> the best essays on the theme: Why Clearcut Logging Is Beneficial
> for B.C. (Poeg, 1989).

Librarians providing information on scientific research to nonspecialist environmentalists need to be aware that the source of
information may determine its content, and that libraries must provide access not only to government and industry reports but to the
often conflicting studies of environmentalists, in order to provide a
balanced collection.

Review Sources

Balancing information with a scientific focus may be found in reference sources devoted entirely to environmental information, such as
World Resources (a serial) or *Our Common Future*.[3] Most works
become known to librarians—and hence, become part of the library's
collection—primarily through convention review media. Environmental works are no exception.

While the conventional reviewing journals do not provide a
special subject category of reviews for books on the environment,
reviews of these texts seem to be found most often with those of
general science works. Occasionally, a special review is dedicated
exclusively to environmental books; in 1986, for example, *Choice*

featured a lengthy and detailed bibliographic essay which reviewed more than 80 environmental science and ecology texts, and which updated a similar essay published in 1972 (Smith 1986). Single-book reviews are, of course, more frequent.

But selection based solely on the basis of standard review media will mean that unreviewed texts (usually those published by small and/or local publishers, or groups like Greenpeace) are not likely to become part of the collection. James Danky has commented that selection is often based on "procedures [which] have tended to discriminate against the inclusion of alternative materials" (Danky 1982). Conventional selection procedures themselves, therefore, may function as an impediment to accessing a full range of environmental information. Access to current scientific information which may be useful to environmentalists is available presently through a variety of topical indexes such as *Environment Index/Abstracts*. Access to much alternative material can be found through *Alternative Press Index*. These abstracting and indexing tools index hundreds of periodicals, but, perhaps in part because the cost of periodicals is increasing, only a small percentage may actually be available even in a large public library. This information is theoretically accessible, but not practically available, therefore creating a problem common to social change organizations (Durrance 1984).

Branch and small libraries usually do not subscribe to specialized indexes, and environmentalists must depend, instead, on general indexes such as *Reader's Guide to Periodical Literature* which include "environment" as a search subject, but which are not likely to index periodicals of a more technical nature. Furthermore, current technical information with a specifically Canadian focus may not be thoroughly indexed by American services (such as Bowker or Wilson), and the information-seeker must again turn to a general index such as *Canadian Periodical Index*.

Electronic Databases

Online databases are seen by some librarians as the solution to limited in-library resources, but impediments to information access exist in the electronic format as well. Online databases do provide access to the most current information generated within the scientific establishment, as well as to environmentally significant studies within the fields of politics, law, commerce and medicine[4] and full text or numeric databases can eliminate the problem of document availability. But in the U.S., although many online databases are still maintained by the Environmental Protection Agency (EPA), the Department of Energy (DOE), and other government agencies, the federal government has begun to privatize some of them.

The EPA network of approximately 30 databases, known as the Chemical Information Service (CIS), was turned over to a private company (Fein-Marquet Associates) after government and private sector panels concluded that the service had several major "systems deficiencies" and that "none of the [government] agencies had the resources to make the necessary improvements to CIS" (Freeman and Smith 1986)[5] Some American librarians believe that privatization of government databases threatens equitable access to the information available on those databases. Nancy C. Kranich, for example, has noted that not only has the cost of access to now-privatized databases increased—while libraries "are not funded to insure that the public has adequate access"—but that:

> the private sector has a tendency to censor information on the basis of marketplace. . . . As a result, the public is threatened with the complete elimination of access to specific segments of data with limited commercial value but with substantial significance in terms of policymaking, research, scholarship, and accountability (Kranich, 1989).

Librarians committed to freedom of information in the U.S. are, therefore, fighting the privatization trend.

In Canada, while an online database compiled and maintained by Environment Canada is still being developed, environmental information is currently available through CAN/OLE, a database network maintained by CISTI (Canada Institute for Scientific and Technical Information); the WATDOC (Water Resources Reference Center) network; and the Geographic Information System (GIS), as well as through commercial databases of both Canadian and U.S provenance.

Although Greenpeace researcher Bob Lyons obtains much of his information from online databases, he doe not use the library to access this information. Most of the databases useful to environmentalists are not available in libraries because the electronic format is too costly—even for a library such as the Vancouver Public Library, which subsidizes online search services in the interests of economically equitable access for patrons. Lyons feels the public library system should do more to provide access to inexpensive databases which carry information useful to social change organizations.

The Media

An overview of environmental information sources must include some mention of the news media, especially as a recent poll suggested that television and newspapers are the major sources of environmental information for most Canadians ("Media top list for information" 1989).

News coverage of the environment has been, at best, uneven. A study of network TV news coverage of environmental risks concluded that while "the media are not biased against environmental risk stories . . . they do favor dramatic news" (Greenberg, et. al. 1989). Visually exciting stories such as "refinery explosions . . . receive major coverage, but factual information—for example on asbestos, radon [or] pesticide exposure"—is not likely to "attract attention from television journalists" (Greenberg, et al. 1989), although it may receive minor coverage in a newspaper. The Southam newspaper conglomerate recently offered a special series on the environment and currently features a regular column by well-known environmentalist David Suzuki, but the *Globe and Mail* cancelled that same column because it ran counter to the "views of its upscale 'establishment' readers" (Jones 1989).

However, since newspapers do provide a substantial percentage of what the public knows about the environment, online news databases as well as the classified subject clippings file may be seen as

significant services libraries can provide. A "see also" reference, directing patrons from environmental news clippings to the vertical file,
indexes, and other reference materials might also serve to compensate
somewhat for the biases or inadequacies of the news media.

The cross-disciplinary nature of environmental studies, the weak-
ness of the federal Access Act, and the lack of standardized methods
of reporting scientific data have been shown to function as impediments to full access to information for environmentalists. Librarians
must not only be willing to advocate for access to information, but
also be knowledgeable about these impediments, and about the
complexities surrounding various sources of environmental information.

Particularly in recognizing that information exists in a political
context, librarians can work toward the ideal of not only providing
access to "all information that is not secret" (Darling 1979), but of
improving access to information which is now secret, well-hidden, or
distorted by governments and the private sector.

Anna de Soledade Vieira, in her study, concluded by asking
readers: "If we accept environmental information to be a possible way
to a global solution, are we, information professionals, conscious that
the light seemingly at the end of the tunnel may be in our own hands?"
(Vieira 1985). Librarians can respond to the current groundswell of
popular interest in the environment by providing citizens and environmentalists with access to information they need for the good of
all; even more is at stake than the future of the library.

Footnotes

1. Numerous directories for environmental groups are also found in general
   works such as *Directories in Print* and *Directory of Associations in Canada*.
2. A list of environmental libraries in B.C. is found in *Focus*; many of them
   allow public access to their collections only on a restricted and discretionary basis.
3. World Commission on Environment and Development, *Our Common
   Future*, (Oxford: Oxford University Press, 1987), and World Resources
   Institute, International Institute for Environment and Development, and

United Nations Environment Programme, *World Resources, 1988-89*, (New York: Basic Books, 1989).

4. In 1986, Freeman and Smith listed six "commercial databases devoted exclusively to the environment" (p. 253) and numerous others which contained information critical to environmental studies, but which were specific to the areas of chemistry, toxicology, land and aquatic resources, and energy. The 1989 *Directory of Online Databases* lists forty-five environmental databases. A list of databases searched regularly by Greenpeace researcher Bob Lyons includes not only scientific databases such as the *Biological and Agricultural Index*, but government sources such as *BNA [Bureau of National Affairs] Environment Reporter* and *CQ [Congressional Quarterly] Weekly Report*.

5. This incident was also noted in *Library Journal* 109 (July 1984): 1274 and in David J. Huddart, "Environmental databanks on the Chemical Information System," *Aslib Proceedings* 40 (May 1988): 137.

References

ACRL Library Access Task Force. "ACRL Guidelines for the preparation of policies on library access: A draft." *College and Research Libraries News* 50 (May 1989): 386-392.

Bechler, Hilda, Community Learning Services for a Sustainable Future, environmentalist. Interview with the authors. September 30, 1989, New Westminster, British Columbia.

Blake, Fay. "Let My People Know-Access to Information in a Postindustrial Society." *Wilson Library Bulletin* (January 1978): 392-399.

Blanke, Henry T. "Libraries and Political Values: Neutrality or Commitment?" *Library Journal* 112 (July 1989): 39-43.

Bohn, Glenn. "Latest on Pollution by B.C. Pulp Mills a Mixed Picture." *Vancouver Sun,* September 16, 1989.

_____. "Feds' Report Details Coastal Waters Toxins." *Vancouver Sun.* November 18, 1989.

Canadian Library Association. *Statement of Intellectual Freedom.* (Ratified by the Board of Directors and Council at the 29th Annual Conference in Winnipeg, June 1974 and amended November 17, 1983 and November 18, 1985).

Carr, Adrienne, Western Canada Wilderness Committee, environmentalist. Telephone interview by author. October 11, 1989, Vancouver, British Columbia.

Commission on Freedom and Equality of Access to Information. *Freedom and Equality of Access to Information*. Chicago: American Library Association, 1986.

Danky, James P., and Elliott Shore. *Alternative Materials in Libraries*. Metuchen, New Jersey: The Scarecrow Press, 1982.

Darling, Richard L. "Access, Intellectual Freedom and Libraries." *Library Trends: Libraries and Society*. 27 (Winter 1979): 315-326.

Durrance, Joan C. *Armed for Action*. New York: Neal-Schuman Publishers, 1984.

Freeman, Robert R., and Mona F. Smith. "Environmental Information." In *Annual Review of Information Science and Technology*. Vol. 21. Edited by Martha E. Williams, 241-305. New York: Knowledge Industry Publications, Inc., 1986.

Gaines, Matthew J. "Sources of Environmental Pollution Information: Radioactivity." *Aslib Proceedings* 40 (May 1988): 147-156.

Gladstone, Arthur, ed. and comp. *Environmental Information Guide for B.C.* end Edition. Vancouver, British Columbia: SPEC, 1977.

Greenberg, Michael R., et al. "Network Television News Coverage of Environmental Risks." *Environment* 31 (March 1989): 19.

Herner, S. "Environmental Impact Statements as Information Resources." *Government Publications Review*. 11 (July/August 1984): 261-268.

Huddart, David J. "Environmental Databanks on the Chemical Information System." *Aslib Proceedings* 40 (May 1988): 133-37.

Jones, Evan. "Suzuki, A Broken Record." *Ubyssey*, November 3, 1989.

Joy, Albert H., Nancy L. Eaton, and Rodney K. Goins. "Access to Canadian Government Publications on Acid Rain." *Government Publications Review*. 16: 31-39.

Kranich, Nancy. "Information Drought: Next Crisis for the American Farmer?" *Library Journal* 114 (June 15, 1989): 22-27.

Ludlow, Robin, "Environment: Poll Shows Activists and Scientists Are Held More Credible Than Industry, Government." *Vancouver Sun*, October 4, 1982, B2.

Lovenburg, Susan L., and Frederick W. Stoss. "The Fugitive Literature of Acid Rain: Making Use of Nonconventional Information Sources in a Vertical File." *RSS* 16(1-2): 95-104.

Lyons, Bob. *Dire Straits: Pollution in the Strait of Georgia, B.C., Canada*. Vancouver, British Columbia: Greenpeace, 1989.

_____. Greenpeace, environmentalist. Interview by author. November 2, 1989, Vancouver, British Columbia.

Macfarlane, Ronald G. "A Case Study of Information Transfer by Social Change Organizations." In *Alternative Library Literature, 1984/1985: A Biennial Anthology.* Edited by Sanford Berman and James P. Danky. Jefferson, North Carolina: McFarland & Co., 1986.

McNeeley, Jeffrey A. Review of *World Resources 1988-1989,* by World Resources Institute, International Institute for Environment and Development, and United Nations Environment Programme. In *Environment* 31 (April 1989): 25-28.

"Media Top List for Information." *Vancouver Sun.* October 4, 1989.

Moulder, David S. "Sources of Environmental Pollution Information: the Marine Environment." *Aslib Proceedings* 40 (May 1988): 139-146.

Parfitt, Ben. "Forests: Fighting Forever? Business and Preservationists Wage a Public Relations War Over the Province's Resources." *Vancouver Sun.* May 30, 1989. B4.

Poeg, Kalevi. "Money Talks." *Adbusters* 1 (Summer 1989): 55.

Rankin, Murray. "Information and the Environment: The Struggle for Access." In *Environmental Rights in Canada.* Edited by John Swaigen. Toronto: Butterworths, 1980. 285-332.

Roberts, Hon. John, Secretary of State. *Legislation on Public Access to Government Documents* (Ottawa: Minister of Supply and Services, June, 1977). *See* Rankin, 1980.

Robson, Barbara. "Information Web Offers Environmental Facts." *Winnipeg Free Press* August 8, 1988, p. 23.

Rubin, Ken. *Testing the Spirit of Canada's Access to Information Legislation.* Ottawa: [n.p.], 1984.

Ryder, Dorothy E. *Canadian Reference Services, A Selective Guide.* 2nd Edition. Ottawa: Canadian Library Association, 1981.

Smith, R. L. "Ecology and Environmental Science Books." *Choice* 23 (February 1986): 829.

Southam, Inc. *Highlights from the Southam Environmental Polls.* [n.p.], October, 1989.

Vierie, Anna de Soledade. *Environmental Information in Developing Nations.* Contributions in Librarianship and Information Science [Series] 51. Westport, Connecticut: Greenwood Press, 1985.

von Stackelberg, Peter. "White Wash: The Dioxin Cover-Up." *Greenpeace.* 14 (March/April 1989): 7-11.

Walton, Dr. W. H., and Christine M. Phillips. "Green Information for a White Continent—Environmental Information for Antarctica." *Aslib Proceedings* 40 (June 1988): 187-94.

West Coast Environmental Law Association. *Freedom of Information Act. Commentary.* West Coast Environmental Law Association Access to Information files. Vancouver, British Columbia.

Yeats, Trina, West Coast Environmental Law Association, technical researcher. Interview by author. October 14, 1989, Vancouver, British Columbia.

POVERTY AND DEVELOPMENT IN SOUTH AFRICA AND THE ROLE OF LIBRARIES

Mary Nassimbeni

"Poverty is a profoundly political issue." With these powerful words, the authors of *Uprooting Poverty: the South African Challenge*(1), Professor Francis Wilson and Dr. Mamphela Ramphele, both of the University of Cape Town, introduce their report of the Second Carnegie Inquiry into Poverty and Development in Southern Africa. The report, an analysis of the nature and causes of poverty and a formulation of strategies for action, was launched at the University of Cape Town on 24 January 1989. It represents a synthesis of about six years' wide-ranging and multidisciplinary research (into such areas as economics, labor and industrial relations, unemployment, agriculture, health, urbanization, housing, education and illiteracy) by 22 Southern African universities. It is an overview of 300 research papers prepared for the Second Carnegie Inquiry which was held at the University of Cape Town in 1984, and the findings of a number of papers published by the inquiry in the post-conference series, mainly concerned with issues uncovered by the conference which required further investigation.

The Report

The first nine chapters explore the definitions, nature, manifestations and symptoms of poverty and make chilling reading, particularly when seen in comparison with the privileged situation of the rich and elite minority. In one of the keynote conceptual papers prepared for the inquiry, Ellis points out the importance of relativity and differentials in any assessment of the distribution of resources and services conferring wealth on the beneficiary group. He observes pertinently (2. p. 10):

> In measuring resources it is usually the *per capita* supply of resources that matters. Thus the propaganda sheets explaining that vast sums of money have been spent on housing, education, etc. for some "beneficiary" group convey no information about the possible increase of welfare implied, until these figures are converted into *per capita* figures, and the distribution of these resourses among the population made clear: The real *per capita* distribution of such resources among the members of the group considered should be compared with those for other groups, to assess the relative benefits provided.

The second part of the book (three chapters) moves beyond a description of the nature of poverty in its many manifestations to an analysis of the complex of multiple factors that cause it: "three centuries of racist laws and practices in which the roots of South African poverty lie" (1, p. 310). The final section of the report (four chapters) deals with strategies for eradicating poverty and for transforming society. The title of the book reflects the authors' belief that society is a living organism constantly changing and that the removal of poverty involves "not only pulling up the roots of processes that impoverish people but also planting (and nurturing) those needs that will produce good fruit" (1, p. 5).

The First Carnegie Inquiry

The Second Carnegie Inquiry was held some 50 years after the First Inquiry which examined in depth the "Poor White problem" in South Africa. The report of this investigation was published in 1932 (3). A team of university researchers and church representatives undertook the investigation under the auspices of the Carnegie Corporation of New York as a result of a visit in 1927 to South Africa of the president and secretary of the corporation. The Carnegie Commission was successful within the limits of its brief: to investigate the causes of poverty among the whites who had drifted from rural areas to urban areas in the hope of employment in spite of their lack of skills and training; and to plan actions to combat the process of impoverishment (3, p. x). The Commission failed to examine the equally, acute problem of poverty among blacks since this was outside its brief (3, p. x), with the result that there was a significant lacuna in their investigation which remained unaddressed until the Second Inquiry.

Extent of Poverty

The Second Inquiry revealed the striking extent and pervasiveness of poverty, particularly among black South Africans. This is reflected in the Gini coefficient (which measures inequality between a country's rich and poor) of 0.66, the highest of the 57 countries for which data are available (1, p. 4). The authors found that poverty is concentrated mainly among black people (i.e. among colored, Asian and African people, to use official categories), but mostly Africans (1, p. 9).

Education: An Index of Inequality

A commonly used and telling index of disparity and inequity in the distribution of resources is the different levels of spending for various racial groups by the different education departments. Education is not located in one ministry because the government is irrevocably committed to the concept that education is an "own affair" (4). This costly system means that there are separate departments of education for the different race groups, with consequent fragmentation, inequalities and disparities. While there is increased pressure and demands by blacks for education and educational facilities, those institutions and facilities controlled by the white administration are underutilized, with schools closing and being used for noneducational purposes rather than being used by those who suffer educational deprivation (5, p. 14).

Apartheid is expensive, a fact conceded by the Minister of Education and Culture in the (white) House of Assembly because it necessitates duplication, triplication and quadruplication of facilities" (6, p. 2). This astonishing acknowledgment vindicates a study (received with skepticism and some hostility by the progovernment press) made by Professor Michael Savage of the University of Cape Town in which he demonstrated that 12 cents out of every Rand (100 cents) are spent by the state to maintain and enforce apartheid in South Africa (7, p. 2). He estimated that the GNP would have been 50 per cent higher in 1986 without the wasteful direct expenditure on a segregated society (7, p. 2).

Illiteracy

Illiteracy, a dimension associated with education, is one of the major indicators of poverty identified in the report. Although statistics are contradictory, it is safe to say that it is widespread and that attempts to eradicate it have been inadequate (1, p. 141). The seriousness of the problem is reflected in the conclusion by Wilson and Ramphele that illiteracy is as serious as and perhaps more resented than bad housing, because it is both cause and effect. It results from poverty, but also causes poverty because it is a major cause of unemployment (1, p. 348). In a paper prepared for the inquiry, researcher Wedepohl notes that, in spite of efforts by government departments, industrial programs, and church and other volunteer groups "in 1980, out of an estimated 6 (up to 9) million illiterates in South Africa, all the above efforts taken together assisted no more than 25,000 persons (0.3% of 7.5 million) to attain literacy" (8, p. 6). Wedepohl identifies as a major problem in literacy training the lack of appropriate post-literacy bridging materials. Literacy organizations have tried to meet this need by producing their own material, exemplified in such booklets on unemployment, history, etc., as those produced by Operation Upgrade, a nationwide, church-based literacy agency (9, p. 81).

Libraries and Illiteracy

Librarians in South Africa have recently been thinking and conferring about the possible role that libraries might play in the eradication of illiteracy (10; 11; 12; 13; 14). In the recent report of the investigation into the role of libraries in the development of South Africa the point is made that libraries are missing an opportunity to cooperate with a literacy organization such as Operation Upgrade which has extensive roots in the community and relationships with many community organizations (14, p. 24). The authors report that books on health, do-it-yourself skills, alcoholism, farming, money management, etc., offered by Operation Upgrade to a large library system for selection were rejected, presumably because they did not meet book production standards (14, p. 24). Although "libraries seemed at a loss how to act in regard to literacy" (14, p. 24), there appears little excuse for this state of affairs, given the burgeoning literature on illiteracy both in South Africa and outside its borders emphasizing the urgency of the problem and offering ideas on how libraries might make a contribution. The reaction of the librarians reported here seems to parallel a manifestation noted by the authors in another context, viz. the professed ignorance of librarians with respect to the needs of developing communities and of relevant research in other fields that might inform their own work or future initiatives (14, p. 245). (The significance of this important report is discussed elsewhere in this paper under various rubrics.)

Towards Transformation

While the Second Carnegie report does not elaborate a role for libraries in the eradication of illiteracy, the role of the library in the transformation of society is referred to in the third and final section of the book, called "Towards Transformation" (1, p. 257), in which the authors outline an agenda of action against poverty. They refute the argument that strategies against poverty in the current political dispensation should be rejected on the grounds that they serve to legitimize the status quo. They argue, instead, that some strategies have to be pursued within the constraints of the current unjust system and that one should operate even in the small spaces allowed (1, pp. 7-8). Their position is supported implicitly by, *inter alia*, Dr. Motlana, an influential civic leader who commented thus on this apparent paradox (15, p. 203):

> I appeal to all my people to use all avenues open to them (or force open those presently closed to them like Menlo Park High School and Pretoria University), to acquire as much knowledge as possible, now.

In the same address, one of whose themes was the inequitable distribution of resources, he linked the liberation struggle to the struggle "to open all places of learning to all our people" (15, p. 204), echoing the clause in the Freedom Charter which states that "all the cultural treasures of mankind shall be open to all, by free exchange of books, ideas and contact with other lands" (16, p. 265). This clause of the Freedom Charter, adopted on 26 June 1955 at the Congress of the People in Kliptown, is resonant with as yet unfulfilled possibilities for libraries and information centers in South Africa, and in accord with professional practice in the Anglo-American model in which the library is viewed as a democratic educational agency.

Underlying the thinking of Wilson and Ramphele about strategies for uprooting poverty and for transforming an unjust society is the concept of "empowerment," a shift in power in favor of the poor. To this end they identify a number of agencies (1, p. 261)

that can, even within the present political context, not only
make a difference in people's lives in existing circumstances, but
also help, by transforming power relations, to shift the balance
of power towards the poor as well as laying the foundations
which help determine the shape of society in the long run.

The library is one such organization.

Libraries and the Carnegie Inquiry

It is useful to quote the extract referring to libraries in the report for
it raises a number of issues that warrant deeper investigation within
the scope of this article (1, p. 296)

> In a paper on libraries and poverty prepared for the Carnegie
> Inquiry, Mary Nassimbeni reminds us of the fact that the
> founding of free library services was part of the great drive in the
> 1930s and 1940s to improve conditions for poor whites. The
> first Carnegie Commission had drawn special attention to the
> deprivation of children (white, particularly Afrikaans-speaking)
> in those schools—especially in the rural areas—where libraries
> were inadequate and suitable reading materials unavailable.
> Much was done to rectify the situation and facilities improved
> enormously for whites. Despite strong efforts, manifest in such
> developments as the Carnegie Non-European Library, Trans-
> vaal, which began in 1931, we find that in the 1980s when the
> vast majority of those who are poor are black, library facilities
> are primarily available only to whites. In the Cape Province, for
> example, according to a 1985 study, three-quarters of all libraries
> are closed to black South Africans. Clearly there is much work
> to be done, not only in opening existing libraries to all, but also
> in building and stocking new ones. Where they are imagina-
> tively run, whether in schools or in neighborhoods, libraries are
> heavily used even by those who are not considered highly
> literate. In the process of establishing such libraries, resource
> centers or reading rooms, attention will have to be paid to the
> training of suitable librarians and the development of appropri-
> ate strategies so that each center can better meet the needs (such

as illiteracy, unemployment, or simply a desire to know more
about the wider world) of those living nearby.

The situation with respect to the opening of library facilities to
all groups does not appear to have improved much since the observations made in 1986 in the paper referred to in this extract (17). In
November 1987, for example, Natal's provincial secretary, Mr. Roy
Hindle, issued a circular to all local authorities telling them that the
parliamentary standing committee responsible for Natal had "placed
great emphasis on the opening of libraries to all population groups"
(18, p. 50). He noted that fewer than half of the libraries run by local
authorities affiliated to the Natal Provincial Library Service were open
to all races and appealed to local authorities to consider opening their
libraries. In February 1988 it was reported that several local authorities
had rejected the request; they included Ladysmith and Newcastle,
both of which said that black people had adequate facilities (18, p.
50). The conclusion is that the government, while ostensibly in favor
of desegregated facilities, appears unwilling or unable to force recalci-
trant municipalities to open their facilities.

In order for libraries to play a role in reconstruction, existing
facilities should be shared by all groups and, in areas where there are
no facilities services should be established, sensitive to the needs of the
communities thus to be served. In a recent survey of information needs
and sources in black urban communities in the Witwatersrand, a vast
urban conglomeration, researchers found that libraries are almost
entirely disregarded except in so far as they are study centers for Vista
and Unisa university students "Who comprise under 1 per cent of the
population (19) Such low use of public libraries as there is, is mainly,
by school children. Very few educated black people are members of a
public library. The reasons provided for this were as follows:

—Existing services do not cater for the needs of the urban black
   community and are irrelevant to specific community issues.
—They are perceived to be "white" institutions linked to local and
   regional authorities which lack legitimacy in the eyes of the
   community (19, p. 69).

Respondents in the survey suggested ways of increasing community acceptance and of enhancing the relevance of holdings to community needs (19, p. 69). One suggestion was that community representatives be involved in advising on the selection of materials, etc. A successful example of this can be seen in the Funda Centre in Soweto. This library, catering mainly for university students, receives community input by way of representatives on the library committee which is responsible for policy. It was also suggested that libraries eschew formal associations with black local authorities which enjoy very poor standing with the people they purport to represent. The new type of library premised on these guidelines should be promoted as different from its earlier counterparts.

The same study found that in the delivery of appropriate services the role of the librarian was perceived to be pivotal. The librarian should be sensitive and responsive to community needs and have not only the traditional professional skills but also communication and negotiating skills (19, p. 70). This suggestion reinforces the recommendation, made by Nassimbeni in a paper on curriculum revision, that decisions about library services be negotiated with the community and that librarians will need to be trained in a panoply of skills which are currently absent from the traditional curricula (20, p. 159). The investigation into the role of libraries and development also indicates the need for the establishment and maintenance of library services on a more democratic and participatory style than is currently the practice (14, p. 34).

The authors of the survey in black urban communities make a number of recommendations about the future role of libraries in black communities:

—The development and delivery of literacy programs.
—The provision of support for literacy programs run elsewhere (e.g. industrial programs).
—The meeting of study needs.
—The provision of assistance and advice for pensioners.
—The development of life-skills programs.
—The promotion of work-skills programs (designed to help certain groups obtain and perform particular jobs.

—The teaching of child-care skills.

—The provision of alternative education programs by way of nonformal education, adult education, etc.

—The promotion of parental development programs through encouraging reading in the home, etc. (19, p. 71).

These guidelines are consistent with the broad recommendations made by Wilson and Ramphele, who place libraries and information centers on the national agenda for action in eradicating poverty—notwithstanding the finding of the investigation into libraries and development referred to earlier that developers and development agencies had low expectations of librarians in this area (14, p. l2).

Turning to another issue raised in the extract quoted from the Carnegie report, viz. that of school libraries, it can be noted that while there has been considerable development in white schools, there is a massive backlog of such facilities in African schools. In a survey of school libraries in South Africa published in 1986, the distribution of school library books for the various racial groups underlines this point (21, p. 814). The average number of books per pupil in each of the different groups was as follows: 2.4 for Africans, 2.5 for coloreds, 5.5 for Indians, 10.6 for whites.

There has been, however, some progress since the publication of the paper (17) referred to in the extract from the Carnegie report relating to the role of libraries, notwithstanding the deficiencies in the various sectors already noted. A very significant development has been the commissioning by the South African Institute for Librarianship and Information Science (SAILIS) of an investigation into the role of libraries in the development of South Africa (referred to *passim*). The report of this investigation (14), published in 1988, represents an impressive advance in thinking which is consistent with the recommendations and suggestions made in the extract from the Second Carnegie report quoted at the beginning of this section. While the report does not claim any relationship with the Second Carnegie Inquiry, its very title, with the explicit reference to development in the context of libraries, links it conceptually to the Carnegie Inquiry, one of whose main themes was development. Both reports acknowledge the contribution made by the development of free library services in the upgrading of the poor whites consequent upon the publication of the First Carnegie Inquiry (1, p. 296; 14, p. 59). Furthermore, both reports conclude that libraries have the potential to make a difference and that they can be positive forces for change and development by better meeting needs in areas such as illiteracy, unemployment, etc. (1, p. 296; 14, p. 230).

No doubt, the role of the library in reconstruction and development will be canvassed from different perspectives. A hint of the potential differing positions likely to be adopted by educators and practitioners is apparent in the publication of an entire issue of the *Wiits Journal of Librarianship and Information Science* devoted to the theme of "South African librarianship in crisis (22). The editor of this issue is to be commended for bringing together a number of thought-provoking papers which examine the possibilities of alternative approaches to professional practice and ideology which challenge "conventional assumptions and attitudes inherent in writing on South African librarianship" (23, p. 3). Collectively, the papers attempt to locate librarianship in the current sociopolitical context, which, it is claimed, most researchers have failed to do, preferring to avoid contentious issues (23, p.3). Whatever the source of thinking about change, whether from a radical, liberal or even reformist perspective, there is sufficient evidence that options are being seriously considered both within and outside "established" circles, a situation, it could be argued, that is to be preferred to inertia and complacency.

References

(1) Wilson, F., and Ramphele, M. *Uprooting poverty: the South African challenge.* David Philip, 1989.
(2) Ellis, G. *The dimensions of poverty.* Carnegie Conference Paper no 4. University of Cape Town, 1984.
(3) *The poor white problem in South Africa.* Report of the Carnegie Commission. Pro Ecclesia, 1932.
(4) *Race relations survey 1987/1988.* South African Institute of Race Relations, 1988.
(5) Cosser, E. *SAIRR Social and Economic Update,* February-May 1988 (5).

(6) *SAIRR Social and Economic Update,* update 4, fourth quarter, 3 October 1988.

(7) Heavy Cost of divided society. *Sunday Times.* 27 September 1987.

(8) Wedepohl, L. *Illiteracy and adult basic education in South Africa.* Carnegie Conference Paper no. 263. University of Cape Town, 1984.

(9) Wedepohl, L. *A survey of illiteracy in South Africa.* University of Cape Town, 1984.

(10) Fouchè, B. Bridging the gap: the role of libraries in the promotion of literacy. In Hauptfleisch, T. (ed.). *Literacy in South Africa.* HSRC, 1979, 79-88.

(11) Kesting, J. G. *Literacy promotion, formal education and public library use.* HSRC final report. University of Cape Town, 1984.

(12) *Libraries and literacy.* Papers from a workshop presented by the South African Institute for Librarianship and Information Science (Western Cape Branch): 17-18 April 1984. University of Cape Town, 1984.

(13) Shillinglaw, N. The role of the public library in the development of South Africa. *South African Journal of Library and Information Science,* 1986, 54 (1), 39-44.

(14) *The use of libraries for the development of South Africa.* Final report on an investigation for the South African Institute for Librarianship and Information Science. UNISA, 1988.

(15) Motlana, N. Reflections. *English Academy Review,* 1987, 4.

(16) Suttner, R., and Cronin, J. *Thirty Years of the Freedom Charter.* Ravan Press, 1985.

(17) Nassimbeni, M. Libraries and poverty. *South Africa Journal of Library and Information Science.* 1986, 54 (2), 56-60.

(18) Mackay, S. *SAIRR Quarterly Countdown,* first quarter, 15 April 1988.

(19) Bekker, S., and Lategan, L. Libraries in black urban South Africa: an exploratory survey. *South African Journal of Library and Information Science* 1988, 56 (2), 63-72.

(20) Nassimbeni, M. The imperative for change: curriculum revision in South Africa. *Education for Information,* 1988, 6 (2).

(21) Overduin, P. G. J., and De Wit, N. *School librarianship in South Africa: a critical evaluation.* University of the Orange Free State, 1986.

(22) *Wits Journal of Librarianship and Information Science* July 1988 (5).

(23) Merrett, C. South African librarianship in crisis: alternative viewpoints. *Wits Journal of Librarianship and Information Science, July 1988, 5.*

SECTION THREE:
SCHOOL MEDIA CENTER CONCERNS

BEYOND THE CHIP: A MODEL FOR FOSTERING EQUITY

Delia Neuman

> O wonder!
> How many goodly creatures are there here!
> How beauteous mankind is!
> O brave new world
> That has such people in't!

William Shakespeare
The Tempest
V. i. 181-184

Miranda's excitement over Shakespeare's magic island has been echoed many times over the centuries. Today, those echoes might easily refer to the "many goodly creatures" described elsewhere in this special issue: CD-ROMs, artificial intelligence, hypertext, and more. Indeed, there is no question that the tools currently or soon to be in educators' hands offer unique and unprecedented possibilities for improving instruction and increasing learning. The challenge lies in exploiting those opportunities for all segments of "beauteous mankind,": female as well as male, handicapped as well as nonhandicapped, inner-city and rural as well as suburban, minority as well as majority, disadvantaged as well as privileged, average learners as well as those at both ends of the ability spectrum. The purpose of this paper is to address that challenge, first, by identifying probable obstacles to achieving educational equity through and with emerging technology and, second, by offering a two-tiered model for the school library media specialist to apply in addressing this critical issue.

COMPUTERS AND EQUITY

History does not suggest that equitable access to and use of the newest technologies will happen automatically or ever easily. A number of studies and reviews of equity in computer based education have described a full spectrum of problems associated with this first and simplest educational incarnation of the chip.[1] At the most basic, or "counting" level, it has become a truism that wealthy school districts own more computers than impoverished ones and that they augmenttheir numbers so rapidly that the gap between rich and poor schools is widening rather than shrinking. At a more subtle level, Daniel Watt's often-quoted finding suggests a less visible but arguably more pernicious problem in the ways the equipment is used:

> "When computers are introduced into suburban schools, it is often in the context of computer programming and computer awareness courses. In less affluent, rural or inner-city schools, computer use is more likely to be in the context of computer-assisted instruction of the drill and practice variety. Affluent students are thus learning to tell the computer what to do while less affluent students are learning to do what the computer tells them."[2]

An ERIC search completed for this paper revealed over 130 documents dealing with various aspects of the computer equity issue. This collection includes research reports, position papers, conference presentations, and suggestions for resolving inequities. It documents inequitable patterns not only in regard to financial status but in regard to race, gender, geography, handicapping condition, and level of academic ability as well. Throughout this literature, authors have chronicled widespread inequity in access to computers, described patterns of inequitable distribution and use of computers within and across schools, and delineated disturbing implications of such patterns for individuals and society. The picture is bleak. As Lipkin noted,

> Computer literacy . . . represents the basis for creating a further schism between the "haves" and the "have nots." . . . Thus, the economically and educationally disadvantaged are prime candidates to join the ranks of this new category of disadvantaged—the computer nonliterate.[3]

Although assessments of the impact on equity of the newer technologies are not yet available, it is clearly time to consider that issue. History suggests that technological inequity in education appears early and endures indefinitely. And even a basic understanding of the new technologies suggests that they are so different, so powerful, so little understood—and initially, at least, so expensive—that opportunities for inequity are likely to increase. It is startling to realize that the serious issues of equity occasioned by the simple microcomputer will become even more critical and subtle as more powerful and sophisticated tools appear in the schools. Without careful and active attention, our "brave new world" could become more like Huxley's than like Shakespeare's.

Evidence of such attention is beginning to appear. In addition to documenting and explaining current problems, the literature is starting to suggest that the newer technologies can offer an escape route from present inequities rather than a road to future ones. At the federal level, at least three major documents of interest to school library media specialists incorporate such a viewpoint into their wide-ranging and informative treatments of technology and education. *Transforming American Education: Reducing the Risk to the Nation* presents to the Department of Education the report and recommendations of the National Task Force on Educational Technology convened in 1984 by then-Secretary Terrel H. Bell.[4] *The Librarian in the Information Age* provides similar information gathered under the auspices of the Office of Library Programs of the Department of Education.[5] *Power On! New Tools for Teaching and Learning* presents the results of the Office of Technology Assessment study commissioned by the House of Representatives Committee on Education and Labor and its Subcommittee on Select Education.[6] All three documents reveal an awareness of the problems of the past and present but suffuse these with a recognition of the promise of the future. Perhaps the following excerpt from *Transforming American Education* best exemplifies this approach:

Information technology represents a powerful array of tools that when creatively applied and appropriately integrated will meet three fundamental goals:

1. Improving the quality of learning.
2. *Increasing equity of opportunity, access and quality* [emphasis added]
3. Ensuring greater cost effectiveness.[7]

Professional organizations that represent school library media specialists are taking a similar tack. The Association for Educational Communications and Technology (AECT), for example, was involved with the Department of Education Task Force throughout its work and continues to serve as the primary disseminator of its findings.[8] The American Association of School Librarians (AASL) played a prominent role in the development of the American Library Association (ALA) Presidential Committee's Statement on Information Literacy, which addresses the importance of technology in an "information age school."[9] And AECT and AASL together, acknowledging the enormous and continuing effect of emerging technologies on school library media programs, issued a joint challenge in *Information Power: Guidelines for School Library Media Programs*: "To ensure equity and freedom of access to information and ideas, unimpeded by social, cultural, economic, geographic, or technologic constraints."[10]

Publications on computing and education offer background information on equity issues as well as concrete suggestions for addressing them on a day-to-day basis. Articles have been sprinkled throughout this literature for several years in such journals as *Educational Technology*,[11] *Electronic Learning*,[12] and *Journal of Educational Computing Research*.[13] Perhaps the most consistently helpful and easily accessible of these resources is *The Computing Teacher*, which has published a number of "equity" articles[14] and offers an occasional column entitled "Action for Equity"[15] and has devoted two issues [16]to technology and the kinds of students for whom equity has traditionally been a problem. In a similar vein, *School Library Media Quarterly* recently published a special issue in which excerpts from *Rethinking the Library in the Information Age* are infused with questions suggesting the importance and subtlety of this topic.[17]

The assumption underlying much of the emerging literature is the same one that has fueled the hype for many previous technological advances in education: the latest gimmick will solve all our pedagogical, motivational, financial, and societal problems. But history has demonstrated that such an assumption is never borne out. On the contrary, as noted above in the discussion of computers and equity, the introduction of new technology can exacerbate existing problems. If this recent history repeats itself, the advent of the emerging technologies will signal an unbridgeable widening of the gulf between those who are in society's mainstream and those who, for whatever reason, are in its eddies. Without deep commitment, strong leadership, careful planning, and consistent attention to equitable implementation, the promise of the "goodly creatures" will be subverted.

Equity and the School Library Media Specialist

A variety of factors have conspired to place the school library media center and its professional staff in the ideal position to meet the challenge posed by the implementation of new technologies in educational settings. Traditional headquarters for media as diverse as the study print and the videocassette, the library media center offers the natural home for the newer technologies as well. More knowledgeable about the instructional uses of media than any of their colleagues on the instructional team, library media professionals embody the experience and expertise necessary to exercise the commitment, leadership, planning, and implementation mentioned above. Library media professionals touch all segments of the instructional enterprise rather than focus on any particular component of it; therefore, they have a broad perspective on the needs and abilities of various groups of students across the school. And charged by *Information Power* to ensure unimpeded access to information and ideas, library media specialists have the support of their major professional organizations to tackle the equity issue.

No single group or individual, of course, can resolve all existing inequities or prevent every new one. But inequity is often the result of oversight, of the absence of an advocate for those who are over-looked. And no one else within the school community is so uniquely suited to play the "equity advocate" role as the school library media specialist. While many people and organizations within and beyond the school have made important contributions to equity, no one else occupies such a potentially effective position for exerting both imme-diate and long-term influence. Tradition, training, perspective and national mandate all suggest that the school library media specialist can—and should—play a key role in using both existing and emerging technologies to overcome problems and to enhance for all students.

A Model for Fostering Equity

Accepting the role of equity advocate does not necessarily imply undertaking a grand initiative. For the most part, it means infusing everyday activities with an awareness of the issue and looking for opportunities to address it carefully and systematically. The literature on computer equity suggests that a successful approach must comprise two tiers, general and specific. Each tier itself includes a series of closely related steps for enhancing equity within the school library media center and across the wider constituency the library media specialist serves.

General Steps for Equity

At a general level, addressing equity has four major dimensions. The first—gathering and interpreting information—not only draws on the traditional skills of the library media specialist but provides the basis upon which the latter three rest. The other dimensions, which involve using the information in ways that can affect policy and planning at a variety of levels, are critical to establishing a context in which efforts for equity can achieve success.

Become knowledgeable about both the potential value and the potential problems in regard to equity that are inherent in each of the emerging electronic tools. This paper and the referenced cited in its tables and references offer a baseline for becoming informed about the issue. Reading the documents, contacting staff members of the projects cited, and gathering additional information are obvious first steps. Table 1, "Selected Sources of Information on Technology and Target Groups," lists the names, audiences, and services and publications of a range of agencies and organizations that provide information about the uses of technology for particular groups for whom equity has been a problem. The popular press also provides leads to current developments that have implications for equity: *Time* magazine's "Video" column, for example, has covered such stories as the federal government's Star Schools Project (a demonstration project in distance education) and the introduction of commercial, for-profit television programming into the classroom. When one has become attuned to the issue of equity, questions about uses of and access to technological breakthroughs become self-evident.

Table 1. SELECTED SOURCES OF INFORMATION ON TECHNOLOGY AND TARGET GROUPS

Source	Target Audience	Services and Publications
Apple Computer Office of Special Education and Rehabilitation 19925 Stevens Creek Blvd. MS 43S Cupertino, CA 95014 (408) 974-7910	Handicapped students and adults	National Special Education Alliance Electronic information exchange *Apple Computer Resources in Special Education and Rehabilitation* (comprehensive resource guide)
Center for Special Education Technology Council for Exceptional Children	Handicapped students	Resource inventories Electronic bulletin board Regular publications

Source	Target Audience	Services and Publications
1920 Association Dr. Reston, VA 22091 (800) 873-8255		
Computer EQUALS Lawrence Hall of Science	Female students, minority/disadvantaged students	Curriculum materials Reports Newsletter
University of California Berkeley, CA 94720 (415) 642-1823		Technical assistance *Off and Running* (teaching manual)
IBM National Support Center for Persons with Disabilities P.O. Box 2150 Atlanta, GA 30055 (800 426-2133	Handicapped students and adults	Resource guides Electronic information exchange Reports on new products
ISTE University of Oregon 1787 Agate St. Eugene, OR 97403 (503) 686-4414	Minority/disadvantaged students, handicapped students	*The Computing Teacher* (journal) *Yes I Can! ECCO's Equity in Technology Project* (book; Summer 1990)
PEER NOW Legal Defense and Education Fund 99 Hudson St. (12th floor) New York, NY 10012 (212) 925-6635	Female students and adults	Reports Technical assistance Newsletter *Debugging the Program* (kit)
Sex Equity in Education Women's Action Alliance 141 Fifth Ave. (212) 532-8330	Female students and adults	Staff development Various materials *The Neuter Computer* (resource guide and teaching manual

Raise awareness of equity concerns among administrators, teachers, school board members, and others in decision-making positions. Planners and decision makers at all levels—local, district, state, and national—must be reminded to "think equity" and to take steps to achieve it. Raising awareness can be accomplished both informally, through day-to-day contact and discussion, and formally, through making presentations at meetings, scheduling speakers for in-services and other programs, and designing information sessions about the problems and possibilities for equity in the implementation of new and expensive technology. The school library media specialist can fill a critical role by providing information to decision makers that can bring important issues to light and lead to suggestions of alternatives that minimize inequity.

Consider long-range and policy implications for equity as well as immediate needs. Focusing on immediate needs can introduce practices that result in unintended inequity. The present pattern of male-dominated computer use, for example, results more from inadequate vision than from conscious efforts to exclude other groups. Nevertheless, that pattern is not only likely to transfer to the new arena of networked computers but also to continue indefinitely into the future unless its long-term implications are recognized and considered. As an advocate for equity, the school library media specialist must draw upon knowledge of past practices to suggest farsighted approaches for the future. Policies and plans must promote equity for tomorrow's students as well as today's.

Provide informed and committed leadership for equity as the acquisition and implementation of new technologies are planned. Volunteering to serve on appropriate committees within the educational system as well as within professional organizations will provide opportunities to exercise leadership and influence policy. Unless people who are knowledgeable about and committed to using technology to promote equity serve in such capacities, opportunities will be lost. Advocacy implies active involvement, and the library media specialist can provide a vital service by working diligently to acquire information, to provide it to appropriate individuals and groups, and to propose and support general policies and specific plans that promote equity at every level.

Specific Steps for Equity

The library media specialist can take a number of measures to enhance equity within the library media center as well as beyond it. The following seven specific steps, like the four general ones outlined above, are based on the literature on computer equity but are clearly applicable to promoting equitable access to and use of the more advanced technologies as well.

1. **Determine the adequacy of the numbers and types of hardware and software available at school.** According to *Power On!* the current national average of installed computers is one machine for every thirty public school students, while the desired ratio "often cited by school district personnel and educational technologists" is one for every three.[18] These overall statistics obviously mask differences in needs and numbers across a variety of factors, particularly school level. Nevertheless, the figures suggest that, in practice, assessing the adequacy of existing resources will almost always identify such a large hardware need that the acquisition of additional equipment will be justified.

Determining the exact configuration of equipment needed will, of course, depend upon local needs, goals, and curricula. Assessing the adequacy of the software for the equipment will also depend upon an examination of local conditions—curricular goals and objectives, teachers' and administrators' priorities, student population, and gaps in the existing collection. In any event, while simply asking for "more of everything" will not solve equity problems, having more will certainly improve the chances of spreading the resources among more kinds of students. And including on purchase orders such items as software thought to appeal to girls (e.g., programs that incorporate nonviolent fantasies) and adaptive input and output devices designed for the handicapped (e.g., guarded keyboards for the physically impaired and large-print monitors for the visually impaired) will open the spectrum of the resources to a much wider audience.

2. **Determine additional funding needs, explore additional sources of funding, and make funding for additional hardware and software part of long-term plans.** Electronic technology is far more expensive than chalk and slate, and the new technologies will require a substantial initial investment and a long-term commitment to maintenance and upgrading. Clearly, district and building budgets as currently constituted cannot absorb the full costs. In addition, such traditional sources of "extra" funds as the PTA are also unlikely to be

adequate. Planners and policymakers must exercise vision and creativity in recognizing the need for ongoing expenses for the new technologies—and for achieving equity through them—and in devising ways to meet this goal.

Many of the most glaring examples of inequity exist across district lines rather than within districts or schools; long-term, widespread solutions to these problems must await national political attention. Nevertheless, individual districts and schools can take steps to address their own immediate needs. Both the public and the private sectors offer sources of additional funding, and the school library media specialist should investigate these. The federal government and almost all state governments provide some funding for technology and education. Foundations and corporations are also emerging as important sources for grants of funds and equipment for school initiatives in technology: computer companies like Apple, IBM, GTE, Commodore, and others have all supported various programs. Standard Oil of Ohio (now BP America) funded the first three years of the equity projects of the Educational Computer Consortium of Ohio noted below. In addition, local businesses as well as national corporations are becoming increasingly aware of the need to assist in the funding of educational improvement in order to serve our nation's changing student population and to maintain our country's position within the world economy. The Committee for Economic Development, for example, provides general information about business involvement in education.[19] The National Business Roundtable booklet entitled *Business Means Business in Education* lists almost 200 examples of school/business partnerships across the country, a number of which are designed to address equity.[20]

3. **Ensure equitable scheduling for all segments of the student body.** Is all the school's computer time being used by the gifted and talented classes? By the Chapter 1 students? National data suggest that the former scheduling pattern is more likely, but both patterns result in restricted access and disparate applications. Until the additional funding requested in Step 2 results in the additional hardware and software mentioned in Step 1, the library media specialist should take care that patterns of inequity in regard to both old and new technologies are avoided. Despite the constraints imposed by curricular,

logistical and other considerations, equity requires that all students have reasonable access to computers and to whatever other electronic tools appear in the schools.

Equipment location is a key element in scheduling this access. The school library media specialist should take the lead in arguing for the placement of equipment in a central location, accessible by all students, rather than only in labs and classrooms restricted to particular student groups. Locating old and newer technologies where students can use them on their own time—at lunch, during study hall, and before and after school—is a particularly important strategy. It will enable the school library media specialist to schedule periods of open access to the equipment so that students who might otherwise have limited or no opportunities to use it can explore its possibilities.

4. Identify and remove both overt and subtle biases from curricula, course outlines, and uses of technology by different groups. Both kinds of bias are problematic, but the subtle aspects of inequity are more difficult to pinpoint and to address. In her interviews with the experts, Zakariya uncovered a number of the more elusive aspects of computer inequity. [21] For economically disadvantaged students, the problems center on the absence of programming instruction and enrichment activities and the use of the computer exclusively for drill and practice and for business and vocational courses. For girls in nonacademic tracks, the problems often involve curricular offerings leading to lower-paying computer operator jobs rather than to the computer-related jobs in drafting and accounting pursued by boys in such tracks. For handicapped students, the lack of special software and a similar lack of information about adapting "regular" software to meet special needs leaves many of those needs unmet. For all students. unnecessarily difficult prerequisites for computer courses can restrict these offerings to academically gifted students with a special talent for mathematics.

Many of these subtle inequities seem to be the unforeseen consequences of laudable attempts to address students' individual needs and aspirations. Nevertheless, using computers in these ways perpetuates stereotypical patterns and consigns many students to be servants rather than masters of the technology. Such subtle and complex issues will certainly provide the most challenging obstacle to the equitable use of the emerging technologies as well as of the microcomputer.

The library media specialist is ideally placed to work at forestalling the subtle problems that are sure to emerge. Responsible for providing services across the curriculum, the library media specialist is likely to be more aware of the scope of the curriculum than anyone else in the school. In addition, through maintaining collections of syllabi and guidelines as well as systematically collecting curriculum information,[22] library media specialists have a unique vantage point for identifying any possible biases across the curriculum and within individual courses. Capitalizing on this perspective, actively planning for equity, questioning assumptions about the "appropriate" uses and users of each new tool, and keeping the issue alive in the local environment are especially critical strategies for fighting subtle and unintended inequity.

5. **Actively promote appropriate use by target groups.** Every school employee, of course, can contribute to efforts to foster equity. In particular, however, female, minority, and handicapped personnel should be encouraged to offer technology courses and advise technology clubs so that target students will recognize that technology holds something for them, too. Recruiting these students into such activities is a similarly straightforward promotional strategy. Scheduling classes specifically for target students is also an option: learning to use a word processor can benefit resource-room English classes as well as advanced ones; remote instruction can benefit the vocational student who wants to learn about auto mechanics as well as the physics whiz who wants to learn about superconductivity. Using peer tutoring to help target students learn CD-ROM database searching can have multiple benefits: not only can it expand opportunities for the tutees, it can make the tutors partners in enhancing equity in the present and sensitize them to the issue for the future.

Building positive attitudes toward using technology is a critical element in promoting appropriate use; once again, the school library media specialist has a key role to play in this complex and subtle area. Only when students perceive using the equipment as personally attractive—nonthreatening, useful, and empowering—will they exert the effort necessary to take charge of the technology. If equipment is housed in the library media center, staff can promote uses of it that are likely to build such perceptions. When students can use the technology for their own purposes (e.g., to create personal products and to explore intriguing applications) and in an informal atmosphere (e.g., in collaboration with one another), they can be guided to discover the importance of technology as an attractive tool that expands their own abilities and affords them a measure of personal control.

6. **Develop strategies for using various technologies effectively with target groups.** Reaching target students, like counting pieces of equipment, is a simple step compared to the steps that follow. Fortunately, a number of efforts for promoting equity with microcomputers can serve as models for promoting equity with the newer technologies. Table 2, "Exemplary Efforts to Promote Equity in Computer Access and Use," summarizes several such efforts for enhancing equity both within and beyond the school library media center. The strategies range from such simple approaches as scheduling special classes during and after school to such elaborate ones as planning and outfitting a mobile unit to deliver the technology and related instruction to targeted students' homes.

The details of the projects can be learned either by reading the appropriate references for this article or by contacting the individuals listed in the table. In addition, some common elements extracted from the projects suggest general ideas that can be adapted to other settings. Many of these ideas are noted in the steps above as well: securing additional equipment, increasing the amounts and kinds of access necessary for target groups through innovative scheduling, and locating materials designed to promote equity with target groups. Other major strategies involve moving beyond the library media center itself to involve parents and other members of the community in efforts for equity: providing training for parents as well as students, finding ways to get hardware and software into the homes of those who would not otherwise have access to these resources, offering summer camps and special technology fairs for target groups. One of the most ambitious projects—Playing to Win—is a privately funded Computer Center visited by approximately 700 economically disadvantaged people each week either to use one of the Center's computers or to borrow one to take home (see Table 2).

Table 2. EXEMPLARY EFFORTS TO PROMOTE EQUITY IN COMPUTER ACCESS AND USE

Project and Contact Person	Target Audience	Strategies
Computers and You David Autor Glide Memorial Methodist Church 330 Ellis St. San Francisco, CA 94102 (415) 922-7593	Minority/disadvantaged families	Walk-in computer center After-school classes Preschool program
Detroit Public Schools Geraldine Carroll Lawton Building 9345 Lawton St. Detroit, MI 48206 (313) 494-0915	Minority/disadvantaged families	Parent workshops Harware/software lending Telecommunications
Equity in Technology Projects Alice Fredman c/o ECCO 1123 S.O.M. Center Rd. Cleveland, OH 44124 (216) 461-0880	45 projects: minority, disadvantaged, female, learning disabled, and physically disabled students	Telecommunications Science projects After-school courses Parent/child teams Parent/child workshops Hardware/software lending Peer tutoring In-school courses
Fairfax County Public Schools Marvin Koontz Office of Instructional Technology 4414 Holborn Ave. Annandale, VA 22003 (703) 978-0075	Minority/disadvantaged students	Computer labs Grants Long-range plan
Houston Independent Patsy Rogers Dept. of Technolgy 5300 San Filipe	15 projects: minority/ disadvantaged students	After-school courses Harware/software lending Hardware discounts Techmobile

Project and Contact Person	Target Audience	Strategies
Houston, TX 77056 (713) 960-8888		Parent/child training Computer camps Technology fairs
Playing to Win Antonia Stone 1449 Lexington Ave. New York, NY 10128 (212) 410-1694	Minority/disadvantaged families	Walk-in computer center Technical assistance Publications
Project MiCRO Carol Edwards Southern Coalition 1293 Peachtree St. NE Suite 226 Atlanta, GA 30309 (404) 874-5199	Minority/disadvantaged students Female students	Teacher training In-school courses Parent involvement

7. **Explore ways the new technologies can be used to promote equity.** Like the microcomputer before it, emerging technology is being touted as the great equalizer. As reported by Bruder, equity is in fact the primary impetus behind distance education: the satellite dish will increase access and opportunities for students who live in remote areas; who endure illnesses and physical disabilities that keep them out of classrooms; who need remediation that requires individual rather than group attention; and who attend schools that cannot afford the latest technology, the most advanced courses, and the most skilled teachers.[23]

Clearly, the tools appearing on the horizon can vastly expand the horizons of all these groups. Demonstration projects in various parts of the country are already exploring some of the possibilities.[24] It is equally clear, however, that widespread equity will never occur unless specific plans are made in each school to include those who are too often overlooked. Will teleconferencing permit electronic field trips to museums and labs? Fine—as long as handicapped students get to go, too. Will interactive television enable students to take courses not offered locally? Fine—as long as minority students get to take them, too. Will networking allow students across the country to collaborate on science and communication projects? Fine—as long as females collaborate, too. Will expanded online services empower students to gain and use more information than they dreamed existed? Fine—as long as these undreamed of possibilities are made available and attractive to all the students in the school. Will someone make sure that they are? That is the key question.

Conclusion

Left to chance, the opportunities presented by the new technologies will elude the same groups who have been underserved by the computer revolution. Inclusion of these groups will not happen automatically, and exclusion will have dramatic consequences for both individuals and society. Assumptions about the equity benefits "beyond the chip" are at present just that—assumptions. To bring them to life in the day-to-day business of the school, someone—the school library media specialist—must exercise awareness, commitment, leadership, planning, and careful implementation of a model involving both general and specific steps. Without such a catalyst, equitable participation by all students will be as illusory as the wonders on Shakespeare's island.

On that island, Prospero responds to his daughter's naive enthusiasm with the cynicism of one who knows that promise often goes unfulfilled: her "brave new world" is "new to *thee*," he chides, knowing from experience that "such people" can be monsters rather than models. The challenge for the school library media specialist, then, is to prevent either Prospero's pessimism or history's precedent from prevailing with the new technologies. The challenge is to preserve Miranda's faith in her "many goodly creatures"—to discover ways to use these powerful and exciting new tools to maximize educational benefits for all students.

References

1. Ronald E. Anderson, Wayne W. Welch, and Linda J. Harris. "Inequities in Opportunities for Computer Literacy." *The Computing Teacher* 11:10-12 (Apr. 1984); Henry J. Becker, *Instructional Uses of School Computers:*

Reports from the 1985 National Survey, Issue No. 2 (Baltimore: Johns Hopkins University, Center for Social Organization of Schools, 1986); Henry J. Becker, *The Impact of Computer Use on Children's Learning: What Research Has Shown and What It Has Not* (Baltimore: Johns Hopkins University, Center for Social Organization of Schools, 1987); Henry J. Becker and Carleton W. Sterling, "Equity in School Computer Use: National Data and Neglected Considerations," *Journal of Educational Computing Research* 3: 289-311 (3, 1987); J. Hayes, *Microcomputer and VCR Usage in Schools—1985-1986* (Denver, Colo.: Quality Education Data, 1986).

2. Daniel Watt, "Education for Citizenship in a Computer-Based Society," in *Computer Literacy,* eds. R. Seidel, R. Anderson, and B. Hunter (New York: Academic Press, 1982), p. 59.

3. John P. Lipkin, "Equity in Computer Education,: *Educational Leadership* 4:26 (Sept. 1983).

4. National Task Force on Educational Technology, *Transforming American Education: Reducing the Risk to the Nation* (Washington: U.S. Department of Education, Office of Educational Research and Improvement, 1986).

5. U.S. Department of Education, Office of Library Programs, *Rethinking the Library in the Information Age,* Volume 1, Section 3 (Washington: U.S. Department of Education, 1988).

6. U.S. Congress Office of Technology Assessment, *Power On! New Tools for Teaching and Learning* (Washington: U.S. Government Printing Office, 1988).

7. *Transforming American Education,* p. 111.

8. *Transforming American Education* was reprinted in *TechTrends* 31: 10-24 and 35 (May-June 1986).

9. American Library Association Presidential Commission on Information Literacy, *Final Report* (Chicago: American Library Assn., 1989).

10. American Association of School Librarians and Association for Educational Communications and Technology, *Information Power: Guidelines for School Library Media Programs* (Chicago: American Library Assn., 1988), p. 5.

11. Richard A. King, "Rethinking Equity in Computer Access and Use," *Educational Technology* 27: 12-18 (Apr. 1987); Bernadette Martin and J. Dixon Hearne, "Computer Equity in Education," *Educational Technology* 29: 47-51 (Sept. 1989).

12. Fran Reinhold, "Sorting Out the Equity Issues," *Electronic Learning* 4:33-37 (Feb. 1985); "Technology and the At-Risk Student," *Electronic Learning* 8: 36-39 and 42-49 (Nov.-Dec. 1988).

13. Becker and Sterling, "Equity in School Computer Use," 1987; S. M. Chambers and V. A. Clarke, "Is Inequity Cumulative: The Relationship Between Disadvantaged Group Membership and Students' Computing Experience, Knowledge, Attitudes, and Intentions," *Journal of Educational Computing Research* 3: 495-518 (4, 1987).

14. Kay Gilliland, "EQUALS in Computer Technology," *The Computing Teacher* 11: 42-44 (Apr. 1984); Pat Sturdivant, "Access to Technology: The Equity Paradox," *The Computing Teacher* 11: 65-67 (Apr. 1984); Jo S. Sanders, "The Computer: Male, Female, or Androgynous?" *The Computing Teacher* 111: 31-34 (Apr. 1984).

15. Carol Edwards, "Action for Equity: Project MiCRO," *The Computing Teacher* 16: 11-13 (Feb. 1989); Ellen Richman, "Action for Equity: Equity in Technology," *The Computing Teacher* 15: 35-37 and 58-59 (Feb. and Mar. 1988).

16. *The Computing Teacher*, Theme issue "Equity," 11 (Apr. 1984); *The Computing Teacher*, Theme issue "At Risk Students," 17 (Nov. 1989).

17. "Setting a Research Agenda," *School Library Media Quarterly* 17: 123-25 (Spring 1989).

18. *Power On!*, p. 74.

19. Committee for Economic Development, *Children in Need: Investment Strategies for the Educationally Disadvantaged* (New York: Committee for Economic Development, 1987).

20. Business Roundtable, *Business Means Business About Education* (New York: Business Roundtable, 1989).

21. Sally B. Zakariya, "In Schools (As Elsewhere), the Rich Get Computers; the Poor Get Poorer," *American School Board Journal* 171: 29-32 (Mar. 1984).

22. See, for example, Michael Eisenberg, "Curriculum Mapping and Implementation of an Elementary School Library Media Skills Curriculum," *School Library Media Quarterly* 12: 411-18 (Fall 1984).

23. Isabelle Bruder, "Distance Learning: What's Holding Back This Boundless Delivery System?" *Electronic Learning* 8: 30-35 (Apr. 1989).

24. Chris Clark, "Distance Education in United States Schools," *The Computing Teacher* 16: 7-11 (Mar. 1989); Steven M. Ross, Lana Smith, Gary Morrison, and Ann Erickson, "An Apple a Day and at Night: A Distance Tutoring Program for At-Risk Students," *Educational Technology* 29: 23-28 (Aug. 1989).

FACTORS INFLUENCING THE OUTCOME OF LIBRARY MEDIA CENTER CHALLENGES AT THE SECONDARY LEVEL

Dianne McAfee Hopkins

Access issues, particularly as they relate to intellectual freedom and schools, are of continuing concern to library media professionals at all levels.[1] Nationally, access to information and intellectual freedom are among the priority areas and goals of the American Library Association (ALA) as adopted by ALA Council at the summer 1986 ALA Annual Conference.[2] In a similar way, the American Association of School Librarians' long-range plan, adopted by the board of directors at the summer 1989 ALA Annual Conference, includes both access to information and intellectual freedom as priority areas of the association.[3]

Although interest in intellectual freedom is widespread, many unanswered questions must be studied to provide information that can profoundly influence the professional preparation of library media specialists as well as the treatment of challenges to materials in school library media centers. One of the important questions to address is, "What are the factors that are most likely to influence the outcome of challenges to school library media materials found in public schools?"

The question addresses basic, legitimate concerns dealing with barriers to access for minors, as well as the broad issue of human rights.

This article examines factors, suggested by a review of research in library and information science, as possible influences on the outcome of challenges to library media materials. The focus of this article is a report of an intellectual freedom study of Wisconsin's public middle, junior, and senior high school library media centers conducted by the author in spring 1988.

For purposes of the study, "challenge" is defined as an oral or written complaint about the appropriateness of school library media center material(s). "Outcome" is defined as the resolution of a challenge about the appropriateness of school library media material(s). The three outcomes investigated included retention, restriction, and removal. In retention, material that is thought to be appropriate for the school library media center remains on open shelves and is readily accessible to users of the library media center (LMC). In restriction, material that is thought to be suitable for some students in the school but questionable for others is given limited access, such as placement on a restricted shelf for access only through the library media specialist or other authority figure. In removal, material that is thought to be inappropriate for the school and its students is taken out of the school library media center altogether.

Conceptual Framework

The conceptual framework upon which the proposed intellectual freedom study is based is represented in Figure 1 and was developed and discussed by Hopkins.[4] The conceptual model suggests that the outcome of a challenge to library media materials is affected by five major factors:

- the existence of a district materials selection policy and the degree of its use when material is challenged;
- selected personal and professional characteristics of the library media specialist;

- school environment, including the influence and power of the school principal as well as the support of the teaching staff;

- community environment, including the influence of local information media in bringing challenge issues to the attention of the community and in seeking to influence school decisions by expressing opinions;

- initiator of the challenge as a determinant of the decision, including whether challenges are internal (e.g., initiated by principals or teachers) or external (e.g., initiated by parents).

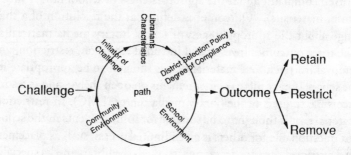

Figure 1. Factors Influencing Challenge Outcomes

These factors are conceptually based on research in library and information science; research in educational administration, including formal and informal organizations within schools, school climate, and supervisor/subordinate relationships; communications research including information media (such as newspapers) and community interactions; and behavioral science research relating to personality, power, and authority. In library and information science research, the conceptual framework is strongly influenced by the research and discussions of Busha, England, Farley, Fiske, Pope, and Serebnick.[5] Educational administration research is based on research compilations of Hoy and Forsyth, and Silver.[6] A summary of selected studies in library and information science cited in Hopkins follows.[7]

Materials Selection Policy

A number of studies have been conducted that relate to the use of the materials selection policy during a challenge. The studies show a positive relationship between retention of challenged materials and the existence and use of a materials selection policy. Studies/surveys supporting this relationship include Bracy, Fiske, Jenkinson, "Limiting What Students Shall Read," McDonald, Wisconsin Department of Public Instruction, and Woodworth.[8]

Characteristics of the Library Media Specialist

Characteristics of librarians of all types have been the focus of several studies in intellectual freedom. Among the characteristics examined are years of professional service, internal sense of status, age, internal sense of pressure, and level of formal training. Among the library and information science studies/surveys addressing one or more of these characteristics are those of Busha, England, Farley, Fiske, Pope, and Wisconsin Department of Public Instruction.[9] Studies suggest that certain characteristics of the library media specialist will influence the outcome of challenges to library media center (LMC) materials.

School Environment

As used in this study, the school environment includes the influence of the principal and teachers with whom the library media specialist works and support structures within the school. Among the library and information science studies addressing one or more of the areas are those by Busha, Farley, Fiske, and Pope.[10] The research suggests that library media specialists are influenced by administrators as well as support networks such as those that may be provided by teachers.

Community Environment

The community environment reflects the area in which the school is located. The conceptual framework focuses on the role of information media such as newspapers during a challenge, the size of the community as well as support structures outside the school. Studies/surveys from Busha, England, Fiske, "Limiting What Students Shall Read," Pope, and Wisconsin Department of Public Instruction examine one or more of these aspects.[11] The studies suggest that community environment may influence the outcome of challenges to LMC Materials.

Initiator of the Challenge

Previous research suggests that a factor influencing the outcome of a challenge is who initiates the challenge. Studies/surveys that examine the initiator include Fiske, Jenkinson, Wisconsin Department of Public Instruction, and Woodworth.[12]

Studies suggest that the outcome to a challenge may be dependent on whether the initiator is a member of the school community such as a teacher or principal or outside the school such as a parent.

Methodology

The Wisconsin exploratory study was designed to test several of the factors suggested in the conceptual framework. This study's population included the head library media specialists in all of Wisconsin's public middle, junior, and senior high schools, based on data provided by the Wisconsin Department of Public Instruction. One library media specialist in each of Wisconsin's 606 library media centers at public middle, junior, and senior high schools received the survey instrument. A total of 534 usable surveys, or 88%, were returned for purposes of analysis. Respondents provided general background information about themselves and the school environment. Those reporting oral or written challenges during the period, September 1985 to the time of study in spring 1988 also provided information about the nature of the challenges and the challenge process that occurred during the time period of the study.

The questionnaire was pretested in the following order: (1), graduate-level students in a class in the School of Library and Information Studies, University of Wisconsin-Madison; (2) selected district-level library media directors; (3) selected school library media specialists in public and private secondary schools. After each pretest, the questionnaire was revised. Following the pretest by school library specialists, the questionnaires were printed and mailed to schools in April 1988 with an addressed, stamped return envelope. Respondents were assured that the questionnaire was voluntary and that responses would be confidential. The cover letter indicated the endorsements that the study received from the Wisconsin Educational Media Association (WEMA); the Wisconsin Association of School Librarians (WASL), a division of the Wisconsin Library Association (WLA); and WLA's Intellectual Freedom Committee. One follow-up mailing with a second survey instrument and an addressed, stamped envelope was sent to those not returning the instrument within three weeks of the first mailing.

Selected definitions adopted by the Intellectual Freedom Committee, American Library Association (ALA), June 27, 1987, were used in the actual instrument. The definitions used were the following: *oral complaint*—an oral challenge to the presence and/or appropriateness of the material in question; *written complaint*—a formal, written complaint filed with the school or library that challenges the presence and/or appropriateness of specific material.

Analysis of the Data

Highlights of the report are provided in two parts. One provides general status information, while the other examines the factors influencing the challenge outcome. In some instances, respondents did not answer all questions; therefore, information reported reflects only responses received on each question. Percentages are rounded off. In the interest of brevity, highlights focus primarily on the outcomes of retention and removal, with occasional inclusion of the outcome of restriction in the discussion.

Highlights, General Status Information

District Materials Selection Policy

1. **Existence of Districtwide Policy.** A total of 95% or 506 of the respondents indicated that there was a district materials selection policy; 4% or twenty (20) indicated that there was no district materials selection policy; 1% or seven (7) indicated that they did not know. One respondent did not answer.

2. **School Board Approval Interval.** Four hundred fifty-nine (459) of the respondents who reported having materials selection policies indicated the time span since the policy had been approved. A total of 3% or fifteen (15) respondents indicated that the policy had never been approved; 59% or 270 indicated approval in the last five years; while 38% or 174 indicated policies in use that had been approved six or more years previously.

3. **Use of Policy During the Challenge.** A total of 229 challenges were reported by 26% of respondents (see "Complaints" section below). The use of the materials selection policy was reported by respondents in a total of 191 challenges. The policy was reported as used fully or partially in 60% (114) of the challenges, while in 40% (77) of the challenges, the policy was not used at all.

Characteristics of Library Media Specialists

1. **Education of Library Media Specialist.** Educational levels for the 534 respondents were obtained. A total of 35% (184) of respondents reported the highest degree earned in their educational background as being a bachelor's degree or postbachelor's study; 59% (313) reported master's degrees or postmaster's study; and 7% (37) reported two master's degrees, specialist degrees, or Ph.D. degrees.

2. **Sense of Pressure.** All respondents were asked: "To what extent do you feel under pressure by others to restrict or curb selections of materials beyond budget or curriculum constraints?" Of the 527 respondents answering this question, 4% (19) responded "definitely";

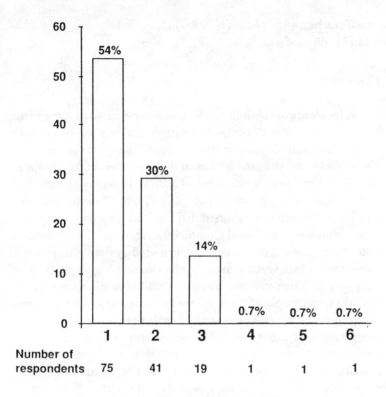

Total Complaints: 229

Total respondents: 138

Figure 2. How Many Complaints

the majority, 68% (356), felt that they were under minimal pressure; 29% (152) reported that they felt under no pressure.

Those indicating feeling under pressure identified the following major sources of pressure (respondents could identify one or more sources): parents—checked by seventy-nine (79) respondents; ultra-conservative group/organization/church—forty-nine (49) respondents; district administrator—forty-three (43) respondents; community members other than parents—forty-one (41) respondents; teachers—thirty-six (36) respondents; school board—thirty-four (34) respondents.

Complaints

1. **Incidence of Complaints.** Respondents were asked if there had been any oral or written complaints regarding library media materials in the school since September 1985. (Note: Library media specialists employed for less than three years in the school were asked to speak only for the period in which they had been at the school.) Of the 534 respondents. 26% or 138 answered "yes"; 72% or 383 answered "no"; and 2% or thirteen (13) reported that they did not know.

2. **Number and Type of Complaints.** A total of 229 complaints were reported in the three-year period covered by the study. Figure 2 shows that 54% or seventy-five (75) reported one complaint; 30% or forty-one (41) reported two complaints; 14% or nineteen (19) reported three complaints; 2% or three (3) reported four or more complaints. In the great majority of challenges (80% or 156), the complaints were about books. Magazines were complained about in 13% (26) challenges; films/videos and others accounted for the remaining twelve (12) or 6% of the challenges reported. The type of material complained about was specified for 194 of the 229 challenges reported.

3. **Reasons for Complaints.** From twenty-six possible choices, respondents identified six primary reasons for challenges to materials: family values—forty-four (44) challenges; sexuality—forty-one (41) challenges; morality—thirty-three (33) challenges; immaturity of students—twenty-seven (27)challenges; profanity—twenty-six (26) challenges; obscenity—twenty-four (24) challenges. Respondents were able to check as many reasons as appropriate for each challenge. Thus, one challenge could have had several reasons checked for the complaint.

4. **Initiator.** Respondents reported that 51% or 107 of the challenges were initiated by parents; 17% or thirty-five (35) were initiated by teachers; 9% or nineteen (19) were initiated by principals; all others

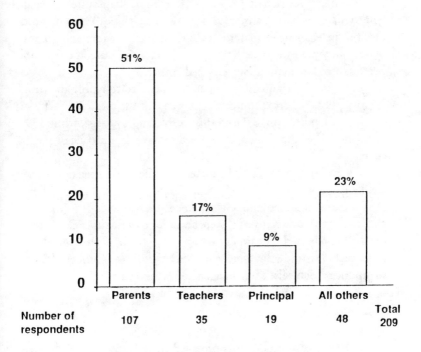

Figure 3. Who Initiated Complaint

(including district administrator, other community members, organized groups) accounted for 23% of the challenges.(See Figure 3.)

5. **Outcome.** Complaint outcome is reported in terms of whether material is retained, restricted, transferred, or removed. Of 187 complaints reported in these categories, respondents reported that 64% or 120 complaints resulted in challenged material being retained on open shelves: 15% or twenty-eight (28) complaints resulted in challenged material being restricted; 3% or six (6) complaints resulted in challenged material being transferred; 18% or thirty-three (33) complaints resulted in challenged material being removed. In remaining complaint outcome categories not reported here, the outcome had not been resolved or respondents checked "other."

6. **Media Coverage.** Respondents were asked to report any community public information media coverage of the challenge. Of 226 challenges reported on, 87% or 196 received no coverage, while 13% or thirty (30) of the challenges received print and/or broadcast media coverage.

7. **Challenged Books.** The material challenged varied in the 299 challenges reported. Of 156 challenges to books, only 10% or fifteen (15) were questioned more than once. Of these, eight (8) were challenged twice each, two (2) were challenged three times each, three (3) were challenged four times each, and two (2) were challenged five times each. No titles, therefore, emerged a significant number of times to produce a viable list of challenged books for reporting, in this study.

Others Involved in Challenge

1. **Principal.** Respondents provided their perception of the role of the principal during the challenge. A summary of Figure 4 shows that 50% or seventy-seven (77) of the respondents saw the principal as providing a leadership or support role to the library media specialist; 49% or seventy-six (76) viewed the role of the principal as being unsupportive, either by leaving the process up to the library media specialist entirely, or by questioning the value of the material being challenged.

2. Teachers. Based on 131 challenges, teachers were generally viewed as supportive in the challenge process. In 70% or ninety-one (91) challenges, teachers were identified as being openly or quietly supportive. In 30% or forty (40) challenges reported, teachers were

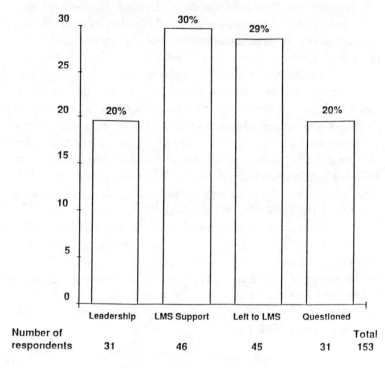

Figure 4. Role of Principal

viewed as staying out of the process or questioning the value of the material being challenged.

3. Assistance Provided Inside the District. Respondents were asked to indicate who inside the district provided assistance during each challenge. Six possible choices were offered, more than one choice could be selected. While no assistance within the district was sought in 102 challenges, assistance was reported in 156 challenges as follows: teachers in school assisted in forty-nine (49) challenges; the principal in school assisted in forty-three (43) challenges; other library media specialists within the district helped in thirty-nine (39) challenges; the district library media director aided in twenty-five (25) challenges.

4. **Assistance Provided Outside the District.** Respondents were asked to indicate if assistance was provided outside the district. A total of ten choices were given. including the public library system, Department of Public Instruction, and library media associations. No assistance was sought in fifty-one (51) challenges. The only choice listed a substantial number of times was the Cooperative Children's Book Center (CCBC), a review, examination, and research collection of children's and young adult books located on the campus of the University of Wisconsin-Madison. The CCBC was selected forty-five (45) times. The CCBC, which has provided intellectual freedom reference review services since 1978 for Wisconsin school and public librarians, has been honored for its intellectual freedom services by its selection as the 1989 winner of the John Phillip Immroth Memorial Award, presented by the American Library Association's Intellectual Freedom Round Table. The CCBC has also been selected as the 1989 winner of the Robert B. Downs Intellectual Freedom Award given by the University of Illinois at Urbana-Champaign's Graduate School of Library and Information Science. (For more information about the intellectual freedom services of the Cooperative Children's Book Center, see appendix A.)

Summary, General Status Information

Respondents overwhelmingly reported having material selection policies that were approved, yet those reporting challenges to materials reported that the policy was not used at all in 40 percent of the instances in which library media center materials were challenged. The majority of library media specialists in Wisconsin's middle, junior, and senior high schools have master's degrees or above. Very few library media specialists reported feeling definitely pressured by others to restrict or curb selections of materials beyond budget or curriculum constraints.

Approximately one in four library media specialists reported a challenge relating to the availability of library media materials in the library media center. Of those reporting complaints, the majority reported one complaint, with one or two complaints accounting for 84 percent of those responding to the number of complaints question. Family values and sexuality were reasons given the highest frequency of times by respondents as the basis for the complaint.

While parents accounted for a slight majority of challenges (51 percent), teachers or principals were reported as initiating 26 percent or about one in four of the challenges. In terms of the outcome to the challenge, most of the challenged materials were retained on open shelves, while slightly more than one in three challenges resulted in the restriction, transfer, or complete removal of material. Most challenges received no media coverage in the community. In most instances, titles of challenged books varied considerably throughout the state.

Principals were reported as providing leadership or support to the library media specialist in half of the challenges reported. Likewise principals were reported as being unsupportive in half of the challenges. Teachers were generally viewed as being supportive of the library media specialist in a majority of challenges.

Finally, while many respondents did not seek assistance outside the district during a challenge, those who did overwhelmingly sought the intellectual freedom services of the Cooperative Children's Book Center, a review, examination, and research collection of children's and young adult books and related resources available to Wisconsin adult residents including school and public librarians.

Highlights, Challenge Outcomes

The outcomes of retention, restriction, and removal were examined more closely in selected findings to provide some basic information useful in initially addressing the question, "What are the factors which influence the outcome to challenges to materials in middle, junior, and senior high school library media centers?" The primary focus of the highlights will be on the outcomes of retention and removal.

Where deemed important, explanatory information occasionally includes the outcome of restriction. Differences in the number of challenges reported is based in part on responses to complaint outcomes that were not selected for further testing, such as "not yet resolved" or "other."

The SAS (Statistical Analysis System) Program was used to provide frequencies and cross tabulations. The GLIM (General Linear Model) Program was used to test hypotheses. Hypotheses were tested on contingency tables using a generalized incremental chi-square technique. A nominal point 0.05 rejection level was chosen. However, since twenty-eight (28) tests were planned, the Bonferroni correction (.05 divided by 28 = .00179) was applied to yield an actual rejection level of 0.00179. This yields a chi-square value of 9.746 for the single

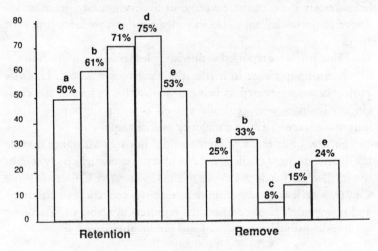

a = never   (8 respondents)
b = last 2 years   (36 respondents)
c = 3-5 years   (49 respondents)
d = 6-10 years   (55 respondents)
e = 11+ years   (17 respondents)

Total - 165

Figure 5. When Policy Approved

degree of freedom tests. Associations were deemed significant at the 0.05 level.

Materials Selection Policy

1. **Approval Interval.** Retention and removal of challenged materials were examined based on the time span since the policy was approved. A Summary of Figure 5 shows that districts with policies never approved (8) or approved more than eleven years previously (17) had the lowest retention rates of 50% and 53% respectively. Districts with policies approved 3-5 years previously (49) and 6-10 years previously (55) had the highest retention rates of 71% and 75%, respectively.

Those districts with policies never approved, policies approved in the previous two years, and policies approved more than eleven years previously had the highest removal rate, 25%, 33%, and 24% respectively, while those with policies approved 3-5 years before had the lowest removal rate at 8%.

The following statistical hypotheses were tested:

- Districts with policies never approved and policies older than eleven (11) years have a lower retention rate when material is challenged. x^2 = 4.28 (not significant)

- Districts with policies approved 3-5 years ago have a lower removal rate. X^2 = 6.69 (not significant)

- The highest retention is in districts with policies approved between 3-10 years ago. x^2 = 99.11 (significant)

2. **Use of Policy and Outcome.** Retention, restriction, and removal of challenged material were examined based on the reported use of the policy. Figure 6 indicates that where the policy was reported as not used at all (72 challenges), the retention rate was lower (53%) than when the policy was used fully (55 challenges or 71%) or partially (50 challenges or 72%). Where the policy was reported as not used at all, the removal and restriction rates combined (44%) were higher

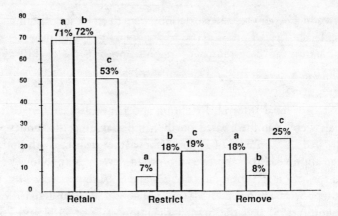

a = full use   (55 respondents)
b = partial use   (50 respondents)
c = no use   (72 respondents)

Total - 177

Figure 6. Use of Policy

than the same categories where the policy was reported as fully (25%) or partially (26%) used .

The following statistical hypotheses were tested:

- When the policy is not used at all, there is a greater likelihood that material will be removed. $x^2 = .07$ (not significant)

- When the policy is not used at all, there is less likelihood that material will be retained. $x^2 = 16.925$ significant)

Characteristics of the Library Media Specialist

1. Sense of Pressure. Retention or removal of challenged material was examined based on the library media specialist's sense of pressure. Library media specialists who experienced challenges and who reported a "definite" sense of pressure were more likely to report a low retention rate. Of a total of 179 respondents, those reporting a "definite" sense of pressure reported a 25% retention rate (twelve respondents), as compared to 68% for those indicating they felt "somewhat" under pressure (66 respondents); 69% for those reporting "hardly any" pressure (75 respondents); and 62% for those reporting "no" pressure (26 respondents). The twelve (12) library media specialists reporting a definite sense of pressure were also more likely to have challenged material removed (42%) than those checking other categories, i.e., somewhat (24%), hardly at all (15%), not at all (23%).

The following were tested:

- The more definitely library media specialists feel under pressure, the lower the likelihood that material will be retained. $x^2 = 14.36$ (significant)

- The more definitely library media specialists feel under pressure, the higher the likelihood that material will be removed. $x^2 = 10.45$ (significant)

2. Education. Retention and removal of challenged materials were examined based on the level of formal education reported by the respondents. Figure 7 shows that sixty-seven (67) library media specialists reporting bachelor's degrees or postbachelor's study were less likely to report retention of materials than the 113 reporting master's degrees or above, i.e., 60% retention compared to 65% of those with master's or postmaster's, and 78% of those with two master's or more. Similarly, those reporting bachelor's degrees or postbachelor's study were more likely to indicate removal of materials than those with master's degrees or two master's or more, i.e., 24% removal compared to 15% of those reporting master's or postmaster's, and 11% of those with two master's or more advanced degrees.

The following statistical hypotheses were tested:

- The higher the degree earned, the greater the likelihood that challenged material will be retained. $x^2 = 28.87$ (significant)

- The higher the degree earned, the less likelihood that material will be removed. x^2 (significant)

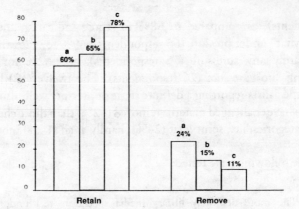

a = bachelors or postbachelors (67 respondents)
b = masters or postmasters (104 respondents)
c = 2 masters, specialist, Ph.D. (9 respondents)

Total - 180

Figure 7. Earned Degrees

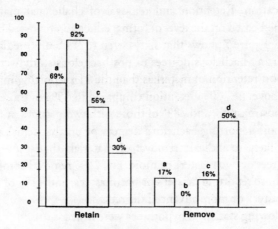

a = Leadership (29 respondents)
b = Support (38 respondents)
c = Left decisions to LMS (32 respondents)
d = Questioned (20 respondents)

Total - 119

Figure 8. Role of Principal and Outcome

School Environment

1. Role of Principal. Retention and removal were examined based on the role of the principal as reported by the library media specialist. A summary of Figure 8 reveals that the highest retention rate of 92% resulted when the principal was viewed as supportive to the library media specialist compared to the lowest retention rate of 30% when the principal was said to have questioned the suitability of the material. The highest removal rate, 50%, resulted when the principal was reported as questioning the suitability of the material, while the lowest removal rate, 0%, resulted when the principal was viewed as supportive to the library media specialist.

The following statistical hypotheses were tested:

- The more the principal is seen as supporting the library media specialist, the more likely the challenged material will be retained. $x^2 = 45.44$ (significant)

- The more the principal is seen by the library media specialist as questioning the value of the challenged material, the more likely challenged material will be removed. $x^2 = 11.033$ (significant)

- When the principal is seen by the library media specialist, as questioning the material, it is less likely that material will be retained. $x^2 = 25.33$ (significant)

- The more the principal is seen as supporting the library media specialist, the less likely material will be removed. $x^2 = 8.109$ (not significant)

2. Role of Teachers. Retention and removal were based on the role of teachers in the school where the challenge occurred. Figure 9 shows, that the highest retention rates were found to occur when teachers were viewed as openly (38) or quietly (39) supporting the library media specialist (74% and 69%, respectively), while the lowest retention rate, 17%, was reported where teachers were viewed as questioning the material (6). Where the teachers are openly or quietly supportive of the library media specialist, the removal rate is lower

(8 % and 10%, respectively) than where they are reported as staying out of the process (20) or questioning material (40% and 50%, respectively).

The following statistical hypotheses were tested:

- The more teachers openly or quietly support the library media specialist during a challenge, the greater the likelihood that material will be retained. $x^2 = 75.87$ (significant)

- The more teachers openly or quietly support the library media specialist during a challenge, the less likelihood material will be removed. $x^2 = .591$ (not significant)

- The more teachers question or stay out of the challenge process, the greater the likelihood that material will be removed. $x^2 = .306$ (significant)

Initiator of Challenge

Retention and removal were examined based on who initiated the challenge. Figure 10 shows that challenges initiated by school board member(s) and parents (94) were more likely to result in retention than those initiated by principals (17) or teachers (30), i.e., 73% and 71% compared to 41% and 47%, respectively. Challenges initiated by principals or teachers were more likely to result in removal than those initiated by school board member(s) or parents, i.e., 58% and 47% compared to 18% and 26%, respectively

The following statistical hypotheses were tested:

- Challenges initiated by school board members have a greater likelihood of resulting in retention. $x^2 = 91.29$ (significant)

- Challenges initiated by parents have a greater likelihood of resulting in retention. $x^2 = 53.05$ (significant)

- Challenges initiated by principals or teachers have a greater likelihood of resulting in removal or restriction. $x^2 = 1.363$ (not significant)

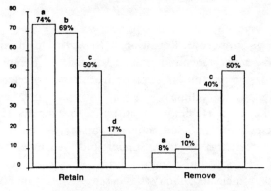

a = openly supportive   (38 respondents)
b = quietly supportive   (39 respondents)
c = stayed out of process   (20 respondents)
d = questioned material   (6 respondents)

Total - 103

Figure 9. Role of Teachers

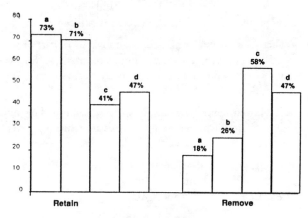

a = school board   (11 respondents)
b = parents   (94 respondents)
c = principal   (17 respondents)
d = teachers   (30 respondents)

Total - 152

Figure 10. Initiator and Outcome

Other

1. Active Support for Retention or Removal During the Challenge. Those actively involved in the debate for retention or removal of materials were examined in terms of the outcomes of retention and removal. Respondents chose from twenty-two (22) potential support groups and could select all those that applied. See Figures 11, 12, 13, and 14. Respondents indicated active support for retention or removal within the district as including support provided by school board member(s), district administrators, district library media coordinator/director, principal(s), library staff in school, library media specialists in the district, other librarians located elsewhere, parents, teachers, teacher organizations, etc.

The following statistical hypotheses for active supporters of retention were tested (see Figures 11 and 12):

- The likelihood of retention is greatest when school board members, district administrators, and principals are active supporters of retention. $x^2 = 100.98$ (significant)

- There is a greater likelihood of removal or restriction when active support for retention is limited primarily to the district library media director and other library media staff. $x^2 = 69.55$ (significant)

- The lowest removal rate results when school board members, district administrators, and principals are active supporters of retaining materials. $x^2 = 15.42$ (significant)

- Challenges with no active support for retention are more likely to result in removal than those with active support for retention. $x^2 = 5.248$ (not significant)

The following statistical hypotheses for active supporters of removal were tested (see Figures 13 and 14):

- The likelihood of removal or restriction is greatest when district administrators support removal. $x^2 = 4.091$ (not significant)

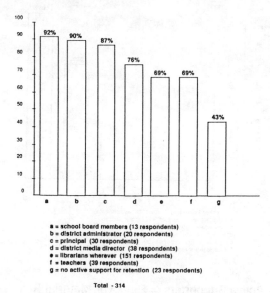

Figure 11. Active Supporters of Retention: Material Retained

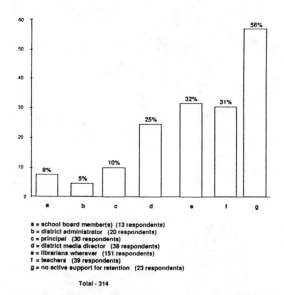

Figure 12. Active Supporters of Retention: Material Removed or Restricted

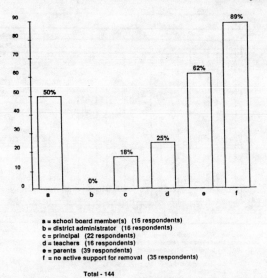

a = school board member(s)   (16 respondents)
b = district administrator   (16 respondents)
c = principal   (22 respondents)
d = teachers   (16 respondents)
e = parents   (39 respondents)
f = no active support for removal   (35 respondents)

Total - 144

Figure 13. Active Supporters of Removal: Material Retained

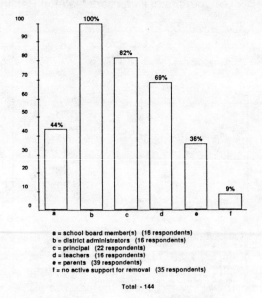

a = school board member(s)   (16 respondents)
b = district administrators   (16 respondents)
c = principal   (22 respondents)
d = teachers   (16 respondents)
e = parents   (39 respondents)
f = no active support for removal   (35 respondents)

Total - 144

Figure 14. Active Supporters of Removal: Material Removed or Restricted

- The likelihood of removal is least when parents and school board members actively support removal. $x^2 = 5.254$ (not significant)

- Challenges with no active support for removal are more likely to result in retention than those with active support for removal. $x^2 = 50.71$ (significant)

2. Assistance Outside District: Cooperative Children's Book Center (CCBC). Restriction and removal were examined based on those who sought and received assistance from Wisconsin's Cooperative Children's Book Center (CCBC). Of thirty-two (32) challenges in which assistance from the CCBC was sought, 78% or twenty-five (25) of the challenges resulted in materials being retained and 6% or two (2) reported that materials were removed. This compares to a retention rate of 69% for ninety (90) challenges reported as not seeking assistance from the CCBC. and a removal rate of 15% for nineteen (19) challenges in which assistance from the CCBC was not sought. The overall retention rate for all those reporting challenges was 64% for 120 challenges, with an overall removal rate of 18% for thirty-three (33) challenges.

The following statistical hypotheses were tested:

- Those using CCBC services had a higher likelihood of retention than those that did not. $x^2 = 29.04$ (significant)

- Those using the CCBC had a lower likelihood of removal than those that did not. $x^2 = 12.04$ (significant)

Summary, Challenge Outcomes

When one looks at challenges to library media materials as they relate to outcome, i.e., retention, restriction, and removal, additional insights are provided in comparison to a general reporting of results as in the first part of this report. In terms of the materials selection policy, the amount of time since the policy was approved relates to outcome. Districts with policies approved between 3-10 years previously had significantly higher retention rates than those districts with policies never approved, newly approved, or approved more than eleven years previously.

The use of the policy also reflected the outcome. Where policies were not used at all during the challenge, the retention rate was significantly lower and the removal rate was higher than when policies were used fully or partially.

In terms of characteristics of the library media specialist, library media specialists reporting a definite sense of pressure, although few in number, also reported greater removal rates and lower retention rates than those reporting less or no sense of pressure. In terms of highest educational attainments, those with master's degrees or above were significantly more likely to report that challenged material was retained than those with bachelor's or postbachelor's study. Similarly, those with master's degrees or above were less likely to report that material had been removed.

The role of the principal as viewed by the library media specialist definitely affected the outcome of challenges. When principals were viewed as being supportive of the library media specialist, challenged material was significantly more likely to be retained. The retention rate was higher (92%) when principals were viewed as supportive compared to the retention rate of 69% when principals were viewed as assuming a leadership role. Where the principal was viewed as questioning the appropriateness of the challenged material, it was significantly less likely that challenged material would be retained.

Where teachers were viewed as being openly or quietly supportive of the library media specialist, there was a significantly greater likelihood that challenged material would be retained.

The initiator of the challenge was significant. Challenges initiated by school board members and parents were more likely to result in the retention of materials than those initiated by others.

In terms of outside support during a challenge, it was found that those using the intellectual freedom services of the Cooperative Children's Book Center had significantly higher rates of retention and significantly lower rates of removal than those that did not.

In terms of retention, there is a significantly greater likelihood of retention where principals, school board members, and district administrators are viewed as active supporters. In addition, where there is no active support for removal reported, there is a significantly greater likelihood of retention of the challenged material.

Major Factors

Major findings of this study of the outcome of challenges to library media material in Wisconsin's middle, junior, and senior high schools between 1985 and 1988 show that the outcome of challenged library media center materials is influenced by the following factors:

- How recently a materials selection policy has been approved or if the policy has never been approved;

- How a policy is used during a challenge, especially nonuse;

- Educational level of the library media specialist, with those with master's degrees or above reporting the highest rates of retention;

- The role of the principal, with highest retention of materials relating to the library media specialist's view of the principal as being supportive during the challenge;

- The role of teachers, with high retention of materials relating to the library media specialist's view of teachers as supportive during the challenge;

- Level of active support for removal with least likelihood of removal when parents and school board members actively support removal;

- Outside assistance provided by the Cooperative Children's Book Center, with higher retention rates for those using the CCBC's intellectual freedom service;

- Who initiates challenges, with challenges initiated by school board member(s) or parent(s) more likely to result in retention of materials than those initiated by officials and staff inside the school.

Discussion and Recommendations

Because this study focused on Wisconsin, results are not generalizable to challenges to library media center materials in states outside Wisconsin. However, because the results of this study support the conceptual model based on research findings, particularly in library and information science and educational administration, there is reason to suspect that similar results may be found in a more broad-based study. Further testing is essential, especially nationally based testing. The author will be conducting a national intellectual freedom study during the 1989-90 school year based, in part, on the Wisconsin study.

This exploratory study suggests that attention is needed on the internal school environment during challenges to library media center materials, including the role of the principal and teachers as initiators of challenges and as persons influential in the outcome of challenges. Those inside the school environment make a difference in the outcome to challenges. The study suggests that preservice as well as continuing professional development focus attention on dealing with challenges that have been initiated by persons inside as well as outside the school. This study suggests that, through education of library media specialists and through practice, there should be a recognition of the importance of prior internal understanding of intellectual freedom issues and advocacy for intellectual freedom when challenges occur. It also suggests that the existence and use of material selection policies continue to be important in challenges. At the same time, the study also suggests that external support, such as that provided to Wisconsin library media specialists by the Cooperative Children's Book Center (CCBC), may also empower the library media specialist to provide the local leadership necessary to affect the outcome of challenges in positive ways.

References and Notes

1. The author gratefully acknowledges the receipt of a Minority Faculty Research Award provided by the University of Wisconsin-System's Insti-

tution Race and Ethnicity and the receipt of research support from The Graduate School, University of Wisconsin-Madison, which were instrumental in the completion of this study. Appreciation is also expressed to the associations which endorsed the study and to all Wisconsin school library media specialists who participated in this study. 2. "ALA Strategic Long Range Plan," *American Libraries* 17: 462-63 (June 1986).

3. "ASSL Long Range Plan," approved by the American Association of School Librarians Board of Directors, Summer 1989, American Library Association Conference.

4. Dianne McAfee Hopkins, "Toward a Conceptual Model of Factors Influencing the Outcome of Challenges to Library Materials in School Settings," *Library and Information Science Research* 11: 247-71 (July-Sept. 1989).

5. Charles H. Busha, *Freedom Versus Suppression and Censorship: With a Study of the Attitudes of Midwestern Public Librarians and a Bibliography of Censorship* (Littleton, Colo.: Libraries Unlimited, 1972); Claire St. Clere England, *The Climate of Censorship in Ontario: An Investigation into Attitudes Toward Intellectual Freedom and Perceptual Factors Affecting the Practice of Censorship in Public Libraries Serving Medium-Sized Populations,* Ph.D. diss. (Toronto, Canada: University of Toronto, 1974); John J. Farley, *Book Censorship in the Senior High School Libraries in Nassau County, New York,* Ph.D. diss. (New York: New York University, 1964); Marjorie Fiske, *Book Selection and Censorship* (Berkeley, Calif.: University of California Press, 1959); Michael J. Pope, *Sex and the Undecided Librarian: A Study of Librarians' Opinions on Sexually-Oriented Literature* (Metuchen, N.J.: Scarecrow, 1974); Judith Serebnick, "A Review of Research Related to Censorship in Libraries," *Library Research* (now *Library and Information Science Research*) 1: 95-118 (Summer 1979).

6. Wayne K. Hoy and Patrick B. Forsyth, *Effective Supervision: Theory into Practice* (New York: Random House, 1986); Paula Silver, *Educational Administration: Theoretical Perspectives on Practice and Research* (New York: Harper & Row, 1983).

7. Hopkins, "Toward."

8. Pauletta Brown Bracy, *Censorship and Selection Policies in Public Senior High School Library Media Centers in Michigan,* Ph.D. diss. (Ann Arbor, Mich.: University of Michigan, 1982); Fiske, *Book Selection;* David Jenkinson, "The Censorship Iceberg: The Results of a Survey of Challenges in School and Public Libraries," *School Libraries in Canada* 6: 19-22, 24-30 (Fall 1985); Association of American Publishers and others. *Limiting What Students Shall Read* (Washington, D.C.: Association of American Publish-

ers, 1981); Fran McDonald, *A Report of a Survey on Censorship in Public Elementary and High School Libraries and Public Libraries in Minnesota* (Minneapolis: Minnesota Civil Liberties Union, 1983); Wisconsin Department of Public Instruction, "Censorship of IMC Materials in Wisconsin Schools, Part I: Focus on Middle/Junior High Schools" (Madison: Wisconsin Department of Public Instruction, 1980); Wisconsin Department of Public Instruction, "Censorship of IMC Materials in Wisconsin Schools, Part II: Focus on Elementary Schools" (Madison: Wisconsin Department of Public Instruction, 1981); Wisconsin Department of Public Instruction, "Censorship of IMC Materials in Wisconsin Schools, Part III: Focus on High Schools" (Madison: Wisconsin Department of Public Instruction, 1981); Mary L. Woodworth, *Intellectual Freedom, The Young Adult, and Schools*. rev. ed. (Madison: University of Wisconsin—Extension, 1976).

9. Busha, *Freedom*; England, *The Climate*; Farley, *Book Censorship*; Fiske, *Book Selection*; Pope, *Sex*; Wisconsin Department of Public Instruction, "Censorship."
10. Busha, *Freedom*; Farley, *Book Censorship*; Fiske, *Book Selection*; Pope, *Sex*.
11. Busha, *Freedom*; England, *The Climate*; Fiske, *Book Selection*; Association of American Publishers, *Limiting*; Pope, *Sex*; Wisconsin Department of Public Information, "Censorship."
12. Fiske, *Book Selection*; Jenkinson, "The Censorship"; Wisconsin Department of Public Instruction, "Censorship"; Woodworth, *Intellectual*.

Appendix A. Cooperative Children's Book Center

Based on an article by Cinny Moore Kruse, director, Cooperative Children's Book Center, that appeared in the December 1988 issues of Channel DLS, the newsletter of the Division for Library Services, Wisconsin Department of Public Instruction.

The Cooperative Children's Book Center (CCBC) is a review, examination, and research collection of children's and young adult books and related resources available to any adult resident of Wisconsin and housed at the University of Wisconsin-Madison. Funding for the CCBC comes from the Division for Library Services of the Wisconsin Department of Public Instruction (DPI) and from the School of Education on the Madison campus. The School of Library and Information Studies also provides support to the CCBC. The CCBC was established in 1963.

In 1977, Ginny Moore Kruse, director of the CCBC, established the Intellectual Freedom Information Services. Further development was made possible through a 1978 grant from the Evjue Foundation, a local foundation associated with the Madison newspapers, and a Library Services and Construction Act grant from the Department of Public Instruction in 1982. Since its establishment, hundreds of librarians, teachers, and administrators have been assisted in responding to book challenges all over the state of Wisconsin. Supervised by the center director, the service is coordinated by a one-third time staff member. Five to six on-call reference assistants provide staff support.

An extension of CCBC reference and information functions, the intellectual freedom services produce a number of resources once set in motion by a telephone call. These resources include:

- A telephone summary of review citations, awards, and distinctions for the book in question is provided when a call is received.

- Photocopies of information described in that summary, articles on the relevant literary genre, and other material developed specifically to answer the question being posed are mailed the day the call comes in.

- The caller is sent an information packet containing statements and policies based on the First Amendment from the American Library Association and other professional sources and articles on book evaluation, selection, and censorship.

- The CCBC director will consult by telephone with a requesting librarian or educator one or more times, as necessary.

- The caller gets information about professional assistance available from the Department of Public Instruction, the Wisconsin Library Association, the Wisconsin State Reading Association, the Wisconsin Council of Teachers of English, and other sources; the CCBC offers to make an initial contact with one of these groups only if the caller wishes such assistance.

- If applicable, the librarian or educator is offered open-ended loan of a CCBC-produced slide tape on realistic elements in fiction for the young.

- The center makes a follow-up contact in two months to see if further information might be useful.

The CCBC intellectual freedom services are continually revised and refined on the basis of written evaluations from users. The CCBC Advisory Board, which represents center users, also reviews intellectual freedom services annually. This group and the CCBC Executive Board of DPI and University of Wisconsin-Madison funding agency representatives have assigned the highest priority to intellectual freedom services, after provision of walk-in and telephone reference assistance during public service hours.

SECTION FOUR:
MANAGEMENT APPROACHES

FUNDING FOR PUBLIC LIBRARIES IN THE 1990S

Arthur Curley

Public libraries in the United States are struggling to emerge from a decade and more of crisis. The most obvious manifestation of that crisis has been severe revenue shortages, leading to major reductions in services and resources development. Financial strategies for the 1990s must begin with an assessment of that crisis, for its roots lie deep in the history of the public library movement and in conflicting forces within the nation's framework of values.

The Library as Anomaly

The public library is something of an anomaly in American society; revered as fundamental to the nation's values, yet without mandate or secure fiscal niche at any level of government in most areas of the country. In the spontaneous nature of its origins, and the voluntary basis of its continuance, are rooted both the strengths and weaknesses of this remarkable institution as well as the causative background to the financial predicament we confront as we enter the final decade of this century.

"Funding for Public Libraries in The 1990s," by Arthur Curley in *Library Journal.* Vol. 115, no. 1 (January 1990), pp. 65-67; reprinted with permission from Reed Publishing, USA, copyright © 1990 Reed Publishing, USA.

That the birth of the public library movement occurred in the United States, in the mid-19lh century, is a matter of some irony. The decision to serve a universal audience hardly sprung from a superabundance of private resources.

By 1850, the oldest and largest library in the country, that of Harvard University, contained only 84,000 volumes; the Library of Congress merely 50,000. In fact, only five libraries in the country held over 50,000 books, and the entire national composite amounted to barely two million.[1]

The inadequacy of the young nation's library resources was dramatically underscored by the provocative challenge of Fisher Ames that

> we have produced nothing in history. Our own is not yet worthy
> of a Livy; and to write that of any foreign nation where could
> an American author collect his materials and authorities? Few
> persons reflect, that all our universities would not suffice to
> supply them for such a work as Gibbon's.[2]

Charles Coffin Jewett, who would set about to correct this assessment upon his appointment in 1858 to the superintendency of the Boston Public Library, maintained at mid-century that "not one American library could meet the wants of a student in any department of knowledge.[3]

The Rest is History

On the other hand, the fallow soil of a new nation would prove particularly receptive to the zealous idealism that was the principal motivating force behind the movement to create the public library. New England in the 1840s was a still fervent disciple of the Enlightenment, committed to the concepts of humanism, of human perfectibility, of democratic promise, the center of the universal free education movement and of the growing Abolitionist cause.

As Sidney Ditzion summarized,

the main currents of 19th-century American thought, no matter what their origin or direction, supported the foundations and growth of the free public library movement. That such a confluence of diverse ideologies, meeting on the common ground of a system of free schools and libraries, was at all possible is to be attributed to the adjustability of the American mind to shifting forces and changing conditions. It was this flexibility that could start with a common heritage—the democratic premise—and could modify, distort, or even pervert it to suit the requirements of widely varying points of view. The tax-supported public library not only answered the criteria inherent in the democratic premise but also offered an instrument as responsive to varying social requirements as democracy itself.[4]

The idealistic origins of the public library have remained a force to shape its mission and philosophy for nearly a century and a half; unfortunately, the naivete so characteristic of an idealistic movement placed greater reliance on noble inclinations than on a rational legal and financial framework to insure support for the infant institution, and this too continues as an operative force to our present time.

The famous Act of Authorization to Establish a Public Library in the City of Boston, enacted in March 1848 by the legislature of the Commonwealth of Massachusetts, represented the culmination of a fervently idealistic movement. The statute also contained the provision that "no appropriation for the said library shall exceed the sum of $5000 in any one year.[5]

The cautious solons need not have feared: the initial appropriation by the Boston City Council, and that after a delay of three years, was the princely sum of $1000.[6] Edward Everett, the first president of the Library Trustees, had become the major colleague and catalyst in the ultimate success of George Tichnor's 20-year struggle to establish a public library; yet, the uncertainty in the minds of even these determined founders of the proper relationship between public mission and public support is evident in Everett's 1850 letter to the Mayor, in which he pleads that

if the city government would provide a suitable building for a public library, it would be so amply supplied from time to time by donations, that only a moderate annual appropriation for books would be wanted.[7]

The Boston Public Vision

The first report of the trustees of the Boston Public Library, issued in July of 1852, has been cited on innumerable occasions for its visionary articulation of the philosophy that would influence the mission of public libraries everywhere; but, again, the visionary confidence seems to falter on the matter of public financial support:

> If it were probable that the City Council would deem it expedient at once to make a large appropriation for the erection of a building and the purchase of an ample library, and that the citizens at large would approve such expenditure, the Trustees would of course feel great satisfaction in the prompt achievement of an object of such high public utility. But in the present state of the finances of the city, and in reference to an object on which the public mind is not yet enlightened by experience, the Trustees regard any such appropriation and expenditure as entirely out of the question. They conceive even that there are advantages to a more gradual course of measures. They look, therefore, only to the continuance of such moderate and frugal expenditure, on the part of the city, as has been already authorized and commenced, for the purchase of books and the compensation of the librarian; and for the assignment of a room or rooms in some one of the public buildings belonging to the city for the reception of the books already on hand, or which the Trustees have the means of procuring. With aid to this extent on the part of the city, the Trustees believe that all else may be left to the public spirit and liberality of individuals.[8]

The faith of the trustees in private philanthropy was soon rewarded by the great generosity of Joshua Bates as was the case in New York with that of John Jacob Astor, and universally through Andrew Carnegie's gifts of public library buildings to over 1500 communities in the United States alone a half-century later. To be less than grateful for such generosity would be boorish, indeed; private philanthropy was both an important predecessor, and at times a stimulant, of tax support. But a case may also be made that philanthropy discouraged communal responsibility, even unto the present time in which many a beleaguered library has been urged by public officials to seek private funds in lieu of additional tax support.

The Gradual Shift to Public Support

The shift from private to predominantly public support was a matter of considerable gradualism; there were, after all, nearly 700 private academic and subscription lending libraries in the United States in 1850, many of which would become the basis of future public libraries. Getz contends, in fact, that "for more than their first 100 years the line between private and government support of libraries was never crisp."[9] This is much more than a matter of historical curiosity, for the long identity crisis that it signifies continues to complicate the legitimate search of public libraries for a rational support structure.

Another characteristic of the challenge we confront as we plan for library funding in the 1990s is the great diversity of taxation structures throughout the country. The principal source of support for financing public libraries in the United States is local taxation; but, as Robbins-Carter concludes:

> local government financing varies from state to state and within states there are usually a number of local government financing options open to communities and/or counties; thus, it is not possible to present an accurate picture of a "typically" financed public library.[10]

Most major urban public libraries are either legally or de facto departments of municipal government, in competition with police or fire or sanitation for scarce funds distributed at the discretion of elected officials; a very few have power to seek special levies by referendum; the New York Public Library is a private corporation. Libraries in some parts of the country are creatures of county government, some are local but receive supplemental services or funds from county sources, others have separate district status with tax millage formulas determined by state statutes and voter referenda. Such diversity presents a serious obstacle to funding strategies based on comparative research or to effective lobbying on a nationwide, or even statewide. basis.

The Role of Government in Our Affairs

The traditional concern of state governments was service to rural and unincorporated areas; by the 1980s nearly all 50 states provided some form of support for library service. The pattern varies widely from support for cooperative or regional services to direct per capita aid. In a few states, modest aid to major urban libraries has been achieved, in recognition of service beyond local borders or resources of more than local importance; but by far the prevailing pattern has been small support to virtually all communities rather than significant aid for the special few.

The role of the national government in library affairs, beyond support of the splendid libraries of the national government, has been extremely limited, in large part precisely because the initial library movement sprung from local initiative; and continued resistance to national support and coordination reflects the lasting effects of that historical identity crisis, for the appropriate role of government in the development and support of library resources remains unresolved. As Wedgeworth has noted. "inconsistencies in public library financing are only the superficial manifestations of the confusion that exists over public support for libraries."[11]

As we devise financial strategies for the 1990s, however, the confusion we confront goes beyond that of the library's place in the public sector to a national crisis of confidence toward the public sector itself. For most of this century, following the demise of spectacular personal philanthropy in the wake of progressive tax legislation, local public support remained modest but healthy, even during the Depression years, reflecting a comfortable relevance to the values and aspirations of most American communities .

As one library administrator remarked recently,

For over one hundred years, public library funding was a consensus decision made by public officials. The message was clear:
Libraries—no matter how large or small—must be supported.
Taxpayers willingly financed library services. . . . Then, along
came the 1970s. . . . Suddenly, libraries didn't appear quite so
high on the priority list as public works projects, governmental
infrastructures, water and sewer facilities, streets, or public
safety. Once regarded as an essential service and birthright for
every American . . . libraries were forced into budget-cutting
positions.[12]

The response of the library profession to this undeniable crisis
was essentially defensive, at least initially. The mid-1970s ushered in
a virtual obsession in the library profession with cost-accountability,
cost-benefit analyses of services formerly deemed essential, market
research, performance measurement, and back-to-basics redefinitions
of mission.

Professional management techniques are certainly useful to effective budget development and presentation; too often, they merely
masked a crisis of confidence. An institution that is largely the
embodiment of intangible values can be only diminished when a
material monetary standard is applied to every function, when only
that which is tangibly measurable is valued. Planning, managerial, and
political skills will be essential to the development of effective funding
strategies for the 1990s; but they are not enough. It was not so much
such skills, as it was the ideals of visionary founders and early cham-
pions, which launched the library movement. It is not libraries that
have fallen out of favor in America, it is the larger public sector itself.
Small comfort, this, but we can ill afford a flawed analysis of our crisis.

Reacting to the Explosive 60s

A skeptical attitude toward the public sector and a distrust of government have long been latent in American society. The reactionary
swing in the national consciousness, reflected in the political balance
of power, began as a corrective to excesses of the explosive 1960s.
Traumatic national frustration with the debacle of military failures in

Southeast Asia soon led to anger and distrust toward government, as did the scandals associated with the Watergate incident. Simultaneous disenchantment with the great expense yet minuscule apparent success of governmental efforts to create an ideal "great society" virtually free of poverty or injustice unleashed a backlash that has not yet abated. The 1980s continued to witness the triumph of political campaigns based on promises to do less, to dismantle government, to enhance the private sector at the expense of the public.

Yet the 1980s also saw several stunning reaffirmations of popular belief in the importance of the public library, particularly in instances (such as bond issues) when the electorate could vote directly on library issues.[13] California was the scene of the most influential tax limitation referendum of the 1970s, the infamous Proposition 13, which sent a shock wave of retrenchment across the country. But, in 19888, the people of California approved a $75 million bond issue for library construction and renovation, and the citizens of both Los Angeles and San Francisco have voted over $100,000 million each for new central libraries.

Similar successes, by direct popular vote, have occurred in Detroit, Cleveland, Atlanta, Miami; extensive revitalization programs are underway in New York, Boston, Chicago, and Philadelphia. That very degree of separateness from the center of government, that uncertain status in the public sector, which so contributes to the fiscal instability of the public library serves also as a buffer in this era of antagonism toward government.

Strategies for public library funding in the 1990s must include legislative efforts to increase the ability of libraries to go directly to the public; creation of a national public library network; establishment of direct support for major research-level public library resources as a basic national responsibility; full federal funding of the depository library system; special state legislation incorporating equalization and compensation factors for urban public libraries serving multi-community metropolitan areas and population concentrations with high degrees of special needs.

But, more than all else, these strategies must be based on a reassertion of the fundamental relationship of the public library to the cultural, educational, civic, and economic health of the nation. Strategies based on a diminution of mission, on fees for access to information in any format, on the privatization of public responsibilities can only be counterproductive. E. J. Josey, in his 1984 presidential address to the American Library Association, urged that

> Librarians . . . need to integrate their goals with the goals of greatest importance to the American people. . . . We need to foster and to reaffirm the inseparable relationship between libraries and democratic liberties.[14]

That relationship, so confidently assumed for over a century, helped shape the noblest goals of the public library movement; reasserted, it offers the best hope for revitalization of the public library—and of the humanistic values it represents—in the 1990s and well beyond.

References

1. Getz, Malcolm. *Public Libraries: An Economic View.* Johns Hopkins, 1980, p.3.
2. Ames, Fisher. *Work.* Little, 1954, Vol. 2 p. 440.
3. Shera, Jesse H. *Foundations of the Public Library.* Univ. of Chicago Pr., 1949, p. 205.
4. Ditzion, Sidney H. *Arsenals of Democratic Culture: A Social History of the American Public Library Movement in New England and the Middle States from 1850 to 1900.* American Library Assn., 1957, p. 51.
5. Commonwealth of Massachusetts, Statutes . . ., 1848, Chapter 52.
6. Whitehill, Walter Muir. *Boston Public Library: Centennial History.* Harvard Univ. Pr., 1956, p. 22.
7. *Ibid.,* p. 21.
8. Boston Public Library. Report of the Trustees of the Public Library of the City of Boston, July 1852. Boston: City Document 37, 1852.
9. Getz, p. 3.
10. Robbins-Carter, J. *Public Librarianship.* Libraries Unlimited, 1982, p. 329.
11. Wedgeworth, R., "Prospects for and Effecting Change in the Public Library," *Library Quarterly,* Oct. 1978, p. 534.

12. Walters, Suzanne, "Funding Strategies for Survival." *The Bottom Line,* 1987, p. 4.
13. Turock, Betty, "A Fiscal Agenda for the 1990s." *The Bottom Line,* 1988, p. 3.
14. Josey, E.J. *Libraries, Coalitions, and the Public Good.* Neal-Schuman, 1987, p. 2.

WHAT DO OUR "SENIOR CITIZENS" WANT FROM PUBLIC LIBRARIES?

Bryce Allen and Margaret Ann Wilkinson

In the spring of 1987, an in-depth study of services offered to seniors by eight public libraries of different sizes in southwestern Ontario (Wilkinson and Allen, 1988), coupled with a number of articles in the library literature, raised three major issues needing further investigation. All of these related to the marketing of public library services to seniors.

The first was market segment definition. Following Kotler and Andreasen's (1987) customer-centered view of marketing, it was deemed essential to identify the market segment (or segments) towards whom public library services might be directed. The second issue was the viability of various approaches to service development. Following Kotler and Andreasen, once again we wanted to determine

"What Do Our 'Senior Citizens' Want From Public Libraries?" by Bryce Allen and Margaret Ann Wilkinson in *Canadian Library Journal.* Vol. 47, no. 2 (April 1990), pp. 105-110; reprinted with permission from the Canadian Library Association and *Canadian Library Journal,* copyright © 1990 *Canadian Library Journal.*

The support of the Government of Ontario through the Ministry of Culture and Communications in gratefully acknowledged. This project was conceived and directed by E. S. Beacock, Adjunct Professor at the School of Library and Information Science, University of Western Ontario.

This article deals with only some of the responses to questions in the instrument; for further details see "What are Users' Views on Seniors in the Public Library?" by Margaret Ann Wilkinson and Bryce Allen in *Library and Information Science Research.* Vol. 13, no. 2 (April, June 1991).

if mass-marketed services, product-differentiated services or targeted services were most likely to be supported by the library user community. Finally, there was the issue of promotion—to determine the level of existing support in the public library community for services to seniors, and how libraries might successfully promote these services.

Method

A short questionnaire was designed and distributed to library users in two Ontario public libraries, chosen because they represented different sizes of library with different service constraints. Several of the survey questions were designed to provide data that could be compared with the important research of Bewley and Crooks (1984).

The first site was a large, urban, multi-branch library system. The second was a library with a central main library serving a small city. Both systems offered a number of programs and services to seniors. Librarians at both locations expressed interest in gathering data on the questions we were investigating and agreed to have their library staff distribute the survey questionnaire to library users. A total of 500 questionnaires was distributed to users by library staff, the number of questionnaires available for distribution at each service point being proportional to the annual circulation from that service point. A total of 345 questionnaires were completed and returned, for a response rate of 69 per cent. There were no major differences between responses from the two test libraries.

Market Segment Definition

Without a well-defined target market, it is difficult to plan specialized services. Both Turock (1982) and Casey (1984) emphasize the importance of community needs analyses and planning of specialized services to meet the needs of special groups of users. Our (1987) study of library services to seniors found little planning for programs and services to seniors. This finding is entirely consistent with the absence of a definition of target market segments.

The survey questionnaire investigated the seniors market in two ways. First, library users were asked to define the population segment they would describe as seniors. The same users were then asked whether they would choose to attend library programs for seniors. The differences between the responses was interesting.

When I'm Sixty-Four?

Figure 1 presents the opinions of library users, in response to Question 1, as to the age at which one becomes a senior citizen. Clearly the most popular response was 65, with 40 per cent of the respondents specifying this age. Of those people who did not choose age 65, 32 per cent specified a younger age, while 28 per cent specified an older age. The

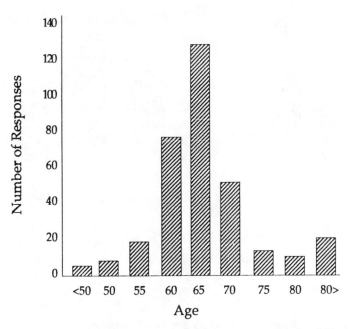

Figure 1. At What Age Does a Person Become a Senior Citizen?

responses to this question did not differ significantly between age groups. People in the older age groups defined "senior" in much the same way as younger library users. This was the first hint that library users under 65 years of age might be considered part of the target market for services to seniors.

Figure 2 presents the proportion of various age groups who said they would probably or definitely attend programs designed specifically for seniors. As expected, younger library users (those under age 55) were considerably less interested in attending seniors' programs. But note the dramatic difference in responses between those people under 55 and those over 55. While we tend to think of 65 as the age at which one becomes a senior citizen, the fact that more than half the respondents over the age of 55 selected themselves for specialized

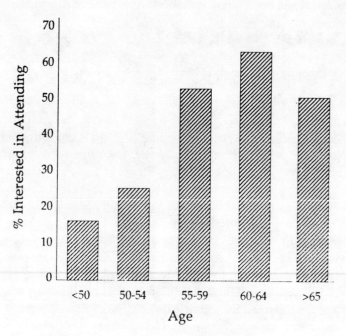

Figure 2. Interest in Attending Seniors' Programs

library activities indicates that libraries could benefit by targeting the over-55 group for services to seniors.

Further analysis of the responses to question 9 of the survey showed that a significant number of those in the 55-and over age group define "senior citizen" as beginning at an age younger than 65. This group of younger seniors may form an important part of the market for library services to seniors.

In one of the communities studied, librarians identified people taking early retirement as one of the growing markets for services to seniors. It seems likely that these professionals recognized a pattern of self-selection for seniors programs, which this research seems to support. Perhaps it is a pattern that should be recognized by the Ontario government. In a 1986 publication entitled: *A New Agenda: Health and Social Service Strategies for Ontario's Seniors,* the younger elderly are defined as those between 65-74 years of age. When considering public library services, however, perhaps this should be revised downward to 55.

Service Development Issues

Following standard marketing theory (Kotler and Andreasen, 1987; Weingand, 1987), it would seem there are three options libraries can choose in developing services for seniors. The first is the *mass market* approach, in which general services are developed for all library patrons. Seniors may, of course, participate in these programs and services if they wish, but no attempt is made to meet their special needs, or those of any other market segment. The second is *product differentiation.* Here, different programs and services are designed to meet the different needs of market groups, but all programs and services remain open to all library patrons. With this approach, a library might design a young adult film program, and a seniors' program on retirement financing, but patrons of any age could attend both of the programs if they wished. The third possible approach is called *targeted* service development. Here, services are offered only to certain groups. A library might for example, develop a program that only seniors could attend, or offer a special service (for example, a no-fine policy) to seniors only.

The libraries we studied tended towards *mass market* or *product differentiated* services, with little attempt to develop targeted programs and services. This approach appears to be fairly common in library service development. Nautrail (1982) found, in her thesis research, that librarians tended to support the general principles of offering specialized services for seniors, as enunciated in the ALA Guidelines, but in practice found a number of practical objections to implementing such services.

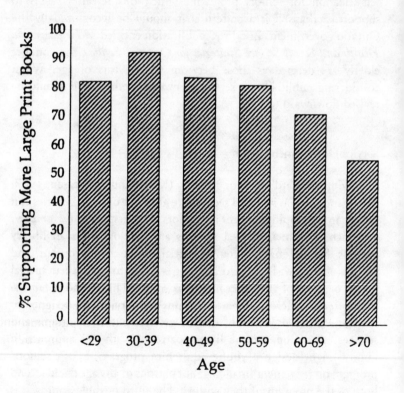

Figure 3. Proportion of Users Supporting Services to Seniors

Product Differentiated Approach

The survey questionnaire attempted to identify the level of support in the library user community for different approaches to service development for seniors. First, our questionnaire asked users whether the library should have more large-print books for seniors to read. This service is a typical product-differentiated service, as large-print books, can be used by many patrons as well as by seniors.

A high level of support for such services was found: 80 per cent of respondents indicated they felt that more large-print books were needed in the library's collection. Interestingly, support for large-print book collections for seniors decreased with age, as illustrated in Figure 3; the 30-39 age group exhibited the highest proportion of respondents who agreed or strongly agreed that the library should acquire more large-print books.

Targeted Approach

To establish the extent of support among library users for services targeted expressly for seniors, our questionnaire asked whether the library should establish programs for seniors that only seniors could attend. There was considerably less support among library users for services targeted specifically for seniors. Only 47 per cent of respondents agreed or strongly agreed with offering targeted programs, as compared with the 80 per cent who supported more large-print books for seniors.

This lower level of support was evident in responses from all age groups—older library users appear to be as ambivalent about targeted services as younger users. However, it is worth noting that despite this apparent ambivalence, half of those over the age of 55 indicated in their response to Question 9 that they would attend targeted programs. One other question addressed the issue of targeted services for seniors: the question about the categories of users who should be able to use the library's home-book delivery service. Only 6.4% of respondents felt that this service should be available only to seniors. Clearly, the preference of respondents was for considering home-book delivery a product-differentiated service.

The conclusions that can be drawn from these results about service development for seniors are clear. It would seem that public library patrons favor a differentiated-products approach, in which specialized services are made available for seniors, but in a nonrestrictive manner. There is less support for targeted services, although many seniors are interested in making use of targeted programs and services.

The fact that younger library users support large-print collections more than the seniors themselves is probably due to stereotyping. Younger patrons may perceive older patrons as requiring large-print materials because of visual handicaps. Older patrons know that this stereotype is unrealistic, and that all seniors do not necessarily have visual handicaps. A recent survey found that only 33 per cent of seniors actually make use of large-print materials (Lawlor, 1988). Librarians should be wary of incorporating stereotypes of this sort when they develop services for seniors.

Promotion of Library Services to Seniors

The questionnaire responses discussed above show that there is a great deal of support among library patrons for services to seniors. But it was important to qualify this support. One way to find out whether support was weak or strong was to determine if patrons would be willing to give up other services in order to provide additional services for seniors.

Our questionnaire asked specifically whether more emphasis should be placed on services to seniors than on services to children. Only 13 per cent of respondents agreed or strongly agreed with this proposition. Again, there was no significant difference between age groups in the responses to this question. This indicates that when hard decisions have to be made, the support for library services to seniors among the library user community may not be very strong. It follows that one of the tasks of promotion of library services to seniors is to strengthen the support among the library user community for provision of services to seniors.

Tabulated Responses to Survey Questionnaire

1. In your opinion, at what age does a person become a senior citizen?

Response	Number	Percent
Less than 50 years of age	5	1.6
50	7	2.2
55	17	5.3
60	75	23.6
65	125	39.3
70	49	15.4
75	12	3.8
80	9	2.8
More than 80 years of age	19	6.0

2. The library should provide more large-print books for seniors to read.

Response	Number	Percent
Strongly Disagree	5	1.6
Disagree	6	1.8
Uncertain	56	16.7
Agree	182	54.2
Strongly Agree	87	25.9

3. The library should have activities (such as films or talks) designed for seniors which only seniors may attend.

Response	Number	Percent
Strongly Disagree	17	5.1
Disagree	95	28.4
Uncertain	65	19.4
Agree	130	33.8
Strongly Agree	28	8.4

4. More emphasis should be placed in this library on services to senior citizens than on services to children.

Response	Number	Percent
Strongly Disagree	43	13.1
Disagree	185	56.4
Uncertain	55	16.8
Agree	36	11.0
Strongly Agree	9	9.0

5. Have you used, or do you know someone who has used the home book delivery service?

Response	Number	Percent
Yes	45	13.3
No	294	86.7

6. What group of people do you think should be able to use the home book delivery service (please check only one box).

Response	Number	Percent
Anyone at all	27	9.1
Anyone confined to home	250	84.5
Senior citizens	3	1.0
Senior citizens confined to home	16	5.4

7. How many library activities (such as films or talks) have you attended in the past six months? If you can't remember the exact number, give an estimate. The number of activities attended is _____ .

Mean	Standard Deviation	Minimum	Maximum
2.6	8.2	0.	90.0

8. Where would you be most likely to find out about such activities?

Response	Number	Percent
Notices in the Library	153	57.5
Newspaper columns	42	5.3
Newspaper advertisement	31	11.7
Radio or TV advertisements	14	5.3
Cable TV	13	4.8
Word of mouth	11	4.1
Other	2	0.8

9. If the library were to offer special activities (such as films or talks) designed for seniors, which only seniors could attend, would you be interested in attending these activities?

Response	Number	Percent
Definitely Not	36	11.5
Probably Not	90	28.7
Uncertain	65	20.7
Probably	91	29.0
Definitely	32	10.2

10. How old are you?

Response	Number	Percent
Under 20	14	4.2
20-29	32	9.7
30-39	49	14.8
40-49	50	15.2
50-54	21	6.4
55-59	27	8.2
60-64	45	13.6
65-69	40	12.1
70-74	25	7.6
75-79	17	5.2
80 or over	10	3.0

It was also important to ascertain the effectiveness of existing library services promotion to seniors. One measure of effectiveness is the number of library programs attended by various age groups. When asked to estimate the number of programs attended in the past six months, all age groups responded with similar numbers. Apparently there are no age differences in library program attendance in these libraries. This result indicates that existing promotional activities for seniors' programs may not be totally effective.

In determining whether different means of advertising and promotion were more successful than others in reaching different age groups (Question 8) we found no age-related difference in the effectiveness of various kinds of advertising generally used for library programs. Older library users were as well informed as younger users about the availability of various services and apparently used the same means of learning about programs and services as did younger users. The result indicates that the libraries surveyed might consider matching their means of advertising and promotion with their market segments to increase users' awareness of services. This means, for example, adopting specialized ways of letting seniors know about the programs and services available for them.

Conclusions

The results of this market research survey shed new light on the provision of specialized library service for senior citizens. When asked to indicate their level of interest in attending programs that were specifically designed for seniors, and that only seniors could attend, a large number of respondents in the 55-65 age group said they would probably or definitely attend. Thus, the target market for library programs and services for seniors could be identified as those users 55 years of age and over, and particularly those individuals in the 55-65 age group who think of seniors as being younger than 65.

In the region studied, 1986 census figures show that 12 per cent of the population were aged 65 and over, and 22 per cent were aged 55 and over. Identifying the target market for services to seniors as those aged 55 and over, instead of as those aged 65 and over, nearly doubles the size of the market. Inclusion of these younger seniors in the market for library programs and services also means a greater variety of levels of activity and of interest in the market. Librarians will have the task of planning, implementing and evaluating services that meet a broader range of interests and needs.

There appears to be widespread support for specialized public library services that, traditionally, have been offered to seniors; provision of such services appears to be a priority not only for seniors themselves, but also for younger adults. This support from the existing user community may encourage librarians to develop additional services for seniors. Mobilizing support from all age groups may encourage greater levels of funding for specialized programs for seniors.

Librarians should also be aware that the users surveyed were ambivalent about services targeted expressly for seniors. However, although opinion was evenly divided on this issue when it was posed as a theoretical question, over half of all respondents over 55 years of age indicated an interest in attending such programs. This is additional evidence of the strength of the market for public library services to seniors.

In terms of promotion, it is appropriate for library workers to build upon this strong market, and strong base of public support, and to present library programs and services for seniors in such a way as to enhance the participation of seniors in these services. Active promotion seems to be called for to inform seniors of the potential that library services hold for them.

Library workers need to take the initiative in planning, establishing, and evaluating programs to meet the special needs of this large user group. Individual libraries are in a position to survey their own user community, and to design the programs that will meet the particular informational, recreational and cultural needs of their senior population.

References

American Library Association. Reference and Adult Services Divisions. "The library's responsibility to the aging." *RQ* 21 (Fall 1981): 27.

Dewley, L. M., and Crooks, S. L. *Urban Public Library Service for the Aging in Canada.* Dalhousie University Libraries and Dalhousie University School of Library Service, Occasional Papers, no. 34. Halifax, Nova Scotia: Dalhousie School of Library Service, 1984.

Casey, Genevieve M. *Library Services for the Aging.* Hamden, CT: Shoe String Press, 1984.

Kotler, Philip, and Andreasen, Alan R. *Strategic Marketing for Nonprofit Organizations.* Englewood Cliffs, NJ: PrenticeHall, 1987.

Lawlor, Patty. "1,100 Seniors Speak Up on Library Service." *Especially for Seniors* (Winter, 1988): p. 1

Nauratil, Marcia J. *An Investigation into the Congruence/Incongruence between Espoused Theory and Theory-in-Use Relating to Public Library Service to Older Adults in Ontario and New York.* Ph.D. dissertation. University of Toronto, 1982. (For a readable summary of this research, see Nauratil, Marcia J. "Serving seniors: commitment or cop-out?" *Canadian Library Journal* 43 (August 1986): p. 265-266.)

Turock, Betty J. *Serving the Older Adult: a Guide to Library Programs and Information Sources.* New York: Bowker, 1982.

Weingand, Darlene E. *Marketing/Planning Library and Information Sources.* Littleton, CO: Libraries Unlimited, 1987.

Wilkinson, Margaret Ann, and Allen, Bryce. *Report on Public Library Service to Seniors in Southwestern Ontario.* (May, 1988). Available from the School of Library and Information Science, University of Western Ontario.

IMPLICATIONS OF TYING STATE AID TO PERFORMANCE MEASURES

Charles Curran and Philip M. Clark

This article is based substantially upon a presentation made by the
authors at the 1989 Spring Conference of the New Jersey Library
Association in Atlantic City. In his letter of invitation, Daniel
O'Connor of the Rutgers School of Communication, Information
and Library Studies stated a dilemma that he and the members of the
New Jersey Library Development Committee wanted us to address:

> Performance measures are considered by some as a valuable
> yardstick useful in evaluating a library and *appropriate for deter-*
> *mining funding levels* [emphasis ours]. Others, however, consider
> performance measures as indicators of the educational and
> economic status of the community being served [and, therefore,
> *inappropriate* determinants for funding levels].

Our purposes in addressing the topic of tying state aid to performance measures are, first, to acknowledge that deriving *any* formula
for the award of aid is a complex and difficult process; second, to
observe that deriving some formula or basis for the award of aid is an
inescapable requirement; and third, to suggest that those who attempt
to wrestle with this complex and difficult requirement may want to
consider the twenty statements, assertions, and questions that we offer.

"Implications of Tying State Aid to Performance Measures," by Charles
Curran and Philip M. Clark in *Public Libraries*. Vol. 28, no. 6 (November/De-
cember 1989), pp. 348-354; reprinted with permission from the American
Library Association, copyright © 1990 by ALA.

Readers will no doubt have additional questions about this volatile issue. We welcome comments and challenges, for we do not believe that a solution, or solutions, to the problem we identify and address here will emerge from dispassionate discussion and nonconfrontational dialogue, nor do we believe that our twenty statements are the last words on the issue.

Our purpose is to suggest a framework for considering solutions and to list some ideas worth exploring by decision makers.

The Twenty Statements

1. The legacy of Standards invites specious comparisons.

The lure of the *Standards* is powerful. While the standardization of record keeping has escaped our mastery, we have always managed to tell our story by reporting *statistics* of one kind or another. Reinforcement comes from supervisory agencies that require such reports and from funding agencies that demand simple, understandable statements of accountability from the agencies they fund. When reports are kept simple it is easy to see that 10 is greater than 5, and when deftly articulated, such reports can assert that not only is 10 greater than 5, it is *100 percent greater!* Big is good; bigger is better.

The same logic that attends this kind of interpretation of the *Standards* is currently being used by some interpreters of *Output Measures* (referred to here as OM).[1] The legacy of *Standards* tempts us to gather some easy-to-obtain numbers and compare results with those achieved by other librarians in like or even unlike environments. We then pronounce some "norm" and anoint it with the oil of legitimacy, goodness, or excellence. We even fund each other on the basis of how closely we achieve one of the norms, in spite of the fact that at least one of the authors of *OM,* Charles R. McClure, discourages such decisions, especially in those organizations that lack the capabilities for gathering the data required to establish reasonable norms.[2] On this point, we invite you to check out Statement 10 and examine the comments made by another *OM* author.

There is mounting evidence that comparisons drawn between libraries serving communities with differing socio-economic conditions (SEC) are unfair and out of focus.

2. Performance Measures tested whether a library could deliver what is advertised.

The Performance Measures spearheaded by Ernest R. DeProspo, Jr., and associates[3] constituted a major departure from the idea of comparing progress toward standards in that they focused, not upon inputs, as most of the *Standards* had, but upon outputs—actual performances by librarians and libraries.

The major intent was to ask and answer the following question: Can a library deliver what it advertises? For example, a catalog is a record of holdings. Its message to clients is that the library owns a listed item. It is also an implied invitation, a promise. It offers a contract to serve what clients pursue when they search for wanted items, a contract which is fulfilled when a patron checks an item out or uses it in the library. Periodical indexes offer the same promise.

By providing the procedure for identifying and searching for items the library claimed to own, Performance Measures enabled librarians to determine how often they could deliver what they said they could.

3. Output Measures test whether a library can deliver what individuals say they want.

Differences between Performance Measures (PM) and *Output Measures* (OM) designed by Van House, Lynch, McClure, Zweizig, and Rodger are substantial. OM asks related but quite different question. Their main thrust, at least insofar as materials availability is concerned, is to determine how often a library can deliver what *patrons* say they want.

In that Performance Measure and Output Measures both look at how librarians and libraries perform, they are similar, but the questions they ask are fundamentally different. PM tested the ability to deliver owned items; OM test the ability to deliver patron-requested items. What *drives* patrons to ask, or not ask, may be a function of socioeconomic conditions, not library policies. Could it be, therefore, that OM measure *community* performance and not library performance? Should we tie state aid to measures that measure the community rather than the library? No one should attempt an answer to this question before investigating relationships between libraries and SEC, and a good place to start such an inquiry would be with Seavey's excellent article, which examines associations between social forces and public library development.[4]

4. Individual characteristics greatly determine what individuals say they want.

If what drives use is "out there," then what can librarians do in their libraries to influence that use? Community-analysis advocates have urged librarians to get out from behind their desks and into the community where they can spread the word, establish connections between their wares and the life of the community, and be observed in the process of doing so. That might chip away some at the nonuser corps, and maybe even bolster demand among users. If, however, SEC drive use, then librarians' efforts to influence use may yield limited results.

What librarians do *in* their libraries to train their staffs, to build and develop collections, to provide comfortable surroundings, to offer programs, to construct attractive displays, and to publicly relate— even markets (which are *out-of-house* as well as in-house activities) may have positive effects among user elites. These activities may have far less, even no, effect upon nonusers. Nonusers are nonusers for personal reasons and for factors associated with socioeconomic conditions—factors beyond the ability of the librarian to influence greatly. There is something intuitively attractive about the notion that if people knew what libraries had to offer, they would flock to those libraries. The fact is that many nonusers, including those who are heavy users of information, know all about the library and prefer to avoid it. Some of our intuitively derived ideas about doing good can misdirect us.

For users, the right information for the right person at the right time may be the right way to go after all. This "right information" does not appear by accident, nor is timely communication achieved through random behavior. The decisions librarians make, in the libraries about the communities, will determine whether information, person and time are "right."

Perhaps the very best we can do in public libraries is to make sure that we have as much as possible of what users want and use. Our ability to influence use may be severely constrained by socioeconomic conditions. Questions raised by D'Elia prompt us to ask whether promotion should be limited largely to practice with users, whose awareness of library programs may be associated with frequency and type of use.[5]

5. Collected individual characteristics of a community are more important determinants of demand than what librarians do in libraries.

Knowing that forces "out there" influence library use more than activities we instigate "in here" may discourage some of us. It should not and it must not. Though we are constrained by reality, we are not paralyzed by it. Nor are we forgiven the responsibility to render an account of our use of resources. We are still required to demonstrate and report our accountability.

Out there in the community there are a tax base, a spirit, attitudes toward learning, and cadres of competitors for the attention of potential users of libraries. There are politics, cultural backgrounds, degrees of affluence, and a combination of access and proximity factors. From these and other ingredients the stew is brewed and the nourishment (tax support) for the library derived. The fact that most of these factors are beyond the ability of the librarian to influence prompts two observations:

- Librarians have to work very hard at changing those factors that can be changed.

- Funding decisions should not penalize librarians and libraries in resource-poor communities.

6. Accountability is best determined by measuring the present self against the past self and by planning to target performance for a future self.

If use is primarily a function of socioeconomic conditions, should librarians be penalized for poor use or rewarded for heavy use where, in both cases, use is characteristic driven, not librarian driven? Funding should not be tied to luck or misfortune. Funding formulas should reward resourceful, responsive librarianship, and funding should be granted on the basis of how well librarians employ the resources they have.

Here the PLA Planning Process model makes its most significant contribution. It "forces" the library staff:

- To make the effort to understand the environment;

- To carve out missions and roles consistent with agreed-upon obligations;

- To establish appropriate goals and accomplishable objectives—objectives that are outcome-related, observable and time-specific;

- To execute those objectives;

- To evaluate performance on the basis of how closely the declared intentions (objectives) have been met;

- To report progress to funders, trustees, and anybody else who wants to know.

Documenting how well the library meets the goals and objectives that the library staff has set is a truer measure of accountability than comparing its collections or turnover with those of another library serving a poorer or richer, but certainly different, community.

In the effort to protect the poor community from even further economic discrimination, decision makers must not rush to adopt measures that penalize the wealthier communities for being wealthier. Rewarding the organization for achievement that is based upon progress toward realistic goals set by the staff may avoid some problems in this area.

7. "Norms" bear a striking resemblance to the old Standards.

The urge to compare may be primal. Anthropologists might observe that humans are and have always been comparing animals. In acting out our primal drives we may get a little sloppy about what is comparable. Our affection for norms is evidence of this, and even when we are counseled by wise people that the norms we identify are suspect, we press on.

One of the authors of OM, Charles McClure, addressed this issue in a letter to a state library agency director.[6] McClure pointed out that using OM for standards was never the intention of their creators (in spite of that annoying reference to "comparable" measures in Statement 10). He insisted that OM should be used "as Self-Diagnostics," and he went on to point out that in a state with a variety of library sizes and resources, the chances for uniform collecting and reporting of data are slim indeed, thus rendering any "norms" that result extremely suspect. He insisted that "using output measures as a basis for standards and comparison is misleading at best, and down-right erroneous at worst."

The numbers that are derived from OM can and should be used as input for managerial decisions about collection development, staff training, and library services. They should not be used to establish standards or norms; and until the methodologies for collection and interpretation are improved, they should not be used as bases for awarding state aid to public libraries.

8. Planning is not a process; it is a one-shot, do-it-and-get-it-over-with event.

This is a totally unwelcome and heretical notion in planning circles. It is the very antithesis of planning. No textbook on planning will proffer this definition. Yet in the realm of practice, librarians may view the obligation to undertake a multistage planning process as an imposition. Planning advocates, especially those in statewide leadership roles, face a formidable challenge: convince busy practitioners that the time spent on planning processes is well worth the expenditure.

Long-range planning is especially vulnerable because it competes head-on with the many routines of library practice. As long-range planning grinds on, fatigue can set in among workers, who see the light at the end of the tunnel getting no closer, the planning procedures stretching out indefinitely, and the ever-present routines beckoning.

Anxious about some of the everyday tasks that seem to be getting shortchanged, staff members may begin to view each of the planning steps as discreet, independent procedures to be performed in sequence and without reference to antecedent or subsequent steps. Data gathered during the important *looking around* stage may be ignored when the planners turn from that to *role setting*. The essential thread is lost in such cases. And so in practice, the planning effort can become a one-shot event instead of the process planners preach about.

One way to avoid this is to deliberately build into the planning effort a series of very short-range objectives to be completed quickly enough to provide encouragement to participants. These little victories can be savored and enjoyed, can provide immediate feedback to busy staff that their efforts are paying off, and can lessen the fatigue that sometimes grips planners. Delaying staff gratification endangers commitment; providing it in doses sustains the planning effort.

9. Searching for the perfect decision leads to frustration.

Planning does not yield a perfect decision; it provides *intelligence* for the *design of satisfactory decisions*. Planning processes enable managers to add systematically acquired data to that which they have gathered and stored through intuitive and impressionistic means.

Planning will not guarantee success; what it guarantees is that librarians who invest in it will get:

- A clearer picture of what business they are in;
- Reliable data on who is using the library and why;
- Useful data on how well the library is able to respond to expressed need;
- Specific indications of where staff training is required; and, most important of all,
- An accurate record of the achievement of goals and objectives.

Managers who understand what the planning process can yield may benefit from the enormous investment of resources required for its completion. Managers who do not understand the possibilities and limitations inherent in the planning process may have their expectations dashed and will only acquire another "I told you it wouldn't work" to add to their arsenals of statements about lame theories.

10. The actors should write the script for this play.

State library agencies, library associations, librarians, funders, maybe clients, and perhaps even the authors of OM—all with their own agendas and definitions of roles—are going to have to come to some understanding about what the measures measure, which measures to use and what to measure, and how to translate results into equitable formulas.

The suggestion that funding be tied to OM has divided the interested parties into several camps. One is the advocate camp. Members of this group see tying aid to performance as a natural outgrowth of disaffection with *Standards,* and they believe in the OM as indicators of comparable performance.

A second camp opposes OM-derived funding, contending that the kinds of performances that the OM record bear a direct relationship to the socioeconomic characteristics of the community—that what the community demands of its library is determined by those characteristics and not affected by what librarians do in libraries. This camp is sustained by the findings of researchers like Kim and Shin, who observed that:

> a library which is unable to generate increased usage is locked into the unfavorable, self-perpetuating cycle of resource disparities. Thus, what might be called [the] "Matthew effect" seems to be operating: the rich get more and more; the poor get less and less.[7]

This camp also points to the findings of D'Elia who, based upon his analysis of materials availability rates, concludes that "data obtained from surveys of *Output Measures for Public Libraries* are apparently useless indicators of library performance."[8]

Why tie funding to useless indicators? protests this camp.

A third camp is composed of the creators of the *Planning and Role Setting*[9] and *Output Measures* manuals. It is they who have spearheaded the use of the manuals and who have been called upon on numerous occasions to teach, consult, and interpret. While they are hardly responsible for all the meanings and uses that have evolved, they must own their published statements. Consumers who read in the OM manual that its purpose "is to define a basic set of output measures for libraries that are . . . relatively easy to use, [and] . . . comparable across libraries"[10] may ask themselves the question, Does this mean the *Return of the Standards!?*

A fourth camp doesn't know it is a camp. It is composed of librarians who have until recently heard no side or only one side of the issue and now find themselves confused about the arguments. They constitute the majority. They must determine what the questions are.

Perhaps clients also are not aware that they are a camp. Without knowing it, they are the ones who stand to gain or suffer from decisions made about OM and funding. Someone needs to inform them, too.

Then there are the library associations, some already on record as supporting the use of OM, others beginning to ask questions in the face of growing interest in tying OM to funding.

This is a classic conflict situation—the clash of advocates, some of whose goals are, or are perceived to be, mutually exclusive. The catechisms of conflict management assert that a necessary precondition for conflict resolution is the belief that all parties are displaying accurate representations of their respectively held positions and that each is interested in a just resolution.

This is a tall order.

The camps are organizing and they are not unarmed. Later in this paper, readers will encounter a suggestion that an expectancy quotient, derived from socioeconomic conditions and sensitive to differences among communities, may help us resolve the problem of the elusive *yardstick* that has until now escaped capture.

In the statements that follow, we attempt to address directly the question, How do you draw fair comparisons among libraries that have greatly varying resources and clienteles? This gets to the heart of the dilemma posed to us. We feel that what is called for is some understandable method whereby the rich, well-educated, motivated communities can be compared to the poor, poorly educated, unmotivated communities. The term *equalization* has often been used to describe this approach; we prefer the term *equitable comparison*.

The following propositions attempt to define performance, restate the emphasis of input and output measures, briefly suggest factors that influence use, propose a model for equitable comparison called the "expectancy quotient," and conclude that we must have minimum levels of acceptable professional practice as well as models of excellent professional practice to emulate.

11. Performance is the result of making the most of what you have.

The sports world has a wealth of behavioral models that chart a course for high performance. The definition of performance chosen here is a "sportsmanship" model that posits, "It's not who wins but how you play the game." Its opposite, the Lombardi/Patton model, "Win at any cost," seems inappropriate within the context of the dilemma we are exploring.

The concept of trying hard, of giving one's best effort, fits within the planning approach that stresses setting local goals and measuring progress toward attainment of those goals. Winning, on the other hand, suggests a competitive contest in which libraries vie for bragging rights as to who is best.

12. All resource measures are economically biased (even when standardized as in per capita measures).

Input measures (i.e., resource measures such as books owned and purchased, subscriptions, staff levels) are money driven. The more money one has, the more one can acquire. Even when one indexes the numbers in per capita computations, the effect of sheer money availability is overwhelming.

State aid base grant programs that call for minimum levels of effort (one book owned per capita, a professional for every 10,000 people) is our traditional way of getting communities to shell out money for libraries. It is hardly an equitable process because of the great disparities among communities in terms of real wealth.

13. Availability, as a concept, is an integral part of performance measures.

Moving from a consideration of input measures (above) to the output or effects measures that are the much-discussed topic of today, we need to step back and consider again why we are so interested in this topic. Supposedly it is because output measures are user oriented and imply, if not demonstrate, the impact of service on individuals. That is rather difficult to discern in a statement like "My CPC is up 23 percent over last year!" or "Charlie didn't make his goal of having a turnover rate of 7 this year."

Somehow, the user orientation is getting lost in our discussions of output measures. The authors continue to favor the imperative that is implicit in the old *Performance Measures for Public Libraries*.[11] which considered the availability of materials, facilities, and staff. The focus was on the probabilities that such services were available to be used, and the idea of testing whether a library could deliver what it advertised was stressed (see point 2 above).

We shouldn't abandon the concept of availability even if we disagree with some of the specific methods used to measure it (as many obviously did). Rather, we should try approaches such as the subject availability measure used at the Ocean County (New Jersey) Public Library. There they test whether or not the patron has a chance to get *some* material at *any* time on any topic they "advertise" as available to the public.

The latest edition of *Output Measures for Public Libraries* has three materials availability measures that supposedly mirror those used in the Performance Measures study: title, subject/author, and browser fill rate. But D'Elia's studies appear to have greatly weakened their credibility. It is time to bring credible availability measures back to the output measures process.

14. Librarians can affect how much a library is used.

And so can the library buildings, their locations, and the quality and quantity of the materials and services offered. If we don't feel we can make a difference, we should hand in our professional licenses.

But we are also conditioned by the communities in which we operate. Lange, in a recent article in *Public Library Quarterly*, points out that such factors as demographics, residential location, community involvement, personal value for the library, and library-related attitudes and behavior help to explain use and nonuse. D'Elia, Zweizig and Dervin, Clark and others have probed these influences as well.[12-15] This leads to the following conclusions.

15. Some people will never use any kind of library. Some people will never use certain types of libraries. For a given type of library and a given type of service, some will use it infrequently and lightly, others infrequently and heavily; some will use it frequently and lightly, others frequently and heavily; some will never use the library but have others use it for them—some lightly and some heavily.

The key question is whether or not we can begin to predict levels of expected use given certain demographic and lifestyle characteristics of communities. Are we not yet at the point where we can expect certain communities with populations that are high on factors that are associated with use to score higher on our use measures than communities with populations not having such characteristics? In other words, can we construct an expectancy quotient for a community—a set of numbers that indicate the maximum expected use after all influencing factors are accounted for?

To do so we must demonstrate and illustrate those factors that have major influences on our use scores. For example, Clark is currently exploring the area of the high-intensity, high-frequency borrower of material. After twelve weeks of observation, it is projected that the 0.3 percent of the patrons who borrow the most could account for 12.5 percent of the total circulation for the year in the library studied. This group of some 300 individuals out of 100,000 registered borrowers is averaging a borrowing rate of one book a day. Such use is probably highly predictable, but it raises other questions such as the hypothesis that the use is predictable but the influencing factors are not.

We should begin listing libraries for comparative purposes on factors that have some correlation to use. Population-size groupings, such as those used in the *Public Library Data Service Statistical Report '88*,[16] are *not* tied to use. We should instead list and group libraries based on community characteristics, such as the average years of school completed, that do have some relation to use.

16. Patron satisfaction is a multidimensional, multiintentional measure.

Most library goal statements contain some language about meeting patron needs. Attempts to measure the attainment of such goals through the use of patron satisfaction surveys are rife with measurement problems. Such surveys are usually spot checks that rarely probe the regular using public and rarer still the population at large. "Are you satisfied with the service you received?" may get a response that differs substantially from one given to the question, "Did you get what you wanted?"

Responses to questions about satisfaction with service are often also tied to the patron's perception of the use to which the survey will be put. We have observed that many patrons are loath to rate a library service as low even though they will write highly critical comments in a general comments section. Obviously, many patrons see surveys as potential devices for cutting services and respond in a way to obviate that possibility.

17. All libraries should be held accountable to perform at a certain level for their intended role with their intended audience.

This statement suggests that objectives that are set must be measurable and that a level of performance be established for those objectives. This reinforces our belief that the initial emphasis on performance measurement is local—that it should be measuring growth toward established goals and only secondarily measuring a library's rank in relation to other libraries.

But we cannot get away from some evaluation of what is and is not acceptable professional practice. Our argument is not with the concept of the norm but with the manner in which some norms are established. If we believe that one of the public library's roles is circulation ("God put us on this earth to circulate books!"—Marvin Scilkin), isn't there a lower limit that is unacceptable despite all the constraints of potential audience, money, proximity, and parking? We think so, but we also believe that the minimum level should be both flexible and objectively determined (i.e., not by the seat-of-the-pants hearsay that seems to have guided previous attempts to set standards).

State library agencies appear to be faced with an imperative from PLA and many public librarians: Local planning efforts should be encouraged and supported. But these agencies are faced with pressures to develop measures of goodness that apply statewide and that show what all libraries are doing. The incompatibility, real and perceived, of local and statewide plans appears to be at the very core of the dilemma confronting the agencies.

18. If there are minimum standards there also must be standards of excellence.

Too often we talk about minimum levels of attainment and less often about truly excellent programs or approaches to service. That is not to say that we do not have lots of assertions of excellence ("how I run my library good" arguments). Rather, we have few if any proven claims of effectiveness.

Altman and Clark, in a paper prepared for the Department of Education entitled *The National Diffusion Network, Its Potential for Libraries,* describe the kinds of rigorous methodologies typically required to establish a claim to effectiveness.[17] Unfortunately, no public library programs have been submitted that meet those criteria. We desperately need efforts in this direction. In fact, we are desperately in need of research that explores the details of use; its frequency, duration, diversity, and intensity.

19. A composite performance measure: The proportion of the community that has contact with the library on a regular basis.

The proportion of the community that has contact with the library on a regular basis is the type of performance measure that would incorporate many of the points we have made in this paper. The proportion of the community suggests that we can aim at something less than the whole. A reasonable proportion might be determined by the potential audience based on demographics and lifestyle characteristics. *Contact* suggests that there are a diversity of ways through which patrons can interact with the library. They can obtain materials, consult librarians by phone or in person, read informative materials prepared by library staff, attend programs, have books delivered to them at home, use copy machines, or accept any number of services.

Depending on the role(s) the library seeks to play, certain contacts will be emphasized over others. *Regular basis* incorporates a frequency measure and assumes that there are recurring needs on the part of patrons. All service agencies from libraries to prisons to restaurants rely on repeat use by individuals to meet their production quotas.

20. There is nothing inherently wrong with tying state aid to performance or in insisting that results be achieved with the money received. But . . .

Among the many caveats that are rightfully part of the issue of *tying state aid to performance measures* issue is the legitimate assertion that if librarians are to be held accountable, they should also be able to influence their destiny. There should be a fair chance at achieving the desired performance level with the resources at hand. Moreover, there should be a recognized audience that can generate the desired numbers given the best efforts of librarians.

As we have said earlier, the actors should write the script for this play, with full awareness of who the audience is and what they want from it.[18]

References and Notes

1. Nancy Van House and others, *Output Measures for Public Libraries: A Manual of Standardized Procedures,* 2nd ed. (Chicago: American Library Assn. 1987).
2. Charles R. McClure, personal communication with authors, 17 April, 1989.
3. Ernest R. DeProspo, Jr., Ellen Altman, and Kenneth Beasley, *Performance Measures for Public Libraries* (Chicago: American Library Assn., 1973).
4. Charles A. Seavey, "The Public Library in Society: The Relationship of Libraries and Socioeconomic Conditions," *Public Libraries* 28:47-54 (Jan./Feb. 1989.
5. George D'Elia, "The Development and Testing of a Conceptual Model of Public Library User Behavior," *Library Quarterly* 50: 410-38 (1980).
6. McClure, personal communication.
7. Chai Kim and Eui Hang Shin, "Sociodemographic Correlates of Inter-county Variations in the Public Library Output," *Journal of the American Society for Information Science* 27: 359-65 (November 1977). See in particular p. 365.
8. George D'Elia, "Materials Availability Fill Rates—Useful Measures of Library Performance," *Public Libraries* 24:106-10 (Fall 1985). See in particular p. 10.

9. Charles R. McClure and others, *Planning and Role Setting for Public Libraries: A Manual of Options and Procedures* (Chicago: American Library Assn., 1987).

10. Van House, *Output Measures,* p. xviii.

11. DeProspo, Jr., *Performance Measures.*

12. Janet M. Lange, "Public Library Users, Nonusers, and Type of Library Use," *Public Library Quarterly* 8, No.1-2: 49-67 (1987/88). See especially p. 58.

13. D'Elia, "The Development and Testing."

14. Douglas Zweizig and Brenda Dervin, "Public Library Use, Users, Uses," *Advances in Librarianship* 7: 231-55 (1977).

15. Philip Clark, "New Approaches to the Measurement of Public Library Use by Individual Patrons," University of Illinois *Occasional Papers* No. 162 (1983).

16. Public Library Data Service, *Statistical Report '88* (Chicago: Public Library Assn./American Library Assn., 1988).

17. Ellen Altman and Philip Clark, "The National Diffusion Network, Its Potential for Libraries," submitted as a White Paper for the U.S. Department of Education's project "Evaluating Federally Funded Library Programs," Spring 1989.

18. The authors deeply appreciate the efforts of Daniel O'Connor who articulated the dilemma that is the focus of this paper. He provided a great deal of basic information, clarification of complex issues, and encouragement. It was at his invitation that we had the opportunity to develop and present these twenty statements. James Benson was of great assistance in delineating the conceptual logic behind the "expectancy quotient." Elaine McConnell and James Wudski of the Ocean County (New Jersey) Public Library were most helpful in enabling us to clarify some of our preliminary thinking. Charles R. McClure generously shared valuable personal correspondence.

ETHICAL BACK TALK

Lillian N. Gerhardt

Code of Ethics

1) Librarians must provide the highest level of service through appropriate and usefully organized collections, fair and equitable circulation and service policies, and skillful, accurate, unbiased, and courteous responses to all requests for assistance.

2) Librarians must resist all efforts by groups or individuals to censor library materials.

3) Librarians must protect each user's right to privacy with respect to information sought or received, and materials consulted, borrowed, or acquired.

4) Librarians must adhere to the principles of due process and equality of opportunity in peer relationships and personnel actions.

5) Librarians must distinguish clearly in their actions and statements between their personal philosophies and attitudes and those of an institution or professional body.

6) Librarians must avoid situations in which personal interests might be served or financial benefits gained at the expense of library users, colleagues, or the employing institution. (*Adopted June 30, 1981, by ALA Membership and ALA Council.*)

Chewing on ALA's Code

Sloppy historians may be tempted in some distant age to label the 1990's "The Ethical Decade" because of the print and video record we leave in this, the first month of the first year of the last decade of the 20th century. The word "ethics" is on every newspaper's front page and on the lips of every newscaster. This ethical din arises from grand scale thievery by legislators and stock manipulators and all the many commissions created to scrutinize big money scandals. It really ignores the fact that ethics go far beyond monotonous, Gargantuan greed.

That ethics involve more than money is especially clear in the codes of ethics drawn up by each and every profession. These generally dwell on the duties and responsibilities that accompany the occupational role and call upon practitioners to police themselves in the scrupulous observance of the principles that sustain their calling.

We're too quiet about ethics in library service. The librarians' *Code of Ethics,* adopted in 1939 and last revised in 1981 by the American Library Association is far less well-known and much less fussed over than the Library Bill of Rights—and that's too bad, because each of the six points in the code deserves the renewal of commitment that results from continuous re-examination and debate. The code has some obvious gaps, too. And, strange as it may seem to *School Library Journal*'s readers, children's, young adult and school librarians are widely believed to be immune to, or above, the temptations implicit in each of the code's points, except those of No. 2.

Maybe the attribution of nearly immaculate virtue by the general public as well as our library colleagues accounts for the unusual and prolonged silence from our sector on those moments in the course of our working days when "the still small voice within" is moved to mutter over the points that do (or don't) exist in ALA's ethical code. Refusing a reputation for spotless behavior is very hard, but somebody should.

To break the silence and shake up codified complacency, SLJ's editorial page, every other month or so across 1990, will pounce on points in our ethics code with revealing stories and many questions about the "bold outrages and corrupt combinations" that boobytrap the ethical delivery of library services to the young. The series will begin in our February issue with point No. 1.

Ethical Back Talk I

1. Librarians must provide the highest level of service through appropriate and usefully organized collections, fair and equitable circulation and service policies, and skillful, accurate, unbiased, and courteous responses to all requests for assistance.

No matter which way you slice it, this first mildly worded statement of principle in the American Library Association's *Code of Ethics* is a stunner. The fact that it leads off—and has to be said at all—tells the world that our ranks can harbor the idiotically organized, circulation poker players and service delinquents as well as unskillful, inaccurate, prejudiced and rude practitioners poised to maltreat information supplicants.

Libraries in schools of any size, for any age level, are particularly vulnerable to the plague of bad practices suggested in point No. 1 because they are less likely to have any taxpayers bellowing or filing complaints. In school-based library collections for the young, embattled parents seldom appear to right service wrongs or to deflect the casual or calculated rudeness that many adults employ to separate themselves from, or to establish dominance over, children and young adults.

It's significant that "appropriate and usefully organized collections" is mentioned first because, despite invasions by computer database files and purchased cataloging, the way a library collection is stored and the access this permits to its holdings remains the librarian's chief professional secret. So, it follows that a collection badly arranged for its users' purposes becomes a matter of unethical practice—as in those K-3 elementary school libraries where the shelving goes far beyond the easy or safe reach of the tallest third grader. (A good talking point when dealing with any architects wedded to such design bizarreties as circular or maze shelving: "Alas. Your aesthetics conflict with my professional ethics.")

"Fair and equitable circulation and service policies" is an aspect of ethical library practice that merits more attention than it gets in youth services circles. I'm thinking of those public libraries where the children's department has no (or heavily restricted) use of the greater breadth and depth of information available in the adult reference department. It's a breach of ethics to fail to negotiate an equitable deal for the youngest library users in such situations. Adults whose grasp of a topic is negligible are usually served, without question, books on that topic in the children's department. They are even encouraged to borrow from the children's department, while too many discouragements and barricades are allowed to stand to keep the patter of little feet away from the adult information collections.

While on the subject of equitable reference services, spare a sob over the teaching of reference skills in our ALA-accredited library schools (or, as many are choosing for their married names, "schools of information studies"). A recent trip through the syllabi of reference courses offered indicates an information gap that stays wide open— the information tools and resources employed by those who work with the young are scanted or absent. Sad to say, when it comes to library services for youth among our leading library schools, ALA accreditation continues to flow to some cesspits of unfair, inequitable attention in terms both of an absence of necessary courses and in the content of existing courses.

In point No. 1, the commonest ethical problem in library services to the young, whether the institutional setting is a public library or school, centers on who takes precedence when both an adult and a minor are after the same item. In school libraries, on Day One, librarians tell students, "This is your library." A month down the road the students may hear, "Bring it back. Mrs. What's-her-face wants it on reserve." In the children's departments of public libraries, similar dilemmas arise when adults reserve and serially renew books children or young adults suddenly find on their recommended reading lists. (Children's librarians are notorious for hoisting and keeping, long past due, the latest Newbery or Caldecott Medal Award books.)

At first glance, the first statement in the *ALA Code of Ethics* seems a bit vague, like a grab bag of besetting sins from which it is easy to walk—or talk—away. Actually, it's best use is as an abbreviated blueprint for what every library policy book or manual of procedures should address. And, if your library exists without such written agreements on these matters, it's impractical (at least) and arguably unethical (at worst) to continue without getting them down on paper.

Ethical Back Talk II

> *2. Librarians must resist all efforts by groups or individuals to censor library materials.*

Of the six statements in the *American Library Association's Code of Ethics*, point No. 2 is the briefest, the most recitable, and the best known both inside and outside library service. Every year, new books are published about some historic or current aspect of its validity. Editorial pages in the library periodical press regularly preach to its text. Writers for the mass media sporadically discover it and gird it with praise. Annually, prestigious awards are presented to librarians who practice it at heroic levels of career-risk where even point No. 2's backsliders rise to do them honor. Unfortunately, the intensity of the admiration for point No. 2 has suppressed its regular re-examination and development.

Point No. 2 is unquestionably attractive to our best instincts to protect our institutions and the audiences they serve. From the time we first meet it in library school by way of ALA's *Code of Ethics* or its restatement in ALA's *Library Bill of Rights,* this puts us sternly on the path of saints and martyrs. It tells us: Go this Road or Walk in Shame. Forevermore, we know how we should behave when some person (ourselves included) or group tries to force material from a library's collection or circumscribe access to it. But, both guiding ALA documents are strangely, even dangerously silent on how to behave with those who would force material into a library collection or misuse a library staff and facilities to distribute materials inappropriate to the library's purpose. Point No. 2 is a story with only one accepted villain: the Censor. It's past time to focus on some others who can run roughshod through a library: the Zealot and the would-be business partners.

I say "strangely silent" because it was recognized long before there were public and school libraries for children and adolescents that the young have always been considered fair game by proselytizers for every sort of cause. This too calls forth the instinct to protect the library's purpose and its intended audience, but support for this from ALA's guideposts to professional behavior is nil. There is no model of library policy on the authority to evaluate and reject a zealot's gifts or on business overdoing business in the library.

The zealots' gift materials in every format can be repellently horrifying or corrodingly seductive. They can be beyond the comprehension of a youthful audience or so hate-filled that they are beneath the intellectual dignity of a human being at any age. But, point No. 2 of the *Code of Ethics* speaks only to the resistance to censorship, not to the fact that gift-bearing zealots often employ the same tactics as censors—blitzkrieg invasions of your working day, hostile publicity and steady pressure on governing boards and school administrators. It's a strange gap in the Code.

I call it a dangerous silence because we have something relatively new to manage: the idea that businesses are, in every instance, the benevolent partners of educational or cultural institutions and often baselessly and recklessly confident that they can do the jobs better than trained teachers, librarians, or museum staff. Just such a case recently came to ALA's Council calling for it to take a position on a brute-sized business deal that may yet affect ALA's public librarians just as it already confronts ALA's school librarians. It involves the offer of free installation, in thousands of classrooms, of expensive television equipment—plus the delivery, free of charge, of a daily news program

"Free" needs some definition in this case. Instead of paying money for the wiring and the TV sets, school administrators pay with the time and attention of their teachers and students, who must watch the program every day whether they want to or not. The programs carry commercials, invade the freedom of teachers to teach, truncate teaching time, and involve required use of unselected materials. Council was silent on all of these matters, opting instead to limply reiterate the importance of written selection policies. It took no stand on forcing the use of materials, on accepting gifts tied with inappropriate strings, or on administrators who bargain away the reading, viewing, or listening time of the young in exchange for equipment they can't afford, simply because they failed at their first function: to win tax money to get it.

Point No. 2 in the *Code of Ethics* didn't help Council in this case because it exists as an arrow without a bow. ALA's Council Committee on Professional Ethics needs to furnish the missing half of point No. 21—an equally noble statement on the duty of librarians to resist the resignation of their selection/acquisition responsibilities to any individual or group, and to ensure that their libraries' users, young or old, are not bartered for free equipment, materials, hamburgers, or whatnot.

Ethical Back Talk: III

> *3. Librarians must protect each user's right to privacy with respect to information sought or received, and materials consulted, borrowed, or acquired.*

The third point in the American Library Association's *Code of Ethics* has three distinct aspects: the one the general public knows about, the one librarians seldom, if ever, talk or write about, and the one that gets completely (usually happily) ignored.

The general public knows that librarians want court orders whenever federal or local police want to go snooping through a library's records in pursuit of evidence of actual or suspected criminal activity. The general public knows about this because heroic resistance to G-persons and DAs and sheriffs on the part of library directors gets prominent, praiseful notice from both the library and the general press.

The aspect of point No. 3 that librarians seldom, if ever, talk or write about is staff gossip about patrons. The silence on this underscores how extremely difficult it would be to locate and to prod into speech or print a practicing librarian who has never traded survival information about patrons who misbehave or hissy speculation on those who exhibit odd-to-weird tastes in their reading or research interests. It is a fact that we tell each other quite readily what a badge-bearing snoop would have to pry out of us with a warrant.

Last but not least (in *School Library Journal's* admittedly biased view), the ignored aspect of point No. 3 is the eagerness with which librarians serving children and adolescents will tell all they know or have observed about a young patron's reading tastes and skills to any parent, concerned adult or teacher who indicates even the mildest interest in the young person's use of the library. (The grand exceptions to this tendency toward the invasion of the privacy of the very young are young adult services specialists in public libraries who regularly witness how much essential hygiene, sex and marriage law information libraries must supply without interference to the young when parents or schools don't—or won't.) However, the whole idea of privacy in our society seems reserved to adults. Only minors who are the perpetrators or victims of criminal acts regularly get privacy protection of these records.

This aspect of point No. 3 deserves more attention than it's ever been given in print. I've searched the literature back as far as it goes: specialists in library services to the young have been, and continue to be, urged to make parents or education colleagues full partners in the effort to develop reading habits or tastes and research skills. Most librarians working with young people could not, I think, be easily persuaded that there is anything wrong or hurtful in sharing what they see and know about young readers with others perceived as helping adults.

But that's not what the *Code* says—and therein lies the problem. Codes for any professional or occupational group are intended to call forth uniform compliance. As with so many other concerns in library service—classification, preservation, fines for overdues—we have to ask, even demand, as a specialist group "Where do we fit? How does this fit with our purposes, and our functions?"

Point No. 3 is quite easy to practice when you equate it only with resisting police attempts at invasions of privacy. Virtuous directors and department heads can keep inevitable staff gossip within bounds through regular reminders about the responsibility for safeguarding the dignity of those served in any library. (It's a guilt trip; librarians should never leave home—for work—without it.) But, specialists in services to the young deserve at least a background statement absolving them from its total observance.

Furthermore, such a background statement requires some guidelines on how and when and with whom these breaches of point No. 3 are appropriate. The ability to ignore point No. 3 in this way—with pleasure and job satisfaction—is something the rest of library service should recognize as an admirable rather than a naughty practice of librarians serving the young.

When you come right down to it, fending off the FBI is easier than stonewalling a concerned parent or teacher who wants to help in the serious, positive work of helping young readers to grow. While this claim would not sit well in a background statement to point No. 3, the statement would show us off at our professional best I between its lines.

Ethical Back Talk: IV

4. Librarians must adhere to the principles of due process and equality of opportunity in peer relationships and personnel actions.

Point No. 1 of the American Library Association's *Code of Ethics* lifts the veil on six ways librarians must police themselves in the provision of responsible library services.

Point No. 2 inspires devotion to the resistance of censorship.

Point No. 3 admonishes librarians to protect library users' privacy.

Point No. 4 just lays there in the lineup like a dead lox dredged from the introduction to a library staff personnel procedures manual.

It's probably there because the ethical codes of the major professions are the starting points for later codes, and those historic guidelines for the conduct of doctors, lawyers and the clergy contain statements on how they should behave toward each other, the responsibility for monitoring entry to their profession, and the duty to help ensure its competent practice.

As it is stated, point No. 4 in ALA's *Code* speaks only to how to behave to other staff members within a given institution, ignores admission to the ranks and stays mum on the matter of competency checks. Point No. 4 is simply not up to the task it was intended to perform: that of guiding librarians on how to treat other librarians in every specialty under any circumstances.

Comparison of point No. 4 with its beginnings in the first ALA *Code* of 1939, the revision of 1975 and its present statement in the 1981 revision suggests that it is the result of a series of evolutionary accidents. Point No. 4 is the platypus of ALA's *Code* unlovely to look upon and confusing as to purpose, intent and application.

In the 1939 *Code,* point No. 4 began as a long passage dictating "Relations of the Librarian Within His Library." This is heavily weighted toward supporting the authority of administrators and safeguarding the library rather than those who work in it. (When you remember that this statement was adopted in a period of trade union victories over owners and managers, it provides a startling contrast to the political coloration of ALA today.)

In the 1975 revision, point No. 4 emerged as: "A librarian has an obligation to insure equality of opportunity and fair judgement of competence in dealing with staff appointments retentions and promotions." While this version is still narrow to the workplace and overly directed to library administrators, it looks good in comparison to point No. 4's 1981 restatement; the addition of such personnel manual doublespeak as "due process" and "peer relationships" neither adorns nor clarifies.

Point No. 4 needs work to make it more all-embracing, lift it off the backs of administrators, and take it beyond the walls of individual libraries. Point No. 4 is most commonly breached, I think, outside a library or away from its administrative offices in ways the statement is too narrow to convey.

For instance, library educators seem exempt from point No. 4. Nevertheless, what they do in terms of their classes affects other librarians. Dropping admission standards to swell enrollment and passing grades for future unmanageables ought to be perceived as maltreatment of library practitioners and an ethical no-no of endless consequence to the profession.

Another example is those letters of reference for colleagues who may or may not be fellow library staff members. The field has always been full of complaints from employers stung by written assurances on the competence of wackos the letter writer wouldn't hire or rehire at the point of a gun.

Another example involves grade-mates in a conspiracy of silence before library administrators in order to keep a lovable incompetent on the job through increasingly lazy (or crazy) years. Unless librarians have been lying to me in large numbers for a long time, there is hardly any big school district, academic or public library that hasn't harbored one of these local legendary cuckoo birds with colleague support.

Other occupational groups or professional callings have enforcers—official committees empowered to discipline and/or lift licenses to practice when their fellows behave stupidly or odiously. Librarians have only their own consciences to check against their own unenforceable code. Armed with consciences as sensitive as mimosa plants and hearts as pure as Ivory Soap, they need the sort of point No. 4 that speaks to all interprofessional behavior such as this variation on the Golden Rule: *Librarians should do unto all other librarians as they would have the others do unto them.*

That would spread the guilt more evenly up, down and across the ranks—like a good ethical code should.

Ethical Back Talk: V

> *5. Librarians must distinguish clearly in their actions and statements between their personal philosophies and attitudes and those of an institution or professional body.*

There is nothing in point No. 5 of the American Library Association's *Code of Ethics* to admire or to inspire. It shot past ALA's Council for adoption without any protest nearly ten years ago, but it deserves plenty.

Let's start with point No. 5's snarl of semantic silly putty. Personal philosophies are convictions that impel the behavior of individuals. Attitudes are physical or vocal demonstrations of a mind-set—the actions or words that show how people think and feel. In point No. 5, both terms are unnaturally forced upon the inanimate workplaces in which librarians practice their profession. That's got to go.

It has to go for more than reasons of clean copyediting. It's got to go because an ethical code for the professional conduct of librarians should serve to guide librarians, and not as protection for the institutions in which they work.

As a guide, point No. 5 can lose you from the start. It asks you "to distinguish" between your personal philosophy and attitude and (presumably) the policies and the regulations of the place where you've accepted a position as a librarian.

So, you "distinguish." You're a children's librarian in a public library that has a policy requiring fines for overdues and it eats your heart out to demand pocket change from children or their financially pressed parents. Or, you're a school librarian who teaches Sunday school and you don't really want to buy the materials that blandly assert that all religious practices of all peoples are equally valid, even those that require the sacrifice of animals. In either case, you have identified matters of serious cross-pressure between your beliefs and the policies of your workplace: the public library's undifferentiated policy on punishing overdues; the school's policy requiring its library to provide curriculum support for the study of various cultures. As a children's librarian, where do you begin to resolve your policy problem? As a school librarian, how do you address your concerns with course content? Having "distinguished," what is it you're supposed to do next? Point No. 5 doesn't say, which is precisely what ethical codes are supposed to do.

Instead of clear guidance, point No. 5 gives you a broad hint on what it takes—beyond incompetence, malpractice or peculation—to get yourself fired. In plainer English, the hint says, "Don't break the rules and never embarrass the shop or its stewards on pain of dismissal." This is the employers' "attitude" on what constitutes insubordination.

What belongs in point No. 5 is what a librarian's conduct should be in seeking, accepting and holding a post.

Point No. 5 should say that librarians must be familiar with the policies and procedures of the organizations in which they accept positions. To be "familiar with" does not mean total agreement. It merely returns to librarians the responsibility for knowing whether they can or cannot live with the existing purposes and current practices of an organization.

Furthermore, Point No. 5 should support librarians by stating that once on the job, librarians have a professional obligation to initiate, through the appropriate channels, the recision or revision of any policies or practices that prevent or impede quality service to the library's users or unduly constrain librarians' free will or intellectual freedom.

It should go without saying that when you can't persuade the governors of "an institution or professional body" to see matters your way, when you've exhausted all the avenues for initiating changes, then the individual librarian must be responsible for "distinguishing" whether or not to bow to duly constituted authority or—to take a walk

Both are incredibly hard choices to make, of course, but there is a third and most admirable possibility. That is, to hang in and to keep trying for the changes you hope to effect, because years are but minutes in the time frames of established institutions. It suggests the need for a dictum in the admonitory language of ALA's *Code of Ethics*: "Librarians must learn to disagree with authority without insult."

But, that ain't ethical, its just down-home political sense—and it can't hope for a space in any revision of point No. 5, which ought to be scrapped as it stands.

Ethical Back Talk: VI

> *6. Librarians must avoid situations in which personal interest might be served or financial benefits gained at the expense of library users, colleagues, or the employing institution.*

Once upon a time, there was a young librarian. On the day point No. 6 of the American Library Association's *Code of Ethics* was scanted during her coursework on "The Library and Society" at her library school, she had stopped on her way to class to put a baby bird back in its nest, so she missed the discussion.

Soon after she got her first library post, a traveling man for ALA convinced her to join the world's oldest, biggest library organization, and she loved it. She became an active, energetic member.

The library partially underwrote her dues for ALA, granted her leave to attend conference and reimbursed some of her conference travel and housing expenses. She was also permitted to use the library's time, space, and communications facilities to fulfill her ALA committee assignments.

Her highly visible, widely admired work in ALA attracted the notice of a library administrator in a distant state, who offered her a better position at a higher salary, which she accepted.

Then, one dark and stormy night when she was completing her pre-slumber ritual of prayer plus a chapter in the *ALA Handbook of Organization,* she came upon point No. 6 and her mind reeled. It said she'd used her first library's funds to pursue her personal interests and to gain financial benefit. It said she'd done this at the expense of the library' s users by not being there for every toddlers' story hour while she was at ALA conference, at the expense of colleagues who'd subbed for her while she was away. She shuddered at the thought of the phone bills that library had paid in support of her ALA committee work.

"O! Lord!," she cried out in anguish. "Is ALA one of those situations that must be avoided?"

And, that's what's wrong with point No. 6. It calls for the paralyzing state of virtue Julius Caesar decreed for his wife—that she be not only free of guilt, but stay forever above suspicion. It ignores the fact that the daily business and professional activities of librarians working in their institutions and for their library organizations present situations that must be managed and cannot be avoided. Point No. 6 turns its back on the fact that mere avoidance requires neither critical self-examination nor corrective action for what could be wrong. It invites the blame-givers and the finger-pointers to slander without evidence of wrongdoing.

All the questions on the following self-test require only YES/NO answers. Most of these arise from situations that membership in ALA casts in your path, while point No. 6 says, "Stay away. These might be nasty."

A. Did you ever attend a meeting at the expense of a vendor, a government agency, or an association?

B. Did you ever accept a speaker's fee?

C. Did you ever participate in the awarding of a bid or a prize to someone you know socially?

D. Did you ever accept a free beverage or free food from a vendor?

E. Did you ever schedule your vacation either immediately before or after distant, week-long professional conferences and then apply for the reimbursement of travel funds?

F. Have you ever kept one of your library's books or films overdue without paying the fine that would be charged a library user?

If you answered "Yes" to all questions, you might be the biggest, freeloading chiseler to ever walk through ALA' s conference exhibits. On the other hand, you just might be decent, well-regarded and sought after—especially for your insights gained from the library materials you finelessly studied past due.

There's another story on point No. 6, and this one is true. A publisher invited a children's librarian to be a guest at ALA's annual Newbery/Caldecott Medals Award banquet, but she regretfully declined because the acceptance of any entertainment from a vendor had just been put off limits by her director. I asked him about this. He told me these were terrible times in his city and no municipal worker could be too careful of giving the appearance of accepting largesse from the business sector. He couldn't expand on this because he was hurrying to a reception of ALA's International Relation Committee paid for by an international distributor with deep pockets and generous impulses toward ALA's commitment to the extension and expansion of library services for all. (Sure makes you think how circumstances alter situations, doesn't it?)

Nobody can really quarrel with the fact that it's ethically wrong for librarians to rip off their users, colleagues, or institutions, but everybody can quarrel with the way ALA's *Code of Ethics* states this point.

Ethical Back Talk: Excelsior!

The American Library Association's *Code of Ethics,* last revised and adopted by ALA's Membership and Council at ALA's 100th annual conference in June, 1981, carried a brief introduction that describes the code's purpose and reasons for its revision. These are as compelling now as they were ten years ago:

> Since 1939, the American Library Association has recognized the importance of codifying and making known to the public and the profession the principles which guide librarians in action. This latest revision of the Code of Ethics reflects changes in the nature of the profession and in its social and institutional environment. It should be revised and augmented as necessary.
>
> Librarians significantly influence or control the selection, organization, preservation, and dissemination of information. In a political system grounded in an informed citizenry, librarians are members of a profession explicitly committed to intellectual freedom and the freedom of access to information. We have a special obligation to ensure the free flow of information and ideas to present and future generations.
>
> Librarians are dependent upon one another for the bibliographical resources that enable us to provide information services, and have obligations for maintaining the highest level of personal integrity and competence.

Starting in the February, 1990, issue of *School Library Journal* and in every other issue thereafter (April, June, August, October, and December) this page has been devoted to a point-by-point critique of the 1981 *Code of Ethics* which creaks in all its parts except for that admirable introduction just quoted. That introduction, in its first paragraph, suggests exactly what ALA's Council needs to do now:

1) recognize once more the importance of codifying the principles that guide librarians in action.
2) publicize these principles within the profession and to the public at large.

3) direct ALA's Committee on Professional Ethics to revise the ethical code to reflect changes in the nature of librarianship and in its social and institutional environment.

4) instruct ALA's Committee on Professional Ethics to make each point in the revision of the code the subject of serial, annual scrutiny for the purposes of necessary augmentation and continuous discussion.

In brief, in order to provide the sort of central, living document its *Code of Ethics* should be, ALA needs to lavish on it the sort of steady attention now reserved for the *Library Bill of Rights,* in which points briefly stated go before the profession and the general public with a solid body of continuously updated interpretative background statements.

In preparing this series of "Ethical Back Talk" editorials, I read the official transcripts conducted before the last revision of the ethical code as well as the relatively few essays in library literature that have been published since its adoption.

Too many of the commentators despair of the effort to produce a viable ethical code for ALA because no mechanisms exist for its enforcement—no committees to point fingers at, to shame, to exonerate, or to cast away those who may be accused of straying f;c m its ideals. These footling calls for organized punishment trivialize the whole idea of personal and professional ethics, which are for inspiration and self-control.

ALA owes its members the finest, most focused set of motivating guidelines for librarians intent on providing the highest levels of skillful library service. Library users need a clearer understanding of what drives this profession than the current *Code of Ethics* has ever been able to convey.

VALUING CORPORATE LIBRARIES: A SENIOR MANAGEMENT SURVEY

James M. Matarazzo and Laurence Prusak

Background and Methodology

The Special Libraries Association, in a report from its Task Force on the Value of the Information Professional, highlighted a need for additional research on how the corporate world values its libraries and information centers. Specifically, the Task Force recommended a further study of the value placed by upper-level executives on both the information professional and the corporate library/information center. This study was conducted in response to that recommendation.

The survey focused on two needs: to enhance the body of research on how work traditionally associated with special libraries is valued, and to identify emerging trends for special libraries. The questions posed to corporate officials were selected to shed new light on these subjects across a broad spectrum of the United States' business and industry. Hopefully, the findings will assist corporate librarians in formulating plans and strategies.

In conducting the survey, we followed an approach different from that commonly found in today's self-referential professional literature. That is, rather than interview the librarians, we interviewed those individuals to whom the head of the library reports. These corporate

"Valuing Corporate Libraries: A Senior Management Survey," by James M. Matarazzo and Laurence Prusak in *Special Libraries.* Vol. 81, no. 2 (Spring 1990), pp. 102-110; reprinted with permission from the Special Library Association, copyright © 1990 by SLA.

officials represented various functions and have different titles. The most common functions reported were finance and administration, marketing, and information services. Titles ranged from manager to senior vice president. Only two of the interviewees had any library experience or library education, an interesting fact in itself.

The survey sample of 164 companies was developed by the authors from an analysis of contributions by the for-profit sector to the gross national product (GNP). Selected firms, chosen by the size of the firm or by its importance to a specific industry, thus represented significant contributors to the major sectors of the U.S. gross national product. The process also gave us a sample representative of United States business while avoiding undue concentration on "information intensive" industries or, conversely, on struggling industries with libraries under obvious survival pressures. As noted in the appendix to the report, the interview list developed has a range and balance that reflect adequately the scope of businesses in the United States.

The study focused on larger companies because they were judged as more likely to have fully functioning libraries and to have had these services for a reasonable period of time. We selected this approach because we wanted thoughtful and seasoned commentary from those interviewed.

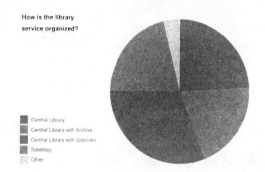

How is the library
service organized?

Central Library
Central Library with Archive
Central Library with Satellites
Satellites
Other

Our expectations were met. Because the executives interviewed must frequently justify the libraries to senior management or to a board of directors, many already had given some thought to our questions and were well prepared to answer them. Their responses focused on issues of library organization, staff sizes, values of services and staff, primary users, and ways to measure a library's value. Trends projected for future library roles also have been summarized.

Library Service Organization

The libraries in the 164 companies follow no common organizational scheme, although use of a central library, in some form, proved most typical. Of the libraries surveyed, 31 percent have a central library with satellites, 24 percent maintain a central library only, and 20 percent support a central library with an archive. On the other hand, 21 percent of the corporations surveyed reported only satellite libraries, and 5 percent have libraries serving a small unit or individual in the organization or collecting specific forms of literature.

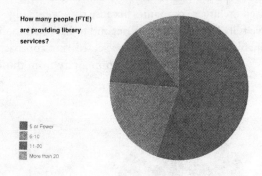

How many people (FTE)
are providing library
services?

5 or Fewer
6-10
11-20
More than 20

Size of Staff

Staff sizes at these special libraries clearly tend to be small. The majority 55 percent) have staffs of five full-time equivalents or fewer. Another 21 percent of the libraries in our sample have staffs of five to ten full-time equivalents. Only 13 percent have staffs of 10 to 20 full-time equivalents, and only 11 percent have staff sizes greater than 20.

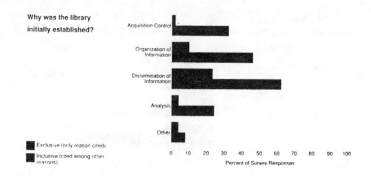

Why was the library initially established?

Reasons for Initial Establishment

Qualitative use of information and its subsequent identification and dissemination cause companies to establish information centers. Those reasons outpaced others cited by the survey respondents for establishing libraries.

The responses reveal a contradiction between the value sought when a company initiates a library and the way that value is subsequently measured. For example, although no respondents cited cost control or employee productivity as reasons for establishment, libraries often are asked to justify themselves using just such categories. Perhaps this contradiction can be explained by the difficulties inherent in measuring qualitative factors.

Fewer than 30 percent of the respondents mentioned data analysis as a reason for establishing the library, indicating a need for improving library capabilities in this area. Librarians are rarely perceived to be information *analysts*. Skills for acquisition, organization, and dissemination of information do not bring with them industry knowledge or the tools needed for analysis. Adding information-analysis ability to the skill base of the corporate librarian is a potential enhancement that should be studied. For example, how much knowledge of business information is considered equal to knowledge of the business itself?

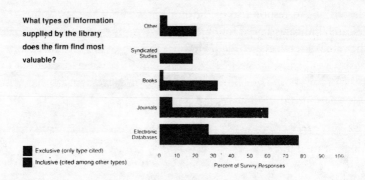

What types of information supplied by the library does the firm find most valuable?

Exclusive (only type cited)
Inclusive (cited among other types)

Value of Services

Librarians usually spend considerable amounts of money, and management must have a clear vision of what the organization receives for that investment. Management does not ask, "How good is the library?" Instead, it asks, "How much good does the library do?"

Based on responses to the survey, librarians must do much more to demonstrate the value of the corporate information center. When asked to identify the library services that added the most value to the company, nearly two-thirds of the respondents did not know and chose not to respond. This lack of knowledge is especially serious because the interviewees not only exercise management control over libraries, but also are the principal evaluators of library managers and staffs. These same individuals also may be asked to justify library budgets and defend against any move to curtail or reduce library expenditures. Given the survey response, some substantive efforts toward demonstrating the value of various library services would seem prudent. Perhaps library managers should conduct appropriate studies on value, then convey those results to senior management.

Our findings in this survey are buttressed by similar results in earlier work. In a 1983 study, MacDonald[1] found that neither librarians nor corporate managers gave high marks to the library when asked if its information helped the firm make a profit. In her study, corporate managers were neutral on the value, while librarians perceived a more positive value for the information provided. Coupled with the fact that more than 60 percent of the corporate managers in our SLA study elected not to respond to or did not know about specific value, the research indicates a need for librarians to demonstrate *in business terms* the value of services provided. Findings in a new work[2] provide a more positive sign: The *most* significant reason given for development of an outstanding corporate library *was* upper management's belief that information is important to the company.

Value of the Librarian

Librarians were generally rated highly by the survey respondents for developing effective services, and responding to changing needs. In addition, more than 40 percent of the executives in this study rated their libraries/information professionals highly in controlling information expenditures. Those who did not rate them as highly acknowledged that the librarians cannot control all of the costs involved.

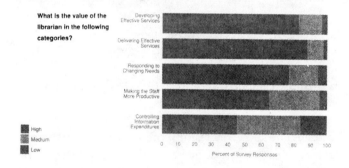

Two factors should be noted in this response. One is the emphasis placed on developing and delivering effective services. Comments by the executives on this question noted that the library's "value-added" performance is enhanced by developing services, not by simply offering menu-type selections to users. Important services include the various customized programs designed for specific users or specific divisions within a company.

A second factor to note is the intuitive nature of these responses. In the absence of any formal evaluation or measurement, the corporate managers of libraries based their responses on impressionistic evidence. To the authors, this practice offers shaky footing in an economy and a business climate that shows little tolerance for any service failing to contribute directly to the business of the firm.

Most Valuable Services

Print materials still show good value, but obviously databases now provide a key value to library users. Almost 80 percent of the survey respondents cited database searching as a key library service.

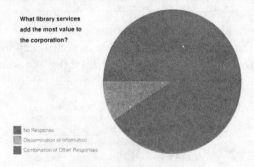

What library services
add the most value to
the corporation?

No Response
Dissemination of Information
Combination of Other Responses

The increased importance of databases presents some potential problems for librarians because it leads to increased pressure from several directions for end-user-initiated searching. Vendors promote this approach for commercial reasons; endusers, especially those with computer knowledge, often see no need for an intermediary to do the searches. In some fast-paced environments, the use of a librarian can be seen as a hindrance—a gatekeeper who adds little value.

To validate the use of an intermediary for database searches, corporate librarians should stress the following:

- The increased proliferation of databases and the issue of choosing the right one for each task;

- The need to apply special skills in a search process, which is more than simply following specific procedures;

• The need for in-depth knowledge of database pricing to control costs.

High cost has discouraged end-user searches to some extent. In several companies where end-user searching is permitted, for example, management seeks to end the practice because of high costs. However, nearly 10 percent of the respondents want to initiate enduser searching where it does not currently exist.

Main User Groups

Primary users of corporate libraries and information centers are technical staffs. Marketing and sales personnel form the next largest user group, followed by operations/administration (which includes the use of tax and law libraries). Such results will surprise no one.

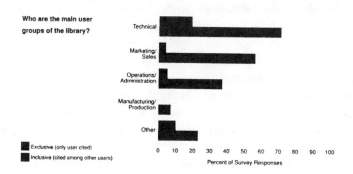

Among the user types listed in the "other" category by respondents were systems/MIS, investor relations, and a specified "CEO" library.

Criteria for Evaluating Libraries

While no one can achieve even a 40 percent plurality in the survey responses, the quality of information made available was the single most important component. More respondents cited "better informa-tion" as a criterion than mentioned other standards. In addition, many of the respondents' answers summarized as "other" concerned is-sues—accuracy, timeliness, and the like—related to quality.

Interestingly, a substantial proportion of respondents declared

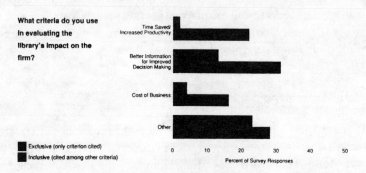

What criteria do you use in evaluating the library's impact on the firm?

- ■ Exclusive (only criterion cited)
- ■ Inclusive (cited among other criteria)

Percent of Survey Responses

they had no procedure at all for measuring the "value" of the library. This issue should be studied further, especially since a library is somewhat of a "discretionary" business need and not an essential operation.

Libraries face an additional problem when assessing value because they have no formal measurements for evaluation. In most other operations, the labor/management ratio and productivity levels can be used by management to determine "value." In functions such as marketing or public relations, proxy measurements (i.e., sales volume) can be used to determine value.

But libraries often exist simply because a firm is so informationally intensive it could not survive without a library, or because a CEO or highly placed individual pushed for the library's establishment and insists on its maintenance.

Without formal value measurements, the library becomes vulner-able if this individual leaves the firm or transfers to another operational area. In a study of five corporate libraries that were "closed," Matarazzo[3] demonstrated that failure of the library manager to for-mally evaluate library services had serious impacts: Corporate man-agement was forced to make a less- than-informed decision about terminating the library service during a period when senior managers were suddenly asked to evaluate call services closely for retention. Curtis and Abrarn,[4] in response to this study of closure, said, "A library's output has to be measured . . . in terms of how, and to what extent, the actions of others are made more productive or their decisions successful. Following this reasoning, a library must be measured in value in user terms."

Five-Year Trends

We presented a series of questions to corporate managers on staff size, budgets, computer applications, size of the library, and general impact of the company library on the business. Near-term projections about library/information service roles were developed from those responses.

In general, the respondents demonstrated a clear appreciation of the growing importance of information technology for corporate libraries. That appreciation, in turn, influenced other responses. For example, the interviewees expect corporate staffs to grow in the future, but foresee no concurrent growth in library size. That expectation can be explained by the increasing use of information technologies rather than the more space-consuming print products; information storage room can be created without increasing the physical size of the library itself. It might also explain the anticipated growth in staff and budgets.

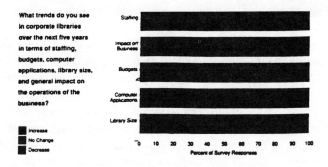

Approximately 10 percent of the respondents added specific comments about the desirability of end-user searching.

Another 10 percent expected the corporate library to be transferred to the same business organization areas as computer services or records management, because corporations will try to group like functions together.

One-tenth of the respondents want the library to occupy less space. Some projected that CD-ROM technology might make this possible, while others speculated that the increased availability of text-online might accomplish the same goal.

A larger segment (more than 40 percent) of those interviewed on future trends want the library to reach a larger audience and therefore generate greater impact on the business. These respondents stressed the importance of attracting new users, and several had just shifted the library's reporting role to the marketing area in order to make the library more visible in the company.

The largest number of comments about future trends concerned the increased involvement of the librarian in value-added functions such as problem analysis and the writing of summary reports. Specific skills mentioned included internal consulting, problem evaluation, synthesis, advanced research, evaluation of information services and products, and high-level analysis using models and spreadsheets.

Implications

Responses to this survey have led the authors to ask a number of questions about librarians' salaries and career paths, about the implications of increased technological applications, and about the overall information work performed in a corporation.

Questions about salary structure stem from a discrepancy between the ratings of librarians and their salaries relative to those of other specialists. For example, librarians received significant praise for developing and delivering effective services and were also rated highly for responding to changing needs and for making staff more productive. With all of these positive statements, we question why librarians' salaries lag so far behind those of other specialists in most companies.

Comparing the SLA salary survey with a similar report for data processing professionals provides one example of this disparity.

Questions about career paths for librarians arise from our review of the survey respondents' backgrounds. It was our original intention to bypass the company librarians and obtain responses from corporate managers with a reporting responsibility for the library function. It is our belief that we succeeded in the quest. We note that only two of those 164 interviewees—the managers responsible for library functions—had any roots in library and information science. What, then, are the career growth opportunities for successful library managers? Does the track lead the library manager out of the library, in a quest for greater remuneration and a more significant role in corporate decision making?

Technology issues lead to questions about future library positioning and roles. More than 10 percent of those interviewed speculated about the future of library/information services in the corporation. Most of these individuals said the increase in technological applications might lead to relocating libraries in MIS, computer services, data processing, or technical systems departments. If such changes occur, the authors believe that selection of library managers to run these departments is highly unlikely—another potential roadblock on the librarian's career path.

In addition, the support for technology in libraries, thus far, seems to focus more on saving space and reducing headcount—by substituting equipment for needed staff and space—than on advancing the library function. Based on the projections in the study, we see corporate libraries in the future with smaller staffs, fewer collections, and as little space as possible. Perhaps the librarian may evolve into an information network manager for the firm.

Finally, we wonder who is doing the information work in corporations? Responses to the survey revealed relatively small staffs, even in the corporate libraries of some of this country's largest firms. In some cases, the small relative size of the library staff can be explained by its serving the special needs of an individual, a department, or an area. Still, although it is not our intention to correlate size of staff to size of the corporation, it does seem unusual that these corporations find themselves with staffs of such modest size. Who provides the information in those firms? This question, as well as others raised by the study, can be resolved in future research projects.

References

1. MacDonald, Arley Ripin. *Managers View Information*. New York: Special Libraries Association, 1983.
2. Matarazzo, James M. *Corporate Library Excellence*. To be published.
3. Matarazzo, James M. *Closing the Corporate Library: Case Studies in the Decision-Making Process*. New York: Special Libraries Association, 1981.
4. Curtis, John and Stephen Abram. "Special Corporate Libraries: Planning for Survival and Success," *Canadian Library Journal*, 40 No. 4, August 1983, pp. 227.

Acknowledgments

The authors acknowledge with gratitude the assistance of the following individuals: Michael Gauthier, principal, Temple, Barker & Sloane, Inc.; Carolyn D. Schroeder, technical librarian, Storage Information Management Group, Digital Equipment Corporation; Debra Maher, associate, Temple, Barker & Sloane, Inc.; Deborah Smith-Cohen, assistant librarian, U.S. Army Cold Regions Research & Engineering Laboratory; and Elizabeth Eddison, Inmagic, Inc. Additional assistance on this project was received from Linda Willey, Robert P. Rich, Donna Doucette, and Sherry Roess.

We also thank Dr. David R. Bender, executive director, Special Libraries Association, for his support and assistance with this project from its inception.

This project was made possible by a grant from the Special Programs Fund (1987) of the Special Libraries Association and a matching grant from Temple, Barker & Sloane, Inc., a management consulting firm based in Lexington, MA. Additional funds were received from the Emily Hollowell Research Fund at the Simmons College Graduate School of Library and Information Science, Mr. Richard Goldberg, and CLSI.

Appendix

We would like to thank the following firms for participating in the survey: Abbot Laboratories / Aetna Life & Casualty / Agway, Inc. / Air Products & Chemicals, Inc. / Alberto-Culver Co. / Alexander & Alexander Services, Inc. / Allied-Signal, Inc. / Alumax, Inc. / Amerada Hess Corp. / American Express Co. / American International Group, Inc. / American Management Systems, Inc. / American Telephone and Telegraph Co. / Ametek, Inc. / AMP, Inc. / Anheuser-Busch, Inc. / Apple Computer, Inc. / Archer-Daniels-Midland Co. / Armstrong Rubber Co. / Armstrong World Industries, Inc. / Avon Products, Inc. / The B.F. Goodrich Co. / Bain & Company / Ball Corp. / Bell Atlantic Corp. / Bethlehem Steel Corp. / The Boeing Company / Boise Cascade Corp. / Borg-Warner / Braxton Associates / Campbell Soup Co. / CBS, Inc. / Chesebrough-Pond's, Inc. / Chi Systems / Cincinnati Milacron, Inc. / The Coca-Cola Co. / Columbia Gas Systems Service Corp. / Combustion Engineering, Inc. / Commonwealth Edison Co. / Compaq Computer Corp. / Computer Sciences Corp. / Consolidated Edison Co. of New York / Consumers Power Co. /Contel Corp. / Continental Illinois National Bank & Trust C. / Control Data Corp. / Coopers & Lybrand / Cray Research. Inc. /Cubic Corp. / Data General Corp. /Dayton-Hudson Corp. /Deere & Co. / Deluxe Check Printers, Inc. / Digital Equipment Corporation / Dow Chemical Co. /Dow Corning Corp. / Dow Jones & Co., Inc. E-Systems, Inc. / Eastman Kodak Co. /Eaton Corp. / Ecolab, Inc., Englehard Co. / Equifax, Inc. / Ernst & Whinney /Ethyl Corp. / Farmland Industries, Inc. / Federated Department Stores / Flour Danial, Inc. / General Dynamics Corp. / General Mills, Inc. / General Motors Corp. / General Public Utilities Corp. / Georgia-Pacific Corp. / Gillette Co. / Goldman, Sachs & Co. / GTE Corp. / Gulf States Utilities Co. / Harvest Slates Cooperatives / Helene Curtis Industries, Inc. / Henkel Process Chemicals, Inc. / Hercules, Inc. / Hewitt Associates / Hospital Corporation of America / Ingersoll-Rand Co. / Inland Steel Co. / Intel Corp. / International Paper Co. Irving Trust Co. ITT Corp. / James River Corporation / John Hancock Mutual Life Insurance Co. / Johnson & Johnson / Johnson Controls, Inc. / Kemper Corporation / Kerr McGee Corp. / Ketchum Communications, Inc. / Kline & Co., Inc. / Land O 'Lakes, Inc. / Laventhal & Horwath / Eli Lilly & Co. / Lockheed Corp. / Loral Electro-Optical Systerns, Inc. / Manville Sales Corp. / Mannon Corp. / Marrion Corp. / Massachusetts Mutual Lifc Insurance Co. / May Department Stores / McDonnell Douglas Corp. / McGraw-Hill, Inc. / MCI Communications Corp. / Mead Corp. / Mead Data Central, Inc. / Media General, Inc. / Medtronic, Inc. Mercer-Meidinger-Hansen / Metropolitan Life Insurance Co. / Minnesota Mining & Manufacturing Co. / Monsanto Co. / Moore Business Forrns, Inc. / Morrison-Knudsen Co., Inc. / Motorola, Inc. / Mutual Benefit Life Insurance Co. / National Seniconductor Corp. / Nationwide Advertising Services, Inc. / Navistar International Corp. / NBD Bancorp, Inc. / NCR Corp. / New York Times Co. / NL Industries, Inc. / Northeast Utilities Noxell

Corp. / NYNEX Corp. / Occidental Chernical Corp. / Ogden Food Products Corp. / Ogilvy & Mather / Ohio Edison Co. / PACCAR, Inc. Pacific Resources, Inc. / Pennwalt Corp. / Philip Morris, Inc. / PPG Industries, Inc. / Prudential Insurance & Financial Services / Rockwell International Corp. / Rohm & Haas Co. / Rorer Group, Inc. / Safeway Stores, Inc. / Scott Paper Co. / Sears, Roebuck & Co. / Security Pacific National Bank / Sherwin-Williams Co. / A.E. Staley Manufacturing Co. / Stanley Consultants, Inc. / Sunkist Growers, Inc. / Texas Eastem Corp. / Thom McAnn / TRW, Inc. / Union Carbide Corp. / Unisys Corp. / Varian Associates / Wal-Mart Stores, Inc. / Warner-Lambert Co. / Wells Fargo & Co.

THE NEW HIERARCHY: WHERE'S THE BOSS?

Joanne R. Euster

A certain seductiveness is evident in discussions of alternatives to hierarchical organizational structures, particularly for a library director who spends some time on the lecture circuit. The speaker gets to discourse on theories and ideas that do not have to be implemented, audiences love the concept, and everybody has a fine time.

As one who is guilty of participation in this game, and who has also collaborated in some experiments in organizational structure,[1] I increasingly speculate about the gap between discourse and action. To be sure, staff seem to unerringly expect greater levels of participation (here come the buzzwords) than management is willing—or able—to accommodate.

There is considerable confusion about the meaning of "participation," "flattening the pyramid," "alternatives to hierarchy," and so forth. Further, in academic libraries where librarians have faculty status, there is no clear understanding of the relative roles of faculty governance and management of an enterprise that more closely resembles a profit-making organization than an academic department. Even without the confusions of faculty status the legitimate expectations of a highly professionalized work force often run counter to organizational needs to "produce" and to keep all the parts of a very complex organization functioning in reasonable synchronicity.[2]

Libraries today must deal with unprecedented forces from technology, high costs, rising user expectations, and pressures for improved quality and accountability. These are well-documented pressures on our libraries, and they show no signs of abating. The root issue, however, is the complexity that these challenges and opportunities (our euphemism for the situation Pogo expressed best: "We are faced with insurmountable opportunities") have created.

The challenge to libraries facing these multiple forces is to develop ways to plan proactively, to change quickly, and above all to ensure that all the relevant information and expertise is brought into play in organizational planning and decision-making. While leadership is a significant element in meeting this challenge, it is important to recognize that our libraries, along with most organizations today, are too complex and interdependent for leadership to reside solely with what might be termed the "designated leaders."

In his book *The Knowledge Executive,* Harlan Cleveland quotes a character in a short story by E. B. White that appeared in *The New Yorker* more than half a century ago: "I predict a bright future for complexity. Have you ever considered how complicated things can get, what with one thing always leading to another? [3] Librarians who have been involved in implementing any major library program recently, taking pains to be sure to involve all interested parties and consider all relevant information, can certainly empathize.

A Revised Concept of Leadership

The recent concern with leadership among librarians, as in our entire society, suggests that more effective leadership might be the preferred solution. Certainly it has a significant role. However, I suggest that not only improved leadership, but a revised concept of leadership, is required.

Although the literatures of management and of librarianship are full of exhortations for more effective leadership, in today's interconnected and interdependent environment, it is patently impossible for any leader to be fully in control of the organization or to know what is necessary to run it. A principal point in discussions of nonhierarchical organizations is that both leadership and expertise must reside at all levels of the organization. This is in fact the very basis that gives professionalized organizations their unique character.

It would be a mistake to assume that this is a leadership failure on the part of librarians. A recent *Wall Street Journal* article on the chief executive of the year 2000 stressed complexity, the speed of change, and the need for team management and collegial working styles.[4]

Any discussion of leadership inevitably also raises questions about the nature of power and where it resides. Power comes from many sources. Obviously it derives to some extent from the position one occupies. Unfortunately, many people see this as the only source of power in organizations. Intuitively, we are aware that power comes from many sources and research supports that belief.[5] A second principal source of power is the knowledge and expertise of people in the organization. People—subordinates, superiors, peers—respond to individuals who have useful knowledge and understanding, and who can be trusted to use that knowledge responsibly and reliably. A closely related source of power is the network of individuals with whom workers communicate, which in turn adds to their store of knowledge.

Whose Hierarchy Is it, Anyway?

Cleveland has coined the term "The get-it-all-together profession" as his definition of leadership. The information and knowledge explosions apply not only to collections and to other sources of information, but to the inner workings of libraries and how they are organized and operated. Interconnectedness and information interdependency *within the organization* have become so pervasive that those nominally in charge—the designate leaders—are completely unable to know enough to be truly "in charge." The result, to quote Cleveland, "Your responsibility increases in direct ratio to your ignorance. If you turn the thought around it is equally valid: your ignorance increases in direct ratio to your responsibility. . . . Of course, none of us is trained for the scary assignment of managing more while understanding less."[6]

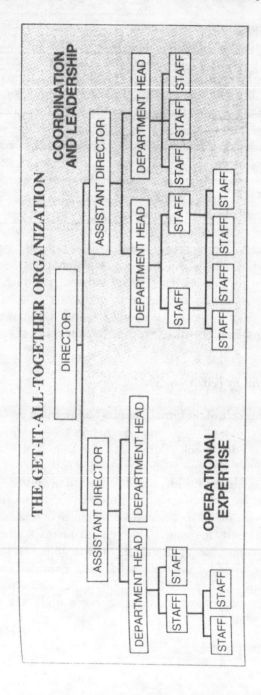

Early in my library career I unexpectedly became library director at the small college where I worked. The task was more than a little intimidating. When a senior director from another college dropped by one afternoon, I confessed my doubts that although I felt that things were going well, I often felt that I had to appear to know more about the library's operations than I really did. My hoped-for mentor leaned back in his chair fussed with his pipe, gestured grandly, and said, "Oh, don't worry. You'll get used to feeling like that!" His message was the same as Cleveland's: the designated leader is never fully in charge.

So, who is? The answer, of course, is Everybody. Or in Cleveland's terms, we now have the nobody-in-charge society led by the get-it-all-together profession.

The concepts of distributed processing and distributed computing, as opposed to centralized processing or computing, are now commonplace. In much the same way, leadership is increasingly becoming a distributed function. For at least 15 years, the literatures of management and of librarianship have discussed and touted participatory management, although the level of participation that has been implemented is the subject of disagreement between managers and staff. I think that it is possible to extend Cleveland's concept of the get-it-all-together profession with some imagery specific to libraries to explain the concept of distributed leadership without organizational chaos.

Leadership in an organization can be thought of as a rectangle, divided roughly diagonally into two triangles. One triangle, with its base at the bottom, consists of expertise, knowledge, and technical know-how. The upper triangle consists of coordination, management, and what is traditionally called leadership. If this pair of triangles is overlaid on the traditional pyramid organization chart, the result is an image of an organization with both expertise and leadership, at all levels.

At the bottom, or where the chart is the widest, there is more hands-on knowledge, technical expertise, and how-to-do-it knowledge, while the leadership/coordination aspect is fairly small. Moving up the pyramid, the expertise triangle gets narrower and the coordination/leadership triangle widens.

In a library, the broad-based triangle represents the business of ordering, cataloging, reference, bibliographic instruction, and so forth while the other triangle represents the process side (*process,* not procedures), where the attention is on how decisions are made, how communication is handled, how all the necessary information and expertise are brought to bear on an issue or problem, etc. At all levels, both expertise and leadership are present, and both are important to the effective functioning of the library.

Defining the distribution of leadership, however, is not enough.

The Information-Based Organization

The problems of complexity and interdependence make mandatory either superhuman intelligence at the top of the organization, or an incredible amount of coordination and information sharing. Few if any administrators disagree with the need for an open flow of information but an optimum information stream is much easier to talk about than to get.

Hierarchical organization structures were designed (among other things) to organize and control the flow of information, yet we now find that they tend to inhibit timely dissemination. Furthermore, there is a fair amount of organizational behavior theory that says that subordinates don't like to—won't—bring bad news to superiors. Yet the greatest problems are always the unanticipated ones, not the ones we can see coming. By its very nature the unanticipated problem is the one we don't know how to look for.

The traditional methods for dealing with information complexity and interdependence have been to 1) increase the vertical flow of information between levels of the organization, and 2) create mechanisms for lateral information exchange among hierarchically unrelated units.

As a result, the paperless library administration, if it was ever a hope, has become a chimera. Memos, newsletters, minutes, electronic messaging create a glut of data shuttling around the organization. Libraries tend to be hotbeds of interconnected committees, task forces, circles, groups, councils, created to deal with the need for information via routes that go around or cut across the hierarchy.

One way of looking at this issue is in terms of the interface between people and automated systems. *In the Age of the Smart Machine*, by Shoshana Zuboff,[7] is a study of several industrial and service organizations. Zuboff spent several years visiting, interviewing, and studying the results of automation. Her thesis is that computers in the workplace can make it possible for management to achieve a level of control over workers far beyond what early proponents of scientific management were able to accomplish, or perhaps even to dream of. But computers also have the ability to empower workers through their "informating" (sic) qualities, which make information the true ingredient of work, even in manufacturing or production environments. Zuboff contends that organizations have a choice as to whether to use computerization merely to automate and control work or to apply it in ways that lead to informated organizations.

In the automated organization, computers are used to make work narrower and more fragmented, limiting the need for understanding and broad skills. In the informated organization, workers are able to use their knowledge and intelligence to understand the complete scope of the system, place processes in context, and make judgments and decisions independently and in concert with co-workers. The managerial and worker domains are less clear, and managers may feel threatened by loss of control and status. Because information and comprehension are the real "products," training and education become essential and integral activities of the organization. In a structure where the core is an electronic database, mechanisms must be devised to facilitate interpersonal communication for problem solving and sharing of information.

Peter Drucker writes in a similar vein in a recent *Harvard Business Review* article,[8] arguing that businesses, even manufacturing concerns, must and will become "knowledge-based" organizations. The reasons? The shift to knowledge workers who resist the "command-and-control" model; the growing need for innovation and entrepreneurship; and the capabilities brought about by information technology, above all.

According to Drucker, with real "management" information accessible throughout the organization, workers can formulate and choose among options, test assumptions, and make decisions. At the same time, an information-based organization will provide top management with immediate and meaningful data on options and decisions. Staff must have the training and specialized knowledge to enable them to convert organizational data into meaningful information for decision-making. Accountability must be built into the system, but ultimately will be based on the organization's mission, goals, and objectives, as understood by operational groups of staff.

A Knowledge-Based Library

What does a knowledge-based library look like? How does it behave? Integrated online systems in a multilibrary setting, for example, have the potential to enable selectors to review the library's holdings, use data, the holdings of other related libraries, and the selection decisions made by other librarians. My ideal system would also include online access to collection development policies and guidelines, and a system—formal or informal—for a selector in one library to confer with another as to which library ought most appropriately to own a title, whether duplication is necessary or access will be sufficient, whether a title might be transferred from one library to the other, and so forth. The process has the elements described above: goals as articulated in collection development policies, immediate access to information via the database, expertise on the part of librarians, and accountability in the form of reports on individual and aggregate collection decisions. Given the collaborative nature of collection development operations, this is an easy example, but others could also be posited.

It appears that there has been a tendency to assume that libraries are knowledge-based organizations, because their business is the provision of information. Although they have been fairly quick to adopt technology to replace manual operations, to gather statistics more quickly and in different combinations, and to provide new information resources to patrons, there is little evidence that to date libraries have taken advantage of information technology to truly "informate" the internal organization. This mismatch represents the critical distinction between product and method of production.

Libraries, by definition, deliver information to patrons. Having an internal organization that is permeated by organizational information is a different matter. A recent SPEC Kit from the Office of Management Services of the Association of Research Libraries (OMS/ARL) points out that although the libraries surveyed on use of statistics gathered them extensively, the primary use was for comparisons with other institutions.[9] There is some irony in the proposition that organizations most dedicated to universal access to information are at the same time among the slowest to take advantage of information and knowledge in their own operations.

The Tenacity of Hierarchy

When considering alternative organization charts in any of the varieties of matrix, intersecting circle, and so forth, the inevitable questions are "Who reports to whom? Where is the quality control? How does work get assigned? Who evaluates (and hires/fires/rewards)? How does the chain of command work? If by some miracle a chain of command is not needed, how does the chain of communication work? Who decides, sets priorities, makes hard choices?"

The facile answer is that in a nonhierarchical organization, people are self-motivated (true), informal communication is vital and must receive intensive management commitment and attention (true), priorities get set by consensus and via reiterative discussion and debate (true), and so forth. All of these premises are correct, but they are also true of a well-run hierarchical organization in this age of complexity.

Whatever the risks or advantages or alternatives to hierarchy, the fact is that few models are in existence in libraries at present. A simple comparison of collections of organization charts such as those assembled by OMS/ARL in 1972 (revised 1977) and in 1986[10] shows very little shift in the way libraries are structured. A survey conducted by this author and Ann de Klerk[11] of Bucknell University of directors of large and small academic libraries yielded much the same result.

Why should this be so, given the demonstrated inadequacies of traditional library organization? There are several reasons: in larger libraries the risks of chaos are substantial if traditional organization is not replaced by something equally effective in coordination; changes in the organization often carry the implication of group decision-making, and while group decisions have higher acceptance among workers, there is also some evidence that they tend to produce mediocre choices; participatory management is seen by some as an abdication of responsibility by administrators; small-scale groups within the library have become an effective overlay for getting coordinative work done; there is a fear that in a participative environment, everyone will be involved in every decision, thereby losing the efficiencies of division of labor.

Whither Structure?

What's the problem? Is there a problem? It is possible that the hierarchy/participation/authority debate is more a matter of problem definition than a matter of substance. Hierarchical structures provide a framework for thinking about an organization and its functions as well as a medium for locating responsibility and authority. On the one hand the need for intra-unit information access is well recognized. The argument for participatory management, however, misses the point. Return for a moment to the selection and collection development scenario above: goals and objectives, information, problem analysis, decision-making, communication. That is *real* participation! On the other hand, administrators are far from innocent. Closed-door decision-making (although I suspect that staff think far more goes on than actually does), inadequate use of available information, slowness to recognize the informating (there *must* be a better word!) capabilities of library automation, the assumption that "management information" is for the use of management alone—all inhibit the shift to knowledge-based organizations.

Organizations are entering a period of growing organizational experimentation. Some experiments will be bold; others cautious. Some will fail, some will succeed. Libraries will learn from them all.

What a new organizational paradigm will look like is, and *should be,* impossible to predict. Will the pyramidal organization chart serve the knowledge-based library well? In an era of widely distributed organizational information, how much middle management will be effective? Will some other model emerge, e.g., fewer positions with line authority and more with coordinative responsibilities? Might the formation of temporary groups for specific purposes and projects replace the traditional departmental structure entirely? A knowledge-based organization will surely also have to focus on training and education; how will this come about? How will it be supported? The number of possibilities is endless. The truth is we simply do not know. Predictions are cheap, guesswork expensive.

What, if anything, should be done? Foremost is the need to recognize and internalize the concept that a library is not only an information service agency, but that operationally it is also knowledge-based. Second is the urgency to design information and communication systems that take advantage of automated and traditional techniques. (Vendors of online systems share responsibility here. Few have provided anything approaching meaningful management information; on the other hand, librarians have not demanded it.) The critical questions shift from "Who has the authority?" and "Who controls?" to "What does a staffer need to do his/her job effectively? What information does that person have that others need to do their jobs effectively? How does it get from point A to point B?" And so forth.

What becomes of hierarchy? Surely it will eventually be redefined. Any such process will be evolutionary. Perhaps in the long run it will become irrelevant, and wither away, with more as yet undreamed organizational structures replacing it. Our next problem is to think creatively about the continuous training that will inevitably be required in the knowledge-based library.

Like the lifelong speaking of prose, libraries have, unaware, become informated organizations already. Might we someday soon look back and observe that our late 20th century concept of organization was narrowed and bounded by two-dimensional paper on which organization charts are printed? How might we think differently about organizational structure modeled in three dimensions on a CAD/CAM terminal?

References

1. Euster, Joanne R. and Peter D. Haikalis, "A Matrix Model of Organization for a University Library Public Services Division," *Academic Libraries: Myths and Realities; Proceedings of the Third National Conference of the Association of College and Research Libraries.* April 4-7, 1984, Seattle, Wash., p. 357-364.
2. Raelin, Joseph A., *The Clash of Cultures, Managers and Professionals.* Harvard Business Sch. Pr., 1986, presents an excellent discussion of the reasons for this dichotomy, which is present in a wide variety of organizations, both public and private sector. Librarians will like his discussion, if for no other reason than that he includes them in his listing of professions.
3. Cleveland, Harlan, *The Knowledge Executive Leadership in an Information Society.* Truman Talley: Dutton, 1985, p. xiii.
4. Bennet, Amanda, "Going Global: The Chief Executives in Year 2000 Will Be Experienced Abroad," *Wall Street Journal,* Feb. 27, 1989, p. Al, continued on p. A4.
5. French, John R. P., Jr., and Bertran Raven, "Bases of Social Power," in Cartwright, Dorwin, ed., *Studies in Social Power,* Univ. of Michigan Pr., 1959, p. 150-167.
6. Cleveland, p. xvi.
7. Zuboff, Shoshana, *In the Age of the Smart Machine: The Future of Work and Hierarchy.* Basic Bks., 1988.
8. Drucker, Peter F., "The Coming of the New Organization," *Harvard Business Review,* Jan.-Feb., 1988, p. 45-53.
9. Vasi, John, *Use of Management Statistics.* (SPEC Kit #153). Assn. of Research Libraries, Office of Management Services, Apr. 1989.
10. *Organization Charts.* (SPEC Kit #1). Assn. of Research Libraries, Office of Management Studies, Oct. 1973, updated 1977, and Organization Chart. (SPEC kit # 129). Assn. of Research Libraries, Office of Management Studies, Nov.-Dec. 1986.
11. de Klerk, Ann, and Joanne R. Euster, "Technology and Organizational Metamorphosis," *Library Trends,* Spring 1989, p. 457-468.

SECTION FIVE:
CHILDREN'S LITERATURE

KILLING BOOKS SOFTLY: REVIEWERS AS CENSORS*

Jean Felwel, Editor and Division Vice President, Scholastic, Inc.:

As long as I've been editor, I've always imagined my nightmare review, probably as it would run in *The New York Times Book Review* where my mother would read it. It would go something like this: "This book must have been edited by a baboon, although I'm probably giving baboons too little credit. The style is plodding, the plot infantile, the book far too long. Perhaps the editor failed to read this book; it would have been better if he or she had decided not to publish it."

Editors are the invisible presence behind a book's creation. There are books that we publish that we have a lot to do with, working happily and critically with an author on the story from its very inception. There are other books that we have far less to do with—sometimes we're signing the book up and putting the "perfect" completed manuscript into production. Then we have merely been the book's sponsor, and there's a whole lot of books in between. But whatever role we play in a book's development, we care very much what reviewers say about the books we publish. Care, yes, because of the possible effect a bad review will have on the book's sales (more about that later). We care because even if a negative review doesn't result in a loss of sales, it can affect an author's self-esteem (maybe even their literary reputation, and that is a different kind of damage). But,

"Killing Books Softly: Reviewers as Censors," in *School Library Journal*. Vol. 36, no. 9 (September 1990), pp. 155-162; reprinted with permission from Reed Publishing, USA, copyright © 1990 Reed Publishing, USA.
* These presentations were made at the YASD President's Program during ALA's 1990 Conference in Chicago.

of course, when we publish, we subject the books and their authors to public scrutiny. And so we must be prepared for what follows.

Having grown up in mass market paperbacks, I wasn't responsible for creating books that were reviewed well, but books that sold well. At the time it was possible to sell books widely that were published originally and exclusively in paperback. The books' titles, covers, and content sold them. It was the *outside* of the book that very much determined the size of its distribution, and young adult readers would determine the longevity of that title in the bookstores. Books like Ellen Emerson White's *Friends for Life,* Julian Thompson's *The Grounding of Group's 6,* Joyce Carol Thomas's *Marked by Fire,* Norma Fox Mazer's *Taking Terri Mueller* were all published as paperback originals. Initial distribution and sales had nothing to do with reviews. B. Dalton was "reviewing" the books. If the buyer liked them, we were in business. If not, the books were doomed.

Original paperback publishing was in no way meant to bypass the reviewing mechanism. It was simply geared directly to the YA population. Happily enough though, some reviewers did pick up on books published only in paperback. *The New York Times Book Review* named *Marked by Fire* one of its outstanding books of the year—a truly bold move by George Woods, the *Times'* ever unpredictable children's book editor at that time. And, of course, many journals had some interesting things to say about Julian Thompson's *Group 6,* the novel about parents who send their teens off to school to be done away with. But for the most part it didn't much matter what the reviewers said—the books initially sold themselves.

I remember an embarrassing, yet instructive incident from my assistant editor days. I was writing jacket copy for a reprint (meaning a book we were reprinting from a hardcover into paperback), and I pulled together all the quotable quotes, wrote some meaningful copy, and even added "an ALA/YASD book" at the bottom of the page. Then I submitted it to the editorial director for approval. He told me to punch up the copy, get rid of the *Horn Book* and *SLJ* quotes ("What 13-year-old," he asked, "has ever heard of them?"), and to cut the mumbo jumbo about ALA/YASD. Now, he was a mass market kind of guy, but I can't help wonder, as I reverentially and proudly go over another editor's copy for the Scholastic books listing the great quotes or library or state awards, if readers really care? Do they pay attention to what *Kirkus* says? Do they really know what *VOYA* is? Do they read the quote, and does it influence their purchase over another book?

My feeling about the power of the review—again at least as it relates to paperback publishing—that it can affect the longevity of the book. Will the title be adopted in classrooms? Will librarians recommend it? Will it appear on reading lists? If the answers are yes, the hook is ensured a long in-print life, but few books are so distinguished. Most YA paperbacks—even with a good review or two and a good cover—could probably go out of print within a few years of initial publication. But that's a speech for another time.

Before I leave the subject of paperbacks altogether, a word or two about paperback series publishing. I don't believe (although someone out there may prove me wrong) Scholastic has gotten more than maybe one review of Ann Martin's *The Babysitters Club,* among all 36 titles. That's okay. I'm not mad. There are 35 million copies of the series in print. These readers don't care what any reviewer has to say about Kristy, Stacey, Claudia, Dawn, Mary Anne, Mallory or Jessi. These books fall under a different review criteria—called "word of mouth." And when the word of mouth is good on a series, it can be a powerful phenomena. No amount of prodding or promoting on the publisher's part can make a series happen if the readers just don't like it. Series like *The Babysitters Club* or *Sweet Valley High* can roll out in volume, month after happy month, while another series can go out in quantity and come boomeranging back to your warehouse. The verdict is clear: they [the potential readers] didn't like the cover, the content or the concept. I guess you could call that a very bad review. So sheer distribution is no guarantee of sales. The world of paperback publishing is a different kind of precarious from hardcover publishing, but it's precarious nonetheless.

Now on to hardcover YA books which I came to publish somewhat reluctantly five years ago with the launching of Scholastic Hardcover. I was used to publishing books that were marketed directly to the kid themselves and, for me, the hardcover seemed like an obstacle to the paperback—an unnecessary delay. Well, I now see the error of that view, the naivete of that thinking. There is something enormously instructive about living through the reviews of the books you publish. It's an education, even if it sometimes seems harsh. Reviews can also bring moments of pure joy. The reason reviews are important, no matter what they say, is that writers write to be read and editors publish to communicate. The reviews are the first acknowledgment that the message is being received. An author has toiled over a book for twenty days or twenty years; someone out there—who isn't his or her mother, editor or best friend—liked it very much. Or didn't like it very much. But they read it.

I'm reminded of a discussion at a YASD Best Books Committee meeting when Ellen Emerson White's novel, *Life without Friends*, was being talked about. Since this novel was a sequel to her first novel, *Friends for Life*, Ellen had labored over just how to incorporate what had already happened in Book 1 into Book 2, without recapping it in twenty pages. She and I had gone back and forth with short versions, long versions, and finally decided to go with the longer one. When someone on the committee started talking about the second chapter, I believe, dragging the book down with explication about the previous book, my heart began to sink. I felt like someone said "Gotcha!" But I almost felt gratified that the book was being discussed at all. It's important to be included. It's important to be noticed. Whether it's good or bad, "ink is ink"—as our marketing people like to say. There's nothing worse than being ignored, and there's nothing more detrimental to a book's sales than being ignored. Even being panned may have its virtues.

As the publisher of Julian Thompson's novels, Scholastic has had to endure some pretty gut-wrenching reviews. In fact we were so struck by how vehement the reviews were for Thompson, pro and con, that against prevailing advertising wisdom we ran an ad that showed just how much people hated or loved him. About *A Band of Angels*, a review in *School Library Journal* had this to say: "Thompson's attempt to deal with important issues is undermined by unbelievable characters and an improbable plot . . . Tongue in cheek asides to readers and an abundance of strong language seem transparent efforts to popularize the novel." While *VOYA*'s review said: "Julian Thompson is a unique voice . . . his faith in the young to build a better world is unbounded . . . all these qualities should make it possible to sell this outstanding author to the outstanding young." *A Band of Angels* went on to earn a Best Books designation that year, mostly due to the efforts of a former librarian, Cathie Macrae, and the kids at her library in Baltimore. But the negative reviews have hurt sales of Julian Thompson in hardcover. Fortunately, the kids find him in paperback and there he's strong.

I don't take issue with the reviews, though, not because I agree with them, but I believe in their right to exist. In my whole career in publishing, I think I've felt only once that a reviewer was being personally vindictive towards an author. Those situations are rare. If an author writes a book and publishes it, he or she holds their work up to be reviewed. Otherwise the book should stay in that bottom drawer. Presumably, if a book is good enough, it will outlive its bad reviews, endure in spite of being panned in some journal or another source. As was the case with Ernest Hemingway's *The Sun Also Rises*, about which *The New York Times* said "[it] leaves one with the feeling that the people it describes really do not matter; one is left at the end with nothing to digest."

So, yes, reviews can hurt sales, but they also hurt feelings—and maybe reviewers would find that surprising. Oneof Scholastic's authors refuses to see any of her reviews, good or bad. We're instructed to send them to her mother who, I presume, knows what to do with them. Some authors insist on seeing everything and don't seem fazed by the negative ones. But an author as widely published and respected as Norma Mazer still reacts strongly to a bad review. She just doesn't want to see it. And, while Julian Thompson insists that a bad review doesn't bother him, he wonders if it affects me.

When Scholastic published Norma Klein's *Going Backward* in 1987, she and I had a discussion about reviews. Norma felt then that reviewers had never been very kind to her work. I think that it bothered her that she never attained a level of literary credibility. Perhaps this became more of an issue for her with her adult novels. She wasn't writing like Laurie Colwin, or selling like Danielle Steele. And when that brat pack of young writers came on the scene—Bret Easton Ellis, Jay McInerney, Tama Janowitz—it seemed like the final insult. Here were first-time novelists treading on her subject matter: getting front-page reviews in book sections, landing on bestseller lists and being interviewed on the *Today* show.

The facts seem all too clear. In order for a young adult book and its author to be taken seriously, in a world outside of YA, it should have been published as an adult book. Isn't that the cruelest review of all? I probably still haven't answered the question that brought this panel together: Will the way books are reviewed influence the way publishers publish? No, I don't think so. At least not for the moment. Unless bottomline publishing swallows us all up, independent thinking and writing and publishing will prevail. But maybe too many books are published today. Maybe the lists should be more selective. Maybe there's something Darwinian in the review process, you know—the old "survival of the fittest." Bad reviews don't stop good books from being published. I think criticism of any kind is healthy. But then I've always liked a good fight.

Debbie Taylor, Young Adult Services Specialist, Enoch Pratt Free Library, Baltimore, MD:

Despite the prestige and reputation of the review media, it is the opinion of local colleagues who know the special needs of young people in a given community that carries the greatest influence. Librarians who review books for purchase in libraries, who work with young people in a community, who work with and influence other librarians, are in possession of a tremendous amount of power. I will hazard a guess that if you ask most librarians how they perceive their role, they will immediately reply that they are conduits to information—a bridge if you will. And, if they do anything, it is to guide their patron; sometimes gently, very gently, as they mold them. Of course, only in the direction that they were headed.

But one role that we as librarian do not cast ourselves is one of a censor. Because we know the power of the written word, we cannot believe we would deny anyone access to any piece of information, whether we agree with it or not. However, we cannot get away from the fact that some librarians/reviewers, more often unconsciously than not, ultimately act as censors because of some of the positions they take with regard to the formats they find unacceptable for their clientele as well as subject matter they deem inappropriate. Sometimes budgetary concerns are blamed for these censorship activities. Other times librarians hide behind the wall of so-called high literary standards.

Many times librarian/reviewers do not carefully think through the impact their selection decision might have on the access young people will have to certain materials and information. In our efforts to guide and protect, we find ourselves engaging in the type of censorship activity we claim to abhor. Very often the needs of particular segments of our readership are denied when librarians do not make concerted efforts to overcome personal objections and biases about reading material that appears in certain formats, such as graphic novels and series books or unfamiliar subject matter.

Censorship efforts of librarian/reviewers are often hard to combat because reviewing is a subjective activity. When a librarian/reviewer refuses to add a particular title because that book is deemed poorly written, challengers have a difficult time proving that the book is actually being turned down because of the subject it addresses. When a librarian/reviewer rejects a title because of budgetary restraints, it's hard to dispute that decision. A librarian/reviewer can, by composing a lukewarm acceptance review, kill a book that addresses subject matter they are uncomfortable with, causing few of their colleagues to purchase, read, or promote that book.

What can librarians do to walk the thin line between selector and censor, especially when library book budgets are tight? How do we keep from using our professional jargon to keep out books that we just don't like? One way to work toward fairness in selection is to be honest with ourselves about the books and subjects with which we are uncomfortable. We must remember that our library collections must reflect the communities that we serve, not as we wish them to be but rather how they are. When we review books about which we have deep personal feelings, we have to be very careful in our evaluation. That may be the time to pass that book over to someone who can give a more unbiased critique of the work in question.

Recently, a colleague brought to my attention Susan Lang's *Extremist Groups,* which has a chapter on Louis Farrakhan and the Black Muslims. I found the chapter somewhat unbalanced in its assessment of Farrakhan and of what he and the group he represents means to a large segment of the black community. Knowing that the chances of receiving a more balanced account in a book written for young people was very slim, I was aware that this may be the only material our library system will have available for young people who are attempting to make up their minds about such controversial public figures. I was reminded that many members of the media portrayed Malcolm X similarly to an earlier generation of young people. My urge to write a counter review for this book was strong but, despite my personal feelings about that particular chapter, the book remains on the shelf of our YA collection. I did urge the librarians who purchased *Extremist Groups* to be aware of shortcomings and to keep looking for publications which presented a more balanced viewpoint on that subject.

When reviewing and selecting books for young people, librarian/reviewers must be mindful of "extra literary considerations," as Maria Salvadore, children's coordinator of the District of Columbia Public Library in Washington D.C., put it. We have to consider community standards as well as literary standards. We reviewers have to be aware of the power we wield. We need to be conscious of the fact that the selection and review decisions we make can open the door to ideas and information or can serve as discouraging barriers to access. We have to remember that with that power comes our responsibility to use it fairly and wisely.

Carolyn Caywood, Bayside Area Librarian, Virginia Beach Public Libraries, Virginia:

I'm a reviewer. I don't feel like a censor, but then censors never recognize themselves. I give advice on books. I have no power to make anyone follow that advice. I don't even know whether anyone does. If this is a picture of a censor I don't know why anyone would worry.

The narrowest definition of censorship is that it is exclusively an act of authority, either by government or church. Most of us feel that anyone who tries to prevent others from gaining access to certain information is acting as a censor. Is that what a reviewer has done when a book is not recommended?

I can't speak for other reviewers, but I have never reviewed a book that I wanted to hide from readers. I have reviewed lots of books I thought were a waste of time, money and trees, but I generally send them to the Friends of the Library's book sale for one last chance to find a reader. If I give a book a bad review and your library still buys it, I will not be offended. You can even write the journal in which the review appeared and tell everyone how wrong I was.

The common pattern in letters arguing with reviews is that they usually question the motives or morals of the reviewer, but rarely his or her credentials. The fact is that the only thing that makes me more qualified than you to write book reviews is that I am willing to take the time to do it. There was no course in my library school to teach writing reviews, and I don't have a second master's degree in literary criticism. The position of unpaid reviewer is open to any librarian who is willing to do the work. I think it is important to keep this in mind as you read reviews. You are reading the opinion of someone much like yourself. There is often an attitude in letters criticizing someone's review that the writer believes that a reviewer has been invested with awesome power and authority. I want to make it very clear that if you think my reviews come carved on stone tablets, that's your problem not mine!

Of course, this could be just a way of avoiding responsibility for what I write. If I'm offering advice, don't I have an obligation to make it the best advice I can give? Why aren't there any standards or ethical guidelines for reviewers to follow? The journals I write for do offer guidance to volunteer reviewers. *VOYA* sends its rating guide with every review book and regularly reminds reviewers to be conscious of their own biases and to recognize when they get a book they can't review. *SLJ* sends a form with a set of guidelines that forces the reviewer to examine all aspects of the book. Journals publish policy statements that explain what they have chosen to accomplish within set limitations. Still there is no professionwide statement of reviewer "shall" and "shall nots." I suspect each reviewer has a personal list, and I have spent this spring sorting out what is on mine.

When I first started reviewing, I wanted to astound readers with the brilliance of my incisive criticism. Gradually, I realized how much effort went into a book, even a lousy book and I became ashamed of being witty at the expense of an author. The function of a library review is not to entertain. The author has not spent months or years on a book with the intent of annoying a reviewer, and I don't think it is honest to write a review that sounds like a personal conflict.

The corollary to this is that some people may like a book even if a reviewer doesn't. Don't sneer at them. No one should be expected to apologize for his or her reading tastes, as Betty Rosenberg explained in her book *Genreflecting* (Libraries Unlimited, 1986). In fact, predicting readers' reactions to a book carries certain risks even though it's an expected part of a review. That is, after all, what a censor does—predict that some people will be damaged by exposure to a certain book or recording. The difference is that the reviewer only predicts where the book may find a readership, if at all. Still, this is an aspect of reviewing that needs careful thought to avoid reinforcing the censor's belief that it is possible for one person to know how a book will affect another.

As a reviewer, I have found it difficult to learn how to praise a book. That is, not merely to *say* it is good, but to *show* how it is good. By contrast, it is easy to point out faults and there is always the temptation to nitpick, to list all the little failings and spend proportionally less of the review on the overall success. Perhaps, too, I'm afraid that a review full of praise will sound gushy. I must remember that literary criticism does not mean a negative attitude. Being critical means looking closely to see how the book works and then describing it clearly for those who have not yet seen it. The best reviews share the flavor of a book, not just the outline. They show rather than tell about it.

One often-cited rule of reviewing is that the review should measure the author's success in fulfilling what she or he set out to do—not what the reviewer wishes had been done. While many reviews have violated this principle, many more have been taken to task for not doing so. A common criticism voiced in Letters to the Editor columns is: "this is a bad book because it perpetuates the oppression of (fill in the blank) and you should be ashamed of recommending it." The underlying assumption is that all authors and reviewers should work toward making the world a better place, as defined, of course, by my values. This can be a hard trap to avoid.

Nothing is dearer to us than our own values, and they shape and color the way we perceive everything else. When the author's view of the world diverges far enough from our own, or even when the author is describing a culture that is drastically divergent, it can be literally impossible to read the book. I know, I have found a genre of books that I feel that way about because of the depiction of the characters. I simply cannot comprehend why characters would behave in the way presented. Before I caught on, I wrote at least one very shrill review. Now I simply recognize my limitation and leave these books to reviewers who are more flexible in handling this genre.

As do all reviewers and all book selectors, we have some biases. We are human beings with value systems. We shouldn't expect to be superhuman and set those biases aside and be objective. All we can ask of ourselves and other librarians in the name of intellectual freedom is to be consciously aware of our values so that we know when we are not able to be objective. For the reviewer, that means admitting there are books he or she is not qualified to judge. For the book selector, it may mean delegating a certain section of the collection. The selector is the reviewer's primary audience and his or her reason for being. Does that mean that reviews should provide whatever the selector wants to know?

I became aware of this assumption through a spate of letters to *SLJ* back in 1981, following the review of *Leakey the Elder,* a photo essay on one of Jane Goodall's chimpanzees. It was the expectation of some book selectors that they would be "warned" by a reviewer anytime an animal's genitals were shown in a science book. The reviewer, Rebecca Keese, felt that the photographs were what one would reasonably expect to find in a science book. She said in reply, "Had *Leakey the Elder* been another *Curious George* I would certainly have been remiss not to mention the fact that genitals were included in the illustrations; mentioned not because the inclusion might be considered questionable, but because such inclusions are not what we expect in that genre of children's literature. The final judgement as to the appropriateness of such inclusions must rest with the individual librarian-selector." I have followed her advice in assuming, for example, that four-letter words in a YA novel should be no surprise to the book selector.

In any case, it lies beyond the power of any reviewer to identify everything that might offend someone. The books I thought were ticking bombs are being quietly circulated, while parents become apoplectic over things I never noticed. Naturally, having said that, I promptly encountered a book where this is not the case. I was reading ALA's *Newsletter on Intellectual Freedom* when I discovered that a series had been challenged in a school library. I had reviewed the most recent book, but my review didn't mention this controversy. I don't think the 400 petition signers in Texas were representative of the rest of the communities in the United States—and probably not even of their own county. I am responsible for giving my opinion of the book, not theirs. In any case, I think all librarians should be reading the *Newsletter on Intellectual Freedom* regularly.

I have to believe that the librarians who read my reviews share the professional foundation of commitment to the *Library Bill of Rights* and the *Statement on Professional Ethics*. It is therefore never appropriate for me to warn librarians about a book. Lester Asheim (in *Wilson Library Bulletin*, Nov. 1983) put it most succinctly when he said, "To the selector, the important thing is to find reasons to keep the book. Given such a guiding principle, the selector looks for values, for virtues, and for strengths which will overshadow minor objections. For the censor, on the other hand, the important thing is to find reasons to reject the book."

The way a book review is written can, I think, invite the reader to respond as a selector or as a censor. By holding an image of the reader as a selector, I hope to avoid inviting a censors' response. Because of this, I have become increasingly uncomfortable with rating systems and codes. I am afraid that they are a temptation to make quick negative decisions. It is not just that I worked hard on the review of a low-rated book and want my effort appreciated, it is also that the review, by telling why the rating is low, helps to keep your decision one of selection. I have also found that if I choose the code before I write the review, then I write to justify the code not to describe the book. Given the number of books to be reviewed and considered for selection every year, shortcut codes and ratings will probably become more widespread—but don't lose track of the danger of relying on them too much.

One strong reason for actually reading reviews is that someday you may have to explain why you purchased the book. While the immediate purpose of reviews is to aid in collection development, they take on a second life by supporting materials selection policies. Every policy that I have ever read says that if a book is challenged, we get copies of all the reviews and quote from them to show we knew what we were doing when we bought the book. I don't actually write reviews with this purpose in mind, but it's a good motivation for stamping out wishy-washy equivocation so that a review can be an effective shield against censorship.

Of course if there is no review of book, it becomes much harder to make a selection decision and to defend it. If a review journal prints only favorable reviews, what are we to make of the omission of a title? Was it lousy or just overlooked? What does the silence mean? The journals for which I review are committed to a wide coverage of book publishing. Each book gets its space on the page whether good, bad, or mediocre. If you disagree with an assessment of a book, you can at least see how the reviewer arrived at his or her conclusion. You can see exactly how bad the reviewer actually thought the book was and you can write a letter if you disagree. In so doing, you can give a book like *Weetsie Bat,* which was recently discussed in *VOYA,* more attention than an initial positive review would have produced.

I see a review journal as an open forum where no opinion is suppressed, and I therefore honestly believe that a negative review—even a misguided review—is in no way an act of censorship.

Hazel Rochman, Assistant Editor, Books for Young Adults, Booklist:

I have to tell you, as an immigrant, I am still unable to take for granted the freedoms of the First Amendment. I grew up in South Africa, where I worked as a journalist. Over many years I saw freedom of thought and expression whittled away by the apartheid regime—until it was forbidden to write against the government or even ask questions about children detained without trial and tortured. The result of that kind of censorship is that most people can shut out; can manage not to know what is happening all around them. So, the fact that we're even having a debate like this is, in a way quite wonderful for me. And the issues are crucial.

Subjectivity

I hope that my reviews—even when you disagree with them—will open up questions about the books and about how we read. You don't have to take my word for it; I would hope you would read other reviews as well. But I am not being a censor when I don't like a book. I know that reviewing is subjective. I try very hard to be fair. But what I do know is that I have opinions—some of them passionate, some of them milder. I try, as far as possible, to be aware of them and not let them get in the way. I have pretty strong views on subjects like abortion and capital punishment. I know that everyone doesn't agree with me. I know that you must have, in your library, books on these subjects supporting views different from my own. I also know that any book you buy will not be the only book on that subject.

One more example about subjectivity. There's a new adult book by Randy Herrod, *Blue Bastard*. At age 17 Herrod served in Vietnam in Oliver North's platoon, and loved it. Sally Estes, my boss, is no fan of North—but that's irrelevant. She knows that there are kids out there who'd love this hero stuff about him. So she said in her review, "the author's simply told, heartfelt memoir shows North in a caring, heroic mode. Compelling and easy to read, this will certainly find a teen audience." Then it's over to you—will you find an audience for it in your library? Our job is to tell you this book is there, and that, for what it is, it's good.

Reviewing is not only a matter of personal taste, there are some basic criteria. Is the book accurate? If the author says that being gay is an illness, that's not true. If a map has the cities in the wrong place, that's an error. Is the book exploitive? I don't believe that there's any subject that's not suitable for YAs. It depends how the subject's handled. I recently reviewed six nonfiction books on violence: some were fine, some fair, some bad. Books must deal with this subject, however disturbing it may be. As a reviewer, I must look at how they deal with it. Does the writer exploit the violence, wallow in the gruesome detail, exhort and harangue us to care? Are the sources documented? What are the sources? Is the writer manipulating us with vaguely authoritative phrases like "Experts say . . . " or "Studies show . . . " The same applies to violence in fiction. Is it there for titillation? For shock value?

In your package you'll find my colleague Steffie Zvirin's very fair, reasoned discussion of Chris Cruther's controversial novel *Chinese Handcuffs*: What's good about it; why she doesn't recommend it. Or take books about the Holocaust. Atrocities were done—by ordinary people to ordinary people. Kids want to know about it, and it's important that they should know. But as survivor Ida Fink said about her Holocaust short stories: "I thought one should speak about these things in a quiet voice."

Is the review fair? Well, that depends on what it says it's doing. If a nonfiction book says it's presenting a wide range of opinions, does it do that? If it's presenting a conservative point of view or a liberal point of view, that's fine, as long as it makes clear that that's the point of view. We want commitment. As Betty Carter [coauthor of a forthcoming nonfiction book to be published by Oryx Pr.] says, we want "passionate nonfiction." There's nothing wrong with giving the history of South Africa from the white's point of view, if you make the point of view clear. But it's distortion to say that you're giving a general history of South Africa and then focus 4/5 of the book on the whites who make up less than 1/5 of the population. It's also distortion to say that when the blacks win it's a massacre; when the whites win it's a brave victory against desperate odds.

When I don't like a book, when the world of the story doesn't hold me, I feel free to leave it behind, and I tell you, in my way, what's wrong with it. I would hope that I would support my criticism and that I would relate the particulars to general issues. And, above all, that I would open up questions, so that, even if you disagree, you'll stop and think about that book and about how we read and what we make accessible to kids. When it's a good book I try as much as possible in the review to give you the world of the book without getting myself in the way. Not by a plot summary—there's nothing more boring than a long plot summary—but I try to give myself over to the world of the book—its people, place, language, ideas, narrative voice.

As a reviewer, I have to stay open to the world of the book; to let myself be drawn in and held there. A good reviewer isn't resistant to new ideas and new forms; isn't standing in the way of the kids who, conformists as they are, also are open to all kinds of new things. You start reading the punk fairytale, *Weetzie Bat,* and you think to yourself, what is this? But it works; the language sings and the characters touch you and what appears to be bizarre is also beautiful and delicate and surprising. If I'm open, I can respond to a great book despite my prejudices. My narrowness is overcome.

Rosemary Sutcliff's *The Shining Company* just swept me away; stirred me with its dark fierce story. Yet, when I think about it, it's not really about what I believe in at all. It tells of glory and comradeship in war and betrayal of oneself. Another example: I'm not a very religious person, but in Cynthia Rylant's *A Fine White Dust,* I believed in the young boy's intense spiritual experience. Or take Amy Ehrlich's *Where it Stops, Nobody Knows.* Ehrlich makes the woman who steals a baby a very good mother to that baby. That may be difficult to accept, but her story makes you believe it—and care, even while you know that this woman did a terrible thing. Or there's the Norma Klein novel *Just Friends.* Well I've like Klein over the years, and Steffie had liked her last book *My Life as a Body* but I'd disliked one of her recent books which seemed to be really self-indulgent about a girl's neurotic relationship with her father, so I didn't expect the new book to be particularly great. To my delight, I found it was. Full of flaws, too preachy, but witty, intelligent, complex. And I thought, if only I'd had such a book when I was growing up, talking about, thinking about, not daring to ask about love, friendship, sex, and intimacy. Here's a book that confronts those things. It doesn't give simple answers; it shows that there are none.

A great book can change all my criteria. Many of us have always been adamant that nonfiction should be fully documented and that it should not indulge in fictionalization. (Much of this is in reaction to those cutesy biographies with made-up conversations and episodes to illustrate the hero's greatness.) Then along comes Tim O'Brien's *The Things They Carried,* which deliberately muddles fact and fiction. It's based on his experiences as a foot soldier in Vietnam. Although he says the book is fiction, he names a character Tim O'Brien. This character goes to war as did the author, thinks as the author does, and has many of the experiences O'Brien has had. What the author is doing is making you think about truth beyond fact. He's showing how we tell stories to try and find ourselves. This book made me see how you can sometimes throw the old categories out of the window.

I try to review the author's book, not one I wish had been written. So if someone writes a farce, I can't criticize it for not being psychologically penetrating. I can't say about Norma Klein, why doesn't she stop writing about New York liberal yuppies? That's her subject; she can write about anything she likes. What I can say is that she is or isn't doing it well, or that she's not saying anything fresh. I can't assume that kids outside New York won't read her stories. I can't criticize Brock Cole for not making his adults responsible and strong. This is his story and it works, and he makes me care about his characters in all their complexity. In the same way, if a story has an unwed pregnant teenager, I can't say, why didn't she get an abortion? Or, if I'm on the other side, why did she consider an abortion? Or, of course there will be those who'll ask, why did she get pregnant?

Role Models

We can't read fiction as a self-help manual, for the message. We've got to stop looking for role models, whether we like them old-fashioned or liberated. In Patrick Raymond's stunning new teenage love story, *Daniel and Esther*, Daniel's view of women is quite sexist. But, first of all, Daniel is a character and that's what he feels. And further the writer makes you care desperately about Daniel and Esther and their love and their parting as the Holocaust looms. Just because we like the role model isn't a reason to say it's a good book. E. L. Doctorow says that one of the things he admires about George Bernard Shaw is that he gave some of the best speeches to the characters with which he disagrees. A good book is rich with ambiguity.

Pleasure

You can't coerce people to read. It has to be a pleasure, and there are various kinds of pleasure in reading. Many readers want formula books. They're what Margaret Atwood calls "hot water bottles and thumbsucking kind of reading." We all need them. and we also need reviews of popular materials. But there are some things—like YA series romances—that you buy for the library but for which reviews are irrelevant. What would my review say? You don't need an assessment of their popularity and quality. You don't want me to describe the characters or summarize the plot or describe the setting, for goodness sake. In a article on marketing formula fantasy in *The New York Times* Book Review [April 29, 1990], David Hartwell compared it with buying a can of tuna fish or a Chevrolet: you know what you're getting.

As a reviewer, I have to keep up with what's popular. One of my favorite kinds of books is one that appears to be formula, that lures you in, sets up the stereotypes, and then startles you awake. But there's also the other side. It's important not to condescend, to assume that all YAs want is what is quick and superficial and popular. Anyone who works with kids know they surprise you. They push you, and you can surprise them too. Within any group there's a wide range of reading interests and reading levels. Within the same reader, there's a wide range; the teenager drifting through *Sweet Valley High* may also love Mahy's *Catalogue of the Universe* or Koertge's *The Arizona Kid* or Brook's *Midnight Hour Encores*.

The Audience

We have to be aware of a varied audience. We find ourselves saying, "Kids won't read this." Who do we mean? Myself as a kid? My son? The kids in my library? Suburban kids? We each live in a small world and talk to people like ourselves and reinforce each other. We think everyone agrees with us. I know that I'm reviewing for all kinds of librarians with all kinds of collections, and programs and users. Some are so busy that they never promote a book. For them anything not immediately attractive will be a shelfsitter. There are those who want to know about what's good and worth telling kids about. I won't perpetuate the idea that those with few blacks in the community don't want books about blacks; or that country people don't want to read about Norma Klein's New Yorkers; or that New Yorkers don't want a wilderness/survival story like Gary Paulsen's *Hatchet*.

Labels

I try to avoid labelling, whether it's that loaded phrase, "for the gifted," or whether it's something like "this may give some problems in some libraries." And, especially now that the *Booklist* policy has a flexibility that allows us to write longer reviews and to use quotes, I try to show you the book, give you a sense of it. I try to support my criticism—positives and negatives—with quotations or examples, with comparisons and connections. For example, I reviewed a book of doggerel verse by Roald Dahl. I know that Dahl isn't for everybody, especially in his vulgar mode. I think that many kids like his vulgarity. I like it, and I try to show and tell you why. I quote a bit of it so you can decide for yourself. Dahl knows about a certain kind of teenage humor (barely out of the bathroom) with sniggering fantasies about teachers and other adults. Another point about labeling and its hidden messages. Should I tell you the race of the character? Since most characters are white, the question really is should I tell you when the characters aren't white? Obviously, if the story is about a racial incident or about a cultural celebration or custom, the ethnicity will be clear. When I reviewed Gary Soto's short stories of growing up Latino in Fresno, California, I said directly that these were stories about a cultural group too little represented in books for young people. But what about when the writer's telling a story in which the characters happen to be people of color and their ethnic identity isn't especially relevant? By mentioning it, I'm reinforcing the stereotype that these people are special, different. Yet librarians tell me that they want to know; they especially want books where ethnicity isn't a big deal, regular stories about all races where the characters aren't a special problem. I try to work it in naturally, to tell you without making it special.

Budgets

I know you have a limited budget and if you buy a hardback poetry anthology, it means several less romances, but what about the kid who also wants something more? Aren't we limiting their choices by giving them access only to what is easy and superficial. If not in the library, where will they find the books that aren't for everyone?

I can't tell you how to spend your money. Or how to balance the diverse demands of your users. I can only tell you what I think is good, and tell you as much as possible about it. And as a reviewer I must bear in mind Lester Asheim's point that the library must provide for the individual; the special case also has rights. I know that you have to buy the book without seeing it and I really try not to mislead you. I also know that I can't make the decision for you. You must decide, in terms of your collection, your audience, and your budget, and whether you'll have time and interest to promote it—and if you will buy it. It's your decision, and it's my job to help you make an informed decision.

Just one last emphasis: *Books must disturb.* As Richard Peck, with his usual concentrated wit, put it: "The illiterate fear that books will give people ideas, when the greater fear is, that they won't."

Roger Sutton, Senior Editor, The Bulletin of the Center for Childrens Books:

I must say I searched in vain for something like a question mark in the title of this program that would give reviewers the benefit of the doubt. "Do we censor?" is a question that must be preceded by another question: can we censor? Carolyn Caywood has already answered this one: reviewers cannot censor; that is, we cannot prevent access to a book. We can however, be censorious, damning a book for its moral or political turpitude, rather than offering informed opinion as to its literary effectiveness, accuracy, and perceived appeal for a given audience. And by opinion I mean just that—I while proud of our professional expertise, none of us is claiming to have the last word.

What much of this discussion has been about, however, is not censorious reviews but negative reviews. They aren't the same thing. It is possible not to like a book for the right reasons. It is possible, for example, to dislike a book by Judy Blume or Norma Klein for reasons other than moral objection. (And we cannot be held responsible for the maintenance of an author's self-esteem, a task better left to his or her editor, family and friends.) To say that a book is "boring" or "predictable" or "confusing" is only censorious when we use those words to cover some deeper distaste, like the librarian I knew who wouldn't purchase *Show Me!* because "it didn't have an index." To say that a paperback romance is "pedestrian trash" may be cranky and officious, but it is not a censorious statement. To label it "sexist (or sexy) pedestrian trash," is. Reviewers hope to evaluate how well something is said; censors keep busy deciding what should have been said—or silenced—in the first place.

The premise of today's program runs along the lines of "if reviewers censor, they should stop." But I am afraid there are many librarians out there who in fact believe the review journals should be doing more flagging and tagging, alerting them to any possible "trouble." They want us to use words and phrases like "problematic," "mature readers," "realistic language," or "sensitive subject." Some librarians want this kind of labelling because they are themselves censors; the great majority, however, are simply afraid for their jobs. All we can do is describe what we believe a book to be about. We hope to do this fairly and thoroughly, but with a sense of perspective. I am not about to start counting each occurrence of the word "goddamn" in every new YA novel, despite letters we have received asking for this assistance. We cannot anticipate your trouble. We cannot promise to mention each time a character dresses as a witch for Halloween. We can't promise to dislike *Weetzie Bat* because you are bothered by Wetzie's unorthodox family. We certainly can't promise to be right.

The Bulletin, SLJ, Booklist, Horn Book, VOYA: librarians are the primary audience for these book review journals. I think the editors of each would agree that our job is to tell our audience enough about a given title so that each librarian can make up his or her own mind as to the suitability of it for a particular collection. I would like to suggest that the best way for us to fulfill this responsibility is by maintaining a prior responsibility to the book in hand, allowing it its say. In my experience, the best books create their own criteria, confounding the imposition of a literary, moral, or sociopolitical checklist. By keeping our attention fixed on what the book is telling us, we reviewers can't go too far wrong.

MEANING-MAKING AND THE DRAGONS OF PERN

Kay E. Vandergrift

Many literary scholars, as well as teachers and librarians who share literary experiences with young people, have been accustomed to studying texts, assuming that meaning resides therein and that a mythical "perfectly informed" reader could extract full meaning from that text. Reader-response criticism reminds us, however, that what a reader takes from a text is not always what someone else presumes to be contained there. Meaning is made as much from what one brings to a text as what one takes from it. Thus, different readers decoding the same text may actually be "reading" very different stories and the same reader may read that text quite differently at different times. Subsequent readings would build on earlier ones and personal interpretations grow with life experiences and in interaction with others who discuss their perceptions of that work.

This article demonstrates a process through which young people are encouraged to believe that their own personal meanings made in response to literature are valid interpretations of a text. They also recognize, therefore, that very different interpretations are also valid and authentic responses to that same text. Through the process of sharing and discussing these meanings they come to an increased understanding of themselves, of each other and of the world of the

"Meaning-Making and The Dragons of Pern," by Kay E. Vandergrift in *Children's Literature Association Quarterly.* Vo. 15, no 1 (Spring 1990), pp. 29-32; reprinted with permission from the *Children's Literature Association Quarterly*, copyright © 1990 by *Children's Literature Association Quarterly.*

text. More specifically this article describes reader imagination and interaction with the dragon lore portions of the Pern novels by Anne McCaffrey in seeking to demonstrate how young readers make meaning.

Pern is an imagined world with medieval overtones in which humans and dragons co-exist and grow in their symbiotic relationship. This metaphoric world also challenges readers to become engaged with it and to respond fully to its potential meanings. Pern is the locus of a number of novels and the complexity and connectedness of these works evokes from the reader a correspondingly complex and connected series of responses. McCaffrey's Harper trilogy was written for young people, but the remaining Pern novels are classified as adult science fiction. This does not, however, make them less accessible or less relevant to a young audience since readers who truly respond to Pern are eager to read all the books, each of which contributes to the total impression of dragon lore in that world.

Pern, like most mythic fantasy lands, is the scene of an ongoing battle between good and evil, between dragons and Thread, a mycorrhizoid spore that destroys all life upon contact. Also true to traditional literature, it is evil. Threadfall, which evokes the good-dragon response. Threadfall is the time when dragons knowingly rise to destroy Thread before it destroys the land and the people. This familiar motif provides a starting point for the interpretation of story events in this imaginative land.[1]

The Model of a Child's Meaning-Making Process in Response to a Literary Text (Figure 1) depicts a circle of meaning and some of the many factors around that circle which either contribute to or provide insight into the process of going from a very personal and private "felt meaning" to the shaping of that felt meaning into language that may be expressed and shared and then to a more common group-developed meaning in an interpretive community. Since I am concerned with interpretive communities in schools and libraries, I also examine the role of the adult intermediary who participates in that community. Readers must keep in mind, however, that this diagram merely attempts to "hold still" or make static enough for observation what is, in reality, a dynamic, on-going process. Making-meaning exists in a moment in time; and any meaning, even a community meaning, is

Figure 1. Model of the Child's Meaning-Making Process in Response to a Literary Text

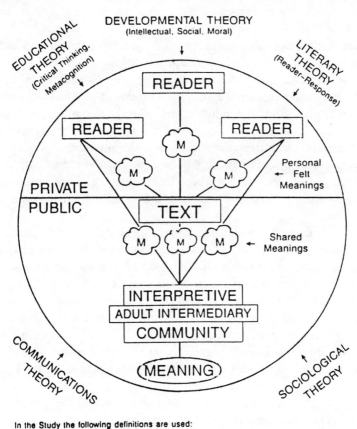

In the Study the following definitions are used:

TEXT: Story or metaphor which stimulates thought about feelings; assumed to be immediately comprehensible, even by the young child, but never fully comprehended.

READER: An active maker-of-meaning in the experience of responding to a text, that is, bringing meaning to and taking meaning from a symbolic form.

MEANING: An event in time, located in the consciousness of a reader so that the text disappears into the reader's experience of it just as the dancer cannot be separated from the dance or the musician from the music.

INTERPRETIVE COMMUNITY: A group of persons who share, exchange and create meanings in response to a text.

ADULT INTERMEDIARY: The adult who shares symbolic experiences with young people and, at best, is both a member of their interpretive community and one who is responsible for encouraging and maintaining the process illustrated in this model.

itself an event in time, likely to change from moment to moment, response to response. The process described here begins with the assumption that readers are creators of meaning, not just consumers of an author's prepackaged and predetermined meaning. The private part of that meaning-making inevitably goes on in the mind of one who reads or hears a story, but the public aspect requires a community of trust, one in which all participants are valued, listened to and respected. Only in a group in which it is safe to attempt to express those felt meanings, to take risks, knowing that those risks will be met with respect rather than ridicule, can one make the conceptual leaps that lead to more insightful, sometimes even startling, meanings. Of course, such an interpretive community, like any other community, takes time and care to develop, but a skillful adult intermediary can facilitate and speed up that process by encouraging all participants to listen carefully and consider seriously the comments and questions of others.

This research was undertaken over a six-month period (beginning in Spring, 1985) as one of several studies to test the above model. Seven young adults (11th and 12th graders, 4 males and 3 females) shared, during three two-hour taped sessions, their visions of the dragons of Pern. Each was an avid fantasy/science fiction reader and all were articulate in discussing plot, characterization, language and other literary elements in the Pern novels. This particular interpretive community was brought together after individual discussions with students during which I discovered a common interest in the Pern novels.

Six major categories of questions were used with the group as a means to collect and analyze data on reader responses. These questions, listed below, were intended to elicit general responses which capture personal experiences with the works but also to refer readers back to the books in an attempt to examine the transaction between reader and text in the meaning-making process. In our first session together, students were asked to write brief personal responses to each of these questions for their own use in retaining and reminding themselves of private interpretations in the midst of subsequent group discussions.

Content: What are these stories about? What key words or phrases describe the stories? Are any of these words or phrases actually used in the books?

Feelings: What, if anything from these books prompted strong emotions? Why does this affect you as it does?

Beliefs: Did particular beliefs surface as you read? What brought them to the surface? How did these beliefs affect your response?

Memory: Where you aware of any connections between text and your memories? What were the similarities and differences between your reading and your memories?

Sharing: What from your reading would you like to share with others?

Different Readings: If you read any of these books more than once, are you aware of any differences in subsequent readings?

Talking with these readers about McCaffrey's novels made it clear that her dragons are far more compelling as characters than those in other dragon stories and than their human companions in these stories. The relatively unstructured responses of these young people referred most frequently to dragons and dragon characteristics; this is evident from the high frequency of their mention of key phrases such as: Impression, bonding, hierarchy among dragons, eating, "between," telepathy, naming, talk and humor, harpers, fire lizards and dragonriders. Thus, our discussions focused on dragon lore. In looking together at specific incidents in the texts, the group was able to share more adequately the various meanings that different individuals made in the process of reading these works and, in so doing, we increased our sensitivity both to the literary works and to each other.[2]

What then attracts readers to Pern and draws them so intensely into the lore of the dragons who inhabit the land? The respondents indicated that what attracted them was exactly what some critics perceive to be the greatest flaw in these works, that is, the rather loosely connected episodic plots with references to characters and events in other Pern novels. One student said she "liked how you meet a character from one book in another one."

McCaffrey has also devised an elaborate hierarchy among dragons that seems to heighten reader involvement. This was very evident in readers' uncertainties about the meaning of color and the relative importance of different dragons. One participant finally decided to go to the blackboard and draw the dragon hierarchy and, with appropriate assistance from colleagues, did so. Students explained that the reader encounters several dragons by name and those named have distinct personalities, but there is always an awareness of large numbers of dragons organized into a dragon power structure. The following is one student's summary of the group's discussion of dragon appearance and structure:

> "Dragons are hatched from eggs with their skin reflecting the light spectrum: the gold dragon is the rare and prized one, a queen dragon; bronze dragons are male and next in importance, because of their size and power and as potential mates for the queen dragon: greens are sterile females, while blues and browns are male, all smaller and of lesser importance in the dragon structure."

In considering the reason for this elaborate differentiation, readers entered easily into a discussion of dragon hierarchy, identifying the queen dragon, a female, as the most powerful of all the dragons. Opinions about distinctions among dragons raised the following question: "Do the colors give a sense of community while names indicate individualization?" Another student suggested that "colors are primary like the sun in our world and add a sense of realness to beings."

The ritual of Impression, when a dragon emerges from its egg and a human is "Impressed," binding them one to the other for life, is fittingly described by McCaffrey:

> A feeling of joy suffused Lessa; a feeling of warmth, tenderness, unalloyed affection, and instant respect and admiration flooded mind and heart and soul. Never again would Lessa lack an advocate, a defender, an intimate, aware instantly of the temper of her mind and heart, of her desires. How wonderful was Lessa. The thought intruded into Lessa's reflections, how pretty, how kind, how thoughtful, how brave and clever! (*Dragonflight* 83).

These readers recognized that the dragon chooses the rider and that the bonding is something beyond the natural. This awareness of caring and loving, as one youngster said, "seems to go beyond the language capability of McCaffrey," leaving gaps in the text and forcing the reader to contemplate the situation and "imagine what it might be like to stand on the hot sands of a hatching ground." In each session with students, a large percentage of the time was spent on discussing Impression; and it was clear that they found the passages in the various texts dealing with this phenomenon to be powerful and emotionally charged. Several indicated that they had re-read those passages many times and tried to imagine themselves in such a scene. The following excerpts from the tapes share some of their thoughts:

> "I would know for sure which was my dragon and would feel so close like a real friend."

> "This made me want to reach out and touch someone (laughter, and teasing) . . . I mean it—the dragons just knew who was right for them. It was a perfect relationship."

> "The fire lizards were different, they Impressed because you fed them, I read about this kind of thing with animals but maybe it is true of kids, babies—maybe babies are like the fire lizards. Later when you meet the right person it's more like dragon Impression."

Thus, the reader's memory, life experiences and relationships with other human beings help deepen the significance of this relationship in Pern. The "personal horizon" (Iser) which each reader brings to story helps to evoke the feelings of such a bonding.

Although the responses to this bonding process were generally very positive, several students did indicate that dragons are frightening in their actions from the earliest stages of Impression when they sometimes maim or kill potential mates. The excerpt that follows was chosen by students to demonstrate this violence, which they, nevertheless, refused to accept as violence in dragon terms:

> . . . the young dragon mauled the boy, throwing him roughly
> aside as if unsatisfied in some way. The boy did not move, and
> Lessa could see blood seeping onto the sand from dragon-in-
> flicted wounds (*Dragonflight* 81).

It is this human waste that disturbs both Lessa and F'lar and leads to
a slightly new pattern for Impression, the bringing of prospective
candidates for Impression to the hatching grounds prior to hatching
and permitting them to touch the eggs in a process perhaps similar to
pre-natal impressions in humankind. One student indicated that she
had participated in a bonding ceremony for a younger sibling which
was similar in many ways. Students recognized this change in the
process of Impression but thought that maybe Lessa was like "some
parents or teachers who complained that it was too violent—like the
TV stuff on violence."

Two of the respondents were very specific in filling in gaps in the
texts to describe the hall for Impression and indicated size factors and
coloration that McCaffrey had not included. For instance, one boy
wrote out the following description:

> "When young people were brought to the hall as potential
> dragonriders it was quite large with precisely seven sections with
> 28 rows in each section and the entire back of the Queen
> dragon's egg nest was a waterfall with the most misty-like colors
> all shiny—the water was hot of course since the eggs must be
> warm."

When questioned about the number of rows and the waterfall the
respondent was *absolutely* certain these descriptions were in the stories
and others in the group indicated "it was logical after all, since the
dragon queen must be calm and water does that." When asked about
the number seven, the respondent indicated "that maybe it was from
childhood reading and all those fairy tales."

Reading about Impression stimulated students to think of a first
puppy, a first love, the parent-child relationship or that with a mate.
They recognized that the concept of respect is integral to this bonding
process between dragon and rider. The mutuality of the two partners
in "sensing each other's needs and desires is so close to what most seek

in human society." Is McCaffrey too much of a romantic in this approach? Some think she is, but most of the young people with whom I discussed these books believe that she has captured a sensitivity to humankind and the nature of a relationship with another lifeform that resembles, at least metaphorically, the relationship of human to human. Fully accomplished, the nature of the bonding between dragon and dragonrider is strong and enduring. Students pointed to the following excerpt to support this:

> But, from the second in which her eyes had met those of the young queen on the Hatching Ground, nothing but Ramoth mattered. Lessa was Ramoth's and Ramoth was hers, mind and heart, irrevocably attuned. Only death could dissolve that incredible bond (*Dragonflight* 91).

They also pointed out that, just as two loving partners often take on the image or reflection of each other, so too with dragons: "Supposedly the dragon reflected its rider as much as the rider the dragon" (*Dragonflight* 89).

It was clear in our discussions that these readers do not view dragons as pets; rather, they are thinking beings who communicate with logic, purpose, humor and emotion. Dragonriders are those individuals in Pern society who have some unknown, perhaps innate, ability to attract dragons. The reader "never knows why a dragon selects one human mate over another." Some young readers, perhaps exploring vicariously the ritual of pairing in their own teen years, created imaginative webs of reason for selection or attempted to compare personal characteristics with characteristics of chosen mates. Others just accepted that there was "no known reason" for particular pairings. When asked if they thought they would have been chosen, almost all responded "yes." From the text, instinct seems to be the only factor in the choice, "but the knowledge that this particular human will be the perfect other half of a mighty dragon is just as magic as falling in love."

Students recognized that dragon and rider ability to communicate telepathically and with intense feelings is what involves us with the individual personalities of the dragons. Telepathic communication of both language and emotions is characteristic of the dragon/rider relationship. There was no question that this fascinated readers, and they spent time wondering if ESP and Telepathic communication were possible for them. In so doing, they remembered examples of possible telepathic experiences from their lives:

> "There was this time when I was small and I just knew my dog was dead and no one would tell me. I know it is possible."

> "Sometimes I know just what my parents will say—no, I mean even the exact words."

> "The thing that is terrific with McCaffrey's dragons—they speak inside your head and even tease you."

McCaffrey has established elaborate names for dragons and riders in Pern, and the Impression ceremony is one of naming as well as bonding. At the time of Impression a rider's name is shortened and it is the rider who announces the name of the dragon. Although some readers thought "this business with the names is somewhat silly," most thought it strengthened the bond. The girls especially appreciated that "both riders and dragons got new names—not like a human marriage when the woman is expected to change hers." At the Impression of young Keevan, students were delighted by the exquisite courtesy of Lessa to young Keevan in asking him the name of his dragon when she could speak directly to any dragon.

> "What's his name, K'van?" asked Lessa, smiling warmly at the new dragonrider. K'van stared up at her for a long moment. Lessa would know as soon as he did. Lessa was the only person who could "receive" from all dragons, not only her own Ramoth. Then he gave her a radiant smile, recognizing the traditional shortening of his name that raised him forever to the rank of dragonrider. "My name is Heth," the dragon thought mildly, then hiccuped in sudden urgency. "I'm hungry" (*The Smallest Dragonboy* 231).

As revealed in the previous quotation, food is very important in dragon lore and references to dragon appetites are often humorous. Once Impression has occurred, the dragon seeks food; and it is the responsibility of the rider to provide moderation, control and direction to the young dragon's appetite. Some weight-conscious young readers commented that they "would like to have someone to help them keep their appetites under control" while another said her "mother is certainly a rider in that respect." The control of food is a critical factor in managing a queen dragon just prior to mating. At this time she may kill animals and drink the blood, but she cannot consume the meat which might inhibit her mating flight. Firestone (phosphine mineral) is a particularly important food in that it is fed to dragons to make the fire which destroys Thread. Students recognized that food and feeding are integral to dragon lore and they make the connection between food and control by the rider, but many "just didn't understand eating firestone which was so deadly."

Members of the group attempted to describe what happens to them as readers as they perceive the dragons and watch them defeat evil in this imaginative land of Pern. There was general agreement when one reader said, "I put myself in Pern to try to help solve the problem, but then I use Pern to think about my own problems." There was also evidence that they "like to imagine the details of some of the things McCaffrey only mentions in the stories," as in the earlier description of the Impression Hall. The immediate problem in each of the novels may be to stop the destruction of Threadfall, but conflicts and power struggles interfere in the accomplishment of this mission In Pern mythical beasts take on tasks that appear impossible, but the novels also place readers in the position of "working things out for ourselves." Questions come to the reader but clues are also provided. For example, the group discussed why all in Pern hold dragons in awe. Several responded with very logical answers supported by actual text. They indicated that, even for those who do not fully value dragon services, "there is a subconscious recognition and fear of their power and might." Indeed, part of the traditional lore of Pern includes the injunction to clear the land of vegetation that borders the Holds and to render tithes of food and clothing to dragonriders. When the Holders choose to ignore these rules, danger and destruction come very close. One respondent made an interesting connection in the following statement:

> "You see rules are important and Pern is filled with them, that's why it is so good. You see the rules are not stupid, they are logical."

The students discussed death, but it was accepted as a normal part of heroic battles. When a dragon's rider dies, a dragon winks into "between," that frozen nothingness which serves as a form of space travel in which dragons move either spatially or through time. Readers pointed out that, although this void "between" is used in fighting Thread, it is very taxing to those who enter and can lead to death for the forces of good as well as of evil. Moreta uses it to save Pern, but she becomes so drained that her exhaustion brings about her own death, that of another dragon and finally the death of her own dragonqueen Orlith (*Moreta: Dragonlady of Pern* 329, 335). To stay "between" is to die in cold nothingness. Thus, the bond is broken; "if a dragon dies and the rider survives, he or she is but a half creature." Students pointed out that such a description is given about Lytol with the death of his brown dragon Larth and of Brekke at the death of Wirenth. The power of "between" is critical to the stories, but it is also "more frightening than death itself," perhaps because McCaffrey leaves no gaps for imaginative recreation. She tells readers that it is a cold vold of nothingness, thus prohibiting that natural reader tendency to specify the unspecified in order to gain imaginative control over it.

Another fascinating aspect of McCaffrey's dragon lore is her inclusion of dragons and riders that are far from perfect, and thus more believable to readers. Although they often fail and reveal weaknesses in personal character, in the long run they will still fight the evil of Thread. A weak dragon may even lead to the very problem that the new weyrleaders will face, as in the case of Jora and her dragon queen Nemorth. A laziness of both dragon and rider eventually led to poor reproductive cycles and consequently fewer dragons to combat Threadfall. It became clear as the discussions progressed that just being a dragon is not enough; it is the development of character through

testing that makes the greatest dragons. This concept of development
of character through testing was described by a student:

> "In each book McCaffrey wants you to know that some kind of
> test is before the dragon. It is not just like the quest in literature
> that we studied but something more. Like in life, you face some
> tough decisions and in a sense you are tested for the future."

Students named Lessa's Ramoth, Flar's Mnementh, F'nor's Canth,
Moreta's Orlith and Jaxom's Ruth as dragons of tremendous importance to the saving of Pern and pointed out that "each had been tested
to be made ready for their important roles."

Several students expressed strong emotional feelings in relation to
the treatment of dragons by the riders. For instance, two students
pointed to the identical incident as disturbing them:

> "I was very angry at the way Meron treated his fire lizard; he was
> cruel and it was good that Canth took care of him."

> "I was frightened and worried as I read that part about the fire
> lizard and even angry with Lord Nabol for being so cruel and
> uncaring."

In describing the actions of Meron, Lord of Nabol, a land holder,
students identified how McCaffrey makes that anger obvious:

> He (F'nor) also saw that the man (Meron, Lord of Nabol) held
> tight to his fire lizard though the creature was twisting and
> writhing to escape. Its agitated screeching rose to a nerve-twit-
> ting pitch. "The little one is terrified," Canth told his rider. . .
> . "The man is cruel." F'nor has never heard such condemnation
> from his dragon. Suddenly Canth let out an incredible bellow.
> It startled the riders, and the other two dragons . . . Canth's tactic
> had achieved the effect he'd wanted. Meron had lost his hold on
> the fire lizard and it had sprung free and gone between
> (*Dragonquest* 322).

On the other hand, students spoke of encountering McCaffrey's concept of "belief and constancy" between dragon and rider, most strongly revealed in the portrayal of Lord Jaxom and his dragon Ruth. There is a constant testing of Jaxom and Ruth to perform the feats common to all other dragons and riders, preliminary to even greater tests, even though Ruth is a small white dragon never expected to survive. Very deftly McCaffrey leads the reader into a deeper understanding of the personal growth of both Jaxom and Ruth in their symbiotic relationship which leads to saving Pern (*The White Dragon* 92, 115-122). The dragon Ruth was much loved by students but not Jaxom; he was admired for having faith in Ruth but perceived as less important.

> "I believed that Ruth would make it and do something so special. He was such a tiny dragon but could just talk to all the others and particularly the fire lizards."

Students recognized that it is the Harpers who are responsible for continuance of the oral tradition, particularly concerning dragons and their roles in Pernian society. The songs and musical stories that Harpers tell are a means of educating, entertaining and indoctrinating the people. Harpers seem to have additional powers as communicators and sense their responsibility for the preservation of Pern. For example, students pointed out that "it is an ancient question song that gives the clue to the solution of Lessa's problem," and once again the destruction of Pern by Thread is prevented. Robinton, a Master Harper, does have a limited ability to communicate with dragons and seems to enjoy this gift. He speaks to Mnementh as he passes announcing his companion's presence and the dragon answers: "'I know. I have told them you are come.' . . . He (Robinton) never expected an answer to his pleasantries but was always extremely flattered on those occasions when Mnementh responded" (*The White Dragon* 37). Readers agreed that they developed a sense of reliance upon the Harpers as fulcrums in the story. "It is the Harpers who always seem to be able to see the direction that has to be taken and lead dragonriders and others toward the path to success."

When asked about what they wanted to share with others from their reading, many of the students of both sexes spoke of the role of women in the McCaffrey books. I asked for specific examples of this in the stories and what follows summarizes their responses: "Females in both weyrs and crafthalls enjoy respect, honor and power in Pern." "Some aspects of the Pern stories reveal a stylized romantic view of women, yet women act independently in Pernian society." "It is the power of the queen dragon that overrides all decisions here, and it is Lessa and Moreta who, in different instances, are the most obvious saviors of Pern." "Women are often the healers of both humans and dragons." When a dragon is wounded in Threadfall, the burning is often so bad that a kind of painkiller (numbweed) is used to kill pain and immobilize the dragon. "Women show no fear in dealing with a wounded dragon" and the reader gets the impression that "women are gifted in such treatments and in other ways too." "It is usually the female characters who possess not only knowledge to do what needs to be done, but also the courage to actually do it." The rides of Lessa and Moreta were identified by several students as indicating such a form of immediate action. One student thought that women knew more than men in the stories but "it didn't matter since the dragons knew everything and even kept some secrets."

Near the end of our time together, the group returned again to our original questions. As indicated previously, these questions served more to record personal responses and as a means of organizing and reporting the data collected on tape than to structure or control the actual discussions. They did, however, also help the group to summarize and reflect upon what had taken place in those discussions. In answer to "What were these novels about?" or "What did they mean to you?" the strongest and most agreed upon response was "the relationship between two beings." This corresponded with the most frequently mentioned key words: impression and bonding. All agreed with the statement that "a mission can be a driving force in life" and that "humor is essential in even the most serious situations." In an attempt to determine which elements or aspects of the texts caused these particular recreations of meaning, we went back and looked again at the incidents discussed in this article.

This return to the texts confirmed that the dragons and fire lizards of Pern share a world of telepathic communication in which a loving exchange is the basis for all that happens. The emotional bonding and the constancy and the power of that relationship is so strong that all else in the stories was secondary for these readers. In their totality, the Pern novels develop quite fully the nature of McCaffrey's dragons and the dragon lore which ties them so completely to her human characters. At the same time, they stimulate readers to make meaningful connections to their lives using the imaginative experiences of the world of Pern to gain insight into the concerns of their own world.

How does what is discussed here differ from what we have most frequently done in analyzing a literary work? Obviously, the major difference is in the starting point. Rather than assuming that meaning is inherent in the structure of the text, reader-response criticism attends first to particular and private meanings made by readers in experiencing that text and then goes back to the printed page to clarify interpretations and share meanings with others. In this instance, discussions with individual readers alerted me to a common interest in McCaffrey's work and caused me to bring this group together.

Therefore, each respondent had already begun the process of using language to translate his/her personally-experienced meanings into expressed meanings prior to any group interaction. This, along with their strong involvement with the Pern novels and their original notes in response to the questions undoubtedly helped students formulate and hold on to their own meanings in the midst of lively group discussions. This is in contrast to the more typical discussion group in schools in which the work to be read is assigned by an adult and often read quickly and with little or no commitment on the part of many readers. In that type of situation, especially in a class-sized group, it is likely that many participants would just accept the expressed meanings of the most vocal members as their own.

The differences of opinion expressed by this particular group of Pern readers were few (Menolly was or was not satisfied to be a harper rather than a dragonrider), and were either resolved using evidence from the text or group members agreed to disagree and "believe in my own interpretation," as in this example. In general, what happened was that each student added perceptions or nuances of meaning to those experienced by others. Thus, as in the model in Figure 1, a larger, more encompassing group meaning resulted from the interaction of the interpretive community. Of course, this group meaning also remains an event in time and does not become a solidified or authorized response to be expected either from other readers or from these students as they reread, reexperience and rethink these stories. The primary value of this type of investigation and analysis is that it values both the literary work and the recreative powers of readers who, in the process of making and sharing personal meanings, become partners in a larger community of meaning.

Notes

1. The terrain of Pern is well documented in Karen Wynn Fonstad's *The Atlas of Pern*. She details, using the texts, the geographic placement of major and minor Holds (homes of common people and governing centers) and the Weyrs (homes of dragons and riders) based on a quasimedieval societal structure in which the Holders, Harpers, Craftspeople, Dragonriders and Dragons live and fight a common enemy—Thread.
2. All of the quotations from McCaffrey's works were selected by the students to make a point during the discussions. Students' own responses are in quotes.

Works Cited

Fonstad, Karen Wynn. *The Atlas of Pern*. New York: Ballantine, 1984.
Iser, Wolfgang. *The Act of Reading: A Theory of Aesthetic Response*. Baltimore, MD: The Johns Hopkins University Press, 1979.
_____. *The Implied Reader: Patterns of Communication in Prose Fiction from Bunyan to Beckett*. Baltimore, MD: The Johns Hopkins University Press, 1974.
McCaffrey, Anne. *Dragondrums*. New York: Atheneum, 1979.
_____. *Dragonflight*. New York: Ballantine, 1968.
_____. *Dragonquest*. New York: Ballantine, 1971.
_____. *Dragonsinger*. New York: Ballantine, 1977.
_____. *Dragonsong*. New York: Ballantine, 1976.
_____. *Moreta: Dragonlady of Pern*. New York: Ballantine, 1983.

_____. "The Smallest Dragonboy," in *Get Off the Unicorn.* New York: Ballantine, 1977.
_____. *The White Dragon.* New York: Ballantine, 1979.

THE PURPOSE OF LITERATURE: WHO CARES?

Natalie Babbitt

An invitation to give the Anne Carroll Moore Lecture is a very special invitation, and I'm grateful for it. I just want to warn you that this was a hard speech to write.

There are a number of reasons for this, one of which is that I've been around in the field of children's books for a long time now, but to tell you the truth, I never have understood why anyone should want to listen to writers give speeches. I'm glad someone wants to listen to us, because it lets us out of the house. But I don't know *why* anyone wants to. After all, we don't know half of what librarians and teachers know about the field, and we are not necessarily either amusing or decorative standing up behind a podium. Still, I suppose we do have opinions—if anyone wants to listen to opinions. (I have a few opinions, though not as many as I used to have.) And it's always kind of nice to get the chance to state one under conditions where nobody can argue back or challenge you.

So I thought I would try to talk, in a general kind of way, about literature and what I think it is—and whether anyone should care what it is one way or another.

I had to give another speech last summer (at the annual children's book conference at Simmons College in Boston), and afterwards, during the question-and-answer period, a young woman asked me why I don't write books about the current societal problems of American children. She was especially concerned, she said, about poverty, drugs, and sexual abuse. These were topics, she said that needed to be treated in books for children because such books could help children to deal with them. My answer was, I'm afraid, rather knee-jerk and glib. "That," I said grandly, "is not the purpose of literature."

I have been thinking about that question, and my answer to it, ever since. And then, only a couple of weeks ago, in *The New York Times Book Review,* an essay by Mark Jonathan Harris raised it once again. He suggested—and I more or less quote—that "because there are no easy solutions to (social problems) . . . most writers simply avoid dealing with (them)," and warned that "it is critical that we not disdain or ignore the experience of one-fifth of our children." Again I found myself saying—this time to myself—"That is not the purpose of literature." But I began to realize that unless I could satisfy myself as to what the purpose of literature is, it wasn't much use to say what it isn't.

By the way, please do not think for one instant that I take lightly the terrible conditions under which so many of our children are living. In a time of great change in eastern Europe—with a chance at last for freedom and democracy in places where things have been very dark for a long, long time—we have this sorrow here, and it is difficult to make sense of the contrast. The changes in Europe are new and exciting; the sorrows here are as old as time and as resistant to solution. But I didn't come here this morning to talk about the sorrows themselves. I came to talk about fiction.

One of the things that makes the children's book field different from the adult book field is that we have a number of implied responsibilities that adult writers simply never think of. All writers are expected, and rightly so, to keep their work free of racism, sexism, and religious bias. But beyond that, I don't think people who write fiction for adults give much thought, if any, to being helpful or useful to their readers. The old maxim that says writers should write about what they know is in full sway, just as much as it ever was, and so subjects and settings and points of view are just as varied as they ever were. It's hard to imagine anyone seriously suggesting—in an Authors Guild meeting, for instance—that everyone from Tom Wolfe to Judith Krantz should start writing about poverty and drugs and sexual abuse, even though these terrible problems are making at least as many adults miserable as children. Writers for adults would probably say—though this is only conjecture on my part since I haven't asked any of them (I would have, but I don't know any)—they would probably say that they are writing in response to an inner impulse, as opposed to one or another need on the part of the reading public.

There have been books for adults written in direct response to pressing social problems. *Uncle Tom's Cabin* is one. Another is *The Grapes of Wrath*. But there aren't many that have lasted. And there aren't many that are written simply to be sympathetic. They tend to be written out of moral outrage and they are directed at the general public, the general reader. Their object is to make a noise and bring about social change, and some have been remarkably successful at this. Then, once the problem has either been solved or has faded into unimportance, most of these books disappear. I really don't think John Steinbeck expected migrant workers to read *The Grapes of Wrath* and be comforted by it, any more than Harriet Beecher Stowe expected *Uncle Tom's Cabin* to be read by slaves.

The novels of Charles Dickens have lasted, and you could argue that Dickens always wrote about pressing social problems. But it's not the same thing. He wrote often about the miseries of his own childhood, and in doing so, he was following that same familiar maxim: he was writing about what he knew, from his own experience, and his own experience is what brings the passion and the truth to his stories and makes them durable.

But neither Mark Jonathan Harris nor the young woman at the Simmons conference were suggesting that writers for children address the general public and raise a cry for change. They were suggesting, unless I misunderstood them, that we write for the children themselves with the idea of bringing directly to them sympathy, encouragement, and the realization that they are not alone. These things are extremely important. They are the things that fiction can bring to readers of any age who suffer from any kind of problem, but only if, like Dickens's novels, they are full of truth.

Truth would make enormous difficulties for the average writer. What is being suggested is a tall order for those who have not themselves undergone the particular, specific miseries that plague so many of today's children. It requires either a great leap of the imagination on the one hand or, on the other hand, research of a kind to which most writers would be (understandably) reluctant to submit themselves. It is an order that leads the writer away from the general to focus on the particular—to write directly to the present needs of one segment of the child population, to think specifically of the audience, to find motivation outside his or her own life. It is an order that could be filled far more effectively and efficiently by social workers and psychologists than by writers of fiction. The world in which we live, which produces the social problems of our children, cannot be changed by writers of children's books because children's books are not read by the general public, and the general public is the only segment of the population with the power to make changes. Children have no power. Yes, yes, I know: you are thinking about Bambi's effect on hunting, and about Dr. Seuss's *The Lorax* and its effect on lumbering. But neither was widespread and neither has had any lasting effect.

There is another piece to this tall order I've been talking about. It may preclude the creation of good fiction. What is *good* fiction, anyway, and why bother with it when there are children in need for whom it may be useless? Might it not be better to bring to those children some sense that they are not alone, than to worry about creating good fiction? Talk about tall orders!

It was at this point in the speechwriting process that I began to wish I'd chosen to talk about something easy, like fantasy. I'm not a critic, and any definition of literature from me is bound to be as full of holes as an old screen door. Is literature fiction that in some way enlarges the soul—by which I mean that it somehow takes the reader beyond his or her own life and experiences and shows him or her how human beings are alike rather than how they are different? Maybe. Recently on television, a poet—whose name I'm sorry to say I cannot remember—said that if you reach down deeply enough into your own psyche, you come to the place where the things you write about are no longer personal but universal. That was good, I thought. That was maybe a satisfying definition of good fiction: it goes beyond the personal into the universal.

But what's the use of universals to a child made miserable by the dreary facts of his or her own immediate existence? Who cares what the soul is doing when the body is besieged by present dangers? Maybe it's a luxury to try to enlarge a soul. Maybe the only souls that can be enlarged are souls in comfortable, well-fed bodies. There's an old saying that when poverty comes in through the door, love I flies out the window—to which I would add that along with love goes philosophy. Maybe those of us who have been fond of saying that all writing is alike, regardless of the intended audience, are full of hot air. It may be true that those who write for adults have no responsibility towards their readers, but it may be just as true that those who write fiction for children do have responsibilities and should be drummed out of the field if they don't make an effort to meet them.

And yet, you see, I have this deeply held conviction, with no clear idea of where it came from, that you can't write a decent book if the subject or theme is prescribed from the outside, by something beyond your experience and your own truths and passions. And so you can see that for me, all this is difficult and complicated. And in addition to all the stuff about trying to enlarge the soul, and trying to meet the immediate needs of the reader, there is a whole other element which we'd better not forget—a book has to be a pleasure to read. If a book isn't first of all a pleasure, then it can't do any good no matter how literary it may be or how useful to present needs, because nobody will read it. Given all these demands, it's a wonder anyone ever undertakes the writing of fiction at all, at least fiction for children. It may, in fact, be impossible to write a book for children which meets all three of these requirements. It may be impossible to enlarge the soul, meet present and specific needs, and please the reader all at the same time.

In my own case, there is no way to meet with any honesty the present and specific needs of those children referred to by the young woman at the Simmons conference and by Mark Jonathan Harris. I don't avoid dealing with those needs because there are no easy solutions. I avoid them because I don't know, first-hand, anything about them. On a scale of one to ten, I am a five. I've never been rich, but I've never been poor, either. The only homelessness I know anything about is the kind you experience in moving—when you've left the old place but are not yet installed in the new place. The only drug I've ever struggled with is nicotine. And I've never gone hungry. There are thousands and thousands of people just like me. But just because we are fives, it doesn't follow that we are innocent lambs, untouched by life, with nothing useful to say in the books we write. We may fall somewhere between the Bronte sisters and Ernest Hemingway in terms of experience of the world, but we are still *human*. And so, in direct proportion to how long we've been around—well, if you've ever moved you know how the moving companies describe your furniture on their worksheets before they put it all into the van: scratched, stained, and marred. That's what we are if we've been around for a while. I'm sure we like to think that we have learned—maybe not a lot, but something.

Here is one thing I have learned. My grandchild, at fifteen months brings out in me feelings I was too young and too busy to face with my own children when they were his age. His beauty is humbling; his trustingness, his vulnerability, his very littleness are sometimes almost more than I can bear. Because I know now what I didn't really know with my own children: no power on earth can protect him from life. No matter what is done for him, no matter how much he is loved and educated, and supplied with books and music and attention to the needs of his soul and his body, he is doomed, simply because he is human, to suffer loneliness, disappointment, anger, despair, confusion, and pain. I yearn to protect him, but I know that protection is impossible.

He will share these woes with every other child in the world—to a greater or lesser degree—because they are all human. But, fortunately this is not all he will share. He will also share common human joys. For there is joy around, always. It is a blighted life, indeed, which has never known a joy of any kind, and books are not for lives like that. Those lives need a kind of care and attention no writer of fiction can provide, however well-intentioned.

So I think a work of fiction—and especially, a work of fiction for children—needs to present life as it really is: a mixture of joy and sorrow, of the solvable and the unsolvable, of the simple and the complicated. I hope my grandchild will be a reader and that he will learn something about the contradictions of life from books before he is thrust out into the world to learn the same thing firsthand.

Thinking about all this and writing it down brought me no closer to defining the purpose of literature or even what literature is. In desperation over the writing of this speech, I finally said to my husband—to whom I don't like to admit I am stumped— "Sam," I said, "what is the purpose of literature?" He looked surprised. "Literature has hundreds of purposes," he said. That was plenty discouraging, I can tell you. It threw me right back onto my own recognizance. Once there, I had to admit that what I used to think the definition of literature was, is plain and simple twaddle. I used to think that literature was the top layer of fiction—the layer that was going to last, or already had lasted, for generations. Up in that layer was *The Odyssey* and *War and Peace* and *The Golden Bowl* and *Dombey and Son* and, well, you get gist. I used to think that all writers should strive to create what I was calling literature because everything else was temporary, if not downright trash. I was wrong. Literature is simply fiction, some good, some not so good, depending on who's doing the choosing. Literature has hundreds of purposes.

It's twaddle to say that writers should sit down and try to deliberately create work of lasting value—and that, by so trying, they should avoid dealing with the social problems of the moment because if they do, their work is doomed to eventual obscurity. If there's anything to be learned in our present-day world, it's that "lasting value" is a term of dubious significance. I've still got my mother's old metal kitchen grater. It has four sides and a handle on top, and you can grate cheese and slice cucumbers with it. On one side are large perforations with such wickedly sharp edges that it looks like a medieval instrument of torture. I don't know what that side is for. My mother probably got this tool when she was married in 1928. So it's 61 years old and still going strong. It has survived my mother, and it will survive me. That's lasting value for you. It is still possible to create kitchen tools of lasting value, but nobody, least of all me, can say what will make a work of fiction survive. And even if we could, I defy any writer to create, by an act of will, a guaranteed lasting work. As a motive for writing, that would be arrogant nonsense. The ages will decide what lasts, not the writer.

So literature has hundreds of purposes, and I for one no longer care. But one question remains: Do we, as writers for children, have any special responsibility? We do. We have a responsibility to do the very best work we're capable of. I still think that means we should each stick to what we know—and do what we do best. Some of us will write movingly and effectively about the current societal problems of children and may be able to bring comfort to those children if only by showing them they are not alone. Some of us will write funny books, light-hearted books—and thank goodness for them. Some of us will write about ideas and snippets of philosophy we find puzzling and interesting. Some of us will write about sports or the solving of cops-and-robbers mysteries, or about aliens from outer space, or about dinosaurs. All of it will be literature, mostly fiction. All will serve one purpose or another. Some will be good, some not so good—again, depending on who's doing the choosing. But, for pity's sake, let us hope that these books will first and foremost bring pleasure to their readers, regardless of which of the hundreds of purposes they serve. Because otherwise it won't matter what they're about, or whether they're good or not so good. It won't matter whether a given writer spent ten weeks or ten years writing one of them because no child will bother to read them. And if a child is forced at gunpoint to read one in school, he will forget it as quickly as possible. Maybe, after all, there is one single purpose for literature—one foremost purpose, anyway. Maybe the giving of pleasure is the purpose. I find I could care about that. The purpose of literature is to give pleasure to the reader.

Of course, somebody will have to define what pleasure is. It could be a topic for some other lecture: what is pleasure, and what is its purpose? I hope nobody will ask me to deal with it.

A CENTURY OF XENOPHOBIA IN FICTION SERIES FOR YOUNG PEOPLE

Paul Deane

For the cultural historian fiction series for young people are rich storehouses of information about twentieth-century American values, tastes, and habits. Three major series—the Rover Boys, the Bobbsey Twins, and Tom Swift—have sold in excess of 300 million copies. Nancy Drew and the Hardy Boys account for 1.5 million volumes a year each, and they and their newest rivals—Sweet Valley High and Sweet Valley Twins—are issued currently at the rate of one book a month. Series reveal changes in language, clothing styles, housing, and transportation. They also reflect the attitudes and beliefs of readers, since authors and publishers are sensitive to what will sell. Furthermore, in overall construction, format, and style, series are calculated to be appealing, and they are aimed at interests that young people already have.

Since 1899, series have dominated children's reading in grades two through six, and in the past decade somewhat beyond, since several series are now pointed at "young adults" and "older readers." Especially in the prejunior high school group, children wish to please and to cooperate; they value adult opinion and are developing acceptable behavior in social and personal relationships; moreover, they are building an ethical sense, and their prejudices are forming. In short,

"A Century of Xenophobia in Fiction Series for Young People," by Paul Deane in *Journal of Youth Services in Libraries*. Vol. 3, no. 2 (Winter 1990), pp. 117-127; reprinted with permission from the American Library Association, copyright © 1990 by ALA.

children are ripe for suggestions found in the reading they enjoy most (fiction) and in the form of fiction (series) they read most.

The extent to which these very popular books, read in massive numbers, foster certain images is an even greater measure of how they reflect the American character. Series do teach, not by assertion but more emphatically by example. Their teaching is embodied in characters whom children like and admire. Since series are black and white in their morality, to readers they reveal definite, uncomplicated ideas reinforced by repetition from book to book and series to series. Though little explicit attitudinizing is done, certain set values, established with slight variation, become taken for granted. In these books, children find object lessons that adults apparently want them to have, as well as views that society evidently wants them to share. Consciously didactic or not, series cannot help affecting the impressions of readers.

Edward Stratemeyer and the Syndicate he formed for the publication of some 800 series, including the Rover Boys, Bobbsey Twins, and Tom Swift, always tried to ensure that "desirable codes of behavior be inculcated in youthful readers."[1] Despite such a positive intention, Stratemeyer and other publishing houses perpetuated many racial and national stereotypes.

Among the best known statements of American principles are the words of Emma Lazarus lodged in the base of the Statue of Liberty for its unveiling in 1886: " 'Mother of exiles.' From her beacon-hand / Glows world-wide welcome." Ironically, little more than a decade later in 1899 the first volume of the Rover Boys series ushered in the golden age of children's fiction series, which present, as J. Frederick MacDonald observed in 1974, "a dramatic picture of race consciousness, xenophobia, and imperialism."[2]

Webster defines xenophobia as fear or hatred of strangers or foreigners. The original sense of the root word *xenos,* however, is quite different. In the ancient Homeric Greek, *xenos* referred to the relationship between a host and his guest, the friend with whom one had a treaty of hospitality. To Homer, any guest was entitled to the rights of hospitality; Zeus himself commanded such rights and would punish those who denied them. Further, the relationship between host and foreigner was hereditary, lasting throughout succeeding generations. Such concepts are more than the theme of the Lazarus sonnet: they comprise the essence of America—the nation of all nations founded and populated by foreigners

Yet fiction series for children contain overall an outright denial of hospitality and tolerance. From 1899 to the present there has been a consistent distaste for and rejection of foreigners in such books. To say that all foreigners in series are villains would be an overstatement; nonetheless, a large number of villains are foreigners. Moreover, foreigners not cast as villains are shown as inferior to Americans—servants, weaklings, clowns. In no series does a foreigner play a major role except as a villain. No foreigner is ever a hero, though he may occasionally assist a hero who is visiting outside his own country. MacDonald is right in saying that "foreigners are second best to healthy, intelligent, rational white Americans."[3] Persons living in other countries are shown as ignorant, unwashed, thieving, and sinister.

Though MacDonald's conclusions are correct as far as they go, his time range and evidence are narrow: "The Foreigner in Juvenile Fiction Series 1900-1945" omits half of the twentieth century and in fact draws most of its evidence from one example of a small list of books published in the first two decades only.

In view of the series' potential for indirect but potent influence, it is important to examine a wide selection of material from the entire century. Conclusions in this article, consequently, are based on a selection of the best-known and best-selling series from the early years of the century to our own time—the Rover Boys, Bobbsey Twins, Grace Harlowe, Don Sturdy, the Hardy Boys, Nancy Drew, Sue Barton, the Lone Ranger, Doris Fein, and the Sweet Valley High books, as well as some lesser-known series, such as Chip Hilton, Uncle Sam's Boys, the Boy Scouts series of Howard Payson, and the Woodland Gang of Irene Schultz. The author's twenty-five year investigation of more than fifty-five complete series and parts of many others, a total of almost 2,000 volumes, indicates that the attitudes revealed in this article are typical of the vast majority of series books in which foreigners appear. These books are so often worlds unto themselves that changes in social attitudes generally are not reflected to any important degree in the series' treatment of foreigners.

Stereotypical Images of Nationality

First, one can always tell a foreigner. In *The Bobbsey Twins at the Seashore,* a heavily tanned lifeguard "looked like some foreigner, for he was almost black."[4] Trying to solve the mystery of the tolling bell, Nancy Drew meets a woman "obviously of foreign birth,"[5] yet the woman turns out not to be foreign; hence, while "obviously" suggests that foreigners are easily identified, implicitly it is seen that they are not. While in Canada to investigate the mystery at Devil's Paw, the Hardy Boys meet two men in the woods: "I'll bet they're foreigners," Joe says.[6] In *The Land of Volcanoes,* Don Sturdy meets Joshki, "obviously of foreign birth, probably a Russian . . . his flat nose and high cheekbones were clearly of Tartar origin."[7] Uncle Sam's Boys also state that "Carl was unmistakably German."[8]

Such statements imply that individual nationalities have immediately recognizable characteristics. The Irish, for example, are red-headed, as witness Nora O'Malley in the Grace Harlowe series or Pat Malone in Burgess' Boy Scout books; both talk with brogues—the more strange since Nora developed hers as the series continued: in high school she had none, but once she married, her brogue became quite strong. Nora has a "charming, sunny nature, and always saw the best if there was any to see"[9]; she is hot-tempered but soft-hearted. Pat Malone shares these qualities. Also in the Grace Harlowe books the maid, Bridget, again Irish, is superstitious, stupid, and easily frightened. All these characters are used for humorous effect; in fact, Nora marries fat Hippy Wingate, who is never taken seriously either. Other nationalities are equally identifiable. In *The Boy Scouts at the Panama-Pacific Exposition* we read, "He has a red face, wears big glasses, and is scrawny enough for a Scotchman anyway."[10] Later in the same book, the reader is told, "The professor is like most Englishmen, for he loves his pipe."[11] The Japanese are fond of the word "honorable," using it often in series. Alain Bakaru, an Arabian in *Don Sturdy on the Desert of Mystery,* talks like a character from Washington Irving's *Alhambra,* suggesting that all Arabians speak like storybook figures. Ramo Stransky, the gypsy villain of *The Mystery of the Moss-Covered Mansion,* is instantly identified because of his earrings and bandanna. Granted that Turk Muslin in the Rick Brant book *100*

Fathoms Down is a bad man, his statement about Otera, the native cook, is still quite strong: "Filthy native swine. Wouldn't change clothes unless told to."[12] In passing the foreign exhibits at the Panama-Pacific Exposition, the Boy Scouts remark that "in some of these squalid villages of foreigners they have some ugly yellow cur dogs hanging around."[13] "Spain is a land of beggars," says Eleanor in Grace Harlowe's *Junior Year at High School*, though Eleanor herself turns out to be of Italian origin in *Grace's Senior Year.*[14] Italians in that book are described as "a race that swear vendettas."[15]

Don Sturdy was told that "life is pretty cheap in this country (Arabia)" and later that "the natives all look alike to our eyes."[16] When visiting among the gorillas, Don was similarly reminded that the "natives presented a grotesque rather than a ferocious appearance . . . low heads, flat faces, a protruding jaw . . . uniform broad grins."[17] John Shephard felt that when Americans are used as villains, no specifically American qualities are associated with them, but that when foreigners are villains, they very often have some stereotyped images of nationality applied to them.[18] The series prove him correct.

Foreign Inferiority

That foreigners are inferior to Americans is a series assumption. Sometimes the idea is stated directly; sometimes it is implied. Often it is put condescendingly or maliciously. In *Sue Barton, Visiting Nurse,* the slum area of New York is a polyglot district: "They were Irish, Jewish, colored, and plain American."[19] "Plain American" says very obviously that there is a difference between blacks, Jews, Irish, and "Americans." When Sue was a student nurse, the supreme irony was uttered by Mrs. McCarthy, a patient with a heavy brogue, who describes Mrs. Pasquale, an Italian, thus: "Them foreigners is always a queer lot."[20]

The most extreme expressions of this kind of feeling are found in the Don Sturdy books, a geographic series that took Don all over the world with apparently the sole aim of proving American superiority. In Egypt Don learns from his uncle that the "natives of a country never do anything. It is the outsiders, after all, who do things."[21] Alain

Bakaru, despite having an "outlandish name," is "much superior to the usual run of natives," although he is "steeped in superstition like all of them."[22]

Don himself comments, "If time were money, these fellows would be millionaires."[23] Twice during *Among the Gorillas* Captain Sturdy wins over the native Africans with "a handful of brightly colored beads."[24]

Treatment of Germans and Asians

Some prejudiced descriptions of foreigners are clearly the products of political events. For instance, *Uncle Sam's Boys with Pershing's Troops,* published in 1919, contains several slurs against people with German names, and *Tom Swift and His Undersea Search* (1920) calls all Germans "huns." Before World War I Germans were approved characters in series. The Rover Boys had a German friend, Hans Mueller, in 1907 (*The Rover Boys in Southern Waters*) and as late as 1913 a fellow student, Max Spangler, who was a German-American (*The Rover Boys in New York*). As soon as war broke out, sympathetic Germans disappeared from the series, and never again were they shown as anything but suspicious figures.

Unquestionably, Asians come off the worst of any foreign people in series. The secret Gentlemen's Agreement of 1907, in which Japan was presumed to have agreed not to issue passports to Japanese laborers emigrating directly to the States, had been intended to curb massive west-coast Japanese immigration while preserving good Japan-U.S. relations. In 1911 two children's series, at least, showed that they were not convinced of Japanese integrity. The most outspoken was *Uncle Sam's Boys on Field Duty,* where Japanese are seen by one old man as a distinct threat to America: he calls them "pesky brown critters" and likens them to "rattlers and grizzlies."[25]; later, the man, asked whether he has ever seen a Japanese person, replies, "Nope, young man, but what's that got to do with hating 'em?"[26] Surely this comment is the essence of prejudice. Anti-Japanese feeling is presented directly in *The Boy Scouts and the Army Airship*: one of the main villains, the sinister Hashishi, is introduced by a one-sentence paragraph—"The man was

Japanese!"[27] In context, the line was designed to raise goose pimples. Later Hashishi is likened to "a small and venomous snake,"[28] and one page later one reads that Japanese "are not friends of Uncle Sam's, however much they pretend to be." Since one of the heroes of the book makes the statement, it was obviously intended to influence readers.

Not until the Doris Fein series in the late 1970s and 1980s does a strong and likeable Japanese character appear. Doris's boyfriend, Carl Suzuki, is a detective on the New York police force when they meet; by 1982 in *Deadly Aphrodite* he is an Assistant District Attorney, and in *Murder is No Joke* (1982) he is planning to go into politics. In *Phantom of the Casino* reference is made to "racially mixed necking" when he greets Doris; Carl proposes marriage to Doris and tells her that she would be a "perfect wife for a rising young legislator."[29, 30] "Carl is a Japanese-American and an extremely proud and honor-bound man."[31] The Fein family has a long discussion about the injustice of Japanese internment during World War II in the course of *Phantom of the Casino*. Things sound fine. We almost feel that foreigners are getting a new chance, until we read in the same book that "Carl is about as Oriental as MacDonald's"[32]; that he grew up in New York eating Jewish food; that he is tall for a Japanese, and that his face reminds you of a typical Ivy Leaguer's.[33] In short, Carl is as far from being a Japanese as one can get. Perhaps this fact makes him acceptable to the Feins and to readers.

The attitude toward Chinese characters is somewhat better balanced—there are honorable Chinese in series—but the image of "the yellow peril" is also prominent. The Hardy Boys faced a number of perilous Chinese. In *The House on the Cliff*, Chinese are the main source of criminal acts, as smugglers of narcotics. In *Footprints under the Window* Louis Fong, also a smuggler, is particularly evil and stereotyped. He was "the most villainous-looking Oriental the boys had ever seen. (He had) a long lean face and high cheekbones. His head was pointed and almost bald . . . a cruel mouth was partly concealed by a drooping wisp of mustache. His eyes were cold and glittering as those of a snake."[34] Sax Rohmer was still producing novels about the worst of Chinese fiends, Dr. Fu Manchu, when the Hardy Boys first appeared; the description of Louis Fong is remarkably close to that of Dr. Fu's. As late as 1986 in Nancy Drew's *Deadly Intent*, reference is made to the People's Republic of China as "the one major country to operate without copyright laws"[35] and the villain, James Li, gives "a demonic laugh"[36] as he leaves Nancy and her friends to burn alive. Although Chinese are not bad characters in the Grace Harlowe books, Ping Wing in *The Great American Desert* is a virtual fool, cowardly and superstitious.

Treatment of African Americans

For the first two-thirds of the twentieth century, blacks filled the children's series; they were Americans, however, not foreigners, and the objectionable attitudes toward them, which also filled the series, were based on color, not nationality. Almost the only foreign black characters in series are found in a very recent title of the Hardy Boys series, *The Revenge of the Desert Phantom* (1985), where the balance is weighted in favor of villainy. Niki Jerusa, the focus of the book, is the daughter of the president of a small African nation. As a classmate of the Hardys, she is of course acceptable; so are her father and one or two others. But the principle menace comes from the Totas, members of a movement to kill President Jerusa and Niki. Charlie, an African who pretends to help the heroes, is actually an opportunist, a greedy and cynical man whose "help" disguises more venal intentions. These again are threatening foreigners who happen to be black Africans. African villages are typically dirty and squalid, natives are unwashed beggars, their "civilization" is chaotic, their culture, nonexistent. Africans are still viewed as children, easily manipulated by the two teenaged Hardy Boys. One seems to be back in a 1930s Tarzan film, or *Trader Horn* at best.

Dialect and Derogatory Designations

Almost without exception in series, foreigners speak with an accent. Sometimes the accent is rendered specifically in phonetics. In the Hardy Boys books, Chinese invariably speak Pidgin English. In the

Grace Harlowe books as well, Chinese dialect is found and is extremely poor: "one blad man," "tlomatoes," even "jlump" are used in *The Great American Desert,*, and Anne says to Grace, "Every 'r' is an 'l' to a Chinaman . . .That's what makes their Pidgin English so quaint."[37] The "r's" are hard to find in the words quoted, however. Sometimes in the Tom Swift, Jr. books, where villains are usually foreigners, they speak with "a slight accent," though it is not reproduced, nor is the country of origin identified: this series is one of the few that invent foreign countries As with black people in series, one finds dialect used to humiliate and to emphasize ignorance and stupidity, even when applied to characters with a positive role such as the Amish people in the Nancy Drew title *The Witch Tree Symbol.* An attempt to be generous is made in *The Bobbsey Twins in Washington,* when the children meet a Chinese family at a play: the father "spoke in English, but with queer little twist to his words, just as we would speak queerly if we tried to talk Chinese."[38]

A very interesting use of foreign dialect is found in *Footprints under the Window.* Louis Fong, the villain, speaks with a strong accent, while Sam Lee, a good Chinese, does not ; hence dialect is used to establish a character distinction. Similarly, Yel Bow in *The Code of the West,* a relatively late entry in The Lone Ranger series, also speaks in dialect, evidently because he too is a hatchet man, conscienceless and hypocritical.

Slang designations of foreigners and foreign countries were found commonly in early series; to modern readers it comes as a shock to find Hippy Wingate referring to a Mexican lariat as made by a "greaser,"[39] or the Rover Boys pointing out "those two dago sailors,"[40] or the villainous Brox of *Don Sturdy in Lion Land* calling African natives "Those niggers."[41] Few such terms are found after 1930 and none at all after 1940.

Positive Images of Foreigners

Positive images of foreigners are found only occasionally and are distinct exceptions to the overall "rule" of how such people are presented. The Chip Hilton series was scrupulously fair to all nationalities. "Steeltown," one reads in *Strike Three*, "was . . . a steel mill town and the men who handled and turned out pig iron and steel for which the town was famous were from sturdy stock. The population was predominantly Polish, Lithuanian, Swedish, and Norwegian. And the boys who played on the high school team were well named. The iron men. . . ."[42]

Although the Sweet Valley High series is not notable for using more than one kind of character or social level, the best portrait of a Chinese person—indeed of a Chinese family—in any series is found in *Out of Reach* (1988). A high school sophomore, Jade Wu has been training as a ballet dancer for several years. When she wins the starring role in the school music and dance show, she faces immediate discord with her father. Jade "wanted to be American in every way. She wanted American clothes, American food, American friends. If she could look American, she would be overjoyed. But Jade was the epitome of Oriental beauty." A major difference from the general series attitude is conveyed in this line. Yet, despite his Ph.D. in physics from CalTech, Jade's father, Dr. Wu, "distrusted Americans and wanted to make sure Jade maintained her ties with Chinese culture."[43]

In this book, then, we find a unique kind of series xenophobia: instead of a white American rejection of Chinese, or foreign, values, we have just the reverse. Moreover, here is found a picture of a cultivated, educated Oriental family. Jade is beautiful, talented, and completely accepted by her fellow students; she even begins a romance with David Prentiss, a white classmate. "'Jade's American,'" Lila observed wryly. 'Just because her father was born in China doesn't mean she isn't American.'"[44] The influence of stereotypes, though, is seen in Jade's dread of anyone's discovering that her grandparents, who pay for her dancing lessons, actually run a laundry; she and David almost part because of his inability to understand why she places such stress on hiding this "traditional" Chinese occupation in America. In the strongest statement to appear in a series, Mrs. Wu explains to her daughter,

> My parents were both born in China. To come to this country took extraordinary effort for them, but they made it . . . You also know what self-sacrificing, selfless, loving people they are. They

spent the best years of their lives giving and giving to my sisters and me . . . That laundry supported us for years . . . I think you should show more respect for your own heritage. To be ashamed of your own family—it's that attitude you should be ashamed of, not your grandparents.[45]

The speech has definite links to a passage in *The Missing Will*, a Woodland Gang series title, in which Mr. Street, the FBI man, explains to the children that "Our one country is made of people from so many different places. It even says on al our coins, 'E Pluribus Unum' . . . Out of many, one." All the characters in the scene begin to name their family backgrounds: Mrs. Tandy's family came from Scotland, Norway, and Arabia; Bill says, "Mine came from Africa, hundreds of years ago . . . and from Viet Nam"; Dave's family is from England and Sweden; Kathy says, "Mine came from Russia and Israel"; Chief Hemster's came from Ireland, Poland, Mexico, and Italy; and Mr. Street is "mostly American Indian, and they were just HERE! Before anyone."[46] Here in this scene is the heart of the Emma Lazarus sonnet, and here, instead of the indirect teaching usually found in the series, the Woodland Gang teaches very directly a most desirable—and American—concept.

However earnestly one may wish to feel that some progress has been made in series' attitudes toward foreigners, one is forced to admit that these few instances are almost isolated ones. Worse yet, a kind of tokenism has emerged in regard to foreigners, especially since the later 1970s. Though still no series with a foreign hero is found, almost a United Nations list of foreign names has come to be applied to minor characters: Linda Ferrare, Barton Novak, and Ann Nordquist in *Deadly Intent*, a Nancy Drew novel, or Narosonia Spatz in *The Camp Fire Mystery* and Beverly Baku in *The Secret of Jungle Park*, both titles in the Bobbsey Twins series. Although these characters are positive ones, foreign names are still tip-offs to villainy, as are Al-Rousasaa in *Dead on Target* and Gustave Laru, Gil Da Campo, and The Dutchman in *Hostages of Hate*, both new additions to the Hardy Boys Case Files. The latter book has the best of such villainous names: Gustave Villen.

The use of such names merely pays lip service to the ideas expressed in *The Missing Will* and in the Lazarus sonnet; they seem to represent no real conviction on the part of authors or publishers that there should be an effort to reshape concepts of foreigners. Although his study covered only the years from 1900 to 1945, J. F. MacDonald was either premature or far too sanguine when he observed in 1974 that "Today such literature (that is, books with stereotypical images of foreigners) is no longer being produced. The few series that have survived are being reedited so as to remove prejudiced and denigrating terminology."[47] Unacceptable terminology may have vanished, but the racial attitudes of the earliest series are still present.

References

1. Christine Maltby Thorndhill, "Skeletons in the Closet: Revision of Racial, Ethnic, and Sexual Stereotypes in the Series Books," *Top of the News* 34:246 (Spring 1978).

2. J. F. MacDonald, "The Foreigner in Juvenile Fiction Series 1900-1945," *The Journal of Popular Culture* 8:534 (Winter 1974).

3. Ibid., p. 534-35.

4. Laura Lee Hope, *The Bobbsey Twins at the Seashore* (New York: Grosset and Dunlap, 1904), p. 115.

5. Carolyn Keene, *The Mystery of the Tolling Bell* (New York: Grosset and Dunlap, 1946), p. 7.

6. Franklin W. Dixon, *The Mystery at Devil's Paw* (New York: Grosset and Dunlap, 1959), p. 165.

7. Victor Appleton, *Don Sturdy in the Land of Volcanoes* (New York: Grosset and Dunlap, 1925), p. 95.

8. H. Irving Hancock, *Uncle Sam's Boys with Pershing's Troops at the Front* (New York: Henry Altemus, 1919), p. 91.

9. Jessie Graham Flower, *Grace Harlowe's Plebe Year at High School* (New York: Henry Altemus, 1910), p. 7.

10. Lieut. Howard Payson, *The Boy Scouts at the Panama-Pacific Exposition* (New York: Hurst, 1915), p. 13.

11. Ibid., p. 15.

12. John Blaine, *100 Fathoms Down* (New York: Grosset and Dunlap, 1947), p. 59.

13. Payson, p. 339.

14. Jessie Graham Flower, *Grace Harlowe's Junior Year at High School* (New York: Henry Altemus, 1911), p. 42.

15. Ibid., p. 42.

16. Victor Appleton, *Don Sturdy on the Desert of Mystery* (New York: Grosset and Dunlap, 1925), p. 14, 17.

17. Victor Appleton, *Don Sturdy among the Gorillas* (New York: Grosset and Dunlap, 1927), p. 73.

18. John P. Shephard, "The Treatment of Characters in Popular Children's Fiction," *Elementary English* 39:675 (Nov. 1962).

19. Helen Dore Boylston, *Sue Barton, Visiting Nurse* (Boston: Little, Brown, 1938), p. 211.

20. Helen Dore Boylston, *Sue Barton, Student Nurse* (Boston: Little, Brown, 1936), p. 55.

21. Appleton, *Don Sturdy on the Desert of Mystery*, p. 3.

22. Ibid., p. 27.

23. Ibid., p. 52.

24. Appleton, *Don Sturdy among the Gorillas*, p. 71, 110.

25. H. Irving Hancock, *Uncle Sam's Boys on Field Duty* (New York: Henry Altemus, 1911), p. 78.

26. Ibid., p. 120.

27. Lieut. Howard Payson, *The Boy Scouts and the Army Airship* (New York: Hurst, 1911), p. 63.

28. Ibid., p. 70.

29. T. Ernesto Bethancourt, *Doris Fein: Phantom of the Casino* (New York: Holiday House, 1981), p. 15.

30. T. Ernesto Bethancourt, *Doris Fein: Murder Is No Joke* (New York: Holiday House, 1982), p. 158.

31. T. Ernesto Bethancourt, *Doris Fine: Deadly Aphrodite* (New York: Holiday House, 1982), p. 11.

32. Bethancourt, *Doris Fine: Phantom of the Casino*, p. 25.

33. Ibid., p. 15.

34. Franklin W. Dixon, *Footprints Under the Window* (New York: Grosset and Dunlap, 1933), p. 6.

35. Carolyn Keene, *Deadly Intent* (New York: Simon and Schuster, 1986), p. 37.

36. Ibid., p. 137.

37. Jessie Graham Flower, *Grace Harlowe's Overland Riders on the Great American Desert* (New York: Henry Altemus, 1921), p. 150.

38. Laura Lee Hope, *The Bobbsey Twins in Washington* (New York: Grosset and Dunlap, 1919), p. 199.

39. Flower, *Grace Harlowe's Overland Riders on the Great American Desert*,. p. 40.

40. Arthur M. Winfield, *The Rover Boys in New York* (New York: Grosset and Dunlap, 1913), p. 211.
41. Victor Appleton, *Don Sturdy in Lion Land* (New York: Grosset and Dunlap, 1929), p. 183.
42. Clair Bee, *Strike Three* (New York: Grosset and Dunlap, 1949), p.155.
43. Kate William, *Out of Reach* (New York: Bantam, 1988), p. 8.
44. Ibid., p. 4.
45. Ibid., p. 109.
46. Irene Schultz, *The Missing Will* (Lake Bluff, Illinois: Black and White and Read All Over, 1984), p. 102-3.
47. MacDonald, "The Foreigner in Juvenile Fiction Series 1900-1945," p. 545.

Bibliography

Appleton, Victor. *Don Sturdy among the Gorillas.* New York: Grosset and Dunlap, 1927.

_____. *Don Sturdy in Lion Land.* New York: Grosset and Dunlap, 1929.

_____. *Don Sturdy in the Land of Volcanoes.* New York: Grosset and Dunlap, 1925.

_____. *Don Sturdy on the Desert of Mystery.* New York: Grosset and Dunlap, 1925.

_____. *Tom Swift and His Undersea Search.* New York: Grosset and Dunlap, 1920.

Bee, Clair. *Strike Three.* New York: Grosset and Dunlap, 1949.

Bethancourt, T. Ernesto. *Dr. Doom: Superstar.* New York: Holiday House, 1978.

_____. *Doris Fein: Deadly Aphrodite.* New York: Holiday House, 1982.

_____. *Doris Fein: Murder Is No Joke.* New York: Holiday House, 1982.

_____. *Doris Fein: Phantom of the Casino.* New York: Holiday House, 1981.

Blaine, John. *100 Fathoms Down.* New York: Grosset and Dunlap, 1947.

Boylston, Helen Dore *Sue Barton, Student Nurse.* Boston: Little, Brown, 1936.

_____. *Sue Barton, Visiting Nurse.* Boston: Little, Brown, 1938.

Dixon, Franklin W. *Dead on Target.* New York: Simon and Schuster, 1987.

_____. *Footprints under the Window.* New York: Grosset and Dunlap, 1933.

_____. *Hostages of Hate.* New York: Simon and Schuster, 1987.

_____. *The House on the Cliff.* New York: Grosset and Dunlap, 1927.

_____. *The Mystery at Devil's Paw.* New York: Grosset and Dunlap, 1959.

_____. *Revenge of the Desert Phantom.* New York: Simon and Schuster, 1985.

Flower, Jessie Graham. *Grace Harlowe's Plebe Year at High School.* New York: Henry Altemus, 1910.

_____. *Grace Harlowe's Junior Year at High School.* New York: Henry Altemus, 1911.

_____. *Grace Harlowe's Overland Riders on the Great American Desert.* New York: Henry Altemus, 1921.

Hancock, H. Irving. *Uncle Sam's Boys on Field Duty.* NEw York: Henry Altemus, 1911.

_____. *Uncle Sam's Boys with Pershing's Troops at the Front.* New York: Henry Altemus, 1919.

Hope, Laura Lee. *The Bobbsey Twins at the Seashore.* New York: Grosset and Dunlap, 1904.

_____. *The Bobbsey Twins in Washington.* New York: Grosset and Dunlap, 1919.

_____. *The Bobbsey Twins and the Camp Fire Mystery.* New York: Simon and Schuster, 1982.

_____. *The New Bobbsey Twins: The Secret of Jungle Park.* New York: Simon and Schuster, 1987.

Keene, Carolyn. *Deadly Intent.* New York: Simon and Schuster, 1986.

_____. *The Mystery of the Moss-Covered Mansion.* New York: Grosset and Dunlap, 1941.

_____. *The Mystery of the Tolling Bell.* New York: Grosset and Dunlap, 1946.

_____. *The Witch Tree Symbol.* New York: Grosset and Dunlap, 1955.

Lazarus, Emma. :The New Colossus." Base of the Statue of Liberty.

MacDonald, J. F. "The Foreign in Juvenile Fiction Series 1900-1949." *The Journal of Popular Culture* 8, no. 2:534-48 (Winter 1974).

Payson, Lieut. Howard. *The Boy Scouts and the Army Airship.* New York: Hurst, 1911.

_____. *The Boy Scouts at the Panama-Pacific Exposition.* New York: Hurst, 1915.

Schultz, Irene. *The Missing Will.* Lake Bluff, Illinois: Black and White and Read All Over, 1984.

Shephard, John P. "The Treatment of Characters in Popular Children's Fiction." *Elementary English* 39:675-76 (Nov. 1962).

Striker, Fran. *The Lone Ranger and the Code of the West.* New York: Grosset and Dunlap, 1954.

Thondhill, Christine Maltby. "Skeletons in the Closet: Revision of Racial, Ethnic, and Sexual Stereotypes in the Series Books." *Top of the News* 34:245-48 (Spring 1978).

William, Kate. *Out of Reach.* New York: Bantam, 1988.

Winfield, Arthur M. *The Rover Boys in New York.* New York: Grosset and Dunlap, 1913.

_____. *The Rover Boys in Southern Waters.* New York: Grosset and Dunlap, 1907.

SECTION SIX:
LIBRARY EDUCATION

WHY LIBRARY SCHOOLS FAIL

Marion Paris

"It was a nice sort of program," said one former library school faculty member. "It wasn't hurting anybody, but it became dispensable" (Paris, p. 100). As another faculty member ruefully recalled, "we shot ourselves in the foot" (Paris, p. 110).

In 1978, the Graduate School of Librarianship at the University of Oregon closed its doors. According to the university's president, it was because of financial problems due to declining enrollments, what he called a "substantial pool" of unemployed and underemployed librarians in his state, and the failure to develop a strong curriculum and faculty (Eshelman, p. 794). Thus Oregon became the first library education program in the United States to be shut down.

In the decade that followed, 13 more would close: Alabama A&M, Ball State, California State at Fullerton, Case Western Reserve, the University of Chicago, the University of Denver, Emory University, the University of Minnesota, the University of Mississippi, the State University of New York at Geneseo, Peabody College of Vanderbilt University, the University of Southern California, and Western Michigan University. (Columbia University's School of Library Service is also due to close; see Appendix.) Other MLS programs have been threatened; at this writing, some barely survive.

One had to ask why, in an era that had been dubbed the information age, and when new roles for librarians and other infor-

"Why Library Schools Fail," by Marion Paris in *Library Journal*. Vol. 115, no. 16 (October 1, 1990), pp. 38-42; reprinted with permission from Reed Publishing, USA, copyright © 1990 Reed Publishing, USA.

mation professionals were emerging, the very programs providing educations for those individuals were under attack and going out of business. In the early 1980s Robert Stueart had proclaimed that "librarianship . . . stands at . . . a gateway of opportunity that few professions have ever experienced and which will probably never come this way again" (Stueart, p. 192). What was happening?

Duped and Discarded

It was a problem that begged to be studied. For aside from the private musings of library educators and other interested parties (including alumni who conjectured loudly in a few cases), little had been publicly said and even less had made it into print. The little that had been published, however, was extremely interesting and turned out to be surprisingly accurate.

Esther Dyer and Daniel O'Connor, writing in 1983, speculated that poor morale, an inability to secure outside funding, and declining university support were behind some of the early closings (Dyer and O'Connor, p. 860). Certainly dwindling enrollments and the soft job market of the late 1970s did not help bolster the cause of library education on many campuses. Basing his opinion on personal experience, Herbert S. White that same year charged that "the problem is not now, nor has it ever really been, one of money. . . . " Rather, he wrote, "it is because of the need to make a political gesture" (White, p. 261-262).

Quality was and is a troubling issue. White again: "The question of quality is not really defined for library education on the campus except in terms of demonstrable perceptions. . . . We prefer to evaluate ourselves and not be judged by others whose appreciation of what we do we distrust" (White, p. 254). The problem of having to "explain" library education to academic colleagues and superiors surfaced again and again. There appeared to be little, if any, relationship between the perceived quality of a program, as determined by a visit from representatives of the American Library Association's Committee on Accreditation, and its eventual demise, although conditional accreditation or complete loss of it did occur prior to several of the closings, including one of those studied.

The study asked six questions:

1. Was there evidence of a financial crisis that called into question the future of academic programs including the MLS?
2. Were university administrators familiar with the mission and programs of the library school?
3. Did university administrators perceive a need for a library school on the campus?
4. Did the MLS program meet the 1972 *Standards* as set forth by the Committee on Accreditation of the American Library Association?
5. Did university administrators entertain alternatives other than closing the library school?
6. Was there an accredited program nearby, or one that extended fee courtesy to out-of-state students?

For complete answers to those questions and detailed but anonymous accounts of four of the closings, the reader is referred to *Library School Closings: Four Case Studies* (Scarecrow, 1988; Professional Reading, *LJ*, September 15, 1988, p. 64). To protect the identities of the many informants who gave freely and willingly of their time, the names of the schools in question were changed to Alpha, Beta, Gamma, and Delta. A number of conclusions are worthy of note.

Not Retrenchment but Politics

Most important, it is an egregious oversimplification to conclude that the four schools were closed solely for financial reasons; although that is what university officials had wanted interested parties—including the press—to believe. Certainly the four universities were not exempt from the pressures that declining enrollment, changing student demographics, rising tuition, and dwindling resources all had exerted upon them simultaneously during the late 1970s. Ample evidence suggests that in each of the four cases, financial reversals—on the university level, the library school level, or both—and institutional responses to those straitened conditions, first prompted the closer scrutiny and subsequent evaluation of the library education programs.

None of the university administrators interviewed by the author, along with only a handful of the library educators, maintained that the schools had closed as part of institutional belt-tightening. The closings were not retrenchment decisions but political ones. Said one of the vice presidents interviewed, "I never closed anything as an austerity move" (Paris, p. 122).

The four cases demonstrate a fundamental lack of understanding and communication between and among the library educators and their university managers, and in each of the four cases, to one extent or another, difficulties that were long-standing and relations that were bitter. The degree to which personality conflicts and simple dislike entered into those relations is astonishing.

Library educators at the four schools believed that their administrations had been out to get them for some years before the termination decisions were finally made. In one case, trouble had been brewing for a full ten years. "I think it was a rigged argument," observed one library school administrator. "My personal opinion now is that they wanted every single one of us gone. They decided years ago to get rid of us" (Paris, p. 122).

It seemed as though the administrators had merely tolerated their library schools, neither giving them undue attention nor ignoring them entirely, until fiscal constraints gave rise to program evaluation, which in turn eventually provided administrators with justification for closing the schools.

Tempers flared, however, about the program evaluation process on several of the campuses. Declared one of the former library school administrators, "I think they could have done the whole thing without throwing in the (program) evaluations. I think the program evaluations, frankly, were eyewash to backstop preconceived notions of what it is they intended to do in the first place" (Paris, p. 63).

In contention is whether or not objective evaluation criteria were employed in a straightforward manner. Some of the library school personnel interviewed believed they were not. For as one faculty member asserted, "they made up the standards to be sure we'd be unable to meet them" (Paris, p. 95). At one of the four universities, no one was able to produce documentation that specified what, if any, the evaluation criteria were. At another, neither were criteria developed nor did a program evaluation occur. "I didn't think we needed any," said a vice president (Paris, p. 138). When asked why he had not fashioned some standards for no reason other than to justify his actions, he replied that in the circumstances such standards were unnecessary.

Restructuring the programs was not an option entertained very seriously. As one administrator remarked, "we couldn't restructure it; we had to kill it," apparently reflecting his opinion that the university had supported the weak program long enough (Paris, p. 89). "Weak sister," in fact, was a term used by one administrator to describe the library school on his campus that he and other colleagues had countenanced in earlier, better times.

In two cases, task forces had been formed to investigate creating interdisciplinary information science programs. The first effort was later described by a former administrator as "an abortion" (Paris, p. 134), and of the second it was said that "the whole thing fizzled out because it never had a champion" (Paris, p. 135). And it never had a home after the library school closed its doors.

And Then There Were Few

In none of the four cases did university managers see a need for an MLS program on their campuses. Admitted one vice president, "it's not like getting rid of economics or English. . . . It was . . . like the arguments over veterinary medicine. How many veterinary medicine graduate programs do you need in this country?" (Paris, p. 91). The notion that the number of library schools in the United States greatly outstrips student demand was given great credence by administrators, who were unanimous in their belief that other schools could take up any slack that might be created in the absence of their own defunct programs. Several university administrators voiced the opinion that the state college down the road that trains teachers might be a good place for a library school. In fact, "let George do it" seemed to be the prevailing administrative attitude, while the Georges became fewer in number by the year.

Many administrators believed that jobs for librarians were in short supply. When some of the library educators labored to correct that misconception (by the early 1980s, the job market was much more robust), their low credibility prevented them from changing administrators' opinions in any way, regardless of the cogency and vitality of their arguments.

Similarly, library educators were unable to convince their managers that the MLS programs should be retained and strengthened. They themselves could not satisfactorily demonstrate why library education is necessary. If library educators could not testify to a need for their programs, then who could? It may be that, at least in part, the library educators' inability to justify the existence of their programs reflects a global uncertainty as to what it is that library schools should be doing, despite some recent efforts to the contrary, most notably the King Research *New Directions* study by José-Marie Griffiths and Donald W. King (Knowledge Industry Publications, 1986).

Where turf battles influenced decisions to close, the library schools were seen as encroaching upon the pedagogical territory of other schools and departments. In particular, business, computer science, and management information systems faculty had become alarmed that MLS curricula threatened their own course offerings.

Admitted a former library educator, "in all honesty, the business school thought this was strictly a competitive thrust the library school was trying." A program initiated in his library school had "raised a lot of hackles over in the school of business" (Paris, p. 52). Information management had suddenly become valuable territory, and leaders of the larger and more powerful academic units were loath to see the library school occupy it alone.

Is Library Education an Oxymoron?

Even more serious perhaps than the fact that the library school did in actuality not threaten other departments to any serious degree, was that the library educators were evidently unable either to defend their instructional domain or to explain to the satisfaction of influential outsiders what the business of education for the information professions is all about. A number of former faculty members believed that their administrators, perhaps holding on to stereotypes lingering from childhood, did not know and did not care.

Quality, as determined by the 1972 *Standards* set forth by ALA's Committee on Accreditation, was a question in only one case. The evidence suggests, however, that the qualitative standards used in the external evaluations of the four library schools not only differed from ALA's but also were much more stringent. Accreditation is not academic armor; it will not guarantee the future of a library education program at a university where administrators have made the decision to close it. Certainly accreditation is important for other reasons, but it will not save a doomed MLS program from elimination.

A serious charge aimed at all four of the programs studied was that their administrations and faculty were isolated from their local academic peers. Those library educators who had served on university committees were often perceived as out of touch and out of date. Recalled one vice president, "the library school had become isolated . . . and (was) not participating. People didn't know them in a social way. They knew them in a scholarly way, but as being out of date. But there was something more here than tiredness; there was dead wood in the sense of not being interested in the way the world was changing" (Paris, p. 90).

It is possible that some of the library educators had failed to reach out from some reluctance (or inability) to "explain library and information science," as several of the faculty informants claimed was necessary when they met with "outsiders." Another vice president charged that "there was hardly a single faculty member who was known to any other faculty member (of the university). . . . No one had met anyone from (the business school), the department of computer science, or the department of management information systems. . . . They didn't know where the computer labs were on campus. Insularity proved to be a disaster" (Paris, p. 109). The sun has set on a world where library educators can afford to be isolated or insulated within their universities. What happened at Alpha, Beta, Gamma, and Delta demonstrates why that is so.

Defining Us Out of Business

Extremely alarming is the fact that library education programs were so easily eliminated as university officials reshaped the missions of their institutions. The new mission of his university, said one library educator, "simply defined us out of business" (Paris, p. 150). More than one faculty member suggested that when formal program evaluations took place, the criteria established by administrators were fabricated to ensure that the library school could not meet them. Mission-redefinition was a weapon deftly wielded by administrators who sought additional justification for eliminating programs they no longer chose to operate.

It is an apocryphal story, but one that is sufficiently chilling that it warrants repeating. A high-level administrator at one of the universities whose MLS program eventually folded was one day overheard asking what a fine university like X was doing with a library school. Many library schools in this country are still in danger of elimination by administrators whose prerogative it is to recast their institutions' missions. It may be cause for alarm to hear that an institution with a perfectly good library school is on its way to becoming "a major research university."

Insufficient or inappropriate faculty research was cited in two of the cases. An external evaluation noted that research was "not visible in current and impressive depth" and that "significant" productivity was necessary (Paris, p. 88). At that same university, after a task force had begun exploring the possibility of a reorganized information management program, a member of the panel warned that "if the university is going to have a library science program, it should be on the cutting edge of current research" (Paris, p. 99). "(The administration) wanted us to become another MIT," mourned a former faculty member (Paris, p. 84).

Related to mission-redefinition is dispensability. Administrators had given up on their library schools. They had declined to make the investments of time or resources that would properly refinance and restructure the programs. Faced with pressure to cut something, administrators chose to eliminate their library schools. "What can we pick off?" was asked on one campus by a vice president. "You can't do everything," he explained (Paris, p. 83).

A similar question was alluded to recently in a *New York Times* article reporting on the imminent demise of a sociology department. Faculty and administrators (nonsociologists) on its campus had asked, "Should there be sociology?" Meanwhile one of the sociologists complained that his colleagues demonstrated "a clear lack of understanding of the nature of sociology" (*New York Times*, p. B6). Should there be library and information studies? It is a question we must be able to answer, for we will be asked by people who are neither librarians nor library educators.

An Apparent Lack of Leadership

Who will lead? At two of the library schools studied, searches for new deans or directors had been long, arduous, and ultimately unproductive. Confided a vice president "this university operates on a strong dean model, and if you don't have one, you're in the bag. I couldn't find one. We were prepared to go out there with our checkbooks and hire some talent away from somewhere . . . (but) the best people don't move just for money" (Paris, p. 103). On the second campus, a vice president recalled the search for a new director. "The amazing thing about it is that it was an embarrassment. They brought in people from unaccredited schools" (Paris, p. 73). Eventually an internal candidate was chosen. An apparent lack of leadership in library education was noted by administrators at all four universities studied.

Private programs may be in greatest jeopardy now than public ones. As tuition and fees continue to climb, it is difficult for many students to justify spending in excess of $15,000 for a degree whose professional practice is financially so unrewarding. As one university administrator put it, "students simply could not amortize the cost of our degree" (Paris, p. 129).

Finally, the library educators had failed to articulate a need for their programs either because they were unable to do so, or perhaps because they themselves were not convinced of that need. Library schools lost turf battles when educators could not effectively explain, for example, how and why their course offerings did not overlap with business or computer science curricula.

The service component of librarianship is one that may have been lost sight of in some quarters. Service, the cornerstone upon which librarianship was founded, is the one aspect of what we do that distinguishes our professional practice—whether children's librarianship or database administration—from related fields, and one that needs to be pointed to with pride and renewed emphasis if library education is to survive. Our information gathering, storing, retrieving, packaging, and dissemination abilities all are based on service.

Library education programs that survive and grow will share at least four attributes: strong, imaginative, forward-looking leadership; sound teaching that will inspire the next generation to be better than the present one; a timely and relevant research agenda; and a strong mission. University administrators will continue to need to be shown why education for the information professions is important to society and likely to become more so in the future. For if library educators cannot explain what it is they do, and why, someone else may tell them. And it may be that they will be told to do nothing at all.

Bibliography

Dyer, Esther, and Daniel O'Connor, "Crisis in Library Education," *Wilson Library Bulletin,* Jun. 1983.

Eshelman, William R., "Death at an Early Age: Library Schools in Oregon and California in Jeopardy," *Wilson Library Bulletin,* Jun. 1977.

Griffiths, José-Marie, and Donald W. King. *New Directions in Library and Information Science Education.* Knowledge Industry, 1986.

Paris, Marion. *Library School Closings: Four Case Studies.* Scarecrow, 1988.

"Professors to vote on Preserving Sociology Dept.," *New York Times,* Feb. 27, 1990.

Stueart, Robert D., "Great Expectations: Library and Information Science Education at the Crossroads," *LJ,* Oct. 15, 1981.

White, Herbert S., "Accreditation and the Pursuit of Excellence," *Journal of Education for Librarianship,* Spring 1983.

Appendix: Goodbye, Columbia

The trustees of Columbia University voted to close the School of Library Service in June of this year (News, *LJ*, January, p. 20; May 15, p. 10-11; June 15, p. 14; July, p. 18), following the *Report of the Provost on the School of Library Service at Columbia University*, April 1990. There is a chilling correspondence between provost Jonathan Cole's main points and Paris's articulation of the reasons for library school closings.

Paris	Provost
A high-level administrator at one of the universities whose MLS program eventually folded was one day overheard asking what a fine university like X was doing with a library school. . . . It may be cause for alarm to hear that an institution with a perfectly good library school is on its way to becoming a "major research university."	The measure of a great university does not lie simply in the number of disciplines it embraces, but in the intellectual vitality of each discipline and the intellectual community among disciplines.—Page 3
A serious charge aimed at all four of the programs studied was that their administrations and faculty were isolated from their local academic peers. Those library educators who had served on university committees were often perceived as out of touch and out of date.	The school remains virtually isolated from the instructional programs, research activities and the intellectual life of the university.—Page 22
The notion that the number of library schools in the United States greatly outstrips student demand was given great credence by administrators, who were unanimous in their belief that other schools could take up the slack that might be created in the absence of their own defunct programs.	Today there are many public institutions that provide excellent professional education in library and information management at a much lower cost than Columbia.—Page 35

YES, VIRGINIA, YOU CAN REQUIRE AN ACCREDITED MASTER'S DEGREE FOR THAT JOB!

Jane Robbins

The function of a professional school is to educate for the broad field, not to emphasize training in its narrow skills. Skills development comes during an internship or during the first years of professional practice in those fields like librarianship where the internship is not a fundamental part of professional education. Education for the practice of librarianship at the professional level takes into consideration not just the first year, but also the practitioner's final year. The aim is to prepare students for a career, not for the performance of narrow tasks.

The actual content of professional education for librarianship is the responsibility of the faculties at each of the schools with a master's level program of education accredited by the American Library Association. The core educational components for librarianship are recognized by all persons who have been initiated into the field, although it is difficult to be precise about the components and even though the components will differ in their manifestations from one educational program to the next.

ALA's Committee on Accreditation (COA) gives the following as the basic content areas that all master's programs must cover:

"Yes, Virginia, You Can Require an Accredited Master's Degree for That Job!" by Jane Robbins in *Library Journal*. Vol. 115, no. 2 (February 1, 1990), pp. 40-44; reprinted with permission from Reed Publishing, USA, copyright © 1990 Reed Publishing, USA.

1) an understanding of the role of the library as an educational and information agency;
2) an understanding of the theories of creating, collecting, organizing, accessing, and preserving information for use;
3) a knowledge of information sources and an ability to assist the user of information in locating and interpreting desired information; and
4) knowledge of the principles of administration and organization to provide information services. [1]

Translated into curriculum structure in master's programs, these four content areas usually constitute what has come to be known as the core. Of 62 schools reporting for the 1988 *Annual ALISE Statistical Report* [2] no school reported fewer than six-hours of course work to be required of students; the most typical requirement is from 12-15 hours.

Because curriculum revision—especially at the core level—is so characteristic of schools, it is difficult to describe a typical core curriculum. The required hours seem to be principally devoted to the traditional content area of librarianship that came into acceptance in the 1940s and 1950s, e.g., courses including a combination of reference, materials selection, cataloging and classification, and administration. The wide acceptance of the addition of courses or course components dealing with the library as a societal institution was complete by the early 1970s and these components remain within typical required courses.

The core curricula of today subsume substantial parts of the traditional core of knowledge, skills, and attitudes related to reference, cataloging, materials selection, and administration with the addition of significant components related to foundations, communication, the research process, media, and, most notably, information technology. The emphasis of the core is that there are elements common to all types of library and other information services that include theoretical and philosophical, as well as practical, fundamentals.

Returning to the traditional core of reference, cataloging and classification, administration, and selection, it can easily be seen that today's core does indeed subsume these elements, but important elements emphasizing conceptual and methodological concerns are added. Especially noteworthy are:

1) the comparison of libraries and librarians with other institutions, professions, and occupations that provide information services;
2) identification of information user needs and behaviors and the roles of information professionals in identifying and responding to them;
3) introduction of technology and information science to all who will become professional librarians;
4) recognition of knowledge of the content and process of research as essential to all library professionals; and
5) acknowledgement of the increasing responsibility of all professional librarians in the management of library operations.

The emphasis on the core curriculum, especially the inclusion in the core of the concerns of, and contributions from, information science and other disciplines, is an indication of the strong desire of library educators to maintain the traditional generalist curriculum.

The curriculum of librarianship, which through the 1960s had been focused almost exclusively toward the library, in most cases continues to emphasize specialization in the profession by the type of library institution, i.e., in school, public, academic, or special libraries. There are indications from curricular changes that this emphasis is declining and that specialization in the field will focus upon type of client served (e.g. indexer/abstractor, collection developer, information interpreter, information manager), deemphasizing the institutional setting of the professional. The addition of components to core curricula is one of the key indicators of this shift.

How are Professions Taught?

Without exception, the ideal of a profession is explicitly connected with a program of study of substantial length in a higher education institution. The linking of employment criteria to educational background is practiced in most professional fields and is evidenced through a variety of combinations of professional association guidelines and standards and governmental regulations and laws. In general, two aspects of professional definition influence the willingness of a society to acknowledge limitations of professional practice to those appropriately educated:

1) the number of different groups (e.g., associations and governmental units) involved in making statements regarding educational requirements for professional practice; and
2) the degree to which that practice has consequence for the well-being of the individuals served.

The profession of librarianship states: "The master's degree from a program accredited by the American Library Association is the appropriate professional degree for librarians,"[3] i.e., the master's degree is the minimum educational requirement for employment in a professional position. While this minimum educational requirement has been upheld in a number of instances, when it has been challenged by individuals, governmental units, or institutions, such has not always been the case.[4] Therefore, librarians are concerned about how they can explain that the master's degree as a minimum educational requirement for professional positions is defensible.

In his recent scholarly analysis, Freidson states that professions are at the least:

> occupations for which education is a prerequisite to employment in particular positions. Formal education creates qualification for particular jobs, from which others who lack such qualifications are routinely excluded.[5]

Professional master's degrees, often known as first professional degrees, are given in a broad range of fields: in business, teacher education, theology, engineering, fine and performing arts, nursing, law, journalism, medicine, social work, and public administration as well as librarianship. These degrees are generally characterized by:

1) one to three years of post-baccalaureate education, with the required length of each master's degree most often determined by
   the content of the bachelor's education: and,
2) preprofessional practice experiences, acquired either during the
   educational process in paid or unpaid field assignments, or
   through classroom experiential exercises (e.g., mock court sessions in law and case studies in management); or, in post-degree
   granting internships such as in medicine.

While some of the fields, e.g., business, engineering, education,
nursing, and social work, allow for employment entry with only the
bachelor's degree, practice at the professional level is circumscribed to
those who have obtained the first professional degree. It is often
maintained that professional education is provided at the master's
degree level, because professional education requires an intellectual
maturity that is gotten most effectively only through attainment of a
bachelor's degree. In librarianship it is further maintained that a
broad-based liberal arts degree is the preferred undergraduate education as librarianship is often practiced in institutions (libraries) that
include broad-based educational missions.

What Makes a Librarian?

Because there are so many individuals practicing librarianship who
are not librarians, the question arises: What is it that professionals
possess due to their professional education experience that others who
perform library-type activities do not possess? The following array of
competencies are derived from the characteristics of professions and
are those that are thought to be attainable most effectively and
efficiently through formal professional education:

1) Understanding of the theoretical foundations of the profession;
2) Ability to meld theory into the practice setting;
3) Ability to use written and oral communication effectively on behalf
   of the profession;

4) Understanding of the societal context in which the profession is practiced;

5) Internalization of the behaviors and norms (the ethics) of the profession;

6) Ability to anticipate and adapt to changes important to professional practice;

7) Scholarly concern for the improvement of professional practice; and

8) Motivation to continue learning related to professional growth.

The critical components in professional competencies are those related to theoretical foundations, societal context, ethics, adaptability, professional improvement, and professional growth within the profession as a whole. Those employed in libraries in positions that do not require the master's degree are not expected to, nor do their duties require, that they have professional knowledge, attitudes, and concerns. The tasks performed by those supporting professional positions are designed and assigned by professional practitioners.

> One criterion of professional responsibility in librarianship is whether the incumbent may reasonably be expected to conduct intellectual analyses of general problem areas such that the results consist of options, plans, and strategies constituting specific resource allocation recommendations and decisions . . . the professional is expected to operate chiefly at the abstract, intellectual level—comparatively infrequently at the procedural or task level, and such tasks or procedures as are carried out by professionals are likely to be only incidental to or supportive of the main function. . . . (Professional) work is conducted within the context of the full professional background in library science so that the specialized activity is comprehended within the scope of a gestalt and not merely the implementation of a narrow specialization.[6]

ALA states:

> Professional responsibilities require special background and education by which the librarian is prepared to identify needs, set

goals, analyze problems, and formulate original and creative solutions for them, and to participate in planning, organizing, communicating, and administering programs of services for users of the library's materials and services.[7]

Attempts to describe professional tasks through task analysis or specific task competencies seem doomed to failure with the techniques presently available. A description of professional practice in any field is not readily amenable to an enumeration of specific duties or responsibilities. As Veaner has pointed out: "(professional) librarianship (similar to other professions) is a gestalt, a complex of flexible, interacting functions, ever-changing and ever-adapting, responsive to continuing developments. . . ."[8]

Quantifying the Work

Despite the fact that professional activity is not readily amenable to task or even job analysis, personnel experts, researchers, and practicing librarians have made many attempts to do so. The most recent large-scale attempt resulted in *New Directions in Library and Information Science Education*.[9] The work reported in *New Directions* attempted to describe and validate professional competencies within the broad field of library and information service. It resulted in lists of general competencies similar to those given above (e.g., ability to use written and oral communication) but included such other universally accepted employee attributes as alertness, effective time management, and accuracy. The outcome of applying task analysis to professional duties and responsibilities usually results in generalities or, worse, trivia:

> it is vital not to be trapped into defining the profession solely via an operational model, that is by means of an inventory of specific, observable tasks or job assignments, though such may be helpful if (it is realized that) . . . task analysis by itself does not account for the qualitative or conceptual aspect of the "task" being performed. Task analysis examines only visible, external,

operational facets, not the internal framework or intellectual and theoretical foundations for the activity.[10]

As Van Rijn points out, task and job analysis techniques are best suited to "blue collar" (that is more routine) positions.[11] Professional work cannot be defined simply by what is done in everyday practice, but rather must be defined against what "upper limits"[12] professionals may be expected to test their expertise. Since this is the case, it is vital that employers, when determining position requirements, analyze each position with neither a focus too narrowly set on position tasks nor too broadly set on professional competencies.

Positions must not be circumscribed to professional applicants because some presently or previously employed librarians are doing work that does not require professional expertise. Also, employers must not require professionals for positions because it either eases their training responsibilities, or is believed to enhance the library's image as an institution that employs a large number of professionals.

Challenges to Requirements

Because professional competencies are relatively easy to describe in terms of expected educational outcomes, but difficult to validate in practice, professions such as librarianship that do not possess the power of legal control over their field's practice may find the use of a minimum educational credential for employment challenged. Challenges to requirements for a minimum educational credential are legitimate *if* it can be demonstrated that the requirement is designed primarily to inflate salaries or limit access to employment.

As it would be extremely difficult to demonstrate that the purpose of the first professional degree in librarianship is either to inflate salaries or to limit access (as opposed to the purpose of assuring employers that those hired will possess requisite knowledge, skills, and attitudes), it becomes incumbent on the profession to assure that all those who desire to obtain the minimum educational requirement for professional practice have access to that education.

In a field such as librarianship that employs relatively few professionals, it is difficult to build an educational infrastructure that
provides easy access; however, the present structure of education for
librarianship can demonstrate that through scholarships and fellow-
ships, admissions criteria, and especially with new technological curricular delivery mechanisms, it does not prohibit access.

Major Concerns in Library Education

A major difficulty facing the profession is its apparent disregard of
educational issues associated with the full range of library employees.
Fully professionalized education accounts for education of the entire
field, including its supporting occupations.

Medicine is clearly the model here. A whole array of allied health
professions that support physicians' work are controlled by the medical profession. While some would argue that librarianship has developed a well-articulated educational continuum through its policy
document, *Library Education and Personnel Utilization,* which states,
"the library profession has responsibility for defining the education
required for the preparation of personnel who work in libraries at any
level, supportive or professional,"[13] in fact there is no educational
structure in place to support a continuum.

Librarianship officially ignores all educational programs (or lack
thereof) with the exception of first professional degree education. The
thousands of persons practicing librarianship throughout the United
States who have had little access to either educational or training
programs are invisible to the profession while highly visible to library
users, employers, and local, state, and national personnel officials.

The category of library employee most fully ignored by the
profession is that known as the library assistant (or library associate).
This category of employee is neither the technical assistant nor clerical
category. Usually employees in this category have bachelor's degrees
(some minimal number of them with minors or majors in librarianship). In larger libraries the tasks performed by those in this category
are relatively easily distinguished from those performed by profession-

als. In smaller libraries this category of employee is often the "librarian."

The profession on the national level has paid too little attention to the educational needs of the library assistant. States have paid more attention to this group often providing those employed in public libraries educational opportunities subsidized by the state library agency. Academic libraries occasionally provide formal training programs for library assistants. (Public schools usually employ only those with some state regulated minimum level of library education.)

Two issues are exacerbating the problem that has arisen because there are no formal educational programs recognized by ALA for those who work in libraries other than those in the professional category, the technical assistant category, and for school librarians as regulated by each state.

There are, of course, a growing number of undergraduate programs in the information field (e.g., Drexel University and the University of Pittsburgh) but these programs explicitly state that they do not represent *library* education, but target education for information systems and information science, respectively.

The first exacerbating issue is that as the complexity of providing library service has risen, librarians have embraced new tasks that are largely management-related. In order to concentrate on these tasks, they have assigned to library assistants some tasks that were formerly performed by professionals. As these tasks require considerable training (and often education in principles so that library assistants may practice judgment in performing them without the need for routine approval from professionals), a considerable portion of professional time is now spent in the training of library assistants.

The second issue, which is closely intertwined with the first, is that the professional tasks of managing the complex information environment of libraries require that librarians spend a large portion of their time studying library use patterns, analyzing the effects of new information technologies on library services, devising effective and efficient materials collection and maintenance plans, managing the library work force, and similar activities. These tasks of the professional are subverted when librarians are required to spend a significant portion of their time in staff education and training.

It is likely, too, that in reality little *education* is undertaken and only task-related training takes place, therefore creating library assistant employees who do their jobs well, but who may in fact optimize the performance of their tasks to the detriment of the larger goal of effective and efficient library service. A response to the need for well-educated support staff that has been practiced by some librarians is to hire entry-level professionals, so that the time required for education and training is not necessary.

Such personnel practice is detrimental to both the new "librarian" and to professional practice in general, for it confuses the articulation between professional and support staff work. Formally recognized education of library assistants should be undertaken in *both* higher education institutions and through educational programs delivered by library associations and state agencies.

The development of higher education-based education for supporting employees is practiced in many fields including health and law. Programs for physician's assistants, nurse practitioners, paralegals, and dental hygienists would be the types of programs that should be investigated by librarianship for program structure and articulation with professional practice. The problems facing social work, business, and journalism among others that have undergraduate as well as master's level formal education programs should also be investigated.

The Validity of the MLS

The master's degree in librarianship from a program accredited by ALA is a valid minimum educational requirement for library practice at the professional level. The master's degree is a valid minimum educational requirement in large measure because it is the standard professed by ALA. Officially recognized professional associations are afforded the responsibility in this society to set minimum educational standards. Any problems associated with access to accredited programs or with the scope and quality of the content of education are, therefore, the responsibility of ALA.

Neither ALA nor individual librarians need be intimidated by the challenges previously made, or inevitably to be made in the future, to the minimum education requirement for the master's degree from an ALA-accredited school. As has been reiterated throughout the literature related to employment of professionals, two concerns must be confronted.

First, the master's degree from an accredited program requirement must not be stated as a minimum qualification unless the prospective employer has made a clear analysis of the position and has determined that the position requires the type of knowledge, skills, and attitudes that are most effectively and efficiently attainable only through formal education. (To assure that the required formal education meets minimum standards, the program must be accredited.) Second, when a position that has been systematically determined to be a professional position is challenged by local, state, or federal inquiry or legal action, the employing unit must steadfastly defend the minimum education requirement set.

So What Should the Profession Do?

One action that ALA could undertake is to start a concerted program to have state library associations begin the process of having their states regulate the exclusive use of the title *librarian* for those who have obtained the master's degree from an ALA-accredited program.

Additionally, states should be urged to create personnel structures for libraries where all support staff working in libraries have *required* access to a librarian for advice and evaluation as stipulated in *Library Education and Personnel Utilization.*[14] As an illustration: library systems (public, school, multitype, etc.) would provide librarian supervisors who would be assigned to those libraries that operate without (professional) librarians. The librarians would work with the support staff-level employees in reaching decisions regarding the full range of library activities and would provide personnel evaluations of these employees for their employers.

Further, a system of articulated higher education-based library education at the bachelor's and master's level should be developed. It would appear that the time has come for ALA, through COA, the Standing Committee on Library Education (SCOLE), and the Office of Library Personnel Resources (OLPR), to address vigorously the full range of educational preparation and standards. SCOLE has appointed a task force on education of support staff issues that is to report in June 1990; it is to be hoped that their work will initiate major developments in education for library practice.

References

1. American Library Association, Committee on Accreditation, "Principles and Procedures Common to All Types of Libraries," ALA, May 1977; revised June 1981, July 1988.
2. Association for Library and Information Science Education. *Library and Information Science Education Statistical Report,* 1986. ALISE, 1988, p. 162-163.
3. The Council of the Association adopted this policy in June 1988.
4. See material included in American Library Association, Office for Library Personnel Resources. *Employee Selection and Minimum Qualifications for Libraries,* ed. by Keith M. Cottam. T.I.P. Kit No. 6, ALA, 1984.
5. Freidson, Eliot. *Professional Powers: A Study of the Institutionalization of Formal Knowledge.* Univ. of Chicago Pr., 1986, p. 59.
6. Veaner, Allen B., "Continuity and Discontinuity—A Persistent Personnel Issue in Academic Librarianship," *Advances in Library Administration and Organization,* 1, 1982, p. 13-14.
7. American Library Association. *Standards for Accreditation.* ALA 1972, p. 5; also, American Library Association. *Library Education and Personnel Utilization,* ALA, 1976, paragraph 8, p. 3.
8. Veaner, p. 12.
9. Griffiths, José-Marie, and Donald W. King. *New Directions in Library and Information Science Education.* Knowledge Industry, 1986.
10. Veaner, p. 11.
11. Van Rijn, Paul. *Job Analysis for Selection: An Overview.* Office of Personnel Management, 1979, p. 12.
12. Veaner, p. 12.
13. American Library Association. *Library Education and Personnel Utilization. ALA, 1976, paragraph 3, p. 1.*
14. Ibid., paragraph 12, p. 3.

SECTION SEVEN:
HISTORICAL PERSPECTIVES AND COL-
LECTING

THOMAS JEFFERSON AND THE LEGACY OF A NATIONAL LIBRARY

Douglas Wilson

Thomas Jefferson once described himself as a man who couldn't live without books. They were for him, he said, "necessaries of life." He consulted books in all of his multitude of endeavors from politics to prosody, from agriculture to architecture, from landscape gardening to the law. He believed that reading and study were the occupations for which he was best suited by nature, as opposed to more worldly activities, such as holding political office. For Jefferson, the pursuit of happiness was the pursuit of knowledge. And, like so many other aspects of the man, his deep regard for books and his faith in the efficacy of learning had important consequences for his country and its emerging culture.

Jefferson's love of books had an early beginning. The tradition in his family is that he had read all the books in his father's library by the time he was five. His classmates in school remembered him as always having had a book in his hand—according to one report, usually a Greek grammar. When Jefferson and his boyhood friend Dabney Carr went off by themselves, their favorite activity was to climb a great hill across the river from Jefferson's home Shadwell, and read under the trees. When he began building a permanent residence on that hill

"Thomas Jefferson and the Legacy of a National Library," by Douglas Wilson in *Wilson Library Bulletin.* Vol. 64, no. 6 (February 1990), pp. 37-41; reprinted with permission from the *Wilson Library Bulletin,* copyright © 1990 by *Wilson Library Bulletin.*

some years later, he set out at the same time to assemble a library on a grand scale.

But that was later. Jefferson's first collection of books was begun when he was a schoolboy and was augmented under tragic circumstances, when, at the age of fourteen, he inherited his late father's modest library. As a college student and legal apprentice in Williamsburg, the young Jefferson added to his collection from the local bookstore, whose account books for two of the years he was there show regular purchases of books by Jefferson in a variety of fields. By the time he began to practice law at the age of twenty-three, he must have had a library that was quite substantial by contemporary standards. Unlike his friend Patrick Henry, he depended in his law practice on the regular recourse to books. In comparing the strengths of these two brilliant young lawyers, Edmund Randolph, a contemporary of theirs, wrote: "Mr. Jefferson drew copiously from the depths of the law, Mr. Henry from the recesses of the human heart." When Jefferson's library was lost in a fire a few years after he began his practice, he despaired of being able to represent his clients without benefit of his books. He estimated the value of this, his first collection, at £200, from which we can calculate its size at between three and four hundred volumes.

Jefferson's first library was lost to the flames that destroyed his mother's house at Shadwell in 1770, not long before he moved across the river to the hilltop. But in just three years he had acquired a collection of more than 1,200 volumes. He seems to have given serious thought at this time to buying the magnificent library of William Byrd of Westover, a princely and, for colonial Virginia, an unparalleled collection, numbering some 3,500 volumes. Jefferson's book collecting in the years that followed was assiduous and resourceful, and it was all the more remarkable in that it was carried on in the face of nonimportation agreements and the manifold disruptions of revolutionary war.

Collecting on a Grand Scale

By the time peace was achieved in 1783, Jefferson recorded the size of his library at 2,640 volumes, a figure that would have been surpassed by very few private libraries in America. But Jefferson was far from satisfied. He had conceived a collection on a grand scale, a library to deal comprehensively with all of his interests and exhaustively with a few of them. He therefore embraced his diplomatic assignment to Europe the following year as an opportunity to expand his library. In the five years he served as an American diplomat in Paris, one of the highest priorities in his personal life was adding to his book collection. Years later he wrote:

> While residing in Paris, I devoted every afternoon I was disengaged, for a summer or two, in examining all the principal bookstores, turning over every book with my own hand, and putting by everything which related to America, and indeed whatever was rare and valuable in every science. Besides this, I had standing orders during the whole time I was in Europe, on its principal book-marts, particularly Amsterdam, Frankfort, Madrid and London, for such works relating to America as could not be found in Paris.

In addition to haunting the Paris bookstores during these years, Jefferson received catalogs from the leading London booksellers and kept up a constant barrage of orders for English books. His principal London book dealer, John Stockdale, even served him as publisher, when, in 1787, Jefferson offered the public his only book, *Notes on the State of Virginia*. By the time he returned to America in 1789 he had, in five years' time, effectively doubled the size of his already sizable book collection and found himself in possession of a splendid library of about 5,000 volumes.

During the next few years, the four years as secretary of state and the three years thereafter spent in Virginia trying to rehabilitate his farms, Jefferson seems to have acquired relatively few books, though he continued to make great use of his library whatever the work at hand, whether foreign relations or fertilizing. But when he returned to Philadelphia as vice-president in 1797, his bibliomania also returned, and he kept up his book collecting in some degree throughout his twelve remaining years in public office. When, in retirement, he decided to offer his great library to Congress in 1814, his collection numbered 6,700 volumes.

But Jefferson's book collecting did not end here. He had hoped that Congress would permit him to keep a small portion of his library—chiefly classical and mathematical books, he said—but when his request was overlooked, he did not remain idle. "I cannot live without books," he wrote to John Adams, and he promptly set out to replace some of those that were most important to him. He already had a small collection of favorites in reserve, the library he had installed at Poplar Forest, his Bedford County, Virginia retreat. Not included in his offer to Congress, these books constituted a collection that ran to 600 or 700 volumes. By the time of his death eleven years later in 1826, his second Monticello library had grown to some 1,600 volumes, a sizable library even by today's standards, and a massive one in his own time.

It would be easy to conclude from this brief rehearsal of Jefferson's compulsive collection building that he was so busy acquiring books and doing the multitude of things that made him famous that he could not possibly have had time to plunge very deeply into this sea of books. But evidence abounds that Jefferson chose his books carefully, that he knew which books were important and what purposes they served, and, most important of all, that he was intimately acquainted with their contents. He was, in short, as avid a reader as he was a collector. Like the rest of us, Jefferson often complained that he did not have the time to do the reading he wanted, but, unlike the rest of us, he somehow managed to perform what can only be described as prodigies of reading. Especially amidst the distractions and difficulties of his retirement, he indulged himself in what he described to John Adams as "a canine appetite for reading." As with so many other things, Jefferson's accomplishments as a lifelong student and as a reader of books simply set him apart and serve to confirm his status as a truly extraordinary man.

Jeffersonian Classifying

What was his library like? Fortunately, we have a fairly full record of his great library, the one he spent forty-five years creating, conveniently arranged into categories by Jefferson himself. It was, as one might expect, noticeably heavy on law and politics. As he explained to the Librarian of Congress, "the law having been my profession, and politics the occupation to which the circumstances of the times in which I have lived called my particular attention, my provision of books in these lines, and in those most nearly connected with them was more copious. . . . " But he aimed at making it broad in scope, to match his inquiring mind. History, both ancient and modern, is well represented. Philosophy, in all of its branches, occupies a third of his categories, though one of the traditional topics—metaphysics—is not only absent but is specifically barred. Appended to the classification table in his manuscript catalog is this instructive note explaining the category "Moral Philosophy": "In classing a small library," he wrote, "one may throw under this head books which attempt what may be called the Natural history of the mind or an Analysis of it's operations. The term and division of Metaphysics is rejected as meaning nothing or something beyond our reach, or what should be called by some other name." In thus pronouncing on metaphysics, he tells us much about the character of his thought.

Prominently represented in all of Jefferson's libraries were the classics. He said on many occasions that the most valuable thing his father had put within his grasp was a classical education. He studied Latin and Greek as a young student and presumably excelled in these studies, as he did in most things he set his mind to. We have overwhelming evidence that he continued reading the classics throughout his life, as attested by the titles in his libraries, the remarks in his letters, the testimony of his family, and the marginal notations in his books. We must bear in mind that as forward-looking and future-oriented as Jefferson was in so many respects he followed the spirit of his age in venerating the classics and believing that the works of the ancients were full of knowledge as well as wisdom. He believed, for example, that the agricultural practices taught by the classical writers—Cato, Varro, and Columella—were often superior to those of the modern age, and, as a farmer, he studied them accordingly. He believed that the works of Livy, Sallust, and Tacitus were the best and most important works of history that could be read, not just because of the masterful writing styles of these authors, but because they castigated the wickedness and wrongdoing of the Roman rulers and thus exposed the basis of tyranny.

There are also many books on "natural history," as natural science was then called. He was a keen student of mathematics, which he characterized as one of his favorite amusements. He was very knowledgeable about plants and biological phenomena, and he kept up with the latest developments in chemistry and physics. Anyone who doubts Jefferson's credentials as a bona fide student of the latest scientific literature should consult the long letter he sent to the president of Harvard College in acknowledgment of an honorary degree from that institution. President Willard had sent the degree to Jefferson in Paris along with a letter that said, in part: "I would esteem it a favor, if you would inform me, what works of most merit have appeared, within these two or three years, in Europe, and particularly in France." If this was intended as an after-the-fact doctoral examination, Jefferson responded with a full reply, which left in doubt only the question of in which of a half-dozen fields he most deserved the degree.

Jefferson's library contained ample "chapters," as he called his categories, on literature and the fine arts, among which he included gardening, a lifelong avocation. There were also many books of a strictly practical nature, manuals of how things work and what would now be called how-to-do-it books. Being a linguist, Jefferson was not limited to books in his native language; he was fluent in French, Spanish, Italian, Latin, and Greek, and, in fact, it is probable that a majority of his books were in languages other than English. One distinguishing feature of his library that he worked hard to achieve was its richness in books on America. In an uncharacteristic boast, he claimed that because of the time, attention, and expense he had put into this aspect of his library, "such a collection was made as probably can never again be effected." As to the future, this may have been an exaggeration, but there is little doubt that Jefferson was the first great collector of Americana on an ambitious scale.

Reading in Retirement

In the original Monticello, the library was in a large room directly above the parlor, the area now occupied by the dome room, so handsomely restored in recent years. In the enlarged and restyled version of the house, the library was incorporated into the suite of rooms at the southern end of the first floor that comprised his private quarters and also contained his bedroom, his "cabinet" (study), and his solarium. When he retired from the residency in 1809, he seems to have embraced his new quarters, as well as his newly acquired freedom and privacy, with great relish.

One gets a better picture of Jefferson's characteristic use of his library in his correspondence with John Adams, a man who was altogether as bookish as Jefferson. Having been friends and then political enemies, their friendship was reestablished in 1812 through the mediation of Dr. Benjamin Rush, and it is quite indicative that they reopened their correspondence with an exchange of books: Adams sent Jefferson a copy of the lectures of his son John Quincy Adams and Jefferson responded in kind with a work fresh from his own pen, the printed brief he had prepared for the New Orleans Batture case, in which he was sued for an action he had taken as president. In their first letters, both were perhaps ill at ease and given to posturing "I have given up newspapers," Jefferson wrote somewhat disingenuously," in exchange for Tacitus and Thucydides, for Newton and Euclid; and I find myself much the happier." Adams replied with a pose of his own: "I have read Thucidides and Tacitus, so often, and at such distant Periods of my Life, that elegant, profound and enchanting as is their Style, I am weary of them. When I read them I seem to be only reading the History of my own Times and my own Life." But soon they were happily and frankly discussing books and authors by the score, from the Bible to Theocritus, from translations of the Psalms to Plato, Theognis, and Joseph Priestley, just to name a few literary topics from the early letters. And Jefferson, who was usually cautious and reserved, soon began to unburden himself to Adams on literary and philosophical subjects with real candor. It was in one of these letters to Adams that Jefferson said of Plato's *Republic*: "While wading thro' the whimsies, the puerilities, and unintelligible jargon of this work, I laid it down often to ask myself how it could have been that the world should have so long consented to give reputation to such nonsense as this?"

For the most vivid picture of Jefferson in his library and for interesting clues to the way he used it in practice, the recollections of Isaac, one of Jefferson's slaves, are without peer. Interviewed many years after his master's death, Isaac recalled:

> Old Master had abundance of books; sometimes would have twenty of 'em down on the floor at once—read fust one, then tother. Isaac has often wondered how Old Master came to have such a mighty head; read so many of them books; and when they go to him to ax him anything, he go right straight to the book and tell you all about it.

This picture of Jefferson on the floor of his study poring over twenty books, comparing one account with another, dramatizes for us the value and utility of a large library with many different books on the same subject, as opposed to the mere mania of owning them. Moreover, Isaac's picture of his master going straight to a book when he was asked a question reinforces our sense, so apparent in other instances, that Jefferson's prodigious and wide-ranging knowledge was largely drawn from his reading. The leading Jefferson scholar, Merrill Peterson, has concluded that "his library expressed much more than the instinct of a collector. Jefferson was dependent on books, tended to take his knowledge from them rather than from direct experience, and approached the world with studied eyes."

Replacing the Library of Congress

Jefferson's importance and wide-ranging influence would be reason enough to pay special attention to his library, that collection of tools and materials that served him as an intellectual workshop. But as we know, this same library was to render yet another important service to American culture as the foundation of the Library of Congress. This fortunate turn of events came about as the result of an otherwise misfortunate event, the burning of the Capitol in Washington by invading British troops in August 1814. All but a few cartfuls of Congress's 3,000 books were lost in the fire, and Jefferson, hearing of this in his retirement a Monticello, wrote at once to offer his library as a replacement. It was not an altogether impulsive act. Jefferson had realized some years earlier that his collection was so choice and so valuable a cultural asset that it ought not to remain, as he said, "private property," and he had considered offering it to the National University that some hoped would be founded in Washington. He had also considered donating it to a new state-sponsored university in Virginia, should one be established. So his mind was attuned to placing his library at the disposal of a public body to serve the common good. The need for a replacement for the Library of Congress was thus an opportunity and in offering his library to Congress, he specified only one thing: Congress must take it in its entirety or not a all. If this condition were observed, he would accept any amount Congress thought fair to offer.

The story of how Jefferson's great library was evaluated, recommended for purchase by the joint congressional library committee, and vigorously debated on the floor of the House is a colorful one, but it turns out in the end to be little more than a lesson in partisan politics. The party that Jefferson had established and led still held a legislative majority, and they found reason to appreciate and praise his library. The Federalists, for their part, found reason to be skeptical of its appropriateness and were scandalized at its worldly contents. And, though the Federalists lined up shoulder to shoulder against it, they lacked the votes to prevent its purchase. Jefferson, of course, knew that his political opponents would seize on the fact that many of his books were in languages that most congressmen couldn't read, that they contained ideas that were considered sacrilegious and immoral, and that they addressed subjects that would be thought, in the language of a Boston newspaper, "finery and philosophical nonsense." And seize upon these things they did. The most vociferous opponent of purchasing Jefferson's library, Cyrus King of Massachusetts, went so far as to say: "The bill would put $23,950 in Mr. Jefferson's pocket for about 6,000 books, good, bad, and indifferent, old, new, and worthless, in languages which many can not read, and most ought not;

which is true Jeffersonian, Madisonian philosophy, to bankrupt the Treasury, beggar the people, and disgrace the nation."

Jefferson had realized in offering his library that objections would be made to replacing Congress's much smaller and more limited collection with his, which was imposing in its size and scope. He had played, as president, an important role in the establishment and nurturing of the first congressional library, and he had donated books to it from time to time. When seated in New York City and then Philadelphia, the national legislators felt little need of their own library because they had the free use of good libraries in those cities. But in 1800, with the government moving to a brand new city on the marshy shores of the Potomac, a congressional library became a necessity. President Jefferson, as one of the best-informed bibliographers of his time, was asked to provide recommendations for the new collection. With his usual care, he drafted a well-deliberated list of titles, and sent it along with an explanatory note:

> I have prepared a catalogue for the Library of Congress in conformity with your ideas that books of entertainment are not within the scope of it and that books in other languages, where there are not translations of them, are not to be admitted freely. I have confined the catalogue to those branches of science which belong to the deliberations of the members as statesmen, and in these have omitted those classical books, ancient and modern, which gentlemen generally have in their private libraries, but which can not properly claim a place in a collection made merely for the purpose of reference.

In so saying, he was not, we should note, implying that a reference library was the only kind Congress was justified in acquiring. We know that his own view of statesmanship was much wider than the mere consideration of laws and treaties, but here he was acting at the request of the congressional committee and playing by its rules at a time when parsimony and modest beginnings were governmental bywords.

In the fourteen years that had passed between the time the Library of Congress was instituted in 1800 and the time it was destroyed in 1814, it had grown considerably. As the only library available to a body of restless politicians living in boardinghouses away from home, the Library of Congress soon became more than a legislative reference library and, in fact, became something of a circulating library for its constituents. Now, with the acquisition of Jefferson's superb collection as its new foundation, talk began to be heard of the Library of Congress as a national library, and the Librarian of Congress did not scruple in promoting this idea to refer to the library on the title page of the 1815 catalog as the "Library of the United States." In 1817 a Washington newspaper announced that "a better nursery or substratum for a great National Library could not be found." It would take a long time for this idea to mature and gather force, many decades in fact, but it was an idea that was destined to prevail.

The first obstacle was Congress's understandably proprietary attitude towards its library. Besides members of Congress, only the president and vice-president were at first allowed users' privileges, which were later extended to members of the cabinet and the Supreme Court. Congress evinced great pride in its library from the beginning, especially when the Capitol was rebuilt with spacious and elegant quarters provided for the collection. When the library was installed in the Center Wing in 1824, it occupied what was called "the most beautiful room in the Capitol; some thought the most beautiful room in the country." But Congress exhibited little interest in sharing its literary resources, much less in the repeated suggestion that its books might form the basis for a national library. It appeared in the 1850s that the Smithsonian Institution would emerge with that honor, but this plan was scuttled by its secretary, Joseph Henry, who, to avoid what he regarded as a deflection of the institute's principal mission of scientific research, not only fired his ambitious librarian but actually deposited the Smithsonian's books with the Library of Congress. However, this fortunate circumstance, while eliminating the major rival for the role of national library, was not sufficient to bring about a change in congressional attitudes. It required the efforts of a strong and resourceful Librarian of Congress, Ainsworth Rand Spofford, appointed by Abraham Lincoln in 1864, to succeed in creating and convincing Congress to sustain a large, comprehensive research library with a national mission. His thirty-five years of dedicated toil were the key to the emergence, by the end of the nineteenth century, of the

Library of Congress as not only the country's foremost library, but also as the flagship and mainstay of the balance of the nation's libraries.

Jefferson's Library Legacy

What is there, we may ask, in the character of our national library that is still traceable to its Jeffersonian origins or is, at least, distinctly Jeffersonian? To put it another way, did its Jeffersonian origins ultimately make a difference in determining the fate of the Library of Congress? There is no doubt that the acquisition of Jefferson's library vastly expanded the scope of the congressional library at a single stroke and demonstrated by its very presence the many advantages thereof. Thereafter, though it might neglect its library from time to Lime, Congress did not seek to restrict its scope and thereby gave passive endorsement to a much more universal and inclusive library. Congress also adopted, albeit for perhaps expedient reasons, Jefferson's catalog and his distinctive system of classification. Jefferson had carefully cataloged his 6,700 books in a meaningful order, not only by creating subject categories but also by carefully arranging the entries within the categories. To make the search for books by author more convenient, he even compiled an author index before sending the revised catalog off to Washington with the books. Although the Librarian altered his arrangements within categories, he printed the catalog in 1815 with Jefferson's index and classification scheme, which the Library faithfully followed until the turn of this century.

In his letter offering his library to Congress, Jefferson had shrewdly anticipated the objection that it was too diverse and all-encompassing for a congressional collection. He wrote: "I do not know that it contains any branch of science which congress would wish to exclude from their collection; there is, in fact, no subject to which a member of Congress may not have occasion to refer." While the arguments and insults of his antagonists are now consigned to obscurity, Jefferson's judicious way of stating the case for a comprehensive congressional library has been frequently remembered and quoted, and it continues down to the present day to inform the expanded mission of the Library of Congress. Referring to this remark of

Jefferson's, the recently retired Librarian of Congress, Daniel Boorstin, elaborated on its meaning at a distance of nearly two centuries:

> Jefferson's books became the foundation of the Library of Congress. But the most important legacy was the searching, outreaching spirit of Jefferson himself. He insisted that no subject was alien to the Congress of a great republic. While no one believed more passionately in the special opportunities of this New World, no one was a more devoted citizen of the whole worldwide Republic of Letters. Jefferson's spirit directs us to become an example, an inspiration, and a resource for all Americans and for people everywhere who wish freely to pursue knowledge.

The extent to which Jefferson's spirit is indeed a living legacy at the Library of Congress is evident in a number of ways. The most obvious is that the beautiful main building, whose great dome and circular main reading room are synonymous with the Library itself, has been officially designated the Thomas Jefferson Building. Houdon's bust of Jefferson occupies a position of honor in the central portion of the Library's Great Hall. And of all the treasures that inhabit this building, none is more prized than the 2,500 volumes of Jefferson's original library that survived the great fire of 1851. But perhaps the most telling manifestation of Jefferson's directing spirit is represented by its policy of access. The great research libraries of the world, private and public, routinely require that those who wish to consult their collections provide endorsements or other evidence that they are qualified researchers and that their research is appropriate to the library. Americans expecting to work in the British Library in London or the Bibliotheque Nationale in Paris, for example, must go well prepared. In the preface to a book on the Library of Congress, Boorstin relates that, as Librarian, he received letters on a daily basis from scholars around the world requesting permission to use the Library of Congress and supporting letters by the score that urged the qualifications and worthiness of these scholars to be granted access to the world's largest research collection. What these scholars did not realize is that prospective readers do not need the Librarian's permission, or anyone else's, for there is no restriction on access to the Library

of Congress. One need not be a certified expert to be admitted; one
need not even be a citizen of the United States. What could be a more
unmistakable manifestation of true Jeffersonian democracy in action?
There could hardly be a more fitting fate for the magnificent collection
Jefferson created than to be the nucleus of a national library that
collects materials in all languages and formats, on all subjects, from
all countries and cultures, and that is open and free to all.

COLLECTING DETECTIVE FICTION

B. A. Pike

It appears from the evidence that people began to collect detective fiction seriously during its so-called Golden Age between the wars. Douglas Thomson's pioneering study *Masters of Mystery* appeared in 1931, and in 1934 John Carter compiled a catalogue of detective fiction and also published an essay on the form, later described as "epoch-making," with the clear implication that this is where it all began. A much later catalogue, issued in 1967, claims that "The serious collection of Detective First Editions started . . . only a few years before the war in the golden age of the thirties, pioneered by such lone devotees as Ellery Queen, Vincent Starrett, and Ned Guymon." A letter written by Dorothy L. Sayers in 1936 confirms that serious collection was undoubtedly gaining a hold by then. She wrote to P. M. Stone, an American admirer of R. Austin Freeman, that he was "lucky to get a first edition of *The Red Thumb Mark* so reasonably," since "There certainly seems to be a bibliographical boom in detective stories"; and she went on to regret not having "thought to start collecting them years ago, as now it is too late to begin!"

After the initial impetus of Thomson and Carter, informed enthusiasm for detective fiction was manifested mainly in America. In 1941, Howard Haycraft published *Murder for Pleasure* and Ellery Queen launched his *Mystery Magazine*. Queen's bibliography of *The Detective Short Story* appeared in 1942, James Sandoe's "Readers'

Guide to Crime" in 1944, and the influential *Queen's Quorum* (of short story collections) in 1948. In 1951 the contents of the "Hay-craft-Queen Definitive Library of Crime Fiction" were published, conferring a status on the listed titles that continues to affect their prices. The first journal devoted to crime fiction was *The Armchair Detective*, founded by Allen J. Hubin in 1967, and the invaluable *Catalogue of Crime*, from which most of this information is taken, appeared in 1971. A first attempt at a comprehensive bibliography of crime fiction was published in 1969 but proved, alas, to be a botched job (done properly by Allen Hubin ten years later.)

Whatever the reason, the British have been much more reluctant to regard detective fiction as anything more than an ephemeral diversion, unworthy of serious attention. When R. A. Brimmell and B. Harding-Edgar jointly brought out a crime fiction list in 1967, it was claimed as "the first such catalogue . . . to be issued in this country"; and since they cited as support for their venture "the recent successful sale of the Symberlist collection and the publication of the catalogue of the Graham Greene-Dorothy Glover collection," they clearly felt the need to justify themselves, as if mystery fiction still needed to be apologized for.

Though two clubs for crime writers were established, the Detection Club in the late twenties and the Crime Writers Association in the early fifties, there was no comparable resource for readers and collectors—no journal, no checklists, no swapping, no sharing. In the absence of any bibliography of detective fiction I made amateurish attempts to compile my own, badgering authors with questions and partial checklists (and generally receiving most helpful and courteous replies); but because of the absence of lines of communication, I had been collecting for some twenty-five years before I realized there were other pebbles on the beach besides myself.

I began collecting around 1950, with paperbacks, which were cheap and readily available. My adolescence coincided with the early days of Pan Books and also with the admirable Penguin policy of issuing simultaneously ten books by a single author. Ignorant of the existence of Haycraft and Queen, I proceeded by trial and error, establishing quickly a taste for good detective fiction that remains with me forty years later. (An early bid to acquire a hardback first edition ended in frustration, however. Having chosen the current Agatha Christie as a school prize, I was ordered to take it back to the shop and exchange it for something less sensational.)

It is impossible, now, not to regret those paperback years and to see them as a waste of valuable first edition time. By concentrating on Pans and Penguins, how many pre-war Agatha Christies did I miss, how many Rex Stouts and Gladys Mitchells? There must have been chances that I failed to take, though I cannot honestly recall rows of classic first editions ripe for the picking—and it may be that Mr. Brimmell and his colleague were right to claim that good crime fiction in decent condition has always been difficult to find and that "almost anything of importance right up to 1940 is scarce and eagerly sought after." Detective stories were enormously popular between the wars and one reason the books have generally become so scarce must be that they were literally read to pieces—and lightly regarded, too, so that there was no reason to preserve them. The original owners of Golden Age books also tended to shelve them without their wrappers, so that, inevitably, these were widely discarded and few have survived. I know of one collector who insists that everything he acquires is fine in the dustwrapper. His collection is presumably choice indeed, but I doubt if it is very extensive.

I came to London in 1956 and gradually began to abandon paperbacks in favor of something more durable. I learnt the hard lesson of the man who persists in wanting his books in their best possible form, buying again and again books I already owned, replacing paperbacks with hardbacks, cheap editions with first editions, books without the dustwrapper with books with the dustwrapper. Despite having come to see upgrading as one of the curses of book collecting, I am still tempted by superior copies of books I already have in less attractive shape and do not hesitate to replace a reissue with a first edition when the chance arises.

In London in the fifties and sixties the obvious place to look for books was Foyle's, which still had a large second-hand department, not to mention an impressive array of recent and current crime fiction. The rest of Charing Cross Road was also a regular haunt and the upper reaches of Albert Jackson's dusty shelves yielded the occasional treasure. Somehow I heard about the few specialist dealers of those years and got in touch with them, visiting Vernon Lay and R. A. Brimmell and receiving lists from Norman Ravenscroft in Penzance. I fondly recall two visits to Vernon Lay, one to his home and the other to the separate house he kept for books in remote North London. I bought *The Man in the Queue* from Mr. Lay for £2 and remain very grateful to him, since I have never seen another copy for sale. Mr. Ravenscroft always included a couple of free books in his parcels (usually, alas, unreadable, though no doubt kindly meant). Mr. Brimmell sold me *The Five Red Herrings* for £4 and gave me a copy of that celebrated catalogue, from which the best items had, of course, already been sold. I still weep for *Sad Cypress* and *Too Many Cooks,* both fine in dustwrapper and each priced at £2. The expensive items were *The Murder of Roger Ackroyd* at £7.10S and *The Mystery of a Hansom Cab* at a staggering £35.

Passing my driving test in 1967 made a considerable difference to my mobility and I began to forage more widely. Despite the ones that got away, I managed to acquire some important first editions. Into the seventies they were still, to a reasonable extent, available, in bookshops, on shelves, waiting to be found: *The Secret of Chimneys* in Hay-on-Wye, *The Garden in Asia* in Totnes, *Flowers for the Judge* in Tunbridge Wells, an inscribed Cyril Hare in Winchester and *The Solange Stories,* exquisite in its wrapper, in Nottingham. I remember an amazing shop in Norwich called The Scientific Anglian, which disgorged among others Ngaio Marsh's first novel, for twenty pence. Best of all was the early morning market at Camden Passage on Thursday of each week, except in the dead of winter. I was happily situated to take advantage of this remarkable institution, since I worked at a school near Old Street and the market is not far from the Angel, a bus ride away. One sometimes had to wait for the legendary Martin Stone to appear, lugging his suitcases and, as it were, pregnant with books, but the wait was almost invariably worthwhile. He opened a crime fiction shop near King's Cross in the early eighties, but for one reason and another it was not a success and, sadly, soon closed.

Until, I suppose, the late seventies, it was worth visiting shops, doing the rounds, breaking a journey to call upon a particular dealer. Prices were still moderate and the competition for books was considerably less than it has since become. It is sad that, as collectors have become more aware of each other and, except by choice, no longer need to operate in isolation, much of the essential pleasure has gone out of the game. The process of collecting has become increasingly difficult and discouraging and I am very thankful that I am not starting now. This is partly because I have made it harder for myself by tightening my personal rules of procedure, but largely because the overall scene has changed so emphatically.

There are now many more specialist dealers and there is even a bookshop in central London devoted to crime fiction (Murder One in Denmark Street). The dealers operate mainly by catalogue through the mail and since they are most likely to find and be offered the interesting books that do turn up, they are now the primary source for new acquisitions. Norman Ravenscroft is, I believe, still living but not trading, so that the doyen of the trade is probably Donald Ireland of Sherborne in Dorset. He is also the only dealer I know who takes wants lists as a serious challenge. Marion Richmond of Ming Books in Watford is organizing the world mystery convention (or Bouchercon) to be held in London later this year. Ralph Spurrier of Post Mortem Books in Hassocks has also become very active in the field. The London Book Fairs are less productive of interesting crime fiction than they might be were circumstances other than they are. The monthly journal *Book and Magazine Collector* offers a further resource, since books are regularly offered in its advertising columns— or one can, of course, advertize one's wants. Unfortunately, the emphasis in this publication is heavily on market values and its obsession with prices does not endear it to me. The magazine *Crime and Detective Stories* (or CADS, for short) was founded a few years ago by Geoff Bradley and is improving with every issue. It provides a valuable forum for enthusiasts, who are its contributors as well as its subscribers. There are also several societies devoted to crime writers, Edgar Wallace, Dorothy L. Sayers, Margery Allingham, and, of course, Conan Doyle among them.

Perhaps in part because of *Book and Magazine Collector* the competition for books is fiercer now than ever before. More people, many of them Americans, are collecting mystery fiction. Many British Golden Age books are now in America, where they are keenly sought and command high prices. If anything exceptional appears on a list at a price most people can afford, the dealer is sure to be besieged by eager callers. It has become almost a ritual to ring for such a book, to listen for the dealer's deprecating laugh, and to grit one's teeth while he says "I could have sold that book twenty times." The only desirable books that are freely available are those that are priced beyond the means of most collectors.

Because there are not enough books to go round the price of those that come onto the market cannot but continue to rise. A first edition of *Lord Peter Views the Body* was on offer in Charing Cross Road a few months ago, but the asking price of £75 must have put it out of the reach of many collectors (though it was eventually sold). I was staggered to see in a recent catalogue an early H. C. Bailey in its dustwrapper offered for £125, not just because the price seems uncomfortably high but because I had already been given an opportunity to acquire the book at £100 (and had not realized that the dealer must have seen that as a favorable price). Values have risen to such an extent that anyone now attempting to assemble a complete collection of, say, Agatha Christie's first editions would need to have literally thousands of pounds for disposal.

It is perhaps worth remarking that, despite the difficulties, such a collection might still be possible to achieve, given that there was no insistence on dustwrappers and that money was indeed no object. I know of two complete Christie collections, one completed within the last two or three years (with the acquisition of *Murder on the Links*). I have also seen complete collections of several other Golden Age writers, John Dickson Carr, Freeman Wills Crofts, Henry Wade, Dorothy L. Sayers, Ellery Queen, Nicholas Blake, and Michael Innes among them. Margery Allingham, though, has proved impossible to complete and no one to my knowledge (not even her surviving sister) has all her works in first edition form. Of all the great writers of that time she is to my mind the toughest proposition to the serious collector. Ngaio Marsh is also difficult, the true firsts of her Geoffrey Bles period being the particular problem. John Rhode's works are probably easier to find than those of his alter ego, Miles Burton, whose books are a staple of many a wants list. Gladys Mitchell's early titles are also elusive and, indeed, until recently, when I was actually offered a decent copy at a price I could afford, I had considered her *Hangman's*

Curfew to be the one book I would probably never find (it is notorious as the title every Mitchell collector lacks). Anthony Berkeley collectors are likely to have the majority of his books under his various names. The one title they are most unlikely to have is *Cecily Disappears*, written under the pseudonym A. Monmouth Platts and unknown, so far as I know, outside the copyright libraries. I'm thankful I don't collect E. C. R. Lorac, since some twenty of her books are extremely rare and hordes of eager collectors are said to be clamoring for them. I am glad, too, that spy fiction and hard-boiled novels are not to my taste, since I am spared the necessity to collect Eric Ambler and Raymond Chandler, both expensive and, like the Scarlet Pimpernel, elusive. Chandler is, I suspect, even more of a cult figure than Ambler, so that his prices are particularly prohibitive.

In general, as one would expect, post-war books cost less and turn up more frequently. It is far easier to catch *The 4.10 from Paddington* (a late Agatha Christie) than *The 12.30 from Groydon* (a pre-war Freeman Wills Crofts). Particular books mark the points at which acquisition becomes easier: *Coroner's Pidgin* for Margery Allingham, *Died in the Wool* for Ngaio Marsh, *The Silent Speaker* for Rex Stout, and *Dead Man's Effects* for H. C. Bailey. All of these coincide more or less with the end of the war and, no doubt, the lifting for printers of restrictions on paper. Certain books from this period are almost common, even though by authors acknowledged as "difficult": *Death in Clairvoyance* by Josephine Bell, for instance, and *The Case of the Missing Men* by Christopher Bush. Others are unaccountably scarce, like Leo Bruce's *Case for Sergeant Beef* or Christianna Brand's *Death of Jezebel* (the latter lent to me years ago by the author, who described her copy as probably the sole survivor of the original edition).

Fewer post-war writers command unvaryingly high prices, though Edmund Crispin is an exception and early Michael Gilbert is coming along nicely (or rather nastily, since I still do not have them all). Crispin's prices range from high to extortionate, but the books still surface, though I have come to despair of some of the wrappers. Certain other groups of post-war books are especially desirable for one reason or another: the early Crime Club titles of Elizabeth Ferrars, for instance, or the long run of Leo Bruce's novels issued in a uniform format by Peter Havies in the fifties and early sixties. The three detective stories published in their youth by the Shaffer brothers are a special case. The wider fame of the authors and the eccentric brilliance of the novels make a powerful dual inducement to seek and hope to find.

A small number of the most popular modern writers have a very large following, so that the demand for their first editions, especially of earlier works, is correspondingly fierce. I heard recently that 2,000 Californians queued to have their copies of her books signed by P. D. James during her latest tour of America. Because she was for many years so little regarded and has now become so extravagantly famous, the three books she published in the 1960s are now pearls of great price. John Le Carre's work before the spy came in from the cold is also very desirable, so much so that a friend recently reported a copy of *A Murder of Quality* on offer at £600. Dick Francis is also in this league. At one time on a count of frequency he outclassed even Richmal Crompton as the most sought-after author in the wanted columns of the *Book and Magazine Collector*.

Others whose work commands prices above the ordinary are Ruth Rendell, Colin Dexter, Ellis Peters, and Anthony Price. Successful television adaptations of their work must surely be contributing to the demand for Rendell and Dexter, and the popularity of Ellis Peters' mediaeval detective, Brother Cadfael, has created an interest in the work of the pre-Cadfael era, with a predictable rise in prices. An odd, rather freakish popularity has attended the novels of the Dutch diplomat Robert van Gulik, whose detective is a Chinese judge active at the time of the T'ang dynasty. These books have been particularly highly regarded in America where, from the prices they were fetching, eccentric millionaires must have been competing for them. It may be, however, that the van Gulik bubble has burst, since I recently overheard two dealers shaking their heads over some disappointed expectations. Perhaps collectors of more modest means might now be able to acquire some of the Judge Dee novels at prices they can afford.

When a crime writer becomes fashionable or, more lastingly, the object of a cult, the first edition dealers begin to take an interest and to force up prices. P. D. James and Dick Francis are much beloved of modern first dealers and even their later, more easily obtainable books invariably appear with fancy prices in modern first catalogues. If a

Dick Francis is signed by the author it is even more outrageously priced, regardless of the fact that he signs so many that unsigned copies may well be rarer (and I'm beginning to worry about P. D. James in this connection.

With the current writers and their new books the question of value for money continually raises its head. As in the Golden Age, there is now so much new crime fiction that a great deal of it must in the nature of things be unworthy of the connoisseur and the serious collector (if they are not one and the same). Since a new novel now costs around £12 my process of selection has had perforce to become more rigorous. Though I am happy to pay up for those authors I rate highly and feel I can trust, I now wait for review copies of the others. In some cases I have even begun to discard books I am unlikely ever to re-read. I take fewer risks nowadays and, sadly, cannot afford to try out new authors.

It has become sound policy to acquire the essential titles as soon as they appear, since modern books tend not to wait around while collectors make up their minds about them. Print runs are reportedly smaller than ever and continuing library demand takes its toll of the relatively few available copies. Once a book goes out of print or into second impression, the first edition may never again be easy to obtain. Anyone now searching for P. D. James's and Ruth Rendell's first novels will know what rarity means. Even quite recent books have already effectively disappeared: Caroline Graham recently had a great success with her second mystery novel, but when her admirers began looking for its predecessor most of them found it was no longer to be had.

Books by unfashionable writers naturally cost less, regardless of their quality. David Williams, Gwendoline Butler, W. J. Burley, B. M. Gill, Peter Dickinson, and Gwen Moffat are all particularly admirable in my view, but I doubt if any of them is very widely or seriously collected. From the collector's point of view this does not matter, of course, and it may even be seen as an advantage, since their prices remain stable. But I am always irritated by the freaks of fashion and the dictates of the market place (and I frequently reflect, rather waspishly, that the forcing up of prices benefits no one but the dealers). I suppose it is comforting to know that such-and-such a title in one's possession was sold last week for £200, but if a book is that desirable no true collector is going to part with it unless he has to. The real evil of fashion and "market forces" is that an author comes to be esteemed according to the prices people will pay for his work and not necessarily for the quality of his achievement. This must be true in other fields than crime fiction, of course, but the principle undeniably operates there. Again and again I hear from dealers that they "can't sell" particular authors, often with proven reputations, as if this were a reflection on those writers and a reason to dismiss them from serious consideration. Commercial facts are one thing, value judgments quite another.

A similar "sheep and goats" situation has arisen between those books that have their dustwrappers and those that do not. Collectors see the wrapper as "completing" a book and there is no denying that, from a purely historical perspective, this is precisely what it does. To collect first editions at all is to subscribe to the view that their primacy is what makes them attractive and worthwhile, and dustwrappers are an essential part of that primacy. The absence of a wrapper is usually seen as a reason to dismiss a post-war book as unworthy of acquisition and its presence inevitably makes it more expensive. On a pre-war book a dustwrapper can add hundreds to the price. Since the effects of this are all-pervasive, it is impossible not to fall into line, but I cannot but regret that dustwrappers have come to play so dominant a part in the game.

Once committed to first editions—and I crossed that line many years ago now—a collector is beset by other hazards than absent dustwrappers, rising prices, and increasing competition for a dwindling supply of books. What an erudite friend of mine calls issue points constitute a subtle trap for the unwary, and I now accept that it is important to establish in advance of purchase that a book is what it purports to be (especially if a stiff price is being asked for it). Extraordinary mistakes can be made, as when a dealer who had better remain nameless offered at an inflated price what he believed to be the true first edition of Ernest Bramah's *The Eyes of Max Carrados*. The book was smaller than the accepted first edition and more elaborate in format, so that the dealer might be forgiven for being mistaken and a purchaser for accepting his claim as true. But the book was published by the Richards Press, as opposed to Grant Richards, and I am assured by one who knows that this is a later imprint that did not come into existence until well after 1923, the year of first publication. The book, in fact, cannot possibly be what was claimed.

Publishing practice is so erratic that it is not really possible to draw up hard-and-fast rules. The best one can do is to formulate guidelines and acknowledge that every rule has its exceptions. When I began to investigate this area for the collectors' guide published recently, I soon realized one could devote one's life to it (literally, since a researcher would have to look at every book to do the job properly).

Meanwhile, one is left with the anomalies, the nonconformists of one kind or another. If pre-war Gollancz books are black with orange lettering, why does *Before the Fact* have green lettering, and why is *The Devil to Pay* blue? Investigation does not really answer those questions but it does indicate that there are, in this instance and so far as is known, the exceptions to the rule. In the same way, *The Mystery of the Blue Train* is only known in undated form, so it is generally accepted as an, if not the, exception to the rule that early Collins and Crime Club books in first edition have the word "copyright" and the year of publication on the reverse of the title-page. Later Crime Club books are dated at the foot of the copyright page (by which I mean the reverse of the title-page), but at least five exceptions are known, of which one is dated at the end of the book and three on the title-page. The fifth exception, *A Policeman at the Door,* is, like *The Mystery of the Blue Train,,* undated—or perhaps I should say that no dated copy has yet come to light. A number of other Crime Club volumes from the late thirties are undated, but they also exist in dated form and so are not generally accepted as first editions. None the less, since they are identical with the true firsts in every respect except that they lack the date, they are obviously variants of the true firsts, and I would dearly like to determine their exact status.

As I suggested earlier, Geoffrey Bles books of the 1930s are a rich source of confusion. To judge by the number of their catalogue appearances, first editions of Leo Bruce's first book, *Case for Three Detectives,* are not uncommon—but caveat emptor, for all is not as it seems. Not only is the red book with the black lettering a later issue but the green book with the black lettering is, too. Only the red book with the white lettering (or what remains after the rest has flaked off) is a true first edition. Most of the Ngaio Marsh titles issued by Bles should be red with white lettering. If *Enter a Murderer* is blue with black lettering it is a later issue, and if *Death in Ecstasy* has black lettering it, too, is not the true first. Only the dustwrappers made the distinctions clear, and since they are almost always absent the confusions persist.

Methuen, Gollancz, and Ward Lock also fail on occasions to identify reissues internally, so that H. C. Bailey collectors are in particular danger of paying handsomely for "first editions" that are nothing of the kind (since Bailey was published by all three). His Methuen titles tend to be rose-red with gold lettering in a fancy framework on the backstrip. My copy of *Mr. Fortune's Trials,* however, is grey with black lettering and the statement within—"First published in 1925"— means precisely that and does not indicate first edition status. What finally determines this is the printer's code at the end of the book, which reads "1026," meaning that it was at the printers in October 1926, and so indicates that it probably came out early in 1927 (as the English Catalogue of Books confirms). In general, Ward Lock's Bailey titles should not be bound in red cloth in the first edition, though, regrettably, they often appear to be. At one time the "red pretenders," as I think of them, were quite common and there must still be collectors who continue to regard them as authentic firsts. Bailey's first book for Gollancz, *Shadow on the Wall,* also turns up in a red binding, with black lettering, and nothing to indicate that it is a later issue. Again, as with Bles, it is the dustwrapper that must have established the point.

The printer's code is the acid test for most Methuen books of the twenties and thirties. If *The Man in the Queue* has 1128 it is the first issue, but 1129 indicates the second. *The Viaduct Murder* first appeared in 1925, was reissued in 1926 with a statement to that effect on the copyright page, and was then reissued in 1929 with no such indication (and only the printer's code to show the book's actual status). It is a sobering thought that this book, Ronald Knox's first crime novel, sells for £50 or more—caveat emptor, indeed.

In many other cases there is confusion over the color of the binding, an issue on which, it seems to me, it is harder to be certain of priorities. Who is to say that the red edition of *Captain Cutthroat* preceded the black or that the green version of *The Moonflower* appeared after the black ? Why did Faber issue Cyril Hare's last novel in both blue and red bindings, and which takes precedence? If brown with black lettering is wrong for *A Daisy-Chain for Satan,* why is it wrong, and what should it be? In most of these cases it is, in fact, possible to adduce indications as to priority, if not irrefutable evidence, but the question of primary color remains a vexed one. My personal answer to all such doubts is to consult the British Library and accept what their copy shows as the "true" color. On a recent visit I down-graded my *Case of the Crumpled Knave* but confirmed the status of my *Bone and a Hank of Hair,* about which there had been some dispute. Not everyone would agree that the British Library copy of a book is beyond question the authentic first edition, but in my experience it can usually be shown that it is.

The American critic Edmund Wilson would, I imagine, have regarded me with intolerant incomprehension and perhaps even with contempt. It was he, of course, who asked the famous question "Who cares who killed Roger Ackroyd?" (a foolish question, to which the answer is obvious). If he had asked instead "Who cares enough about *Who Killed Roger Ackroyd* to pay highly for a first edition?" I might have conceded that the question is less foolish and the answer less easy to justify. Despite this, I hope I have demonstrated why, for me, the whole business of investigating bibliographical points is a fascinating and continually absorbing game and one that, fortunately, is not subject to the rather depressing changes that have overtaken collecting. It makes an admirable supplementary activity and is, for me, a natural extension of my interest in and enjoyment of mystery fiction. John Dickson Carr maintained that writing detective novels was "the grandest game in the world," and in my experience reading, collecting, and exploring them run it very close. If you can't write them, read and collect them.

HISTORICAL RESEARCH IN TRADE CATALOGS

Rhoda S. Ratner

Value of Trade Catalogs

Lawrence Romaine was a man with a mission. In 1960, when he published *A Guide to American Trade Catalogs, 1744-1900*, he was pleading his cause for the historical importance of trade catalogs. In his Introduction, he says, "It is high time that someone compiled and printed a record proving that Americans recognized the value of advertising catalogs and the mail order business even before they recognized the real value of freedom. There are ten thousand volumes that tell and retell the story of the American Revolution. I offer one that will, without bloodshed, convince you of the creative ability, imagination and Yankee ingenuity of the builders of this Republic throughout the 18th and 19th centuries" (1, p. ix).

Romaine was a dealer, collector, and documenter of trade catalogs. In compiling the material for his book, he surveyed over 200 libraries, museums and historical societies, and too often received responses that the collections were "stored in cases and trunks and have never been checked and cataloged" or were "set aside ready to catalog as soon as funds and staff can handle them." While he was grateful that libraries were taking this body of material seriously, he lamented the lack of

"Historical Research in Trade Catalogs," by Rhoda S. Ratner in *Science & Technology Libraries*. Vol. 10, no. 4 (Summer 1990), pp. 15-22; reprinted with permission from *Science & Technology Libraries*, copyright © 1990 by *Science & Technology Libraries*.

funds for "the greatest panorama of industrial development ever printed" (1, p. x).

His closing plea was, "If this volume encourages our library boards and 'angels' to recognize these invaluable records, and to provide funds and staffs to take care of them, not stored in boxes and cartons and trunks, unchecked, but rather properly cataloged and shelved where historians can find them, I shall feel amply paid for the time and effort that has gone into it" (1, p. xiv).

Almost thirty years have passed and the prediction by A. Hyatt Mayer in the Foreword to the book proved accurate: "The new historians of business will find a basic tool in Mr. Romaine's bibliography of American catalogs, for it is the first general listing of these scarce ephemera in any country. Like any pioneer survey, its structure will always endure under the additions that the years must inevitably bring. Henceforth no American trade catalogue can be listed respectably without a Romaine reference, or boasting (while perhaps adding a penny to the price) "Not in Romaine"(1, p. vii).

In those same thirty years, there is ample evidence that trade catalogs are recognized as valuable research tools and that libraries are bringing them under control. Consider for a moment the levels of information that may be gained from a catalog:

—An item advertised in a catalog can represent the leap from patent dream to reality.
—During the last half of the nineteenth century, copy was often written by outstanding authors and historians, and embellished with woodcuts and lithographs executed by the best artists and engravers.
—An artifact will be fully documented as to size, materials and operation.
—Most catalogs will be dated. Some were deliberately undated to preserve the sense of currency. In those cases, the researcher may have the good fortune to be using a copy that was accessioned and date-stamped by a library shortly after publication. It would then be known that the object was produced before a certain date.
—Examples of printing history.

—The illustrations on the covers or within the catalog may represent the workplace, thus displaying labor conditions and procedures and perhaps even the function of tools—both their intended use and their place within a wider context.

—The items offered for sale are indicators of cultural values of the time and ideas about status—how people wished to see themselves.

—The catalog may serve to identify products that no longer exist.

—A series of catalogs can trace the history of technology and skilled workers and the evolution of industries.

—The prejudices of the time—ethnic, sexual or racial—may be demonstrated.

—The catalog may also document the shift of products from the elite to acceptance by the popular culture.

Glenn Porter, Director of the Hagley Museum and Library, summarizes value of trade catalogs as follows:

> Trade catalogs open the doors to a wonderful world of instructive and fascinating things. They can help us to intuit much about the history of marketing and subtle shades of meaning in the material choices of our forebears. For students of those social systems, attitudes and values, and structures of meaning and symbol that constitute the realm of material culture, few printed forms of evidence are as richly rewarding, colorful, or interesting as the trade catalog (2, p. 13).

Major Collections

Meanwhile, what have libraries been doing? In just the past few years, we have seen published guides to major collections at three institutions—Corning Museum of Glass, Hagley Museum and Library, (2) and Winterthur. (4) While each of these libraries include what is generally defined as trade catalogs, there are some differences beyond the obvious.

In the broadest definition of the collection, Hagley terms trade catalogs as printed materials published by a manufacturing, wholesaling, or retailing firm to promote sales through advertising claims; instructions for using the product; testimonials from satisfied customers; and detailed descriptions of the products for sale. Nina de Angeli Walls adds that "although 'trade catalog' originally derived from the phrase 'to the trade,' referring to wholesalers and retailers only, the term now encompasses catalogs and circulars aimed at the ultimate consumer" (2, p. 15).

Corning includes design books, price lists, internal factory record books listing ware, and reprints, as well as trade catalogs that fit the standard definition. Winterthur includes broadsides, broadsheets, pamphlets, manuscripts, and books issued by businesses and individuals to entice the public to buy products.

Libraries have adopted cataloging methods appropriate to their own collections. Bibliographic access, however, beyond company name, is most often by subject. The sixty-two subject categories developed by Romaine for general collections have often been used and adapted to fit specific collections. In variations, the architectural trade catalogs in the Avery Library of Columbia University utilize Sweet's categories (9) and the Smithsonian Institution Libraries use Library of Congress Subject Headings. Shelving arrangements run the full gamut. Catalogs may be arranged by subject, company name, accession number, or by call number when fully cataloged.

A researcher new to this body of literature is in luck if the name of the manufacturer is known. If only the artifact is at hand, however, there are means available to determine who produced what. To begin, Romaine and the three collection guides mentioned above may provide leads. An additional example of a subject-specific guide is *The finest instruments ever made: A bibliography of medical, dental, optical, and pharmaceutical company trade literature; 1700-1939* by Audrey B. Davis and Mark S. Dreyfuss (5). Compared to Romaine's list of 250 medical and dental catalogs, this bibliography includes almost 10,000 citations for nearly 2,000 companies.

A librarian of an earlier time may also be of help. In 1934, the Applied Science library at Columbia University was collecting current catalogs for use by the students. Once the catalogs were replaced by newer editions, single copies were kept for the historical collection. Granville Meixell, Librarian at the time, developed a manual with source lists for those attempting to build and organize such a collection. Her listing of Directories of Manufacturers was an aid in locating catalogs available in 1934. It is reproduced here to serve the present-day researcher as a guide to products produced in the past (6, p. 16).

1. *Directory and Buyer's Guide* (Engineer (London, England)
2. *Engineering* (London) Directory
3. Federation of British Industries. *F. B. I. Register of British Manufacturers*
4. *Fraser's Canadian Trade Directory*
5. *MacRae's Blue Book,* consolidated with *Hendricks' Commercial Register of the United States for Buyers and Sellers*
6. *Thomas' Register of American Manufacturers and First Hands in all Lines*

When an object is not marked as to maker but is clearly identifiable as to type, U. S. Patents may be valuable sources of information. A cumulative index was published in 1873 covering the years 1790-1873 which can be searched by subject or inventor(7). Following 1873, the annual reports of the U. S. Patent Office include the subject and inventor listings as well.

Since Romaine represents a first attempt at a union list of holdings, locating catalogs is often complicated. In Ash's *Subject Collections* there is a heading for Trade Catalogs—Collections; however the listing is not comprehensive. Collections to be added are the Corning Museum of Glassware, Winterthur, the Athenaeum of Philadelphia (nineteenth-century house paint and lighting fixtures), the National Agricultural Library in Beltsville, Maryland (early American seed catalogs), and the Pennsylvania Horticultural Society (Pennsylvania seed catalogs). Historical societies and public libraries sometimes have collections of catalogs of products produced in their regions.

Trade catalogs are often treated as special collections, so the material is rarely available for loan. On-site use is usually possible, but there may be little opportunity for browsing. Dismal as the access picture may seem, it has considerably brightened recently with the advent of six collections in microformat.

1. Henry Francis du Pont Winterthur Museum. *Trade catalogues at Winterthur.* New York: Clearwater Publishing Co. (UPA Academic Editions); [1984].

Eighteen hundred catalogs arranged in 30 subject areas, with most of the catalogs dating from 1870 to 1910. A broad range of subjects including agricultural implements, clocks and watches, musical instruments, furniture, silver and clothing.

2. *Sweet's architectural trade catalog file. Avery Library, Columbia University, 1906-1949.* New York: Architectural Record Co.

Each Sweet's volume consists of catalogs from hundreds of individual suppliers. The complete collection contains 2,334 microfiche.

3. *Architectural trade catalogs from Avery Library, Columbia University.* New York: Clearwater Publishing Co. (UPA Academic Editions); [1988].

One thousand six hundred and eighty-four catalogs covering 16 categories of building products organized in Sweet's catalog classifications.

4. Corning Museum of Glass. Library. *Trade catalogs.* [Corning, N. Y.]: Corning Museum of Glass, [1983].

More than 2,300 foreign and domestic trade catalogs on glass products providing a primary source of information for study of the development of the glass industry throughout the world and the relationship of its products to the societies that created and used them.

5. Hagley Museum and Library. *Trade catalogs from the Hagley Museum and Library: Transportation.* Frederick, MD: UPA Academic Editions; 1989.

Some 1,000 catalogs dating from 1880 to 1940 including the following categories: Aircraft, automobiles, carriages and wagons, firefighting equipment and trucks, railroad equipment, and ships and boats.

6. Victoria and Albert Museum. *Trade catalogues in the Victoria & Albert Museum, London.* London, England: Mindata, 1986.

Illustrated British and European catalogues dating from the late eighteenth century to the outbreak of the Second World War. The 322 microfiche are divided into three broad categories: Industrial/commercial, domestic and household, and fashion.

To the uninitiated, Romaine's enthusiasm about trade catalogs may seem excessive, and yet those of us who are keepers of collections share the enthusiasm. The Smithsonian Institution Libraries considers its trade literature collection as a national resource and a substantial proportion of its resources are allocated to bringing it under bibliographic control. As libraries prepare the materials, commercial publishers have demonstrated their willingness to film and make them available in microformat. This satisfies our common goals of preservation and access.

Taking preservation and access a step further, some libraries in the past have found that the trade catalogs in their holdings did not fit easily into their collections. The Smithsonian Institution Libraries has been the recipient of some gifts as a result, accepting the responsibility that comes with them. Other libraries have also made this commitment.

Thus, the message of this article is twofold. First, there are trade literature collections available to researchers in both hard copy and microformat. Suggestions have been provided on how and where to find them. Finally, readers are urged to consider their own collections. Are you holding uncataloged, unaccessible and perhaps fragile catalogs? Consider contacting one of the libraries who have made the commitment for their preservation and transferring the materials to them. Lawrence Romaine put his trust in us.

Bibliography

1. Romaine, Lawrence. *A guide to American trade catalogs; 1744-1900.* New York: Bowker: 1960.
2. Hagley Museum and Library. *Trade catalogs in the Hagley Museum and Library.* Wilmington, Delaware: Hagley Museum and Library: 1987.
3. Corning Museum of Glass. *Guide to trade catalogs from the Corning Museum of Glass.* New York: Clearwater Pub. Co., 1987.
4. Henry Francis du Pont Winterthur Museum. *Trade catalogues at Winterthur: a guide to the literature of merchandising 1750-1980.* New York: Garland Pub., 1984.
5. Davis, Audrey B.; Dreyfuss, Mark S. *The finest instruments ever made: a bibliography of medical, dental, optical, and pharmaceutical trade literature: 1700-1939.* Arlington, Massachusetts: Medical History Publishing Associates I: 1986.
6. Meixell, Granville. *The trade catalog collections; a manual with source lists.* New York: Special Libraries Association; 1934.
7. United States. Patent Office. *Subject-Matter index of patents for inventions issued by the United States Patent Office from 1790 to 1873, inclusive.* New York: Arno Press: 1976.
8. Ash, Lee. *Subject collections; a guide to special book collections and subject emphases as reported by university, college, public, and special libraries and museums in the United States and Canada.* New York: Bowker: 1985.
9. McGraw-Hill Information Systems Company. Sweet's Division, *Sweet's catalog file. Products for general building and renovation.* New York: Sweet's Division, McGraw-Hill Information Systems Co., 1984.

ABOUT THE EDITOR

Jane Anne Hannigan is Professor Emerita, School of Library Service, Columbia University. She has been on the faculty of the Graduate School of Library and Information Science, Simmons College, and since retiring from Columbia has taught for Nova University and the School of Communication, Information and Library Studies, Rutgers University. In 1984 the American Library Association presented her with the Beta Phi Mu Award for distinguished service to education for librarianship.

Dr. Hannigan has served on the American Library Association Council and Executive Board and on numerous committees of ALA and the Association for Library and Information Science Education. She is a regular contributor to the literature and this is the third volume she has edited of *Library Literature : The Best of 1988, 1989,* and *1990.* In 1990 she was honored by the publication of a Festschrift, *Library Education and Leadership : Essays in Honor of Jane Anne Hannigan,* edited by Sheila S. Intner and Kay E. Vandergrift (Metuchen: Scarecrow Press).